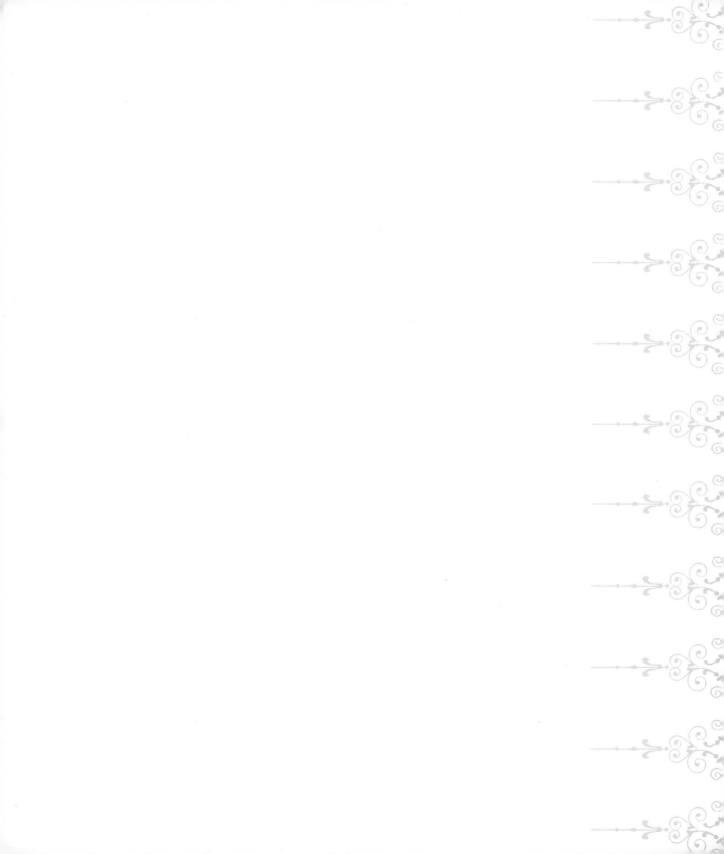

· THE ART OF ·

FRENCH PASTRY

· THE ART OF ·
FRENCH PASTRY

JACQUY PFEIFFER

WITH MARTHA ROSE SHULMAN

PHOTOGRAPHS BY PAUL STRABBING

STYLING BY JOHANNA BRANNAN LOWE

ALFRED A. KNOPF | NEW YORK | 2013

THIS IS A BORZOI BOOK
PUBLISHED BY ALFRED A. KNOPF

www.aaknopf.com

LIBRARY OF CONGRESS CATALOGING-IN-PUBLICATION DATA
Pfeiffer, Jacquy.
The art of French pastry / Jacquy Pfeiffer ; with Martha Rose Shulman ;
photographs by Paul Strabbing.
pages cm
"A Borzoi book."
ISBN: 978-0-307-95935-5 (hardback)
1. Pastry. 2. Cooking, French. I. Shulman, Martha Rose. II. Title.
TX773.P468 2013
641.86'5—dc23
2013017643

Jacket photographs by Paul Strabbing
Jacket design by Carol Devine Carson

Manufactured in China
First Edition

To my little sister Nathalie—

tu me manques tellement

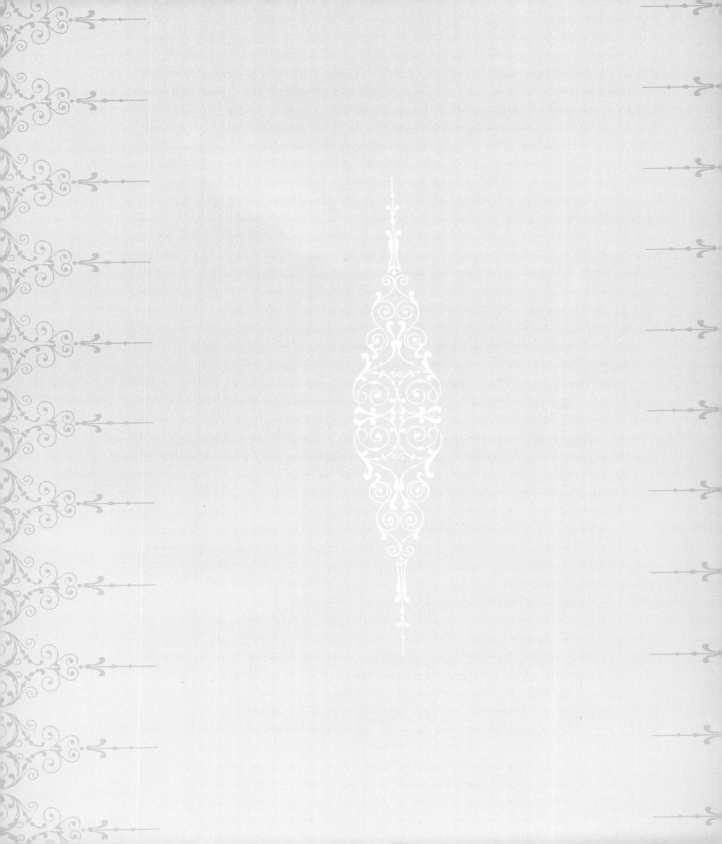

CONTENTS

A LIFE IN PASTRY

*I*WAS RAISED IN MY FATHER'S BAKERY in a small Alsatian village called Marlenheim. My bed was right above the oven (wonderful in winter, but not so great on hot summer nights, since air conditioning was not, and is still not, very common in French homes), and until I was fifteen, the magical aroma of fresh-baked bread was the only alarm clock I knew. My father got up every day at midnight to tend to his dough. His was the schedule of a traditional French baker in the 1960s and '70s, working from midnight to noon and sleeping after lunch from one to four and then again from about nine to midnight. My mother ran the front of the shop. Up at five a.m. every day, she would have the shop ready to open at six—by which time a line had formed outside the door—and would serve customers until we closed at seven p.m.

My mom knew her customers well. She knew the ones who liked their bread light brown and those who preferred it dark and *bien cuit*; she knew who bought croissants, and how many. She knew to set aside a large kougelhof for this neighbor, six cinnamon rolls for that one. Alsatians are exceptionally particular when it comes to food, and a successful

baker must serve them well; they may not complain openly, but if they are unsatisfied they will never, ever return to your shop. My five-foot-tall mom cheerfully churned through one order after another, her cash register a pad of paper on which she quickly tallied up the totals. I worked in the shop one Saturday morning when I was about fourteen years old on a day when my sister Elisabeth, who usually helped out on Saturdays, couldn't. Punk that I was, I thought it would be easy; what could be so difficult about grabbing a loaf of bread and giving it to a customer? My mom smiled, knowing how little I knew about her customers, who expected me to know exactly what they wanted. I could feel them looking over my shoulder to make sure I made no errors as I added up their orders (luckily, I was good at math). By the end of that morning I was so stressed that I begged my mother never to make me work there again. "I'll scrub floors, clean every pot and pan in Dad's kitchen, anything, but please don't make me work the front again!" She smiled and said, "Now you've had a slice of my daily life."

After school, on weekends, and during school vacations my two sisters, my brother, and I were often required to work in the bakery (but not in the front of the shop). We'd try to hide as much as we could, escaping to play in the nearby hills or in the courtyard and barn of our converted farm, but eventually my parents would find us. My father was very strict, and there was always something that needed to be done—greasy sheet pans and kougelhof molds to clean, apples to peel for *chaussons*, *mirabelles*, and *quetsches* to cut up for tarts. On Thursdays there were onions to peel for my mom, who sliced them thin and cooked them in butter for the savory, thin-crusted *tartes à l'oignon d'Alsace* that my dad made once a week. Sometimes I was required to brush his puff pastry *vol au vents* with egg wash, a task he was very particular about, as too much egg wash would prevent the puff pastry from rising.

During the holiday season there were hundreds upon hundreds of Christmas cookies to make and the entire family worked together, listening for hours on end to Edith Piaf, Charles Trenet, Maurice Chevalier, and other famous French stars of the '50s and '60s. Today I love that music, but back then I suffered through it. When school wasn't in session and if my father's assistant didn't show up, my dad would wake me in the night to assist him in scaling 350-gram pieces of dough for baguettes and batards, whose weights are strictly enforced in France. The dough would stick to my inexperienced fingers as if it wanted to be a permanent part of me. At the time it was frustrating to deal with this sticky dough while watching my father shape all of the loaves quickly and efficiently.

But the bakery, which my parents had built with their own sweat and tears, with 250 francs (about $50) in their pocket, was not all drudgery for me. I loved to work with my hands from a very young age, and after school if I wasn't playing soccer or participating in some contest my brother and sisters and I had cooked up, or tending an injured animal I'd res-

cued from the barn, I'd ask my mom for any dough scraps left over from the morning's production. I was happy to spend hours making sculptures or culinary creations out of dough while my father slept. I would bake them in the brick oven, which would still be hot hours after it had been turned off for the day. I loved molding things so much that my mom saved the red wax wrappers from the Babybel cheese we ate because she knew I liked to fashion it into flowers and other shapes. I'd do it at the table every night.

As I got older and watched my father's business grow I began to understand that an artisan can have a good life. Hard work and discipline are required, but we Alsatians are a disciplined lot. My father often told me not to go into the food business—it was too hard—while at the same time I knew that he secretly hoped I would someday take over his bakery. But I wanted to do something more artistic. Pastry was my calling, and so I asked my father to look for a pastry chef I could apprentice with.

My exposure to pastry work had begun at my father's side. Although he was a *boulanger*, not a *pâtissier*—a baker, not a pastry chef—he made his share of éclairs, mille-feuilles, cookies, and cakes. Alsace is a land of traditions. For hundreds of years bakers have been making the same items for each important date on the calendar. A birthday, first communion, graduation, or wedding in our village meant that my father would be very busy in his bakeshop. He could make an excellent sponge cake filled with delicious chocolate, coffee, or vanilla butter cream (butter cream was king when I was growing up in the '60s) and decorated with old-fashioned Victorian filigree piping. If there was a big wedding in the village he'd get thirty, forty, or fifty orders at once because it was the tradition in Alsace that when somebody married off his daughter or son the parents would give filled and decorated cakes to all of the family and friends who came to the wedding as a thank-you. On such occasions, my siblings and I would spend many hours helping my dad, cutting the sponge cakes into three layers, sprinkling them with syrup spiked with kirschwasser, and filling them with butter cream. My dad would ice the cakes, stick toasted sliced almonds on the sides, and pipe the decorations on top. After I began my apprenticeship I often helped in the family bakery on weekends or after work during these busy periods, and by then I could also do the decorating. Piping countless cakes for my dad is how I perfected my skills: pipe a lot, and you will eventually know how to do it.

But the road that stretched between the time I made my decision to apprentice and the time I could pipe filigree onto my father's cakes was an arduous one. I apprenticed with a master pastry chef named Jean Clauss in Strasbourg, twenty kilometers from my village, who trained his apprentices well but was a mean alcoholic. My idyllic boy's life changed forever on the day I walked through his door in September 1976 at the age of fifteen. You will read some of my stories about those difficult days in the pages that follow. I was tempted to give up on more than one occasion, but I had a long-term goal and a vision for my future: I knew that apprenticeship, where you learn all of the fundamentals, was crucial to a career in pastry, and that my tough boss was producing good apprentices. I said to myself, "If I quit, God knows where I'm going to end up," and I knew that if I left I would never be able to face my dad, so I made myself stick with it.

In the end, rather than being beaten down by the rigorous training, I was inspired by it to go on in this beautiful profession. I worked in big bakeries in Alsace, and was even a pastry chef in the French navy when I did my obligatory military service. (What other country but France would assign a pastry chef to a battleship stationed off the coast of Africa?) And since then I have had demanding but amazing jobs that have taken me all over the world.

In 1991 I moved to Chicago to run the pastry operation at the Fairmont Hotel, but by then I knew for sure that teaching was my calling. In a way, I began my career as a teacher when I took my first job overseas as an executive pastry chef and found myself, at the age of twenty-three, in charge of an operation in Saudi Arabia where my production team consisted of thirty-five workers from the Philippines, India, Bangladesh, Sri Lanka, and Pakistan who had never before worked in pastry. It wasn't easy, but I have always loved a challenge. That's what makes the work I have chosen so fascinating: it's a never-ending story. With every subsequent job, from Brunei to Hong Kong to Palo Alto to Chicago, I've trained teams of inexperienced workers. I began giving informal chocolate classes after work and on weekends in the loft where I lived. In 1995, with my colleague Sébastien Canonne, I opened the French Pastry School, the only school of its kind in the United States and now recognized as one of the most prestigious pastry schools in the world.

At the French Pastry School we train pastry chefs and pastry enthusiasts in a kinder and gentler way than my master trained me, but the training is rigorous nonetheless. Like my apprenticeship, it is the crucial beginning of a profession for many and it is vital that the students be both inspired and well grounded. After nearly two decades of standing at the side of students day in and day out as they learn my craft, I know the particular challenges that each new pastry task poses and can predict with certainty the mistakes students are likely to make.

A great cookbook can inspire an enthusiastic cook or baker in the same way that a good teacher can. It can get you started on the right foot. Pastry can be difficult if you don't understand the way it works. That is what I have always strived to help my students understand, and that is what I will show you in the pages that follow. Along the way I'll tell you stories about my life in pastry while I look over your shoulder to make sure you've scaled your ingredients and have them at room temperature before you begin a recipe, that you're not pressing down too hard on the rolling pin when you roll out pie dough, and that you're using a whisk, not a spatula, when you add the flour to the liquids in your *pâte à choux* (because if the flour is at all humid and you add it to the liquids, the liquids will prevail and the flour will lump). You'll learn French classics, but you'll also learn to make some of the lesser-known but equally delicious pastries I grew up with in Alsace.

With each recipe I'll make it clear why you are being asked to use particular ingredients, why the technique works, what can go wrong, and how to correct it if it does. The explanations may seem long, but they are crucial to the success of the task. My goal is to do much more than present you with beautifully illustrated recipes for the perfect sponge cake or apple tart. It is to teach you what it means to be an artisan, which is what you are if you make pastry, whether you are a home cook or a professional. This is what I was trained to be and what I train my students at the French Pastry School to become. Whether you are cooking at home or professionally, you will be mastering a new craft as you work your way through these pages, and you too will be able to call yourself an artisan.

THE CRAFT OF FRENCH PASTRY

*T*HIS IS A BOOK DESIGNED TO TEACH YOU the beautiful craft that I learned as a teenager and that it has been my great joy to teach to hundreds of students over the years. It's a manual of sorts with a personal touch, meant to guide you through a thorough repertoire of French pastry. The recipes, written for the home cook, have much more information in them than you'll find in recipes that professionals and even the students at the French Pastry School work with. You can consult them time and again for the details that we share with our students every day at the school, and this knowledge not only will help you with those recipes but also will make you a better cook in general.

I believe that it is possible to master a craft or a skill at home as long as you have two things: one will come from me, the other comes from you. I will give you the proper information and tools to allow you to understand how to execute a given recipe, but your contribution—the patience and persistence to work at it—is just as important. Many of you have learned to play an instrument, to knit a beautiful sweater, or to excel in a sport. You did not learn to play that Bach chorale well enough to play for an

audience just by looking at the music on the page and playing it once. First you memorized the keys on the piano, then practiced scales, then played the piece and practiced it over and over and over again. When you learned to knit, you first mastered the different stitches and how to manipulate them, then you made a scarf before you tackled making a sweater. In pastry it's the same: you must learn to make and pipe proper *pâte à choux* and pastry cream before you can make good éclairs.

Some—perhaps most—pastry skills, like piping those éclairs, won't come easily the first time. But if you're willing to practice, your hands will eventually know what to do. That is the beauty of being an artisan: the more you practice your craft, the better you get at it. With my help it will at least be less frustrating at the beginning, because I will tell you how to hold the pastry bag and demonstrate with pictures how high above the sheet pan to hold it, what angle to hold it at, when to stop piping, and how to cut off the little tail at the end. And I'll always be there to refer back to if you're making a recipe and something doesn't seem right.

You'll also be getting some chemistry lessons

as you work your way through this book. It's very important to understand the chemistry of pastry, because pastry works (or doesn't) the way it does because of the way ingredients react with each other. Making French pastry without understanding some of these underlying principles would be like trying to fix a car without any knowledge of mechanics. But once you understand both the technique and the chemistry involved you'll be able to execute the recipes successfully a hundred times in a row.

The messages in these pages (and I may repeat myself from time to time, but I've observed with my students that repeating the message helps to get it across) are those that it is my privilege to impart to every class that passes through the doors of my school. I hope they will inspire you to become a true artisan. Then, whether you make this craft your profession or your hobby, you will have many happy customers.

HOW TO USE THIS BOOK

Many of the recipes that follow, especially those in the first chapter, are like little pastry master classes. They represent the fundamentals and classics of French pastry, the pastries that customers have been telling bakers they love for centuries. My students sometimes want to jump ahead and get creative, but I always insist that they master the classics first. There is no need to reinvent the wheel, and I want them to show me that they can make a good regular croissant before they create an original one.

You will not be able to execute the classic recipes in Chapters 2 through 6 without mastering the fundamentals, so it's important that you begin this book by becoming comfortable with the recipes and techniques in Chapter 1. Do them more than once. Each of the recipes is followed by a list of subsequent reci-

pes in the book for which they are required, and this may help you decide what pastries you want to move on to once you've gotten some of the fundamentals under your belt.

One of the most important lessons in pastry is to make sure you give yourself plenty of time. Treat each pastry as a project in itself whose successful outcome will be a wonderful dessert for you and your family and friends to enjoy. Don't decide to tackle a pastry with several components, such as *religieuses* (PAGE 104), on the day of your dinner party, when you also have to make the main dish, starter, and sides. A *religieuse* is a wonderful dessert, but it does involve making *choux* pastry, pastry cream, and fondant, then filling the cream puffs, coating them with fondant, sticking one small puff on top of a larger one, and, finally, finishing them with piped *mousseline* (PAGE 41). Organize yourself to make complex pastries like *religieuses,* a croquembouche, or a gâteau St. Honoré in the same way you would prepare for a crafts project. Get all of your materials together and set aside a Saturday or Sunday afternoon. When you've succeeded in making your pastries, serve them to your friends, take some to neighbors, or bring them to a potluck. Or, if you want to serve them for your next dinner party, you can always make the choux pastry ahead and keep it in the freezer.

If you have to juggle pastry with other commitments, there are plenty of wonderful recipes that don't have as many steps, like Paris-Brest (PAGE 101) or one of the tarts in Chapter 6 (pie crust can always be made ahead). Whatever recipe interests you, read it through from start to finish twice before you plan on serving it, and ascertain whether you are comfortable with the basic components of the pastry before you begin to work on it. This way you can block out the time that will be required and you won't be stressed by the time you finish. Learn how to freeze components so that you can use them weeks later and whip up a fantastic dessert in no time. Once you're familiar and confident with the fundamental recipes you'll be able to skip some of the long explanations and jump into the action right away.

SCALING INGREDIENTS: WEIGHING VS. MEASURING

It is always funny to see the reactions of my students during the first week of class when I tell them that it is important to scale their ingredients and that precise scaling equals consistent pastries. When they hear that they will have to scale every ingredient they will use for the next six months, they all look at each other in disbelief. Some get angry, some scared, and some are sad that they won't be able to use their grandmother's vintage measuring tools to make all the pastries they're about to learn. The disgruntled students ask me how they're going to adjust to scaling, and I reassure them that people have been scaling ingredients for centuries and that it is very easy to get used to this precise system. "You put a man on the moon! I think that you will be able to manage putting ingredients on a scale until it registers the right weight."

Then comes my favorite part. To prove my point I always take a measuring cup, fill it with flour, and scale the content in front of them. I write the result on the board: 123 grams. Then I measure another cup of flour and scale it again: 125 grams. I repeat this procedure another eight times, and it never fails: each measurement registers a different weight in grams.

This proves the simple point that any measurement done with cups or tablespoons is not precise enough for pastry. The more measurements you do with cups, teaspoons, or liquid measuring cups, the bigger the inconsistencies you will have with your

ingredients and in the recipes—and inconsistencies are deadly in pastry. You must always be sure about the way the ingredients are going to interact if you want to be sure of a recipe. If your measurements vary, you will never be certain that a cake will work out the same way twice. But if you scale your ingredients, every recipe in this book will work, again, and again, and again.

The degree of variation in weight when you use measures is not surprising. The amount of flour or confectioners' sugar held in a cup is a function of many things, including the humidity of the flour, whether or not it is packed into the cup, how long it has been sitting in the bag before being scooped, whether or not it has been sifted, and the dimensions of the cup itself. They are not all the same. As for liquids, no two people are going to measure milk in a cup at exactly the same point on the line in the cup. And when it comes to measuring spoons, there is a tremendous variation in volume from one manufacturer to another. (Do the experiment yourself if you don't believe me!)

Did you know, for example, that 200 grams of flour measured on a scale would represent $1\frac{1}{2}$ cups plus 1 tablespoon plus $1\frac{1}{4}$ teaspoons? You will see that in each recipe I have provided a grid with approximate measurements for each ingredient—but I do not want you to use those measurements. They are just to give you an approximate idea of the amount of an ingredient that the weight represents, since you may have never worked with scaling before. *I cannot vouch for the recipes if you use the measures.* Every professional chef would agree that the approximations prove my point.

The prep time for all of these recipes is also considerably faster when you use a scale. So I am proposing that you use one piece of equipment, a scale (well, okay, two pieces, because a precision scale in conjunction with your main digital scale set for gram weights will allow you to accurately weigh out very small quantities of ingredients like spices and salt), and that you scale all ingredients, whether they are liquids, solids, eggs, apples, nuts, flour, or spices. It's very efficient to put a bowl on a scale, zero out the scale, and pour or scoop in the amount of flour you need—and there will be fewer items to wash up when you've finished. Most importantly, the recipes will work. That's why it doesn't take long for my initially skeptical students to be won over by this system.

NOTES ON BAKING

Many pastry recipes require multiple steps, including a crucial one, the baking process. It's important to understand this delicate phase. Baking at home is different from baking in a professional pastry kitchen, where we use commercial convection ovens with many shelves. For this reason all of the recipes in this book were tested in a home kitchen using a regular oven. My coauthor Martha's oven is a vintage gas Wedgewood, and mine is an electric oven from KitchenAid. Though my preference has always been for gas ovens, both of these ovens yielded similar and successful results.

Here are some general words of advice when it comes to baking:

- When I bake at home I *always* put the baking rack in the center of the oven. This is where you will get as close as possible to the same heat and performance as a commercial oven. Unless specified otherwise, adjust your oven rack accordingly for most of the recipes in this book.
- If you place the rack lower the product will bake more from the bottom, and the reverse will happen if you place the rack closer to the top. So if

you are baking a pizza, it makes sense to lower the rack, as you want the crust to be baked more from the bottom. On the other hand, if you want to brown the top of a lemon meringue pie, it is logical to place it closer to the top of the oven.

- Today home ovens can be convection ovens or conventional ones. Convection ovens have a fan that blows the heat around so that it circulates evenly in the oven, which is very efficient for pastry. If you have a convection oven you can place two sheet pans at a time in the oven on different shelves. Make sure to rotate your product top to bottom and front to back midway or two-thirds through the baking, and when you do, open and close the door quickly. In conventional electric ovens the heat comes from coils surrounding the interior of the oven. The same idea applies to gas ovens, where a flame heats the interior. For conventional ovens I recommend that you bake only one sheet pan at a time, because if you use more than one at once the heat does not have a chance to circulate in the same way.
- Using the right temperature to bake a product is absolutely critical. It is important to check the actual temperature of your oven once in a while by inserting a probe or oven thermometer, to verify that the temperature in the oven matches the set temperature that you need for your recipe. Should your oven be off, I recommend that you bring in a technician to calibrate it for you. It's not uncommon for home ovens to need to be recalibrated from time to time.
- Another recommendation I have for you is best illustrated by the statement "Curiosity kills the cake." Many bakers are very curious or impatient, and they open the oven door multiple times during the baking process to see how their pastries are coming along. I always tell my students to think twice before opening the oven door and

only to open it for a very good reason. Home ovens are not as efficient as commercial ovens and they lose a tremendous amount of heat when you open the door. This drop in temperature will interrupt and affect the baking process in a big way. A product will bake perfectly if the baking process is continuous and uninterrupted.

· Don't be afraid to bake things enough! I have been running the French Pastry School for seventeen years and I see the same problem session after session: people do not bake things for long enough. Consequently their products are pale in color, are bland in flavor, and have a chewy texture that is not easy to digest because the gluten has not been broken down sufficiently. A slightly darker crust will bring character to the flavor profile and great texture to your baked goods.

· It is important for you to understand that some baking mediums are better than others. Today when it comes to choosing baking equipment such as molds or sheet trays (we call them sheet pans in the profession) there are many materials to choose from—metal, ceramic, glass, and silicone. In most of Europe, professional pastry chefs use sheet pans made of blue or black steel, which in my opinion is the best metal for baking because it conducts heat very well. It has many advantages: you can bake straight on this sheet pan without using parchment paper or a silpat;

all you have to do is to grease the surface lightly with butter. They can be pricy, but they will last you a lifetime if you care for them. Usually I wipe them clean right after my product is baked when the mold is still warm. I wash them very rarely, as the steel can rust.

In the United States most sheet pans are made out of aluminum or a mix of metal that includes aluminum. This is not the best choice, as aluminum is a poor heat conductor. You also can never bake straight on the metal as it sometimes produces a grayish residue that will end up in the baked product.

Another option is to use silicone molds or silpats on sheet pans. Silpat liners and molds have revolutionized baking in general. They never need to be greased and are extremely practical and easy to use. They definitely make a pastry chef's life easier, as they are light, flexible, and never rust. However, if you need your product nicely browned—for example, if you are making puff or *choux* pastry—silpats will create a buffer and not allow the same baking as parchment paper.

Finally, clay or tempered glass does not conduct heat very well. These materials can be used for baking, but only for a limited number of items, such as crème brulée or bread pudding. I do not recommend using tart pans made out of porcelain, clay, or glass. For this I would always use a steel mold.

ESSENTIALS

EQUIPMENT ESSENTIALS

One of my pastry maxims is "Use the right tool for the right job." A beautiful and well-made tool is a thing of beauty and will simplify the task that it is meant for. You do not need hundreds of one-time gadgets that clutter your kitchen drawers for pastry. Here is a list of fundamental tools that should allow you to make most of the recipes in this book. You'll use them often and cherish them forever.

DIGITAL SCALE

Digital scales are crucial for successful pastry. They're the best choice when we want precision. I recommend using the Doran Scale PC400. It's made in the United States, is built like a tank, and is very accurate. It goes from 1 gram to 2270 grams (5 pounds), and is where you should be ready to invest money in order to ensure the accuracy of all your recipes. For very small quantities of crucial ingredients such as baking powder you will also need a mini pocket scale that scales to $\frac{1}{10}$ of a gram. These are not expensive and can be found online. Source: **www.doranscales.com**

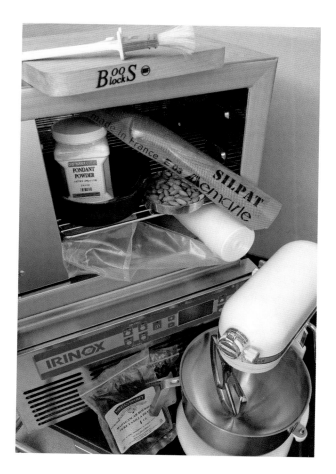

DIGITAL CANDY THERMOMETER

Today you can find glass thermometers and digital ones. I've tested both types with my students, and after cleaning up broken glass session after session, I've determined that the digital ones are the safest to use. I like the ones that are used to take the temperature of meat in an oven. They have a base that has a timer, a thermometer function, and an alarm that rings when the product reaches a set temperature. They come with a probe attached to a long flexible wire that cannot be submerged in water or manhandled, otherwise it will not function anymore. I suggest buying a replacement probe from the beginning so that you will have a plan B if the first one breaks. I shy away from infrared thermometers, as they measure only the surface of the product you are cooking or baking. Make sure that you buy a thermometer that will go higher than 300°F and that can be set for Celsius or Fahrenheit. I like the Therma K and Thermapen models from ThermoWorks.
Source: **www.thermoworks.com**

KITCHENAID MIXER WITH WHISK, PADDLE, AND HOOK ATTACHMENTS

If you are going to be serious about making pastry you will need a stand mixer, and you can't do better than a KitchenAid. You will be called upon to use one in just about every recipe in this book.
Source: **www.kitchenaid.com**

IMMERSION BLENDER

You will need one for several emulsions and creams in this book. This practical tool is very efficient for blending and reconstituting liquid mixtures.
Source: **www.kitchenaid.com**

CUTTING BOARD

Plastic cutting boards work, but I am old-fashioned and use wooden cutting boards. I like to place a piece of rubber shelf liner underneath so that the board does not slip on the counter while I am using it. You can also put a damp piece of paper towel underneath to keep it from slipping. Never submerge wooden cutting boards in water or they will warp. It's crucial to have a separate one for pastry if you chop a lot of onions and garlic on your cutting board.
Source: **www.johnboos.com**

WOODEN ROLLING PIN

All kinds of rolling pins are on the market, made of plastic, metal, marble, and even silicone. But I recommend heavy wood. The best is beech or boxwood, hard woods that do not easily warp. They are more expensive than regular rolling pins, but if you take care of them by cleaning them with a plastic scraper and then a very slightly damp paper towel, you will have them for a lifetime. Never submerge a wooden rolling pin in water, as it will swell or warp and never be straight again. I grew up using dowel rolling pins, but you can also use rolling pins with handles. Avoid using tapered French rolling pins, as they have an uneven thickness and make rolling very difficult.
Source: **www.backmann24.com**

PARCHMENT PAPER

Try to find silicone-coated parchment paper, as it prevents the product from sticking to it. You can buy parchment paper at your local grocery store, but restaurant- and baking-supply stores sell convenient packs of parchment paper already sized for sheet pans.
Source: **www.amazon.com**

SILPATS

Silpats are silicone baking sheets that changed the way we bake. You can bake on them and freeze product on them, and they will change your life when it

comes to rolling out pie dough and laminated dough. I recommend that you get one full-sized silpat ($14\frac{1}{2} \times 19$ inches) for rolling out dough and two sized for a sheet pan (11.62×16.5 inches) for baking. Do not store them folded in a drawer, as they will eventually break at the fold. You can roll them up loosely, but ideally silpats like to sit flat when they are not in use. We hang them by clips on pants hangers at the French Pastry School. They are much more expensive than parchment paper but are a worthwhile investment since you will use them hundreds of times. Nothing ever sticks to silicone.
Source: **www.demarleathome.com**

FLEXIPAN SILICONE MOLDS

Food-grade silicone molds can be used for baking or molding various pastry products. Just like silpats, they do not release a smell and are extremely user friendly, as they do not need any greasing or special treatment before baking. They are also lightweight and dishwasher proof.
Source: **www.demarleathome.com**

DISPOSABLE PASTRY OR PIPING BAGS

They are called both pastry bags and piping bags, but are exactly the same thing. You can find different kinds on the market. Some are made out of cloth, but my favorite ones are disposable and made out of heavy plastic that is slick on the inside so that the mixture in the bag slides out easily; the outside of the bag is slightly sticky to provide a good grip. For sanitation and efficiency purposes, pastry professionals throw them away after using them once, but you can always wash them thoroughly after each use. I prefer the disposable bags that come in a roll as they take up less space in your cabinet. You should have one roll of large (18-inch) bags and one roll of smaller (12-inch) ones.
Source: **www.backmann24.com**

PIPING TIPS

You should get a set of round and star-shaped piping tips. Make sure they are heavy duty and made of stainless steel.
Source: **www.backmann24.com**

SMALL, MEDIUM, AND LARGE SAUCEPANS WITH LIDS

Make sure that they are heavy duty and made of stainless steel. It's important when you make things like caramel and pastry cream that you use the right-sized pan. If you use one that's too big the product you are cooking will burn because too much of it will be exposed to heat. If you use one that's too small it could be unsafe, as your product could boil over. I like the Matfer brand.
Source: **www.amazon.com, www.matferbourgeatusa.com**

SMALL, MEDIUM, AND LARGE MIXING BOWLS

Make sure that they are heavy duty and made of stainless steel. Glass bowls can break or chip and are not allowed in commercial pastry kitchens because of that risk.
Source: **www.amazon.com, www.matferbourgeatusa.com**

MICROWAVE-SAFE BOWLS

You should get one small and one medium microwave-safe bowl for heating chocolate and butter. These can be made of plastic. You can also use glass, but you need to be very careful that no glass chips fall into your food preparation.
Source: **www.amazon.com**

TWO 9-INCH METAL TART RINGS OR PANS

To make tarts there are many different choices out there, but I recommend a metal pan or ring made out of galvanized metal or stainless steel. I prefer rings, as they are bottomless and sit straight on the sheet pan, which is extremely practical for the professional baker. Tart pans with bottoms are very

practical for home use. I like the Matfer brand.
Source: **www.amazon.com**, **www.backmann24.com**,
www.matferbourgeatusa.com

STRAINER AND SIFTER
Make sure they are made of stainless steel and have
a fine mesh.
Source: **www.backmann24.com**, **www.amazon.com**

PLASTIC WRAP AND ALUMINUM FOIL
I recommend that you buy large rolls of
heavy-duty aluminum foil and plastic wrap at a
restaurant-supply or big-box store. Heavy-duty
wrap and foil are thicker and will protect your
product better than regular wraps and foils.
Source: Restaurant-supply and big-box stores

CHEESECLOTH
Great for straining liquid mixtures and trapping
herbs and spices that are sitting in broth.
Source: Your local food store

LARGE AND SMALL STAINLESS STEEL HAND WHISKS
The wires must be stainless steel; the handle should
be stainless steel or plastic. In addition to a regular
whisk you should also have a balloon whisk, which
is more efficient and does a better job of whisking
egg whites and folding them into batters. It is very
nice to have one, but you can do without. I prefer the
Matfer brand.
Source: **www.amazon.com**, **www.matferbourgeatusa.com**

HIGH-HEAT RUBBER SPATULAS
I recommend buying a large one and a small one.
The large, wide ones are very useful when it comes
to folding mixtures. They have to be made of high
heat–resistant rubber so that they don't melt when
you make caramel. You will only be able to get all the
batter out of a bowl efficiently if you use a spatula or
a bowl scraper (as opposed to a spoon). If you also
use spatulas for savory foods, I recommend that you
have two and dedicate one to pastry, as the rubber
can retain savory flavors.
Source: **www.amazon.com**

BOWL SCRAPER
This is a rectangular hard plastic scraper that has a
round edge; it is very efficient for scraping out product from a mixing bowl.
Source: **www.backmann24.com**, **www.amazon.com**

FLAT AND OFFSET METAL SPATULAS
You should have one medium (9-inch blade) flat
spatula, one medium (9-inch blade) offset spatula,
and one small (4-inch blade) offset spatula. An offset
spatula has an L-shaped blade that drops down from
the handle. The blades should be stainless steel but
the handles can be either plastic or wood. Just like
knives, if you take care of these spatulas you will
only have to buy them once in your lifetime.
Source: **www.backmann24.com**, **www.amazon.com**

ICE CREAM SCOOPS
Scoops are very useful for scooping ice cream but
also for calibrating the size of cookie batters that will
then be baked. I recommend getting scoops in three
sizes: 25 millimeter (1½ teaspoons), 35 millimeter
(1 tablespoon), and 56 millimeter (4 tablespoons).
Source: **www.amazon.com**

ROUND AND FLUTED COOKIE CUTTERS
The best are made out of stainless steel and will last
you a lifetime. A set of round cutters in graduated
sizes will have all sorts of uses beyond cookies, such
as shaving chocolate (SEE PAGE 000). I like the Matfer
brand.
Source: **www.amazon.com**, **www.chefrubber.com**,
www.matferbourgeatusa.com

VEGETABLE PEELER

Each chef has a favorite kind of vegetable peeler. My rule of thumb is the same as it is for all equipment: use the peeler that is the most efficient and comfortable for you to use. In pastry we use them for shaving chocolate as well as for peeling fruits and vegetables. Most people like Y-shaped peelers.
Source: **www.kitchenaid.com**

RULER

In pastry not only do we scale everything, we also measure many of the items we make. I recommend investing in a stainless steel ruler that has inch and centimeter gradations.
Source: An office-supply store

CERAMIC RAMEKINS

These provide a very nice presentation for many individual desserts, such as the Frozen Coffee and Chocolate Mousse on PAGE 289. I recommend Revol, a company that specializes in small dishes of all shapes and kinds.
Source: **www.revolusa.com**

SAFE SHOES

Always make sure that you wear closed-toe shoes with soles that grip when working in a kitchen. Like many things you will read about in this book, I learned this the hard way, when a paring knife fell off the counter and pierced my big toe. Kitchen floors can be wet and slippery, and you never know when something hot will splash from the stove. Wear shoes that are comfortable to stand in for hours at a time. I like the clogs made by Dansko.
Source: **www.dansko.com**

SHEET PANS (AKA SHEET TRAYS OR COOKIE SHEETS)

In pastry we do not use the flat cookie sheets or lightweight jelly roll pans that you can buy in the super-market. It's very important to use heavy-duty sheet trays, which professionals call sheet pans. In the trade a full tray is much larger than the size we will be using in this book, which should measure 11 × 17 inches. You should have at least two of them; if you have four you won't be sorry. A half-sized sheet pan is also a convenient size for toasting small amounts of nuts and cooling pastry cream. You can find sheet pans in restaurant-supply stores and online.
Source: **www.chefrubber.com**; black steel sheet pans can be found at **www.dr.ca, www.matferbourgeatusa.com**

PARING KNIFE

You will need a paring knife for several tasks. It does not have to be very expensive but try to find one of good quality.
Source: **www.backmann24.com, www.chefrubber.com**

SPIDER

A spider is a flat, round slotted wire skimmer that is used for fishing items out of liquid when you want all the liquid to stay behind. Spiders are particularly useful for deep frying.
Source: **www.amazon.com**

PASTRY BRUSHES

We use pastry brushes all the time in pastry—to brush egg wash onto dough or glaze onto finished baked goods. You can also use them to brush sugar crystals down into a saucepan when making caramel. When dry, they are very useful for brushing flour off pastry. I recommend one small brush and one medium one. The bristles should be soft.
Source: **www.backmann24.com**

CAKE PANS

You will need a 7-inch (18-centimeter) cake pan or Flexipan mold for smaller cakes like the Black Forest

Cake on PAGE 259. For all other cakes a standard 9-inch cake pan will be fine.
Source: www.chefrubber.com, www.backmann24.com, www.demarleathome.com for Flexipans; www.amazon.com for metal pans, including an 18-centimeter pan by Matfer

BREAD PAN(S)

You can make pound cake and *pain d'épices* recipes in a regular 5 × 9–inch bread pan, but the longer, skinnier pans produce a more attractive loaf. Matfer produces very nice 9.9 × 3.1–inch and 10 × 3.5–inch pans.
Source: www.amazon.com, www.matferbourgeatusa.com

PIZZA STONE

A pizza stone does not conduct heat like metal but instead provides a constant and gentler heat that bakes product more slowly and is very efficient at creating a crust. That is why true artisan bread is always baked in an oven lined with a brick bottom.
Source: www.amazon.com

BREAD SCORER (RAZOR BLADE FOR SLASHING BREAD)

Many breads are slashed right before the shaped loaf goes into the oven so that they don't tear as they open out when they bake. This tool does the job very efficiently.
Source: www.backmann24.com, www.amazon.com

DOUGH (BENCH) SCRAPER

A dough or bench scraper is a rectangular metal or plastic scraper topped with a handle; it is very convenient for scraping up leftover dough residue on the counter.
Source: www.backmann24.com, www.amazon.com

LATEX OR HEAT-RESISTANT GLOVES

You will need to wear protective gloves when you work with hot caramel, and they also protect your hands from getting sticky and gooey when you coat pastry with fondant.
Source: www.amazon.com or your local pharmacy or hardware store

KITCHEN TIMER (OR TWO)

I recommend the type that also has a probe thermometer.
Source: www.kitchenaid.com, www.thermoworks.com

ELECTRIC HOME ICE CREAM MAKER

You will need one to make any of the ice creams in Chapter 5.
Source: www.amazon.com

PIZZA WHEEL

This tool is useful for cutting raw dough as well as pizza.
Source: www.kitchenaid.com

MICROPLANE

Great for zesting citrus and grating nutmeg. They come in different sizes. Get the smallest size for citrus and nutmeg.
Source: www.amazon.com

KITCHEN SCISSORS

We use them all the time in pastry. Invest in a good pair of stainless steel scissors that will last forever.
Source: www.kitchenaid.com

APRONS

Get used to wearing an apron as it will not only protect you from getting dirty but will also protect your body from splashes or even flames. I recommend a bib apron.

CHEF'S KNIFE

This is the most important tool a hot food chef can have, and it's important for the pastry chef too. You need one with a long blade—10 inches is ideal—for cutting pieces of puff pastry, chopping nuts, cutting up fruit, etc. Use a heavy-gauge stainless steel knife with a good grip and keep it sharp by regularly sharpening it with a knife sharpener and honing it with a steel.
Source: **www.backmann24.com**, **www.chefrubber.com**

PIZZA PADDLE

We use pizza paddles for sliding breads and pizzas onto baking stones in a hot oven and for taking them out.
Source: **www.amazon.com**

OVEN MITTS

I prefer cloth mitts to silicone as they are less slippery.

PLASTIC CONTAINERS, SUCH AS 1-QUART YOGURT CONTAINERS

Useful for storage.

OPTIONAL NONESSENTIALS

ELECTRIC KNIFE

I use one rarely, but when it comes to cutting a Napoléon or slicing cooked meat finely, nothing comes close. They should not cost a lot and there are plenty of models available online. Some are cordless, other are not.
Source: **www.amazon.com**

COMMERCIAL CHILLER AND BLAST FREEZER FOR HOME USE

If you want the ultimate cooling system that does not take up much space and runs on regular 110-volt power, Irinox, a company that makes commercial refrigerators and freezers, has recently released a refrigerator/blast freezer for the home, the EF 10.1 Multi Fresh. This freezer goes to 0°F and allows you to cool hot mixtures in very little time. Its small size and versatility make it a very attractive piece of equipment for the home cook.
Source: **www.irinoxusa.com**

VACUUM-SEALING MACHINE

We are all guilty of turning our freezers into time capsules and keeping things in there for too long. In my experience, after a month anything that is just wrapped in regular plastic wrap will smell and taste like the freezer. A vacuum-sealing machine is not necessary for making successful pastries, but it is a great way to keep ingredients and finished product tasting fresh for months (if not years), because the plastic used with these machines is much thicker than ordinary plastic wrap.

We all clean our freezer out once in a while, and the value of the items that we throw away would definitely pay for such a machine. When you are researching brands, the quality of the bag and the way it is sealed are the most important factors to consider. I recommend the VacMaster Pro 140 because of its robust construction and great performance.
Source: **www.vacmaster.aryvacmaster.com**

DOUGH DOCKER

Docking dough is the process of poking small holes in the dough to allow the steam to escape. A fork will work just fine, but if you are making a lot of puff pastry you might want to invest in this roller with spikes for docking pastry.
Source: **www.backmann24.com**, **www.amazon.com**

SPECIAL TOOLS FOR SHAVING CHOCOLATE

You can find special tools called manual shavers for chocolate decorations, but you can also use Y-shaped vegetable peelers and large round cookie cutters. They do the trick well.

Source: **www.dr.ca, www.chefrubber.com, www.amazon.com, www.kitchenaid.com**

ST. HONORÉ PIPING TIP

A piping tip with a round opening on the top and a V cut on the side.

Source: **www.backmann24.com**

ACETATE STRIPS

Acetate strips are used to line the inside of cake molds when you are making mousse cakes to prevent the mousse from sticking to the mold. They are never used in baking, as the plastic would melt. I also use acetate strips to make chocolate decorations. I spread the tempered chocolate on them and make the desired shape, and when the chocolate is hard I peel away the acetate, leaving the chocolate in the shape. It's useful for decorating the Black Forest Cake on PAGE 259.

Source: **www.chefrubber.com**

COMMON SENSE ADVICE

If you have long hair, I recommend that you put it in a ponytail, not only for sanitation purposes but also as a measure of safety. No one wants to get his or her hair caught in a mixer while it is on. I also recommend that you remove dangling pieces of jewelry and heavy rings so they don't become an unwanted part of your cake.

ESSENTIAL INGREDIENTS

One of the most important lessons that I learned as an apprentice was to respect my ingredients. Nothing can beat a perfectly ripe peach or a fragrant Tahitian vanilla bean. Just like good equipment, quality ingredients are essential to making successful pastries.

Using the best flour, butter, and chocolate you can get is the first step toward making successful pastry. These ingredients will ensure a consistent result. Not only do they taste better, they are also usually free of fillers and chemicals. If you begin with cheap ingredients you'll be fighting an uphill battle that is impossible to win.

Additionally, pastry ingredients react with each other in very specific ways, and for this reason we are specific about what type of ingredients to use in each recipe. Do not try to make substitutions and expect to get good results. We have tested all of these recipes with whole milk (3.5 percent fat), 35 percent cream, and 82 percent French-style Plugra butter. If you try to use, say, nonfat milk and lower-fat butter, then the ingredients will not interact with each other in the same way. Also, some low-fat or low-sugar products contain substitute ingredients that are not necessarily good for you.

Remember also that all ingredients are alive and should be kept in a cool and dry place. Most kitchen cupboards work fine, but avoid warm and humid places, as they favor bacteria growth. Nuts and nut flours are high in fat and will be more stable if you keep them in the refrigerator or the freezer; just remember to bring them to room temperature before you begin your recipe. Some ingredients, such as baking powder, lose some of their strength if they are well over the expiration date. Some, such as flour, attract bugs after a while, so it is important to rotate your ingredients and use the oldest ones first. We call this system FIFO: First in, first out.

Common sense should tell you that miracles don't happen in pastry: if you are using an ingredient that has the word "imitation" on its label, you will end up with an imitation cake.

Here in the United States we find mostly cane sugar, but you might also encounter beet sugar, which is the main sugar used in Europe. They are interchangeable, and both offer great results. My recipes call for granulated (white) sugar, turbinado sugar (also known as "sugar in the raw"), brown sugar, and confectioners' (powdered) sugar. I explain my choices in each recipe in the "Understanding Ingredients" section. I do not have much experience in baking with sugar substitutes or other types of sweeteners such as agave nectar.

Powdered sugar, confectioners' sugar, and 10x sugar are the same; they are all regular granulated sugar that has been ground up very finely into a powder. We use it in recipes because of its fine texture versus the grainy texture of granulated sugar. The "x" denomination on the label refers to the fineness of the grinding, which ranges from 4x to 14x. Most grocery stores carry 10x sugar, and this is fine for baking.

Sugar keeps very well in an airtight container at room temperature and does not spoil, as it does not contain any water.

SEA SALT

Sea salt is harvested from the sea with little processing; it has a great flavor that suits pastry very well. Use only fine sea salt. Table salt is mined underground and is more processed than sea salt. While it is great for cooking, it is saltier than sea salt, too much so for pastry making. Kosher salt is also unsuitable for pastry because the crystals are larger and do not dissolve in the same way as fine sea salt.

Sea salt keeps very well at room temperature in its original container.

HONEY

I use a small amount of honey in quite a few recipes for its flavor profile and also because of its very strong sweetening power due to its high glucose and fructose content, which acts as a great natural emulsifier by breaking large droplets of fat into tiny ones. I usually use a good clover honey for my recipes, but you can be adventurous and follow your sense of smell and taste buds. Know that honey can have a strong flavor, so taste it before you use it if you are not using clover honey, which is fairly neutral. Acacia and sage honeys are also very versatile. I usually do not use chestnut honey for pastry making because it is very bitter and will definitely change the taste of your finished product.

Should your honey crystallize in the jar, microwave it at 50 percent power for about 30 seconds to a minute, and it will turn to liquid again.

Honey keeps nicely at room temperature in a sealed jar for months; once opened, clean the exterior of the jar carefully after each use so it doesn't attract ants.

CORN SYRUP

Corn syrup is an inverted sugar, which means that an acid has been added to it. This prevents it from hardening or crystallizing. Because of its anti-crystallizing properties, it is added in small amounts to recipes that involve heating sugar, such as caramel, Italian meringue, and sugar candies, as well as to ice cream and sorbet recipes. It absorbs moisture in baked products and helps them to stay moist. Corn syrup comes in different flavors, but I recommend that you use the clear version so that it does not change the flavor of your pastries.

FLOUR: CAKE, ALL-PURPOSE, PASTRY, AND BREAD

Using a good flour from a reputable source is extremely important, as it is one of our staple ingredients and used in so many of our recipes. I recommend King Arthur Flour because it is consistent and of a very high quality.

All flours contain starch and a certain amount of gluten, which is the protein in wheat. The amount of gluten will change from one flour to another. In my "Understanding Ingredients" sections I explain the reason for my flour choices.

Flour has a limited shelf life, so it's best not to stockpile it. Buy what you need for the recipes plus a little extra for the pantry and store it in tightly lidded containers. If you have a lot more than you need, keep it in a cool place. The bad news is that once you find bugs in your flour, they are probably also in your rice and cereals. Then you have to throw out all of these products and start fresh.
Source: www.kingarthurflour.com and most supermarkets

ACTIVE DRY YEAST

Active dry yeast is a living ingredient. You can find it in supermarkets, but it will only be fresh and active if many people buy it; if it sits on the shelf for too long, it will become moldy and eventually die, which makes it inactive. All my recipes are calibrated with active dry yeast, which is what I recommend for a consistent product. Active dry yeast keeps very well at room temperature in the small packets that it comes in.

VANILLA BEANS, EXTRACT, OR PASTE

Nothing can mimic the flavor of a real vanilla bean. Tahitian beans are my favorite because they are the most floral. But you can use others depending on the intended use and your preference. Mexican beans have spicier overtones, while the ones from Madagascar have sweet and creamy overtones.

For liquid vanilla, you are forbidden to use vanillin, or imitation vanilla, as it is an artificial product made with chemicals. The brand of vanilla I recommend—the only one I use, in fact—is made by Nielsen-Massey, an Illinois-based company that has been around since 1907.

All vanilla products keep best in an airtight jar at room temperature, away from light. When buying any type of extract, follow your senses and pick what tastes or smells natural. Use vanilla judiciously—a little bit goes a long way.
Source: www.nielsenmassey.com

FRENCH-STYLE, 82 PERCENT FAT BUTTER

Butter is another crucial ingredient in our recipes. It is important to use one containing 82 percent fat, which is the fat content of good butter in France. If the fat content is 82 percent, the butter will contain 2 percent protein and only 16 percent water. This will make a stable product that will bake nicely in the oven. The solid ingredients in a recipe are what make the product hold its shape. Pastry made with butter that contains a lower amount of fat, and thus a higher amount of water, will collapse slightly in the oven. The water will also create a lot of steam in your oven and slow down the baking of your product. My students and I have been using Plugra butter for many years; it is a very consistent product with a great flavor profile.

Butter keeps well in the refrigerator for two weeks; you should be sure to use it by then, before it starts to get rancid or pick up other refrigerator smells. It can be kept in the freezer for up to a month. The price varies depending on where you buy it.
Source: Whole Foods Market, www.plugra.com

HEAVY CREAM AND MILK

All of my recipes are calibrated using regular heavy cream that contains 35 percent fat and whole milk with 3.5 percent fat. As much as possible, use organic milk and cream. Heavy cream and whole milk keep well in the refrigerator until their expiration date. Do not substitute fat-free or reduced-fat milk for whole milk, or lighter cream for heavy cream, and expect a recipe to behave the same way.

EGGS

Try to use free-range eggs. They contain less cholesterol and saturated fat, and more vitamins and omega fatty acids. They have great flavor and a firmer yolk and white, which will help your pastries hold their shape better. All my recipes are calibrated using extra large eggs, which weighs 50 to 55 grams on average. To scale them, just crack them in a bowl, whisk them for ten seconds, and scale what you need.

WHOLE NUTS AND NUT FLOURS

It is important to use high-quality fresh nuts so that they can release their true aroma. I like to use almond flour, also called almond powder, because it has the ability to absorb and retain moisture like no other nut flour. I use sliced almonds a lot; I like the way they are thinly and uniformly sliced. I use them to decorate pastries and cakes, and for some of my flourishes like Chocolate Nougatine Crisp (PAGE 59). Hazelnuts are another favorite because of their great flavor. All nuts and nut flours contain a certain amount of oil; but they also contain water, which will eventually make them go rancid. I recommend that you keep them in your refrigerator or freezer, vacuum sealed so that they do not go bad. All my nuts come from American Almond, a company that has been around since 1924. My students have been enjoying the consistency of their products for years.

Source: www.americanalmond.com

APPLE AND NH PECTIN

Pectin is a natural product that is extracted from apples or citrus peel; it acts as a gelling agent and also has the ability to absorb and retain the water in recipes. Once extracted from fruit it is transformed into two different products. The first, usually called pectin, apple pectin, or yellow pectin, helps mixtures set quickly. Once set, the product cannot be re-melted; we call this pectin irreversible. The second one, called NH pectin, is used in jellies and clear glazes for pastry. When you heat up a jelly it usually re-melts; NH pectin is reversible. Both kinds of pectin keep well in an airtight container at room temperature.

Source: www.chefrubber.com and many supermarkets

FONDANT AND FONDANT POWDER

This product comes in both a solid and a powder form. The powder form is rehydrated with water. It is used to glaze éclairs, *religieuses*, and cream puffs. It keeps very well at room temperature in an airtight container.

Source: www.chefrubber.com for powdered; www.lepicerie.com for solid

COCOA POWDER

When baking, it is important to use high-quality chocolate products. Real cocoa powder should be dark brown in color, as it is made from the roasted cocoa bean solids. Cocoa power that is lighter brown or gray probably has fillers in it. I recommend using Barry Callebaut products. They are of a very high quality, are easy to use, and offer a consistent end result. Cocoa powder does not contain water and

therefore keeps very well at room temperature in an airtight container.
Source: Whole Foods Market, **www.callebaut.com**, **www.cacao-barry.com**

CHOCOLATE

Nothing can duplicate chocolate, which is derived from roasted cocoa beans. Chocolate consists of cocoa mass (solids), sugar, and cocoa butter, which is the natural fat extracted from the cocoa beans. I recommend that you use chocolate that has the "couverture" name on its label, which means that it contains at least 31 percent cocoa butter. When cocoa butter melts, it liquefies and brings a great fluidity to the chocolate— it's the cocoa butter that makes the chocolate melt in our mouth when we eat it. Chocolate couverture will have a percentage on the label that indicates the combined cocoa butter and solid content. For instance, a 62 percent chocolate will have 31 percent cocoa butter and 31 percent cocoa solids. Just as in wine making, each chocolate manufacturer has different recipes, mixes, and methods for making their chocolates. I like Barry Callebaut products.

Avoid confectionery chocolate or coating chocolate. These use vegetable fats and waxes that mimic the action and feel of cocoa butter but do not have the same taste.

Chocolate does not contain water and therefore keeps very well at room temperature in an airtight container or wrapped in plastic wrap.
Source: Whole Foods Market, **www.cacao-barry.com**, **www.amazon.com**

SPICES

When it comes to spices, we are completely spoiled in Chicago with Patty and Tom Erd, the owners of the Spice House, a company established in 1957. They are second-generation spice merchants and are extremely knowledgeable in their field.

One of my favorite spices that they carry is cinnamon from Ceylon. I love it because of its floral overtones. It is important to know that although spices do not go bad, they lose their volatile oils and fragrance the more they are exposed to air. It is best to order them in small amounts to ensure their flavor profiles.
Source: **www.thespicehouse.com**

CORNSTARCH

Cornstarch is the white starch of the corn grain. While it is used in cooking as a sauce thickener, we pastry chefs like to incorporate it into some sponge recipes instead of flour because it does not contain any gluten (for recipes such as sponge cake, potato starch would be a good substitute should you run out of cornstarch). Cornstarch is an excellent thickener in pastry creams, contributing a smooth texture because of its lack of gluten. It keeps very well at room temperature in an airtight container or in its original box.
Source: Your local supermarket

BAKING SODA

Baking soda is a white powder with salty undertones. When it reacts with acids in batter it releases carbon dioxide, which then helps the batter to expand. Baking soda is mainly used in pound cakes, pancakes, and other types of quick breads. It keeps very well at room temperature in an airtight container or in its original box.
Source: Your local supermarket

CREAM OF TARTAR

Cream of tartar is a white powder that is a by-product of wine making. Because of its acidity, it is used to stabilize egg white foams or sugar candy mixtures. It is one of the ingredients in baking powder. Cream of tartar keeps very well at room temperature in an airtight container or in its original box.
Source: Your local supermarket

BAKING POWDER

Baking powder is a white powder that acts as a leavening agent; it usually contains baking soda and cream of tartar. It is used in most quick bread recipes and reacts with acids, humidity, and also heat. Baking powder keeps very well at room temperature in an airtight container or in its original box. Try to buy small containers of it, as it loses its strength over time. For all of my baked goods, I use aluminum-free baking powder. It keeps very well at room temperature in an airtight container or in its original box. Source: Your local supermarket

FRUIT

Regarding fruit, apply this simple rule: good fruit makes good pastry. Make sure to let your fruit ripen before you use it. Stay away from bruised, unripe, or overripe fruit. Farmers markets are your best source for fruit. You should always talk to the farmers, as they will be able to guide you in your choices.

Although it's best to stay with the season, if you do need to make a pastry calling for summer fruit in winter it is better to use frozen fruit from the freezer section of your grocery store, as fruit is always ripe when it's frozen. Should you invest in a vacuum-sealing machine, you could stock up on frozen summer fruit so that you have a year-round supply ready to use.

A FEW NON-ESSENTIAL INGREDIENTS

COCOA BUTTER

Cocoa butter is the natural fat extracted from cocoa. It is made up of 100 percent fat solids and does not contain water. Coating products like the caramelized nuts on PAGE 51 with a small film of cocoa butter will

protect them from humidity. Keep what you don't use in a cool place, wrapped airtight.
Source: www.kingarthurflour.com

LYE SOLUTION FOR PRETZELS

You will need this if you make the pretzel recipe on PAGE 351. It is what gives pretzels their distinctive flavor. It is technically sodium hydroxide but is also known as lye or caustic soda. This is a strong alkaline compound that is used for preparing various foodstuffs such as lutefisk, pretzels, bagels, and hominy. Always mix it with cold water, never hot water, always wear latex gloves when you handle it, and keep it away from children and pets.
Source: www.chefrubber.com

PRETZEL SALT

This is a white, large-grained, non-melting salt. It is ideal for soft pretzels, salted bagels, and focaccia.
Source: www.amazon.com

SILICA GEL

This is a desiccant that is very useful for keeping moisture out of items you are storing, like caramelized nuts or nougatine crisp.
Source: www.chefrubber.com

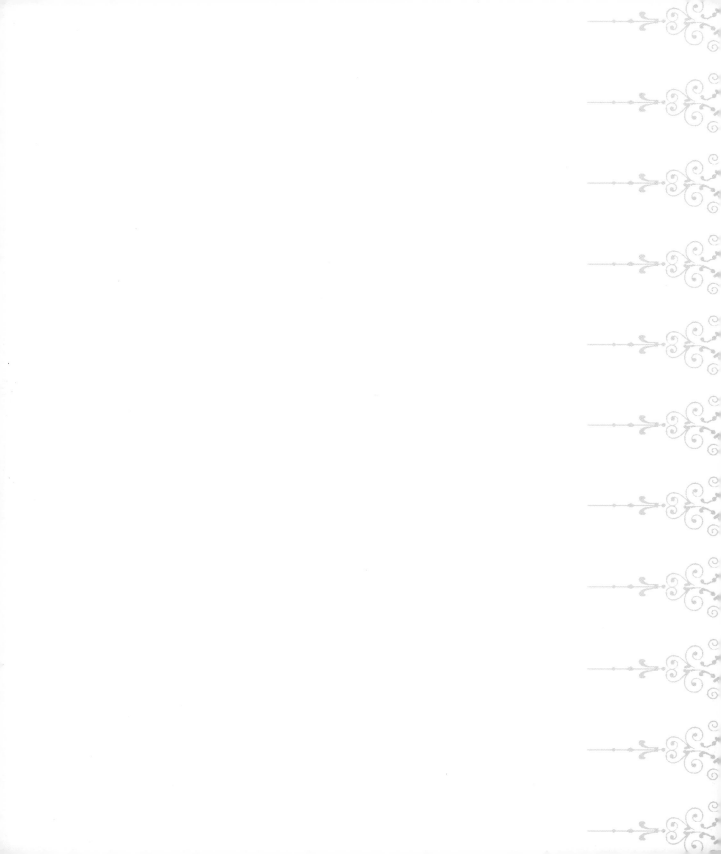

· THE ART OF ·

FRENCH PASTRY

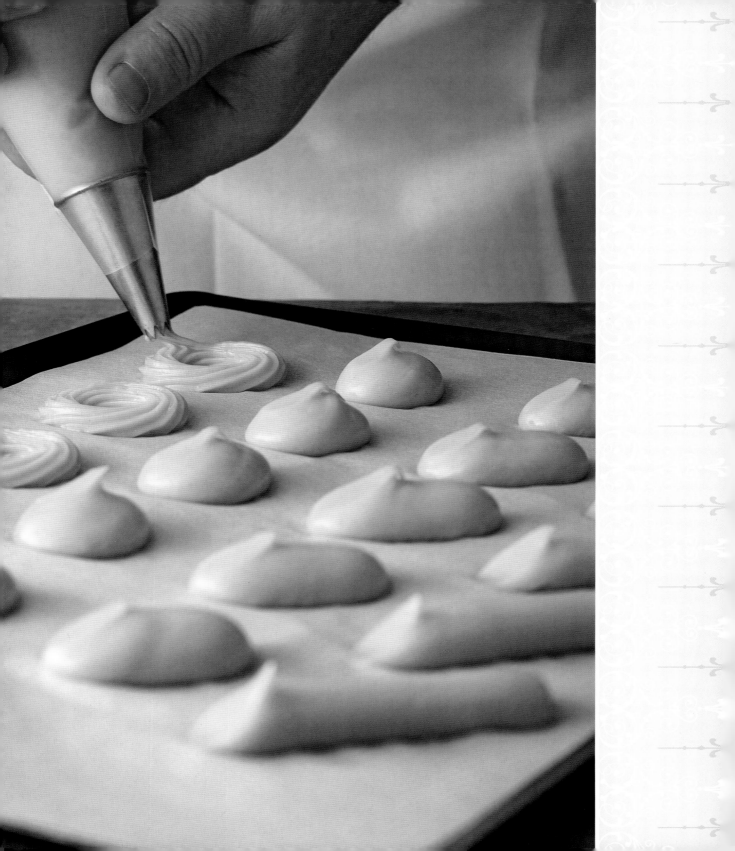

· CHAPTER 1 ·

FRENCH PASTRY FUNDAMENTALS

*T*he recipes and techniques in this chapter are the ones to master first. They will become the pillars of your pastry repertoire and you will see how often you need to refer back to them when you move on to the subsequent chapters in this book. In pastry, as in cooking, many recipes are linked together, and soon you will understand all of these important interconnections. You will see for instance how puff pastry, *choux* paste, and pastry cream are intertwined with each other in many different ways. Pastry is like a tree whose roots are the fundamental recipes that have been created and mastered by chefs over the last few centuries. What valuable work they've done for us, figuring out through trial and error what works and what doesn't! Without these basics, the classics of French pastry and all of the creative modern desserts that followed would not exist.

Take your time as you work your way through the recipes. Do them until they feel very comfortable to you. Remember that it takes a while for your mind and hands to understand how an item needs to be handled and that practice and patience are the keys to successful pastry making. It is only through repetition that you will develop your "pastry muscles"—the ones that are needed to whip a batch of *pâte à choux* or pastry cream—and your "muscle memories"—the ones that know exactly how high up to hold the pastry bag when you pipe éclairs or what puff pastry dough is supposed to feel like and exactly how much pressure to apply when you roll it out. I will explain in detail the chemistry of ingredients and how they change and react during the mixing and baking process, but it will only be through making these recipes over and over that you will really learn and understand what I'm talking about. After that, pastry will start to make sense and you will be able to move on to other challenges with more confidence.

·H "CREATIVITY" AND PASTRY H·

If you are creative it's all the more important that you master these recipes. You need to walk before you can run, and you will run in the wrong direction if you don't have a full grasp of the essentials. I welcome creativity—it is what makes us go forward, and I appreciate my students' desire to express it. But after teaching pastry for seventeen years I have seen many over-creative students forget about what works in pastry and make mistakes. Had they mastered the fundamentals, the mistakes would have been avoided.

One day a student presented me with what he called a "never-been-done-before curry crème brulée." I tasted it graciously, but each spoonful became more painful to swallow; this was definitely not a winning flavor combination. I told the student that there might be a good reason why no one has ever done a curry crème brulée before: curry and crème brulée do not work well together. The student agreed with me but then said that despite its bad taste the combination was "interesting." I responded that an interesting pastry is appreciated (if not enjoyed) once. A classic pastry, made well and with a flavor combination that people have enjoyed over centuries, is appreciated forever. Perhaps that student will become a seasoned pastry chef and will someday figure out a way to achieve a flavorful curry crème brulée that works. But as of now I still have the taste of that dessert in my mind, and not for the right reason.

SUGAR ICING GLAZE

INGREDIENTS	WEIGHT	MEASURE (APPROXIMATE)
Water	40 grams	2 tablespoons plus 2 teaspoons
Lemon juice, freshly squeezed	5 grams	1¼ teaspoons
Confectioners' sugar	150 grams	1½ cups

This is the sugar icing that I use to glaze breakfast pastries or cookies as soon as they come out of the oven. The heat of the product causes the water in the icing to evaporate, leaving a shiny glaze. The addition of lemon juice gives the glaze a nice tangy zing.

METHOD

1 Place the water and lemon juice in the tall container.

2 Pour the confectioners' sugar into the container but do not stir; otherwise you will get lumps. Just push all the sugar down into the water with a rubber spatula or with the back of a spoon. Let sit for 30 minutes at room temperature; this will allow the sugar to dissolve. Before using, whisk the mixture for 5 seconds to make sure that it is free of lumps.

3 Use a pastry brush to coat freshly baked items with the icing.

IT'S DONE WHEN IT'S DONE

The glaze should look shiny and glossy after it has been applied to a hot product. It should dry out on the product, as one of its functions is to protect the product from drying out. If the mixture is lumpy, just be patient and let the lumps dissolve, or strain them out.

STORAGE

Store in a container covered with a lid or plastic wrap in the refrigerator for up to a month. Stir before using, as some of the sugar will settle on the bottom.

BEFORE YOU BEGIN

→ Get out the following equipment and allow all of the ingredients to come to room temperature:

Digital scale, set to metric weights
1 tall plastic or stainless steel container, about 1 quart
1 rubber spatula or large spoon
1 stainless steel hand whisk
1 pastry brush
Plastic wrap

→ Read this recipe through twice from start to finish.

UNDERSTANDING INGREDIENTS

You can control the outcome of a recipe by choosing the right ingredients for the job.

American confectioners' sugar contains 3 percent to 5 percent cornstarch, which is added to prevent caking and so that the sugar does not turn rock solid when exposed to humidity. Because of the cornstarch, the best way to mix the confectioners' sugar and water in this recipe is to just pour the confectioners' sugar over the water, press it down into the water, and let the water slowly dissolve it. If you mix it, the process will go too fast and the cornstarch will cause the mixture to form lumps before all of the water gets to the sugar.

Lemon juice is an acid. When acid is present in a sugar solution it prevents the sugar crystals from fusing back together, which means that this glaze will never solidify completely after being brushed onto your product. If you do want that effect, reduce the amount of lemon juice by half.

SIMPLE SYRUP

INGREDIENTS	WEIGHT	MEASURE (APPROXIMATE) OR OUNCE WEIGHT
Sugar	135 grams	¾ cup
Water	100 grams	½ cup

BEFORE YOU BEGIN

→ Get out the following equipment and allow all of the ingredients to come to room temperature:

Digital scale, set to metric weights
1 medium saucepan
1 rubber spatula
1 jar with a lid

→ Read this recipe through twice from start to finish.

Simple syrup is not just sugar and water: it is the right ratio of sugar to water. The amount of sugar in proportion to the water ensures that the syrup will not easily spoil, as the sugar acts as a natural preservative. This simple syrup is not too sweet, and therefore it can be used for many different recipes.

1 Combine the sugar and water in a medium saucepan and stir together with a spatula. Bring to a boil over medium heat and boil until all of the sugar is dissolved.

2 Remove from the heat and transfer to a jar. Cover with a lid while hot but do not seal the lid. Let sit at room temperature for 2 hours, then seal the lid and store in the refrigerator.

IT'S DONE WHEN IT'S DONE

The syrup should be a clear liquid. You should not see any sugar crystals.

STORAGE

This will keep for 2 weeks in the refrigerator.

JACQUY'S TAKEAWAYS

→ **$50 TRICK:** If you let this syrup cool without a lid, then the surface will be covered with a thin layer of crystallized sugar, which will eventually crystallize the entire syrup. Placing a lid on top of the freshly boiled syrup will allow the steam to rise up, hit the lid, and drip back down to the surface of the syrup, creating a thin layer of water that will prevent it from crystallizing.

INGREDIENTS	WEIGHT	MEASURE (APPROXIMATE) OR OUNCE WEIGHT
Whole eggs	50 grams	1 extra-large egg
Heavy cream (35% fat) or whole milk (3.5% fat)	5 grams	1 teaspoon
Sea salt	0.4 gram	Small pinch

Egg wash is used to glaze bread doughs and pastries before baking. It forms a thin, shiny layer that protects baked products from humidity and also makes them look attractive.

In a small bowl whisk together the egg, cream or milk, and sea salt. Pass through a fine strainer into a small bowl or jar, cover, and store in the refrigerator for up to 2 days.

BEFORE YOU BEGIN

→ Get out the following equipment and allow all of the ingredients to come to room temperature:

Digital scale, set to metric weights
1 small bowl
1 stainless-steel hand whisk

→ Read this recipe through twice from start to finish.

WEIGHING WHOLE EGGS

Eggs vary tremendously in size, even within the same grades of large, extra large, and so on. To scale eggs, break enough eggs into a bowl to reach within a few grams of the amount required for the recipe. In another bowl, break an egg and beat it. Then add that mixture to the bowl with your eggs to reach the required amount.

FLOUR AND BUTTER MIXTURE FOR CAKE PANS

INGREDIENTS	WEIGHT	MEASURE (APPROXIMATE) OR OUNCE WEIGHT
Butter (French style, 82% fat)	40 grams	1½ ounces or 3 tablespoons
Pastry flour	8 grams	1 tablespoon plus 1 teaspoon

BEFORE YOU BEGIN

→ Get out the following equipment and allow all of the ingredients to come to room temperature:

Digital scale, set to metric weights
1 small bowl
1 rubber spatula

→ Read this recipe through twice from start to finish.

I use this mixture of flour and butter to grease metal cake pans used for pound cakes and other recipes that contain a lot of sugar. When sugar is heated it breaks down and gets very sticky. Because the flour is already in the mixture, the need to dust the pans with flour after greasing is eliminated.

Soften the butter and mix in the flour. Use to grease cake pans for pound cakes, sponge cakes, and similar batters (do not use for bread doughs or brioche as they do not contain enough sugar to make the product stick to the pan). Store in the refrigerator or freezer and bring to room temperature before using.

INGREDIENTS	WEIGHT	MEASURE (APPROXIMATE) OR OUNCE WEIGHT
Butter (French style, 82% fat)	60 grams	2 ounces or 4 tablespoons
Turbinado sugar	88 grams	⅓ cup
Cake flour	70 grams	½ cup
Almond flour, skinless	70 grams	¾ cup
Ground cinnamon	1 gram	½ teaspoon
Kirschwasser	13 grams	1 tablespoon

Streusel is an Alsatian term for crumble. It keeps well in the freezer and is good to have on hand for toppings and for lining pie crusts (SEE THE WILD BLUEBERRY TART, PAGE 153). I like to keep baked streusel in my freezer so that I can use it as a topping on ice cream for a quick dessert for my friends.

1 Preheat the oven to 325°F/160°C. Line the sheet pan with parchment paper.

2 Cut the butter into ½-inch pieces. Place all of the ingredients in the bowl of a mixer and mix at medium speed until crumbly, about 2 minutes. The pieces should be about ¼ to ⅜ inch in size. Another option is to rub the mixture between your hands. A third way to make this recipe is to mix the ingredients until they form a dough and to press it through a wire rack with a grid formation, straight onto a sheet pan lined with parchment, to get an even crumble that is necessary for the streusel to bake evenly.

3 Spread on the parchment-lined sheet pan and bake 20 to 25 minutes, stirring occasionally, until golden brown and crisp. Allow to cool completely, then transfer to an airtight container or plastic bags and store in the refrigerator or freezer. Store in the refrigerator for up to 3 days or in the freezer for up to a month. Bake and use as needed.

STORAGE

Raw streusel can be stored in the refrigerator for 2 to 3 days. I usually bake it right away and then keep it in an airtight container or airtight bags in the freezer for up to a month.

BEFORE YOU BEGIN

→ Get out the following equipment:

Digital scale, set to metric weights
1 sheet pan lined with parchment paper
1 paring knife
KitchenAid or stand mixer fitted with the paddle attachment
1 rubber spatula or metal spoon

→ Read this recipe through twice from start to finish.

Streusel is easiest to make if the butter is cold rather than at room temperature and soft. If the butter is soft your streusel could easily become dough when you mix it.

Turbinado sugar, also called "sugar in the raw," can be interchanged with granulated sugar, brown sugar, or a mix of the two.

You can replace the almond flour with just about any type of nut flour except for pistachio, which tends to burn very quickly. The best streusels are made with hazelnuts, almonds, walnuts, or pecans. If you want extra crunch you can add an additional 20 grams of finely chopped nuts to this recipe.

You can omit the cinnamon or add different spices, but be very conservative, using no more than 0.3 to 0.5 grams of stronger spices. Spices like ginger, nutmeg, or mace can overpower a dessert quickly. When you eat a dessert that contains spices, the flavor of the spice should be in the background, just like spicy overtones in a good bottle of wine.

The kirschwasser in this recipe brings great flavor to the streusel. The alcohol itself will evaporate during the baking. You can omit it if desired. Kirschwasser is particularly Alsatian, but other types of hard liquor, such as rum, can be used instead.

RECIPES REQUIRING

STREUSEL

Wild Blueberry Tart

(PAGE 153)

Rhubarb Tart with Hazelnut Crumble

(PAGE 179)

Brioche Streusel

(PAGE 307)

PÂTE À CHOUX / CHOUX PASTE

YIELD | ENOUGH FOR ABOUT 80 PUFFS (DEPENDING ON WHAT YOU ARE MAKING)

INGREDIENTS	WEIGHT	MEASURE (APPROXIMATE) OR OUNCE WEIGHT
Whole milk (3.5% fat)	125 grams	½ cup
Water	125 grams	½ cup plus 2½ teaspoons
Butter (French style, 82% fat)	110 grams	3¾ ounces or 7½ tablespoons
Granulated sugar	5 grams	1 teaspoon
Sea salt	2 grams	¼ teaspoon
All-purpose flour, sifted	140 grams	1 cup plus 2 tablespoons
Whole eggs	220 grams plus extra as needed	4 to 5 eggs, as needed
Egg Wash (PAGE 7)	1 recipe	1 recipe

Pâte à choux, the dough that is used to make éclair shells, profiteroles, cream puffs, *salambos,* and *gougères,* makes a miraculous transformation from dough to finished product that is difficult to imagine. Even after all these years of working with it, I am still amazed by it.

Although this recipe makes more than you will need for many of the subsequent recipes in the book that call for it, it is a good amount of dough to work with—not too much and not too little. Because *pâte à choux* can be frozen at the raw stage or the baked stage, making more than you need at any given time is not a problem. Pipe shapes, then freeze what you don't need on a sheet pan. Once they are frozen, put them into a small container or freezer bag and bake them when you want to. Or, if you want to bake them right away, freeze them once they have been baked and cooled. Imagine being able to just whip up a batch of profiteroles at a moment's notice! Making a smaller batch of *pâte à choux* is more difficult because it's not easy to deal with smaller quantities of the ingredients when mixing the batter.

Before proceeding with this recipe, read the section on piping that follows it. At the French Pastry School, students make their first batches of *pâte à choux* just so that they can learn how to pipe. I urge you to do the same. Make an extra batch and practice, practice, practice!

BEFORE YOU BEGIN

→ Get out the following equipment and allow all of the ingredients to come to room temperature:

Digital scale, set to metric weights
1 sifter
1 or 2 sheet pans lined with parchment paper
1 medium saucepan
1 rubber spatula or wooden spoon
1 stainless steel hand whisk
KitchenAid or stand mixer fitted with the paddle attachment
1 dough scraper
1 pastry bag fitted with a ⅜-inch round tip
1 fork
1 pastry brush

→ Scale all of your ingredients and arrange them in the order they will be used in the recipe. This makes it easy to follow the recipe without getting confused.

→ Sift the flour just before you begin. If you sift too far in advance, especially if it's humid, you risk getting lumps in your *pâte à choux.*

→ Read this recipe through twice from start to finish.

UNDERSTANDING INGREDIENTS

Use only whole milk when making pastry, as low-fat milk is too watery.

The flour and eggs work together in *choux* pastry to make the puffs rise. The starch in the flour traps moisture, which escapes in the form of steam during baking. It's the steam that, along with the air bubbles and water trapped by the eggs, will cause the puffs to rise. The gluten in the flour fuses with the egg protein to create a crust. The more eggs you use, the more the pastry puffs.

Butter brings great flavor and should never be replaced by any other fat. Sugar contributes color and just a hint of sweetness, and sea salt fixes the nice golden brown color and enhances the flavor of the dough.

WHISK VS. SPOON OR SPATULA

Some recipes for pâte à choux *say to use a rubber spatula or a wooden spoon when you add the flour to the hot liquids, but if you do this, especially if it's humid where you live, you won't stand a chance when it comes to avoiding lumps. If you add humid flour to a pot full of liquid and don't have a whisk ready to amalgamate it immediately, guess who's going to win the battle? The liquid. You'll have lumps that you cannot get rid of, no matter what you do. The whisk is my answer to this problem, and it works well with my students.*

MIXING THE DOUGH

1 Preheat the oven to 400°F/200°C. Line sheet pans with parchment paper. In a medium saucepan, combine the milk, water, butter, sugar, and sea salt. Stir together with a rubber spatula or wooden spoon, and then exchange the spatula or spoon for a whisk. Bring it to a full boil. Once it comes to a boil and you see that the butter and sugar are well incorporated into the milk, turn off the heat. You don't want to reduce the liquid. It's important to have a uniform mixture at this point; there should be no lumps of unmelted butter.

2 Add the sifted flour to the liquid mixture in one quick addition and immediately whisk vigorously so that the mixture comes together. You have about 30 seconds to do this. No need to panic, but work quickly and efficiently. If you whisk too slowly you risk getting lumps of flour, and once lumps form in a *pâte à choux* you will, unfortunately, never be able to make them disappear. You will see lumps right after you add the flour, but after 30 seconds of whisking it should be a uniform mass.

3 Place the pan back on medium heat, switch back to the rubber spatula or wooden spoon, and cook, stirring all the while, until dry, about 1 minute. What you are doing at this point is cooking the protein in the flour that you just added. The mixture is ready when it congeals in a lump and begins to stick to the bottom of the pan. It will make a sort of hissing sound when it begins to stick.

4 Remove the mixture from the heat and transfer it to the bowl of a standing mixer fitted with the paddle attachment. (Run some water into your pan and let it stand to loosen the thin layer of dough sticking to the bottom of the pan; it will come off easily with a little soaking.)

5 Have 220 grams of eggs (usually 4 extra large) ready, and beat an extra egg to set aside, in case your dough seems dry. Mix the dough on medium speed for 30 seconds, then turn the speed to low and begin adding the eggs, 1 at a time, beating on medium speed until each egg is incorporated into the dough before adding the next one. Each time you add an egg turn the speed down to low so that you don't get splashed with egg if it catches the paddle at the right moment (so much for your white chef's jacket!). Once you've added 2 of the eggs, stop the mixer, take off the bowl and paddle, and scrape the bottom of the bowl to mix in the layer of dough adhering to the bowl. Then return to the mixer and add the remaining eggs following the same procedure.

6 Now you must ascertain whether the *pâte à choux* is the right consistency. Stop the machine, take the bowl and beater off, and scrape up any dough that is sticking to the bottom. Beat briefly to incorporate. Pull out the beater.

If the consistency is right, when you pull the paddle up the dough sticking to the paddle should hang down in a V shape (SEE PHOTO).

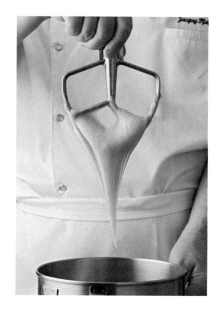

If it does not, the dough needs more liquid, either some beaten egg or a little warm milk. But you must be careful adding liquid, because if you add too much your *pâte à choux* will turn to soup and you'll have to begin all over again. There's no fixing a soupy *choux* pastry by adding flour—I know, I've tried. So add a teaspoon of egg or milk at a time, and each time you add and beat in a little more, check the consistency again. Adjust until you get the V-shaped ribbon when you lift the paddle from the dough.

7 Once your dough is the right consistency, transfer enough *choux* pastry to a pastry bag fitted with a ⅜-inch round tip to fill the bag halfway. See PAGES 15-20 for instructions on filling the bag and piping. Pipe the desired shapes—1¼-inch rounds (for all cream puffs), 1½-inch ovals (for Salambos, PAGE 93), 3- to 3½-inch strips (for Éclairs, PAGE 97), 1-inch rounds (for Croquembouche, PAGE 109)—onto a sheet pan lined with parchment paper. Continue piping with the remaining *choux* pastry. Brush the surface of the pastries evenly with a little bit of egg wash. With the tines of a fork, make a slight impression on the surface. This will help the puff to rise evenly.

At this point the *choux* pastry can be frozen unwrapped on the sheet trays. Once frozen, wrap the pieces in plastic wrap and store in a container or in freezer bags. Before baking, place on parchment paper–covered sheet pans and allow to return to room temperature.

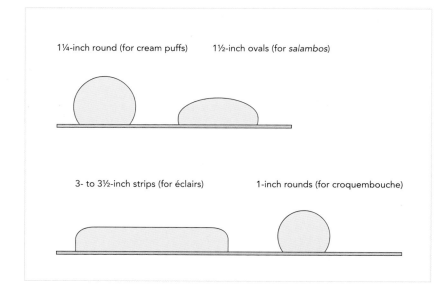

1¼-inch round (for cream puffs)   1½-inch ovals (for *salambos*)

3- to 3½-inch strips (for éclairs)   1-inch rounds (for croquembouche)

BAKING INSTRUCTIONS

1 Make sure that the oven is fully preheated to 400°F/200°C before you bake the pastries. The high heat causes the protein in the eggs and flour to congeal together and create a soft shell, and forces the water in the *pâte à choux* to steam, which is what makes the pastries puff. If the oven isn't hot enough your product will be flat and dense. Place a sheet pan in the oven and bake until the pastries rise, which should take 10 to 12 minutes.

2 Once the pastries have risen, lower the oven temperature to 325°F/160°C. You now need to bake them long enough for them to form a crust so that they'll hold their shape and dry out completely. Otherwise they'll be doughy, and in France we do not like doughy pastries. This should take 25 to 45 minutes, depending on the size of the pastries.

3 When they are done they are very golden. Remove from the oven and allow to cool. You can freeze them at this stage as well. Freeze them on the sheet pan; once they are frozen, transfer them to an airtight container or freezer bags.

IT'S DONE WHEN IT'S DONE

The *choux* pastries should be dark golden brown on the outside and hollow with a little moisture in the middle.

STORAGE

At the raw or baked stage *pâte à choux* can be kept frozen for about 1 month. Usually we do not keep baked *pâte à choux* refrigerated for more than 1 day because it will become soggy.

THAWING INSTRUCTIONS

Let the baked *pâte à choux* thaw out at room temperature and then flash them in a 400°F/200°C oven for 1 minute.

Thaw unbaked *pâte à choux* at room temperature before baking.

JACQUY'S TAKEAWAYS

→ Too much heat in the oven will create too much steam and will make the product crack or result in a misshapen pastry, which makes it hard to glaze.

→ **$50 TRICK:** If you have added too many eggs to the mixture and created soup, do not add more flour to it, as you will get instant lumps (don't waste your time, I have made that painful mistake before). The only way to fix this is to make an additional base (flour, sea salt, sugar, milk, and water) and add it to the soft *pâte à choux* (the soup), mix it together, and then adjust with more eggs if needed.

·⊣ PIPING PÂTE À CHOUX ⊢·

If you learn to pipe *pâte à choux* you will be able to pipe anything, from meringue to *macarons*. At the French Pastry School we begin piping lessons during the first week of classes. Each student makes a big batch of *pâte à choux* and then practices piping it onto a silicone silpat. The silpat is great because once you finish piping what's in the pastry bag, you can just put the empty bag into a tall container and scrape the *pâte à choux* off the silpat and into the bag with a flat-edged scraper. Note that I said, "put the empty bag into a tall container." *Never* lay the empty bag down on the surface where you've been piping; the residue on the sheet pan will get onto the outside of the bag and make it slimy (this is one of my pet peeves).

THE MOST IMPORTANT THINGS TO ASK YOURSELF WHEN YOU PIPE

1   Am I holding the bag correctly, with my right-hand thumb and index finger acting as a clip at the top of the bag (if I'm right-handed), my other three fingers holding the bag from underneath, and my left hand guiding the bag?
2   How high above my sheet pan is the tip of the pastry bag?
3   What is the angle of my piping tip?
4   Am I leaving enough space between each piece and staggering the rows?

FILLING THE BAG

1   Outfit a pastry bag with the desired tip. Make sure that you cut enough off the end of the bag to allow the piping tip to stick out $\frac{1}{2}$ inch but make sure that you don't cut off too much, which would allow the tip to slip out of the bag once it is under pressure. Otherwise whatever you are piping can ooze out of the bag between the bag and the piping tip. Place the bag in a tall (at least 5-inch) container that is about 4 inches wide, with the piping tip pointed down, or, if the container isn't quite tall enough, the tip can be on its side on the bottom, and fold the edges of the bag over the sides of the container. It's important to have a cuff that is at least $\frac{1}{3}$ the size of the bag. You can also hold the bag and fold the cuff down over your hand, but it's easier to fill the bag if it is resting in the container.
2   Using a rubber spatula or a wide plastic scraper, fill the bag halfway. To ensure that the bag is filled compactly so that you don't have air bubbles, unfold the cuff, lift up the bag, lay it down flat on the counter (*making sure that you are not laying it down where there is any residue*), and, using

the flat edge of a dough scraper, scrape the filling from the wide end of the bag toward the tip to push the filling down toward and into the tip and to push out all the air bubbles.

3 Lift up the bag and (assuming you are right-handed) use your right-hand thumb and index finger to clamp the bag shut at the top of the filling. The right-hand thumb and index finger will continue to act as a clip at the top of the bag so the filling cannot come out of the top while you pipe. Your other three fingers will hold on to the bag from underneath. The bag will rest on them, but be careful not to clutch or squeeze the bag with these fingers. The pressure comes from your thumb and index finger at the top of the bag and the three other fingers as well. Your left hand will act as a guide and will be the only way you control the bag. This is important, because the way you guide the bag, the angle at which you hold it, and the height you hold it above your sheet pan will determine the shape of the item you are piping. Twist the top part of the bag with your thumb and index finger until the filling is under pressure and about to come out of the tip. Now grab the bag with your free hand and the three free fingers of your "clip" hand. Your free hand and fingers of your clip hand should always be under the bag.

GENERAL TIPS ON PIPING

When you are learning to pipe it's important to pipe only one thing for 30 to 45 minutes at a time. You should master one shape—for example, cream puffs—before going on to others, such as éclairs, teardrops, Paris Brest, or *salambos*. Then practice only one of those for the next 30 to 45 minutes. It may be boring, but I can assure you that if you pipe éclairs for 45 minutes your hands will know how to pipe éclairs for the rest of your life. Once you've mastered one shape, the others will come more easily.

THREE IMPORTANT FACTORS DETERMINE THE SHAPE OF THE ITEMS YOU PIPE

1 The first factor is the distance between the end of the tip and the sheet pan. Let's say you are piping cream puffs. If the tip is only ¼ inch away from the sheet pan (SEE FIGURE 1), the mix will come out completely flat. The higher you go, the rounder it will get, until you reach a breaking point after an inch, when it will be out of control. If the tip is ½ inch above the sheet pan, the puff gets rounder and skinnier (FIGURE 2). At ¾ inch above the sheet pan the puff is nice and round (FIGURE 3). If the tip is too high (FIGURE 4), the product comes out with no control.

2   The second factor is the angle at which you hold the tip. When you pipe a cream puff the tip is pointed almost straight down at a 90-degree angle and held ¾ inch above the pan. It is pointed straight down and held ¾ inch the pan if you pipe a circle for Paris-Brest (PAGE 101) or a spiral for, say, Gâteau St. Honoré (PAGE 253), or Vacherin Glacé (PAGE 281). If you hold the bag at a 45-degree angle ½ inch above the pan and pipe without moving the bag, you will get an oval puff. If you want an éclair you use the same angle, but you need to move the bag in a line as soon as the product emerges from the tip. When you reach the length you want (3 to 3½ inches in our recipe on PAGE 11) you must stop pressing, dip the end of the tip quickly, and touch the sheet pan so that you force the tail to stick to the pan, and then with a very quick motion swing up and away to slice off the tail.

3   Whatever shape you are piping, once the correct size is obtained you have to get rid of the tail—the little tip we see on Hershey's Kisses—because we don't want these on our cream puffs. It is crucial to stop pressing on the pastry bag and to stay at the same height with the tip (FIGURE 5). With a quick flick of the wrist, cut the little tail on the top of the puff with the edge of the piping tip (FIGURE 6). Some chefs use more of a gentle swirl to lose the tail. If you pull straight up you will get a Hershey's Kiss; the tail will dry out or burn when you bake the *choux* pastry, or it will prevent you from getting an even coating if you are dipping the puff in caramel or fondant. Figure 7 shows what happens if you continue to press on the bag once you've obtained your puff. Figure 8 shows what

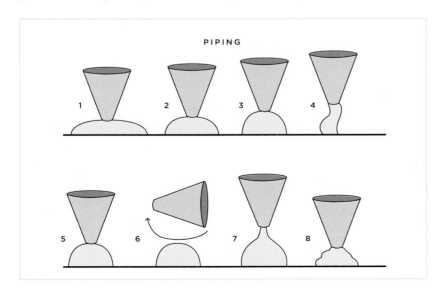

PIPING

CREAM PUFFS

1 Hold the bag with the tip ¾ inch above the sheet pan at a slight (90-degree) angle and pipe the desired size while keeping the bag still.

2 Once the desired size is obtained, stop pressing. With a quick flick of the wrist, cut off the little tail at the top of the puff with the edge of the piping tip.

3 The puff should be nice and round. Keep the tip ¾ inch above the sheet pan and continue to pipe the first row of puffs. Remember to stagger the puffs when you begin the next row.

OVALS (*SALAMBOS*)

1 Hold the bag with the tip at a 45-degree angle, ½ inch above the pan, and pipe without moving the bag.

2 Once the *pâte à choux* hits the sheet pan, move away from the initial blob while still piping.

3 Once the oval has reached the desired length, stop pressing. With a quick flick of the wrist, cut the little tail at the top of the oval with the edge of the piping tip. Keep the tip ½ inch above the sheet pan and continue to pipe the first row of ovals. Remember to stagger the puffs when you begin the next row.

happens if you don't keep your hand steady while you pipe, or if your hand shakes at the end.

4 Make sure to leave enough space between each piece—1 to 2 inches, depending on the product—so that they will not touch each other when they rise during baking. Stagger the rows so that there will be enough space around all sides of each piece.

Professional bakers use a machine called a depositor, which has 10 tips in a row that can be set at a certain height and angle above the sheet pan. They deposit, say, 10 *macarons* from ½ inch above the sheet pan; then the sheet pan moves and they deposit 10 more from the same height. The sheet pan moves, but the tips remain at the same height above the pan.

Like many skills in my profession, you will get good at piping by . . . piping. Don't overthink it; read my instructions twice but then pipe until you get into the rhythm and until your hands instinctively mimic the depositor. When I demonstrate piping cream puffs to my students, I say out loud, "Tac, tac, tac, tac, tac" with each puff, encouraging them to get into a cadence. I hope that this little trick will help you as much as it helps them.

HOW TO PIPE DIFFERENT SHAPES

It helps to draw the size of the pieces you want to make on the parchment paper before you begin, then flip the parchment paper over so that the pencil marks don't bleed onto your product. Whatever shape you pipe, remember to stagger the rows and leave enough space between each piece so that they have plenty of space to puff during baking.

CREAM PUFFS

1 Hold the bag with the tip ¾ inch above the sheet pan at a slight (90 degree) angle and pipe the desired size while keeping the bag still.

2 Once the desired size is obtained, stop pressing and cut the tail off. With a quick flick of the wrist, cut the little tail at the top of the puff with the edge of the piping tip.

3 The puff should be nice and round. Keep the tip ¾ inch above the sheet pan and continue to pipe the first row of puffs. Remember to stagger the puffs when you begin the next row.

OVALS (*SALAMBOS*)

1 Hold the bag with the tip at a 45-degree angle, ½ inch above the pan and pipe without moving the bag.

2 Once the pâte à choux hits the sheet pan move away from the initial blob while still piping.

3 Once the oval has reached the desired length, stop pressing and with a quick flick of the wrist, cut the little tail at the top of the oval with the edge of the piping tip.

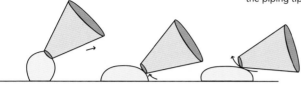

ÉCLAIRS

4 Hold the bag with the tip at a 45-degree angle, ½ inch above the pan. As soon as the product emerges from the tip begin to move the bag in a line until you reach the desired length.

5 As soon as you reach the desired length stop pressing, dip the end of the tip quickly to touch the sheet pan so that you force the tail to stick to the pan.

6 With a very quick motion swing up and away to slice off the tail.

PARIS-BREST

1 Hold the bag vertically over the sheet pan with the tip pointed down, ¾ inch above the pan and pipe 2-inch rings.

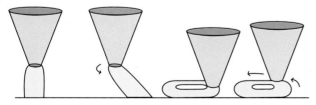

2 When the ring is complete, stop putting pressure on the bag and with the flick of your wrist cut the tail off the pastry.

ÉCLAIRS

1 Hold the bag with the tip at a 45-degree angle, ½ inch above the pan. As soon as the product emerges from the tip begin to move the bag in a straight line until you reach the desired length.

2 As soon as you reach the desired length, stop pressing. Dip the end of the tip quickly to touch the sheet pan so that you force the tail to stick to the pan.

3 With a very quick motion swing up and away to slice off the tail.

PARIS-BREST

1 Hold the pastry bag vertically over the sheet pan with the tip pointed straight down, ¾ inch above the pan, and pipe 2-inch rings.

2 When the ring is complete, stop putting pressure on the bag and with the flick of your wrist cut off the tail of the pastry.

TEARDROPS

1 For flat teardrops (for example, for Fours de Lin, PAGE 205), hold the pastry bag with the tip at a 45-degree angle, close to the sheet pan (about ¼ inch away). For rounder teardrops (needed for the Lemon Cream Tart with Meringue Teardrops, PAGE 163), move the bag away from you for ½ inch so that a bulb forms.

2 Continue to press on the bag and swing the tip toward you while you progressively stop pressing, so that the teardrop ends in a tail.

3 Note: If you stop pressing abruptly the teardrop will not have a tail; if you continue to press while you swing the tip toward you the tail will be too long.

MACARONS

1 Hold the bag vertically over the sheet pan ½ inch above the pan with the tip pointing straight down. Pipe 1½-inch rounds and stop pressing.

2 With a quick flick of the wrist, cut the little tail at the top of the *macaron* with the edge of the piping tip.

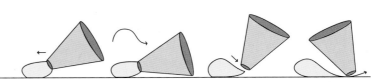

TEARDROP

1 For flat teardrops (for example for the Fours de Lin cookie on page 205), hold the pastry bag with the tip at a 45-degree angle, close to the sheet pan (about ¼ inch away). For rounder teardrops (needed for the Lemon Cream Tart with Meringue Teardrops on page 163) move the bag away from you ½ inch so that a bulb forms.

2 Continue to press on the bag and swing the tip towards you while you progressively stop pressing, so that the teardrop ends in a tail.

3 If you stop pressing abruptly the teardrop will not have a tail.

4 If you continue to press while you swing the tip towards you the tail will be too long.

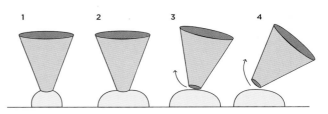

MACARONS

1 Hold the bag vertically over the sheet pan ½ inch above the pan with the tip pointing straight down. Pipe 1½-inch rounds and stop pressing.
2 With a quick flick of the wrist, cut the little tail at the top of the *macaron* with the edge of the piping tip.

MACARONS SECOND METHOD

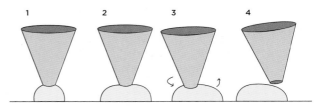

1 Pipe the *macarons* as directed in the above method.
2 Cut the tail with a quick swirl of the piping tip.

BRIOCHE

YIELD | FIFTEEN 2½-INCH ROUND BRIOCHES OR 2 TO 3 LARGE BRIOCHES NANTERRE (DEPENDING ON THE SIZE OF YOUR BREAD PANS)

2-DAY RECIPE

BASE TEMPERATURE | 54°C

INGREDIENTS	WEIGHT	MEASURE (APPROXIMATE) OR OUNCE WEIGHT
POOLISH		
Cold whole milk (3.5% fat)	50 grams	3 tablespoons plus 2 teaspoons
Dry yeast	8 grams	2 teaspoons
All-purpose flour	60 grams	½ cup plus 2 tablespoons
DOUGH		
Whole milk (3.5% fat)	As needed	As needed
Granulated sugar	40 grams	3 tablespoons
Bread flour	340 grams	2¾ cups plus 1½ tablespoons
Cold whole eggs	220 grams	4 extra-large eggs
Sea salt	8 grams	Scant 1¼ teaspoons
Butter (French style, 82% fat), softened	200 grams	7 ounces
Egg Wash (PAGE 7)	1 recipe	1 recipe
OPTIONAL TOPPINGS		
Streusel (PAGE 9), chopped caramelized nuts (PAGE 51), or coarse crystal sugar	50 grams	Scant ½ cup

Brioche, a sweet yeast-raised dough that is just the right balance between sweet pastry and bread, is on my list of top ten favorite desserts (everyone should have a top ten desserts list). In the seventeenth century brioche was called *pain bénit*, which means "blessed bread," a perfect name because of its light, airy texture and buttery flavor.

Brioche is "bready" enough for us to justify eating it with our morning coffee, and when we do it's like eating a buttery, sweet dessert for breakfast. The ideal is to eat it freshly baked, still slightly warm from the oven so that it releases its maximum rich and complex aroma, topped with soft butter and homemade jam. Try it with the raspberry jam on PAGE 80, a heavenly combination.

BASE TEMPERATURE AND YEAST DOUGHS

Yeast becomes activated when it makes contact with warm air and humidity. Therefore, the temperature of your liquid is crucial when making a yeast-raised dough. It works best in a warm and humid environment. A liquid that is too cold will put the yeast to sleep and your dough will rise extremely slowly. Conversely, using a very warm liquid will over-activate the yeast and cause the dough to rise out of control.

BEFORE YOU BEGIN

→ Get out the following equipment and allow all of the ingredients to come to room temperature except for the milk and the eggs:

Digital scale, set to metric weights
1 digital thermometer
KitchenAid or stand mixer fitted with the dough hook
1 rubber spatula
1 dough scraper
Plastic wrap or hand towel
1 small stainless steel hand whisk
1 medium mixing bowl
1 small saucepan
1 sheet pan lined with parchment paper
1 round bowl scraper
1 pastry brush

→ Read this recipe through twice from start to finish.

French bakers use a simple, logical system called the *base temperature* system to figure out what temperature the liquid should be. The base temperature system is the measure of the temperature of the flour and room temperature versus the temperature of the water. French bread that is made in 1 day requires a base temperature of 60°C (140°F): the temperatures of the room, the flour, and the liquid must add up to 60°C. To figure out what the temperature of the liquid should be, the baker takes the sum of the temperatures of the flour and the room and subtracts this from 60; the difference is the temperature he needs for the liquid. The formula works only in the Celsius system; once the calculation is made, you can then convert the temperature of the liquid into Fahrenheit if you wish. Brioche, which is made over the course of 2 days, requires a base temperature of 54°C. The temperature is lower than other breads like Kougelhof (PAGE 297) because the dough rises in the refrigerator overnight, and if the temperature of the dough is too high for this long, the gases created during the long rise will be unpleasant.

For this recipe, let's say that your room and flour are both 20°C.

First, add room temperature to the flour temperature: 20°C + 20°C = 40°C.

Subtract the sum from the base temperature of 54°C: 54°C − 40°C = 14°C. This means that your milk should be heated to 14°C.

If you wish, you can now convert 14°C to Fahrenheit, 57.2°F.

After mixing, the optimum temperature of the finished dough should be 23–25°C/73°–77°F to ensure good, controlled fermentation. Using the base temperature system ensures that the final temperature of the dough remains lower than 28°C/82°F. This is especially important with a buttery dough like brioche, because if the dough is warmer the butter will start to melt.

METHOD

DAY 1

1 We begin by making a quick acting starter called a *poolish* (pronounced "poo-*leesh*"). A *poolish* is a liquid fermentation made with a small quantity of liquid, the yeast, and a small quantity of flour. It is a quick and efficient way to get the yeast activated. Take the temperature of the flour and the room (convert to Celsius) and add them together. Then adjust your milk temperature (in Celsius) so that the sum of the three ingredients is 54°C (SEE ABOVE). Place the 50 grams of milk in the bowl of your stand mixer and add the yeast. Stir together. Sprinkle the all-purpose flour over the top. Let sit undisturbed for 10 to 15 minutes, until cracks form on the surface of the flour. This signifies that the yeast is fermenting. The fermentation of the yeast creates a very slight acidic flavor that contributes a pleasant flavor to the dough.

UNDERSTANDING INGREDIENTS

The reason why I choose to use two different flours is that bread flour in the United States has a very high gluten content, which can make the dough rubbery and the bread chewy. All-purpose flour contains less gluten and will prevent this from happening.

Salt is an acid and controls the action of the yeast by slowing down the speed of the fermentation: too much salt would prevent the dough from rising; not enough would allow the dough to ferment out of control. Never sprinkle the salt straight onto the yeast, as this will kill the yeast. Instead, add the salt as the very last ingredient in the recipe. Sugar starts to caramelize after being heated to over 300°F/150°C and will bring a nice brown color to the brioche. Yeast needs humidity and warmth to be activated. If you deprive it of either of these, the dough will not rise properly.

Butter and eggs add the rich flavor and texture that brioche is famous for. It is crucial that the butter be soft enough to be easily incorporated into the dough when you mix it.

*Larger amounts of dough take longer
to mix. I advise you to not make more
than 3 times this recipe in a KitchenAid
mixer, as the friction this will create is
so strong that it might make the mixer
move around on your counter.*

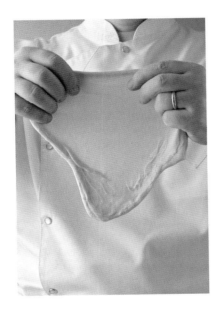

*In pastry shops we always transfer our
dough from the mixing bowl to another
bowl to rise because the stand mixer is a
tool that is used all day long and will be
needed for other tasks. In a home kitchen,
if you don't have anything else planned
for the mixer, you can leave the dough
in the bowl to rise.*

2 Once the yeast has been activated it is time to mix and knead the dough. Because brioche contains so much butter it is crucial that you mix the dough sufficiently, until it is completely elastic, before adding the butter. If it is not elastic enough it will fall apart when the butter is added at the end of the mixing process. Before beginning the mixing process, place an extra cup of milk next to the mixer, just in case the dough is too dry. Add the sugar, bread flour, eggs, and finally the sea salt to the *poolish*. Mix on medium speed for 30 seconds to a minute with the dough hook and observe the dough. If it looks very dry and lumpy add a very small amount of extra milk to it. This can happen if you are in a dry environment where the flour is very dry. The dough should come together after a full minute of mixing on medium speed. Watch carefully and add more liquid if necessary, one tablespoon at a time. Unattended brioche that is very dry in the early stages of the mixing will have lumps that will be impossible to get rid of later on. Mix the dough for about 5 minutes and then stop the machine. Using a rubber spatula or a round dough scraper, scrape the dough that is stuck to the bottom and sides of the bowl and add a tiny amount of all-purpose flour to that area. Mix again for 5 minutes and repeat this 2 more times. Depending on the amount of dough, after about 15 minutes of mixing the dough you should hear a slapping sound and the dough should be very elastic and completely wrapped around the hook. It should now look shiny and you should be able to stretch out a small piece of it like a piece of cloth. This technique is called the windowpane (SEE PHOTO). If you cannot, mix the dough for another 3 minutes.

3 Add half of the soft butter to the dough and mix at low speed to incorporate it, about 2 minutes. At the beginning it will look like the butter will not incorporate, but that is normal. Be patient and don't panic, even if you see a lot of very soft butter on the surface of the dough during the first minutes of mixing. After 2 minutes, stop the machine and scrape the butter and the dough together with a rubber spatula and mix for another 2 minutes. Eventually it will all be absorbed. Add the remaining soft butter and repeat this mixing procedure at medium speed for a total of 4 to 5 minutes. The brioche dough should once again be elastic and shiny and the butter should now be completely incorporated.

4 Place the dough in a medium bowl, dust it with a small amount of all-purpose flour, and cover the bowl with plastic wrap or a hand towel. Let the dough rest at room temperature or in a warm place that is not hotter than 80.6°F/27°C until it doubles in volume. This can take 1 to 1½ hours depending on the temperature of the room. Avoid drafty spots, as drafts can cool the dough so much that it will put the yeast to sleep and stop or delay the fermentation process. On the other hand, leaving the dough in an area that is too hot will do two things: it will make the butter melt out of the dough, and it will overheat the yeast and possibly kill it. You can create an ideal environment for rising in your oven if your oven isn't a gas oven with a pilot light. Fill a small saucepan with 1 inch of boiling water and place it in the cold oven. Set the dough in the oven along with the pan of steaming water and close the oven door. The hot water will provide heat and humidity. This system works very well, as it will also keep the dough away from drafts.

5 Once the dough has doubled in volume it is time to press out the first gases created by the action of the yeast. Failing to do so will allow these gases to increase and create a very foul, yeasty smell. Press down on the dough with your fist or the palm of your hand; you will hear the sound of the gas emerging from the dough. Cover the bowl with plastic and place in the refrigerator for 2 hours, after which time the dough should be cold and it should have risen again.

6 Press out the gases again, cover, and let the dough rest in the refrigerator overnight.

DAY 2

1 After the overnight rest it is time to shape your brioche. Dust your work surface lightly with flour. Line a sheet pan with parchment paper. Using a round bowl scraper, scrape out the dough and place it on your work surface. Cut 55-gram (2-ounce) pieces of dough and place them on the edge of the counter away from you, leaving a lot of space in front of you for shaping the brioche. Making sure that your work area is lightly dusted with flour, place 1 piece of dough in front of you. Lightly dust your hands with flour and place one hand over a piece of dough. Cup the dough and start pressing on it while making clockwise circles. At first you need to press hard so that the dough sticks to the table a little, and then you ease the pressing while tightening the cupping. This will take a few tries until you get the hang of it. Once you get comfortable shaping with one hand try shaping 2 pieces of dough, 1 with each hand at the same time. When I do this, my right hand circles counterclockwise while my left hand circles clockwise. When the shaping is done you should have perfectly round spheres of dough. If the dough sticks to the table too much, stop shaping and dust the work surface again with a very small amount of flour, keeping in mind that over-flouring the dough will make it dry and impossible to shape. Using just the right amount of flour is key; not too much and not too little. After you shape the brioche spheres, place them straight onto the parchment paper–lined sheet pan, leaving 1 inch of space

There's No Substitute for Butter (Certainly Not Shortening!)

Your taste buds will only experience the wonderful flavors of brioche if you use the best ingredients available. This means butter. The opposite will happen if you decide to substitute the butter with . . . *shortening*. Yes, I just said the "S" word. When I teach, I explain the wonders of butter, but sometimes students ask me if they can use shortening or margarine like their grandma uses in her brioche or challah recipe. I answer that, yes, technically they can, but first I invite them to eat a piece of bread topped with some shortening. The response is always immediate—they want to gag at the thought of eating straight shortening. But is it any better when it is incorporated into the recipe so that we don't see it? Shortening, originally invented by soap makers, was at one time presented to the public as a "healthy" alternative to lard or butter, as was margarine (which, I tell my students, is one molecule away from being plastic). Today we all know that these ingredients have a high trans-fat content and are not healthy at all. More significantly for pastry lovers, they will never taste like butter.

Brioche Nanterre

Large brioche called brioche Nanterre is made by placing the dough spheres side by side in a greased rectangular loaf pan. The spheres should sit in the pan comfortably and be in contact with each other while not being squeezed too tightly together, as they will need room to expand. A large brioche Nanterre will take 25 to 30 minutes to bake, depending on its size. Insert a knife in the center of the baked brioche to make sure that it is done.

RECIPES REQUIRING
BRIOCHE

Brioche Streusel
(PAGE 307)
Bee Sting Brioche
(PAGE 311)
Chinois
(PAGE 315)
Brioche Bostock
(PAGE 319)
Cherry Bread Pudding
(PAGE 339)

between each sphere, as they will expand when they rise. You can also place them in individual buttered molds of your choice or silicone Flexipan molds.

2 Using a soft pastry brush, lightly brush the surface of the brioche with egg wash, without allowing the wash to run down the sides onto the parchment paper. Place the brioche uncovered in a warm and, if possible, humid area away from drafts; the temperature should be around 80.6°F/27°C. Let the brioche double in volume; this can take anywhere from 1 to 1½ hours, depending on the temperature of the room.

3 Meanwhile, preheat your oven to 350°F/180°C. Adjust the rack to the center of the oven and remove any racks that may be above it, as they could block the brioche as they rise in the oven. Before baking, very gently egg-wash the brioche again using the flat side of the brush, as they are extremely fragile at this stage. You have the option of sprinkling coarse crystal sugar, streusel topping (PAGE 9), or even chopped caramelized nuts (PAGE 51) on top of the surface before baking. This will contribute great added texture and flavor. Place the brioche in the oven and bake 15 to 18 minutes, until golden brown.

IT'S DONE WHEN IT'S DONE

When brioche is baked long enough and at the right temperature, it will have a golden-brown crust and hold its shape. If you insert a knife for 2 seconds and withdraw it there will be no dough on the knife.

STORAGE

Brioche has a 2- to 3-day shelf life in a cloth bag at room temperature or in a plastic bag if you live in a very dry climate. No matter what, never refrigerate brioche or any other bread. Bread molds faster in the refrigerator than out because of the moisture in the refrigerator. Bread will also absorb all the smells present in your refrigerator.

You can wrap brioche in plastic wrap and freeze it for up to 1 month. To defrost, just take out of the freezer, unwrap, and let it defrost at room temperature for at least 2 hours.

JACQUY'S TAKEAWAYS

→ Making yeast dough requires patience, as you cannot speed up the rising process and hope to obtain a good product. The more patient you are, the tastier your brioche will be.

→ Be careful not to forget about your *poolish*. If you leave it to ferment for 45 minutes to an hour instead of for 15 minutes the yeast will over-ferment and create a foul yeasty smell. You will then have to make a new *poolish*.

CLASSIC PUFF PASTRY (LAMINATED DOUGH) / PÂTE FEUILLETÉE

YIELD | 1000 GRAMS/2 POUNDS/ 1 "BOOK"

2-DAY RECIPE

INGREDIENTS	WEIGHT	MEASURE (APPROXIMATE) OR OUNCE WEIGHT
White vinegar	3 grams	¾ teaspoon
Cold water	180 grams	¾ cup plus 1 tablespoon or 6½ fluid ounces
Sea salt	12 grams	1¾ teaspoons
All-purpose flour	400 grams	3½ cups plus 2 tablespoons
Butter (French style, 82% fat), at room temperature	60 grams	2 ounces
Butter (French style, 82% fat), at room temperature	340 grams	12 ounces
Confectioners' sugar, optional	As needed	As needed

BEFORE YOU BEGIN

→ Get out the following equipment and allow all of the ingredients except the 180 grams of water to come to room temperature:

Digital scale, set to metric weights
2 small mixing bowls
1 small stainless steel hand whisk
1 ramekin or small bowl
1 small rubber spatula
1 large chef's knife
Plastic wrap
1 dough scraper
1 ruler
1 rolling pin
1 full-sized silpat
2 or more sheet pans
Parchment paper
1 fork or dough docker
1 wire rack

→ Read this recipe through twice from start to finish.

My father used puff pastry for his apple turnovers and palmiers, and I remember helping him when I was as young as ten years old. He was so particular about the lamination of the dough and the proper layering that none of us, neither my brother nor my sisters nor I, wanted to be called upon for *pâte feuilletée* duty. If our layers were uneven, resulting in puff that would not rise straight up, my father would be furious because the final product would be unfit to sell. For us even funny, organic-looking warm apple turnovers coming out of the oven were small bites of pure heaven, but that's not how my father saw it.

One of my favorite creations made with puff pastry is mille-feuille (PAGE 116), also called a Napoléon, made of 3 layers of flaky puff pastry separated by 2 layers of pastry cream. It might sound deceptively simple, but when well executed it is unbeatable, one of the eternal classics of French pastry.

Making puff pastry requires patience, perseverance, and practice. I highly recommend that you undertake this recipe in a cold or air-conditioned environment so that the butter does not become soft on you. If you're a novice and you're working in a hot kitchen in the middle of July, now is not the time for this puff pastry lesson. Read on and you'll see why this matters. This is a 2-day operation, so plan accordingly.

Puff pastry dough consists of many alternating layers of butter and dough that are achieved by enclosing 1 large square of butter in 1 piece

The choice of flour is critical for this recipe. I use all-purpose because of its lower gluten content as compared to bread flour. Think of gluten as powdered rubber that is activated by heat and water. As soon as the dough is mixed, the gluten develops and becomes rubbery. Too much of this will result in a dough that will shrink uncontrollably.

White vinegar does two things: it relaxes the gluten, and it prolongs the shelf life of the dough due to its acidity. Without the vinegar the raw dough would turn gray after 2 days in the refrigerator.

Sea salt is the salt of choice for pastry chefs, and the one I recommend for all cooking. It is much healthier for you than rock salt because it is iodized, and it does not taste too salty.

The type of butter you use for puff pastry is crucial. You must use butter with a fat content of 82 percent, because it has less water in it. When you find inexpensive butter in the supermarket the low price is often due to the fact that the butter is loaded with water. This extra water will create excess steam during the baking process, which makes the dough rise tremendously; but more water in the butter also means fewer solids, and your puff will eventually collapse.

of dough, rolling this out, and then repeating a series of folds, turns, rests, followed by rolling it out again. Each turn of the dough results in several layers of butter and dough, until eventually the dough forms a "book" of more than 2,000 thinly and evenly rolled-out sheets. This process is called lamination. When done properly, the sheets all separate when the dough is baked, making it the flakiest dough in pastry.

METHOD

DAY 1

MAKING THE *DÉTREMPE*

The dough base in puff pastry is called the *détrempe*. I recommend that you make this by hand several times before you make it in a mixer so that you will really understand what the dough should feel like. You will need a large work surface—at least 18 inches square and preferably larger.

1 In a small bowl mix the white vinegar, water, and sea salt with a whisk until the salt dissolves.

2 Spread the flour on the work surface in a wide, flat circle and create a 14- to 16-inch-wide "well" in the center. The flour should look like a large lunar crater with a wide, flat well and walls that are about an inch high.

3 Make sure that the 60-gram piece of butter is soft—place it in a small bowl or ramekin and mix with a spatula. Microwave if necessary for 5 seconds at 50 percent power but do not allow the butter to melt. Place the soft butter in the middle of the flour crater and *slowly* pour in the water mixture. It should remain contained within the walls of the crater. If your well is too small or you pour the water in too fast it will break through the walls and flow out.

4 Use one hand only for mixing. If you are right-handed, shape your right hand like a claw and place it in the center of the well with the fingertips touching the tabletop. Move your fingers around in the flour inside the well in increasingly wider circles, working from the center to incorporate flour into the butter/liquid mixture and always touching the tabletop with your fingertips. Use your other hand to bolster up the sides of the crater as you work from the center to the outside of the crater, mixing in more and more flour until all of the flour has been incorporated. Once all the flour is absorbed, continue to mix the dough gently with one hand without kneading it. If you knead the dough you will over-activate the gluten, resulting in rubbery dough that will shrink out of control when baked. Just gently work the dough around on the tabletop with your fingers to homogenize it. The dough should come together and feel and look rough, but it should not feel dry; if it does feel dry add 1 to 2 tablespoons of water to it and gently work it in.

5 Once the dough has come together, use your dry hand to scrape off any dough sticking to your mixing hand, and mix these scraps into the dough. Lightly flour your hands and cup them around the dough. Without kneading it, shape the dough into a ball. The completely mixed dough should look and feel homogenized but will still be rough and a bit ragged.

6 With a chef's knife, cut a ¾-inch-deep cross on top of the ball. This will cut some of the gluten strands in half and therefore slow down the gluten's action.

USING A STAND MIXER

Once you are comfortable making this dough by hand, you will be ready to switch to a mixer fitted with a hook. In a small bowl mix the white vinegar, water, and sea salt with a whisk until the salt dissolves. Place half the mixture in the bowl of your mixer and add the pastry flour and the softened 60-gram piece of butter. Begin mixing at low speed and gradually add the remaining water mixture. Mix only until the dough comes together. It should look rough but you should not see any unmixed flour. It should be a little sticky but not soupy. Turn off the mixer and feel the dough. If you cannot detect any lumps with your hand, the dough is mixed sufficiently. If there are lumps, mix for just a few seconds at a time until the flour is incorporated. I cannot stress enough the importance of not over-mixing. Be careful. The mixer is much more efficient than your hands.

Wrap the *détrempe* in plastic wrap and cool in a refrigerator for 1 hour. Clean up your work area: first use a flat scraper to remove all flour and dough left on the surface, then wash and dry the work surface.

7 While your dough is resting shape your butter block. Using a marker, draw a 7¼ × 9–inch rectangle on a sheet of plastic wrap. Place the 340-gram block of butter on another sheet of plastic, set the marked sheet of plastic on top, and, using a rolling pin, gently roll the butter into a 7¼ × 9–inch rectangle, using the marking on the top sheet of plastic wrap as guidelines. Do not press down too hard and be careful that the rectangle is the same thickness all over. Wrap the shaped butter block in plastic wrap and place it in the refrigerator for 1 hour.

WRAPPING THE BUTTER BLOCK AND LAMINATING THE DOUGH

1 Before you begin, make sure that both the butter block and the dough are properly chilled. They should be at refrigerator temperature, about 40°F. This is crucial. If they are not cold enough, return them to the refrigerator. Both the dough and the butter block should be cold and firm but still somewhat pliable. I recommend that you roll the dough on a full silpat instead of on a table or a board so that if the dough gets too sticky you'll be able to transfer it to the refrigerator on the silpat and salvage it. Once you are more comfortable you will be able to work directly on a work surface dusted with flour. First make sure your work area is ready and that all your tools are close at hand; then take the dough out of the refrigerator.

FIGURE 1

2 Dust the silpat or work surface with flour and place the dough on top. Press the dough flat with the rolling pin, then roll it out to a rectangle that is 18 inches long by 7½ inches wide. Roll gently and evenly in one direction only. Keep sliding the dough on the silpat to make sure that it doesn't stick; if it sticks, stop rolling and dust the rolling surface with a small amount of flour. Roll the dough a little longer and wider than 18 × 7½ inches to allow for shrinkage, because dough always shrinks due to the gluten in the flour.

3 Remove the butter block from the refrigerator and place it on your work surface, leaving it wrapped in plastic. Tap it *gently* on the top surface for 30 seconds with the rolling pin in order to make it more pliable while not changing its shape or size. If the butter is not pliable it will not allow itself to be rolled out. Instead it will shatter.

4 Position the rolled-out dough and the silpat horizontally on the counter (with the long side closest to you). Unwrap the butter and place it on the left half of the rectangle. It should cover half the dough with a very small margin on the sides. Fold the right half of the dough over the butter block and seal

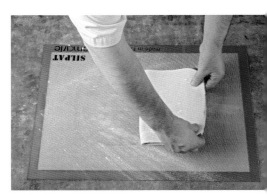

FIGURE 2

all seams so that the butter is completely enclosed in the dough (SEE FIGURES 1 AND 2). You should not be able to see any butter at all. Tap the dough gently for 30 seconds with your rolling pin, turn it, and tap again, continuing until the dough and the butter are bound together. Turn the silpat and dough vertically.

5 Now you are ready to roll out the dough and make the first "turn." The absolute key to this procedure is to make sure that the dough and the butter are cold yet still pliable and that you work quickly so that neither the dough nor the butter becomes too soft. If the butter becomes too soft it will ooze out from the dough; if it is too hard it will crack and break into small lumps during the rolling process (this is why you should never chill the butter in the freezer). Dust your silpat or rolling area generously with flour, place the dough on it, and dust the surface of the dough as well. Slide the dough back and forth on the silpat a few times to make sure that it won't stick. Start rolling out the dough gently and evenly. It is important not to apply too much pressure to one particular area of the dough, as this will result in uneven layers of dough and butter, causing them to rise and bake unevenly. Roll in long continuous strokes over the entire dough and make sure to roll over the ends. Another crucial thing is to roll the dough for only 10 seconds at a time, then stop and check to make sure that the dough isn't sticking to the silpat or table. If the dough does not slide, stop rolling at once and dust more flour underneath to ensure that it will (this principle is the same for all rolled doughs). Also, if the rolling pin gets sticky, stop rolling and dust it and the top of the dough lightly with flour. If the butter feels soft during the rolling and oozes out of the dough, it has become too warm. Stop rolling immediately and place the dough-and-butter "book" in the refrigerator for 30 minutes. If the butter breaks apart and looks like a cracked desert floor the butter is too cold or was not tapped enough to make it pliable. In this case, stop rolling at once and leave the book on the work surface for 5 minutes, flipping it over every 2 minutes so that it will warm up evenly, then continue rolling it out.

6 Roll the dough out to a 12-inch square, then to a rectangle about ¼ inch thick, which should be about 18 inches long by 7½ to 8 inches wide. If you are working on a full-sized silpat it will help to position your silpat vertically in front of you so that the short end is nearest to you.

7 Once you have obtained a ¼-inch-thick rectangle, turn the rectangle horizontally, so the long edge is closest to you, and brush off the surface with a dry pastry brush. Then fold the dough like a business letter—fold the right third of the rectangle over the center third and the left third over the center. This is the first of 6 turns. Using your thumb or a finger, make a slight indent on the dough's surface to register the first book fold. Wrap tightly in plastic (you can also mark the plastic to indicate 1 turn) and refrigerate for 30 minutes.

JACQUY'S TAKEAWAYS

→ Be aware of humidity when making dough of any kind. Flour will always absorb the humidity in the air. In dry conditions you might need to add some extra water when mixing up dough, and in very humid conditions you might have to keep some back. The best bakers are the ones who can feel the weather conditions and act appropriately.

→ Puff pastry can be used for a myriad of things beyond the classic French pastries that we love. Try using it as a savory or sweet flatbread, as the base for elephant ears or cheese straws, or as a crust for a fruit tart.

→ Don't be afraid of puff pastry. This formula works beautifully, and once you get the hang of rolling it out and making the turns, especially if you have a large silpat to roll it on, you won't think twice about making a batch whenever you need one.

8 Flour your work surface or silpat and place the folded dough on top with the open ends facing you and the folded edges to your right and left (SEE FIG-URE 3). Roll the dough out to a rectangle about ¼ inch thick. Turn it 90 degrees so that it is horizontal on your work surface (with what were the open ends to your right and left), and fold it again like a business letter. This is the second turn. With your finger, make 2 small indentations on the top of your dough to mark the 2 book folds that you have made. Wrap airtight in plastic (you can also mark the lines on the plastic) and place the dough in the refrigerator for 1 to 2 hours. This is necessary for the dough and butter to cool and for the gluten to relax, as it has been activated by the rolling.

9 After the rest, repeat the book folds 2 more times, allowing the dough to rest in the refrigerator for 30 minutes between each turn. Mark the dough and/or plastic after each turn. You should have 4 turns with 4 indents. Wrap the dough airtight and let rest in the refrigerator overnight.

FIGURE 3

DAY 2

The next day, make 2 more book folds and mark the dough with 2 indents. The dough is now ready to be used, but before that it needs to rest for 1 hour, or for as long as 48 hours, in the refrigerator. It can also be frozen at this point in its raw stage. To freeze, cut into 3 or 4 equal pieces and roll out to a ¼- to ½-inch thickness. Place the pieces on a sheet of parchment paper and place the parchment paper on a sheet pan. Lay a sheet of plastic over the top of the rolled-out dough, chill in the freezer until stiff, then wrap airtight in plastic. To defrost, just let the sheet of dough come to room temperature on a sheet pan for 30 minutes.

ROLLING OUT THE PUFF PASTRY

Cut the pastry into 4 equal pieces. Line a sheet pan with parchment paper. Roll out each piece of pastry to a ¼-inch-thick square or rectangle, depending on the recipe you are using the puff pastry for, and place on the parchment paper. Make sure to roll the sheets out evenly. Cover with plastic and refrigerate while you roll out the next piece. Place the next rolled-out piece on a sheet of parchment paper and set on top of the first rolled-out sheet on the sheet pan. Cover with plastic. Repeat with the remaining dough. Let the dough rest for 1 hour or longer in the refrigerator before baking.

BAKING INSTRUCTIONS

1 Remove the plastic from between the layers. Unless you have a convection oven, I recommend that you bake 1 sheet at a time in the middle of the oven.

Two other methods for making puff pastry exist. One is called "inverted puff," in which the dough is trapped in the butter instead of the other way around. It's difficult to roll out, but the resulting puff is slightly flakier. The other method is called "quick puff," because all the ingredients are mixed together and rolled out right away. This method is faster but in my opinion does not provide the same flaky result.

Preheat the oven to 400°F/200°C (or 375°F/190°C for convection). The first 15 minutes of baking must be at a high heat in order to transform the water present in the layers into steam. This steam will force the layers to separate and make the puff rise. A cooler oven would create too little steam and a flat puff, which is unfortunately irreparable. Before baking the sheets of puff pastry, place each one on a sheet pan lined with parchment paper and poke it all over with a fork, allowing ¾ inch of spacing between each poke. The holes will allow the steam to escape from the dough so that it rises evenly. You can also use a dough docker, a spiked cylindrical wheel that does the job very efficiently.

2 To further ensure that the puff rises evenly and that the top remains flat, place a wire rack over the sheet of pastry, legs down but not touching the dough. You will remove the rack after the first 30 minutes of baking. Place the pastry in the oven and set the timer for 15 minutes. The puff should have risen. Now turn the oven down to 325°F/160°C and set the timer for 15 minutes. Remove the rack from the top of the puff and continue to bake at the lower temperature for another 30 to 40 minutes, until golden brown all the way through. This amount of time—1 hour total or a little longer—is necessary to ensure that all of the water present in the dough has evaporated, which is what makes the puff pastry flaky. If you leave the dough too long, however, it will burn, so watch carefully.

3 If you want your baked puff pastry to be caramelized, flip the fully baked puff pastry over so that the top is perfectly flat and sprinkle with confectioners' sugar. Place it under a preheated broiler, about 3 inches from the heat, for 1 to 3 minutes, until the sugar is transformed into a golden caramel. Watch very closely so that you don't burn the pastry. This contributes great flavor and texture to the puff.

IT'S DONE WHEN IT'S DONE

A properly baked puff pastry will be golden brown all the way through, including in the center. If it is at all white in the center the dough will be tough and gooey. Underbaked puff pastry is a sacrilege.

STORAGE

Unbaked puff pastry can be stored for 2 days in the refrigerator. Puff pastry can be frozen raw or as a finished baked product. See above instructions, Day 2 **(PAGE 33)** for storing puff pastry after the last turn. Whether raw or baked, make sure to double-wrap in plastic before freezing. You can keep it in the freezer for 1 month.

VANILLA CUSTARD SAUCE / CRÈME ANGLAISE

YIELD | 652 GRAMS (ABOUT 3 CUPS)

INGREDIENTS	WEIGHT	MEASURE (APPROXIMATE) OR OUNCE WEIGHT
Whole milk (3.5% fat)	250 grams	1 cup plus 1 tablespoon
Heavy cream (35% fat)	250 grams	1 cup plus 1 tablespoon
Granulated sugar	68 grams	⅓ cup
Vanilla bean	1½ beans	1½ beans
Egg yolks	150 grams	8 to 9 yolks
Granulated sugar	68 grams	⅓ cup

This quintessential custard sauce goes with a variety of dishes. It has everything you want from a sauce: it's rich, smooth, and feels light at the same time. Custard sauce is a simple mixture of sweetened milk and cream flavored with vanilla that is gently cooked with egg yolks until thick. I make mine with a mixture of milk and cream because I like the richness, but you can use all whole milk if you prefer a lighter sauce. You would substitute an equal amount of milk for the cream listed in the ingredient list.

METHOD

1 Fill a large bowl with ice and set a ramekin in the middle that you can balance a medium bowl on.

2 Set aside 50 grams of the milk (about ¼ cup) and place the rest of the milk, all of the cream, and 68 grams of the sugar in a medium saucepan. On a cutting board cut the vanilla beans in half lengthwise, scrape the seeds into the saucepan with the tip of your knife, and add the pods to the saucepan. Place over medium heat and stir for 10 seconds to make sure that the sugar does not stick to the bottom of the pan.

3 Meanwhile, combine the egg yolks and the remaining 68 grams of sugar in a medium mixing bowl and whisk immediately for 30 seconds; failing to do so will allow the sugar to "burn" the yolks and create small orange lumps. The sugar properly mixed with the yolks will create a buffer around the egg yolk proteins, which helps prevent the coagulation from taking place too quickly. Add the 50 grams of milk you set aside to the egg yolk mixture.

4 When the milk comes to a boil in the saucepan, turn off the heat. Remove the split vanilla pods and place them aside on a plate. Stirring constantly with

BEFORE YOU BEGIN

⤏ Get out the following equipment and allow all of the ingredients to come to room temperature:

Digital scale, set to metric weights
1 large mixing bowl
Ice cubes
1 small ramekin or shallow cup
1 medium saucepan (do not use aluminum)
1 paring knife
1 medium mixing bowl
1 medium stainless steel hand whisk
1 large rubber spatula
1 digital thermometer
1 medium strainer
Plastic wrap

⤏ Read this recipe through twice from start to finish.

$50 TRICK: If you combine the milk with the vanilla seeds and beans the day before and refrigerate it overnight, you will give the water in the milk a chance to absorb the vanilla flavor and you will need to use only half of the vanilla required in this recipe.

This recipe calls for a fair amount of egg yolk. The yolks are important because they contain a natural emulsifier called lecithin. Because one end of the lecithin molecule is attracted to water and the other is attracted to fat, its structure facilitates the melding of the dairy fat, the egg yolk fat, and the water present in both the yolks and the milk. The yolks play a vital roll in the coagulation of the sauce—the transformation of the milk, sugar, and egg yolks from a liquid to a thick mixture with a firm structure. Egg proteins are made of strands that are folded together when the egg is raw. When they start to warm up in the milk they unfold and detach, then once the mixture reaches 165°F/75°C to 180°F/80°C they reattach back together and solidify, allowing the mixture to thicken into a smooth, thick custard sauce.

However, this will not happen properly if you don't stir the mixture constantly and keep the heat low. Without the continuous stirring and low heat the proteins in the yolks cannot unfold and reconnect evenly. If you stop stirring, the proteins on the bottom of the pan closest to the heat will get too hot and you will have scrambled eggs rather than a smooth custard sauce. Tempering the yolks—adding some of the hot milk to

the whisk, pour about 2 cups of the hot milk into the egg yolk mixture. Whisk the egg yolk mixture back into the hot milk in the saucepan. Quickly rinse and dry your medium bowl and place it in the bowl of ice with a strainer set on top, or use a second bowl.

5 Place the saucepan back on low heat. Using a rubber spatula, stir constantly and everywhere until you feel the mixture starting to thicken. Stirring in a figure-8 pattern helps to assure that your spatula touches the entire bottom of the pan. To test whether or not your sauce is thick enough, take your pan off the heat, lift your spatula from the saucepan with some sauce on it and run a finger down the middle. It should leave a canal. Place a thermometer in the saucepan and stir the mixture constantly with the spatula over low heat until the temperature reaches between 165°F/75°C and 185°F/85°C.

6 Immediately strain the mixture into the clean dry mixing bowl set in the ice. The ramekin under the bowl will keep it steady once the ice begins to melt. Stir for a few minutes, then once every few minutes, until the mixture has cooled. It is important that you cool the egg mixture down in 20 minutes or less so that it is safe to use and the salmonella bacteria do not have a chance to reproduce. If you do not have enough ice on hand, place the bowl in your freezer and stir once every few minutes. Once cool, transfer to a container, cover tightly with plastic wrap, and refrigerate until ready to use.

IT'S DONE WHEN IT'S DONE

The sauce should be thick and creamy. It should not be runny or grainy. A runny custard indicates that you did not cook it long enough for it to coagulate sufficiently. If it is grainy, you overcooked and scrambled the eggs.

STORAGE

Custard will keep for up to 48 hours in the refrigerator. We never freeze a vanilla sauce, as the water in it will create ice crystals that will shred through the bonds created by the coagulation. When you defrost it, it will turn into a grainy, watery soup.

EGG SAFETY

If you know how to handle custards safely there is absolutely no reason to worry about salmonella poisoning. The concern with salmonella—more like paranoia—is so far out of proportion that many people feel that just to be safe they should pasteurize or sanitize anything that comes into contact with chickens and eggs, even though the chemicals used in sanitizers are toxic, and this overuse of sanitizers eventually makes you less resistant to diseases and allergies.

Cooks make custards safely every day following simple rules that don't involve poisonous chemicals. The four things to remember are:

1 **Use fresh and unprocessed ingredients.**
They taste much better and are less prone to bacterial infection. The eggs will get cooked in this recipe, but using old ones definitely creates an unnecessary obstacle to success.

2 **Cook the product to the right temperature.**
Bacteria can thrive in fresh egg yolks between the temperatures of 41°F/5°C and 135°F/57°C. This means that once you take a fresh egg out of the refrigerator to let it come to room temperature the egg will soon reach a temperature that is favorable to bacteria growth. But this is no reason to panic, since in pastry we bake or cook all of our products that use egg yolks. When we make custard or vanilla sauce we bring the temperature of the eggs up to a minimum of 165°F/75°C to make it safe; 185°F/85°C will kill most but not all of the salmonella bacteria.

3 **Cool the product quickly and keep it refrigerated until it is consumed.**
It's crucial to cool the custard in less than 20 minutes because that's the amount of time it takes for salmonella to produce a new generation of bacteria. That's why we use the ice bath, or for pastry cream (PAGE 39) the freezer. I have seen people cook a custard perfectly so that most of the salmonella bacteria is dead and the custard is safe to eat, but then leave it to "air cool" for hours on the counter. Since cooking does not destroy every single salmonella bacterium that may be present in the custard, if you allow the custard to sit in a warm environment (between 41°F/5°C and 135°F/57°C) a new generation of bacteria will emerge every 20 minutes. Keeping egg custards in the refrigerator or freezer does not kill the bacteria; it just puts them to sleep. The dormant bacteria will wake up as soon as the custard warms up. You will prevent this from happening if you keep and serve your custard cold.

4 **The same goes for chicken.**
Think about these things the next time you bring chicken leftovers home from a restaurant in a doggie bag or container and stick it in the refrigerator overnight. It will take hours for the cold refrigerator temperature to reach the core of that chicken. My recommendation is that you take the lid off the container and refrigerate it until the chicken is cold, then return the lid.

them before stirring the mixture back into the rest of the hot milk—also helps ensure that the strands unfold and reattach evenly.

Another reason why the operation must happen at a low temperature is that this will give the strands of protein time to trap moisture as they reconnect; this is what makes a custard sauce so creamy. Using high heat would cause a sudden coagulation that would result in a dry and rubbery mixture full of small tunnels. The principle applies to many creamy egg yolk–based desserts: it's why cheesecake is usually baked in a water bath at a low temperature, so the water can act as a buffer and ensure a slow and effective coagulation.

The sugar added to the egg yolks acts as a buffer so that the coagulation will not happen too quickly. But adding all of the sugar at once to the yolks could also make them coagulate because there is a certain amount of acid in the sugar. So we add half the sugar to the milk and half to the yolks before we mix the two together. We also add a small proportion of the milk to the yolks to act as a buffer.

Using low-fat or fat-free milk will not work; the vanilla sauce will be watery and tasteless.

RECIPES REQUIRING VANILLA
CUSTARD SAUCE OR A
VARIATION (THE INGREDIENTS
WILL VARY BUT THE TECHNIQUE
IS THE SAME)

❧

Black Forest Cake

(PAGE 259)

Chocolate and Hazelnut Yule Log

(PAGE 249)

Vanilla Ice Cream

(PAGE 271)

Kougelhof Ice Cream Cake

(PAGE 275)

Vacherin Glacé

(PAGE 281)

Frozen Coffee and Chocolate Mousse

(PAGE 289)

❧

JACQUY'S TAKEAWAYS

→ Do not use aluminum pans when working with eggs, as the metal will react with them and cause the eggs to discolor. This will make the vanilla sauce turn gray.

→ If you overcook and scramble the sauce you can save it by mixing it with an immersion blender for 10 seconds while it is still hot. This will bring it back together and make it usable, though it will not be quite as creamy.

→ To make vanilla sugar, rinse the vanilla beans after removing them from the milk and allow them to air dry thoroughly. Then insert the beans into a container of granulated sugar, or grind the vanilla beans with the sugar, and use in other pastries.

PASTRY CREAM

YIELD | ABOUT 1¼ CUPS (ENOUGH FOR 2 DOZEN 2-INCH ÉCLAIRS OR *SALAMBOS*)

INGREDIENTS	WEIGHT	MEASURE (APPROXIMATE) OR OUNCE WEIGHT
Whole milk (3.5% fat)	250 grams	1 cup plus 1 tablespoon
Butter (French style, 82% fat)	25 grams	1 ounce or 2 tablespoons
Granulated sugar	32 grams	2½ tablespoons
Vanilla bean	½ bean	½ bean
Cornstarch	10 grams	1 tablespoon
Cake flour	10 grams	1 tablespoon
Granulated sugar	32 grams	2½ tablespoons
Egg yolks	60 grams	About 4 yolks, depending on the size of the eggs

I love pastry cream. It is a fundamental recipe—a custard with added starch that can be used to fill cakes, tarts, mille-feuilles (Napoléons), Danish pastries, éclairs, or cream puffs. It can be varied with any number of flavorings, including chocolate, coffee, kirsch, caramel, nut pastes, or orange zest, but my favorite is vanilla. A good pastry cream should be smooth and shiny, which indicates that the fat has been properly emulsified. In addition to being used on its own, pastry cream is used as a base for several other creams that have products like butter, butter cream, Italian meringue, or whipped cream added to it.

METHOD

1 In the saucepan combine all but ¼ cup of the milk, the butter, 32 grams of the sugar, and the vanilla bean seeds and pod. Stir with a whisk and place over medium heat.

2 Meanwhile, in a medium bowl whisk the cornstarch and the flour together with the remaining 32 grams of sugar. Add the remaining ¼ cup of milk and whisk in the egg yolks.

3 When the milk mixture comes to a boil, turn off the heat and remove the vanilla bean (set it on a sheet of paper towel to dry). Whisk half of the hot milk mixture into the egg yolk mixture. Strain the egg yolk mixture back into the saucepan with the remaining milk.

4 Turn the heat back onto medium and whisk the mixture, making sure to whisk everywhere—bottom and sides and bottom edges of the pan—so that

BEFORE YOU BEGIN

→ Get out the following equipment and allow all of the ingredients to come to room temperature:

Digital scale, set to metric weights
1 sheet pan
Plastic wrap
1 paring knife
1 medium stainless steel saucepan
1 medium mixing bowl
1 stainless steel hand whisk
1 strainer

→ Line a sheet pan with plastic wrap.

→ Split the vanilla bean lengthwise in half and scrape the seeds out with a paring knife.

→ Read this recipe through twice from start to finish.

To make good pastry cream you have to allow the coagulation to happen gradually. If it happens too quickly the eggs cannot trap any water, so it will be dry and chalky.

UNDERSTANDING INGREDIENTS

There is no point in using anything other than whole milk for pastry cream. Low-fat or skim milk will make the cream soupy because of the lack of fat and proteins.

Cornstarch and cake flour are used to bind and stabilize the custard and give it a pudding-like consistency. I use half cornstarch and half cake flour (some other pastry chefs use just one or the other). Using all cornstarch would give the pastry cream the glossy consistency of a cheap, fast-food Chinese sauce; using all flour would result in a pastry cream that is rubbery, because of the gluten in the flour, even though cake flour has the lowest amount of gluten of any white flour (between 7 and 9 percent).

The lecithin in the egg yolk binds the liquid and the fat so that the mixture thickens and remains moist; that is why egg yolk is often used to bind sauces.

Butter gives the pastry cream a rich flavor. I add my butter to the milk when I heat it. You could also add butter to the mixture at the end of the cooking to make it creamier.

the mixture does not scorch. As soon as you feel that the mixture is becoming slightly thick on the bottom of the pan, remove it from the heat and whisk for about 30 seconds until the mixture is thick and thoroughly uniform. This will allow a slow and even coagulation of the eggs and result in a nice, creamy pastry cream. Return to medium heat and bring back to a boil, whisking constantly. Cook, whisking for 1 minute to cook out the starch flavor.

5 Immediately remove the pastry cream from the heat and transfer to the plastic-lined sheet pan. Spread in a flat, even layer and place another sheet of plastic wrap directly on top of the cream so that it is not in contact with the air. This will prevent the pastry cream from developing a dry skin. Place the sheet pan in the freezer to cool the cream rapidly and stop the growth of bacteria. This should only take 15 minutes.

6 During the cooling process the pastry cream separates a little, so once it is cold, place in a medium mixing bowl and whisk until it has a uniform and creamy look. Scrape into a bowl, cover with plastic wrap, and refrigerate.

IT'S DONE WHEN IT'S DONE

The pastry cream should be thick, silky, and smooth, with no starchy flavor. You will know that it has cooled properly in the sheet pan when the center of the bottom of the sheet pan is cold to the touch.

STORAGE

Store in the refrigerator in a covered bowl for up to 2 days.

PASTRY CREAM VARIATIONS

MOUSSELINE: Soft butter or butter cream is added to the pastry cream once the pastry cream is chilled.

CRÈME DIPLOMATE: Butter and whipped cream are added to the pastry cream once it is chilled.

CRÈME LÉGÈRE: Whipped cream is added to the pastry cream once it is chilled.

FLAVORINGS: You can add different flavors such as chocolate, alcohol, coffee, nut paste, or caramel to pastry cream. As a general rule (and there are variations and exceptions) we use the following guidelines at the French Pastry School for the amount of flavorings to use:

Alcohol: 2–4% of total weight

Hazelnut praline: 7–10% of total weight

Coffee extract: 3–5% of total weight

JACQUY'S TAKEAWAYS

→ Do not use aluminum pans when working with eggs, as the metal will react with them and cause the eggs to discolor. This will make the pastry cream turn gray.

→ Pastry cream cannot be frozen. The water will turn into crystals that shred through the cream and make the mixture soupy when defrosted.

→ Rinse the vanilla bean and allow it to air dry completely. Once dry it can be reused by placing it in a jar of granulated sugar or ground in a food processor or spice mill to use as vanilla powder.

→ **$50 TRICK:** You can intensify the vanilla flavor in this pastry cream by placing the split vanilla bean in the milk the day before you make this.

RECIPES REQUIRING
PASTRY CREAM

Salambos
(PAGE 93)

Éclairs
(PAGE 97)

Paris-Brest
(PAGE 101)

Religieuses
(PAGE 104)

Croquembouche
(PAGE 109)

Mille-feuille
(PAGE 116)

Hazelnut and Orange Japonais
(PAGE 121)

Gâteau St. Honoré
(PAGE 253)

Bee Sting Brioche
(PAGE 311)

WHEN I BEGAN MY APPRENTICESHIP with Jean Clauss, my first task was producing very large quantities of pastry cream. We made batches at the *pâtisserie* using 8 to 10 quarts of milk each time. The big copper pot we used was 12 inches tall and once it was on the stove it came up to the top of my chest. I was tall for my age, but I still had to reach my arm over the top to stir.

On my first day a second-year apprentice, Claude Lorentz, showed me how it was done. I was familiar with pastry cream, as my father made it at his bakery and I loved to eat it, but I didn't know how to make it. Not for long.

On my first try, I poured the tempered egg mixture back into the pot but didn't begin whisking quickly enough and the milk and egg mixture seized. Because I hadn't given the eggs a chance to coagulate slowly, my first pastry cream was on the dry side, like dry scrambled eggs. I was faster on the second try, but whisking such a big pot of pastry cream was difficult. Claude had helped me stir the first time, but the second time he conveniently disappeared just as I was pouring in the egg mixture. The pastry cream began to seize up, and I had to whisk faster than fast, reaching down to the bottom of the pot so that it didn't scorch and burn (which it did). Lorentz had disappeared because he wanted me to develop a sense of urgency; I had to understand that I couldn't be casual about whisking the ingredients over heat. A sense of urgency is important in a pastry kitchen.

It took me three or four more times making pastry cream until I was comfortable with it. But in pastry you only learn to make a product by making it over and over again.

ALMOND CREAM

INGREDIENTS	WEIGHT	MEASURE (APPROXIMATE) OR OUNCE WEIGHT
Almond flour, skinless	100 grams	1 cup plus 1 tablespoon
Confectioners' sugar	100 grams	1 cup
Cornstarch	3 grams	1 teaspoon
Cake flour	3 grams	1 teaspoon
Butter (French style, 82%)	100 grams	3½ ounces or 7 tablespoons
Sea salt	1 gram	Small pinch
Vanilla extract	3 grams	¾ teaspoon
Whole eggs	60 grams	1 large egg plus 1 to 2 tablespoons
Dark rum	20 grams	1 tablespoon plus 2¼ teaspoons

This is a fundamental recipe used in pastry, made with eggs, almond flour, starch, and sugar. It's sometimes mixed with pastry cream; then it's called *crème frangipane*. Almond cream is used as a filling for tarts or breakfast pastries. It is always baked in pastries and never served raw.

METHOD

1 Sift together the almond flour, confectioners' sugar, cornstarch, and cake flour. Tap in any almond flour that remains in the sifter.

2 Make sure your butter is at room temperature. Place the soft butter, the sea salt, and the vanilla in the bowl of a stand mixer fitted with the paddle and mix at medium speed for 1 minute.

3 Turn off the machine, scrape down the sides of the bowl with the rubber spatula, and add the nut flour mixture to the machine. Mix at medium speed for 1 minute. Gradually add the egg and mix at medium speed until it is incorporated, which should take no more than 2 minutes. Add the rum and mix until incorporated.

4 Use right away or transfer to a plastic container and refrigerate.

BEFORE YOU BEGIN

→ Get out the following equipment and allow all of the ingredients to come to room temperature:

Digital scale, set to metric weights
1 sifter
KitchenAid or stand mixer fitted with the paddle attachment
1 rubber spatula
1 bowl scraper
1 plastic container
Plastic wrap

→ Read this recipe through twice from start to finish.

Almonds have the highest water absorption power of all nuts due to their slightly lower fat content. They also have a milder flavor than other nuts, which is why they're used for this cream, as it leaves room for other flavors to be highlighted. Even when baked, the filling stays moist for a few days, because the water in the recipe is absorbed by the nuts. If you wish to make this cream with another nut, use the same proportion of nut flour but use half almond flour and half of the other nut. Almond flour is sometimes called almond powder. They're the same ingredient.

RECIPES REQUIRING

ALMOND CREAM

Raspberry and Hazelnut Tart

(PAGE 169)

Chinois

(PAGE 315)

Brioche Bostock

(PAGE 319)

IT'S DONE WHEN IT'S DONE

The finished product should look shiny and creamy. If the cream looks broken it is most probably because either the butter or the eggs were not brought to room temperature. When butter is emulsified and is cold it will break—the butter crystals will clump together and separate from the water in the recipe.

STORAGE

The almond cream can be refrigerated for up to 3 days. The mixture can also be frozen for up to 1 month. In this case, first divide into 100-gram batches.

JACQUY'S TAKEAWAYS

→ The important thing to watch for is to not incorporate too much air into the cream. Doing so will fill it with air bubbles that burst and make the cream rise when it's baked in pastries, only to deflate and collapse in the end. Additionally, if the baked almond cream is porous, any humidity in the air will make the finished product soggy.

→ **$50 TRICK:** If your almond cream or any other butter mixture separates and breaks during the mixing, it is because your butter or eggs were not at room temperature. All you need to do is to warm up the bottom of the bowl slightly so that the fat can come to room temperature and incorporate with the rest of the ingredients. Simply take the mixing bowl out of the mixer, put an inch of hot tap water in a large mixing bowl, place the mixing bowl in the water for 20 to 30 seconds, then resume beating. You will be amazed to see how it comes together and how much better it looks. In 1980 when I was working as a pastry cook in a pastry shop in Strasbourg, Alsace, I worked with another pastry worker who was very stubborn and never listened to my recommendation regarding the temperature of the ingredients and how they all should be at room temperature before mixing. He would always come to me in a panic with a bowl of broken butter cream or almond cream. I would then ask him to give me ten francs ($1.50) and to leave the room for 5 minutes. I would use this method to warm up the cream a little, remix it, and give him the fixed cream.

IN 1978, WHEN I WAS SEVENTEEN YEARS OLD, I competed in my second big pastry competition, for the title of Best Apprentice Alsace-Moselle. I thought I'd win the contest because the judges loved my almond cream. If I had won I would have then competed against apprentices from all the other French regions for Best Apprentice in France.

Six months before that I'd won the Best Apprentice of Alsace, which was quite an accomplishment for a seventeen-year-old. Competing at such a high level at that age was overwhelming, but I was well prepared for the competition and accomplished all of the tasks required. We had to make various pastries and baked items, as well as a three-foot-tall sugar sculpture.

I got my hopes up because the judges kept coming back to my worktable to taste my almond cream. They thought it was delicious and even asked me for the recipe. It's the optional hint of rum in the recipe that really brings out the almond flavor.

But I didn't win; I came in second. The pastry apprentice who won first place eventually became Best Apprentice of France. His work was definitely better than mine, but at that moment it was very difficult for me to swallow being second best, which in my mind might as well have been the worst place in a competition. I was so enraged that on the way out I carried my towering sugar sculpture to the car and slammed it into a garbage can. Looking back now, I can see that second place was a tremendous achievement for a boy who had only been working in pastry for two years. But you could never have convinced me of that then.

INGREDIENTS	WEIGHT	MEASURE (APPROXIMATE) OR OUNCE WEIGHT
Water	100 grams	About ½ cup
Granulated sugar	300 grams	About 1½ cups
Corn syrup	100 grams	About ¼ cup

A pastry chef once told me that caramel is the cheapest to make but one of the most beloved flavors in pastry. He is right. Who can resist crunchy caramel or a silky caramel sauce? Certainly not me.

There are two different methods for making caramel, a dry one and a wet one. The dry method is deceptively simple, but risky for the beginner. It consists of simply heating one thin layer of sugar at a time in a pan on medium heat until it melts into a light caramel, then adding another thin layer and so on until you have the desired amount. You must use a lot of restraint and control the flame with this method so that the sugar melts without burning. We say in French, "*Quand c'est noir, c'est cuit*"—When it's black, it's cooked. But in the case of caramel, "cooked" means burned, finished, unusable. A very dark caramel is a burned caramel, and once it reaches that stage there is no way to hide the burned flavor.

The wet method used in this recipe involves making caramel with water, corn syrup, and sugar. It is easier to control and I hope that after you master it, your fear of making caramel will be gone. But I will have to ask you for the unthinkable: patience. As in most pastry recipes, patience is key. Like my students, you will struggle with an urge to stir the syrup, but you must resist this urge; if you stir it the sugar will crystallize and your caramel will seize—that is, it will suddenly harden. Just let the sugar do its thing and it will reach the right temperature without crystallizing. If you take your time you can make this caramel in 10 minutes; otherwise it could take an hour and be accompanied by a lot of frustration.

BEFORE YOU BEGIN

→ Get out the following equipment and allow all of the ingredients to come to room temperature:

Digital scale, set to metric weights
1 medium stainless steel saucepan
1 high-heat rubber spatula
1 pastry brush
1 large bowl that your saucepan can sit in
1 digital thermometer
1 wire rack

→ Read this recipe through twice from start to finish.

UNDERSTANDING INGREDIENTS

You can control the outcome of a recipe by choosing the right ingredients for the job. Here are some facts about the ingredients in this recipe.

The water used in this wet method creates a buffer around the sugar, which allows the sugar to caramelize slowly as the water evaporates.

Corn syrup is an inverted sugar that has had water and acid added to it. The acid prevents the sugar crystals from fusing together, so the corn syrup can never harden in crystal form. The presence of corn syrup will have the same effect on the sugar in the caramel, preventing it from crystallizing.

Brown sugar is never suitable for caramel making; the impurities present in the sugar would always make the caramel crystallize.

METHOD

1   Place the water in the saucepan. Pour the sugar into the center of the pan. With a rubber spatula, stir very slowly to mix the sugar and water together, being careful not to wipe or splash the mixture onto the sides of the saucepan. If you do, sugar crystals will adhere to the sides, and once you begin to heat the pan and the sides get hot, the crystals will fall back into the syrup and make the entire mixture crystallize and become unusable. Add the corn syrup and slowly stir together. Examine the saucepan closely: if there is any sugar on the sides, use a clean, wet pastry brush to push it down into the mixture. You will not stir the mixture again until the end of cooking.

2   Fill a bowl large enough to accommodate your saucepan halfway with cold water and place it next to your stove. This will be for quick cooling of the caramel once it reaches the desired color and temperature.

3   Place the pan on medium heat and bring to a boil without stirring. The sugar will dissolve and the mixture will now be a syrup. When the syrup reaches a boil and the temperature begins to climb there will be a lot of bubbles. As it gets hotter the bubbles will get bigger. When you see the bubbles getting bigger, insert a digital thermometer and continue to cook the mixture. Watch the pan carefully; if you see any sugar crystals on the sides, take the wet pastry brush and push them down the sides of the pan—but do *not* stir the syrup.

4   When the syrup reaches 325°F/160°C it will be light golden brown. Immediately remove the pan from the heat and dip it into the bowl of cold water, just for a couple of seconds. This will stop the cooking and prevent the caramel from becoming too dark, as the caramel will continue to heat even after you take it off the burner. The darker it is, the more bitter it will be. Let the caramel sit off the heat until the bubbles subside.

5   When the bubbles have subsided completely you can use the caramel; I like to rest the pan on a wire rack off the counter so that the bottom of the pan does not get cold too quickly and the caramel does not become too thick to use. If you must, stir the caramel, but make sure to use a high-heat rubber spatula rather than a wooden spoon or a cold metal spoon or wire whisk. Do not use a wooden spoon. A wooden spoon is not a good choice because the caramel will stick to the wood, and the only way to remove it is to soak the spoon in hot water for 30 minutes or until the caramel melts. And wood is not happy sitting in water for 30 minutes. If you try to chip off the caramel, you risk chipping the wood as well, and possibly having a wood chip ending up in your food. Remember, always use the right tool for the right job.

IT'S DONE WHEN IT'S DONE

Caramel is done when it is golden brown. A darker caramel will be bitter.

HOW TO KEEP CARAMEL LIQUEFIED WITHOUT COOKING IT TOO MUCH

If you are using the caramel for dipping or decorating pastries, such as the Salambos on PAGE 93, it may begin to thicken before you are finished with your task. Return it to a low heat for a minute and it will be usable again.

Make sure to keep the heat low so that the caramel just gets soft and doesn't become too dark. Patience, as always, is key. You can keep the caramel warm by placing it on a warming tray or a heating pad, as well.

STORAGE

Leftover caramel can be poured onto a silpat, where it will solidify like brittle. Then, once it is cold, wrap it in plastic wrap and crush it with a rolling pin. Keep the crushed caramel in an airtight container with some packets of silica gel, a strong dessicant, at room temperature. Use for sprinkling on ice cream or whipped cream or to add texture to a dessert. Caramel keeps forever; no bacteria will grow in the very sweet and water-free environment.

JACQUY'S TAKEAWAYS

→ Once the caramel is poured out of the pan, fill the pan with water and put it on a medium flame. The hot water will clean the caramel off the pan. Do not even spend a second scrubbing the caramel stuck on the side of the pan—just let it melt away in the water.

→ When making caramel you can make any quantities that you desire following the 3:1:1 rule—3 parts sugar, 1 part water, and 1 part corn syrup. For example, 450 grams of sugar for 150 grams of water and 150 grams of corn syrup. It is a great way of remembering it and might help you out someday if you do not have your recipe book with you: 3:1:1.

RECIPES REQUIRING

CARAMEL

Hazelnut Caramel Curls

(PAGE 376)

Salambos

(PAGE 93)

Croquembouche

(PAGE 109)

Gâteau St. Honoré

(PAGE 253)

Kougelhof Ice Cream Cake

(PAGE 275)

ONE DAY EARLY ON IN MY APPRENTICESHIP my boss Jean Clauss said to me, "Today you're in charge of glazing the *salambos*." This meant that I had to make caramel. Salambos (PAGE 93) are oval puffs made with *pâte à choux*, filled with pastry cream flavored with kirschwasser, glazed on top with caramel, and decorated with a slice of toasted almond.

I was not even sixteen years old and had never made caramel in my life. Jean Clauss told me to get a round 10-inch copper bowl, put it on the gas stove over medium heat, add a thin layer of sugar, wait for the sugar to turn to caramel, and continue feeding each layer of caramel with more sugar. He instructed me to stir in more sugar as the sugar in the bowl turned to caramel.

I stirred slowly, as carefully as I've ever stirred, and Jean Clauss, who was mean, always drunk toward the end of the day, and scary, came by to look over my shoulder from time to time (he was also watching the other apprentices do their jobs). Suddenly he passed by and screamed at the top of his lungs, "STIR FASTER!" and disappeared to check on somebody else. I started stirring like a maniac.

As I began to stir faster the 325-degree caramel spiraled up the round copper bowl, splattered, and landed on my forearm. It was so painful that I went into shock. That day I learned that sugar loves to stick to the skin—and this splatter of hot caramel was about 3 inches long by 1 inch wide. I had no idea what to do so I panicked, left my caramel to burn on the stove, ran to the dishwashing area, and threw my hand into the dirty water—not the best thing for a wound. I would have done anything to make the pain go away. The water, even though it was a little warm, stopped the pain instantly, so I took my hand from the water, grabbed the strip of caramel sticking to my arm, and ripped it off like a Band-Aid. This was very stupid; I could have run cold water on my arm, which would have eased the pain, cooled the caramel, and slowly melted it. All of the skin came off my arm, leaving a gaping wound. It took forever for that wound to heal, at least three months; I have a scar to prove it. From then on I have never stirred caramel too fast again.

CARAMELIZED ALMONDS
OR HAZELNUTS

YIELD | 200 GRAMS (ABOUT 1¾ CUPS)

INGREDIENTS	WEIGHT	MEASURE (APPROXIMATE) OR OUNCE WEIGHT
Almonds or hazelnuts, skinned	200 grams	1⅔ cups
Vanilla bean	¼ bean	¼ bean
Water	20 grams	1½ tablespoons
Granulated sugar	50 grams	¼ cup
Cocoa butter, crumbled, or clarified butter	3 grams	1½ teaspoons

Caramelized nuts are absolutely delicious and when they are prepared well they're also completely addictive. The aroma that emerges from your kitchen as you make them is one of my favorites in pastry.

There are two methods for making these tasty nuts. The first and best way is to caramelize the nuts by adding them to a vanilla-flavored sugar syrup and heating the syrup until it caramelizes (Method 1). This provides the best exchange of flavor, as the heat of the sugar toasts the nuts. The second method is to make the caramel and toast the nuts separately, then assemble them (Method 2). It's easier for some, and a bit more practical, but you will not obtain the same exchange of flavor. However, I'm giving you both methods so you can do what's easiest for you.

METHOD I

1 Place the nuts in a microwave-safe medium bowl.

2 Split the vanilla bean lengthwise with a paring knife. Scrape out the seeds and combine the seeds and pod with the water and sugar in a medium saucepan. Place over medium heat. Bring to a boil, boil for 1 minute only, and turn off the heat. The sugar will have dissolved and you will have a clear syrup in the pan.

3 In the meantime microwave the nuts for 1 minute. Add the hot nuts to the syrup, turn off the heat, and stir with the rubber spatula until the liquid syrup turns white and crystallizes around the nuts. If the nuts and sugar lump up as soon as you mix them together it means that the nuts were not hot enough and caused the syrup to seize up. Stop stirring at once, place the lump in the microwave-safe bowl, and microwave on high for 30 seconds. Return the hot lump to the pan and you will be able to continue the process. Once the sugar

BEFORE YOU BEGIN

→ Get out the following equipment and allow all of the ingredients to come to room temperature:

Digital scale, set to metric weights
1 medium microwave-safe bowl
1 paring knife
1 medium saucepan
1 high-heat rubber spatula or a wooden spatula
1 or 2 spoons
1 sheet pan lined with a silpat
Latex gloves

→ Read this recipe through twice from start to finish.

FRENCH PASTRY FUNDAMENTALS | 51

Nuts vary in size, composition, and fat content, and because of this they don't all roast in the same length of time. If you're making the syrup and roasting the nuts separately for this recipe, it's very important to check the nuts to make sure that they toast all the way through to the center but don't burn. They won't toast properly if the temperature is below 300°F/150°C, as the Maillard reaction cannot take place (SEE PAGE 55). See the chart on PAGE 55 for roasting times for nuts and seeds.

Cocoa butter is the natural fat extracted from cocoa. It is made up of 100 percent fat solids and does not contain water. Coating the nuts with a small film of cocoa butter will protect them from humidity. This ingredient can easily be found online at **www.kingarthurflour.com**. Keep what you don't use in a cool place, wrapped airtight. Clarified butter is the closest thing you can use as a substitute. (See Step 1, PAGE 237, for instructions.)

has crystallized around the nuts, turn the heat back on to medium and wait for 1 minute, or until you see some of the sugar melt.

4 Now stir continuously but slowly over medium heat until the end of the process. Do not stir too fast, because the more you stir, the more you cool down the mixture and the more you disturb the caramelizing process. But if you do not stir enough, you'll allow the sugar and nuts to burn. A medium heat will allow the hot sugar to caramelize slowly without burning and at the same time will be hot enough to roast the nuts. It's a balancing act: if the heat is too low the nuts will not be roasted, but if it's too high the heat will burn the sugar before the heat of the caramel has a chance to roast the nuts. If at any point during the process the mixture begins to smoke, this means that your sugar is starting to burn and you must immediately reduce the heat to a lower setting.

5 Once the sugar has turned into a golden caramel, turn the heat off, quickly remove 1 nut with a spoon, set it on a cutting board—do not touch, as it will be very hot!—and cut it in half with a sharp knife. It should be golden brown all the way through the center. If the nut is still pale in the center, turn the heat back on low for 1 to 2 minutes and repeat the test. Once the right color has been achieved—it should take 4 to 6 minutes—turn off the heat, add the cocoa butter or clarified butter to the pan, and stir the caramelized nuts for 15 seconds.

6 Dump the nuts in a big pile onto the sheet pan lined with the silpat. Immediately fill the saucepan with water and place it in your sink. Put on the latex gloves and remove the vanilla bean and set it aside. Being very careful not to burn yourself, as in the beginning the mixture is extremely hot, separate the nuts with your hands. You can also separate the nuts using 2 spoons. Then place them one by one on the silpat. The trick is to get them separated before the pile of nuts cools down and solidifies, so work quickly. If the pile of nuts does cool and solidifies into a blob, place the blob in a microwave-safe bowl and microwave for 30 seconds, then continue to separate the nuts. Once all of the nuts are separated, let them come to room temperature. Store in an airtight container.

NOTE: Almonds and hazelnuts are the best nuts for this method. Walnuts and pecans will not work; the sugar syrup will get lodged inside the creases of the nuts and will never have a chance to caramelize.

HOW TO SKIN ALMONDS AND HAZELNUTS

It's important to understand that the skin on certain nuts, such as hazelnuts and especially walnuts and pecans, is very bitter. Removing the skin from walnuts and pecans is practically impossible, but it is not difficult to skin almonds and hazelnuts. To skin almonds, place a pan of water on the stove and bring it to a boil. Add the almonds and wait for about 30 seconds. Using a spider, a strainer, or a slotted spoon, take one almond out of the hot water, rinse with cold water, and place it between your thumb and index finger. See if you can squeeze the nut easily from its skin envelope. If the almond pops out, turn off the heat and drain the nuts and water through a colander. If it doesn't, leave for another 10 to 20 seconds, then drain. Rinse with cold water and allow to sit and cool in the colander for 5 minutes. Then skin the nuts; this goes more quickly than you'd think. Once skinned, place them on a cloth kitchen towel so that they dry out. Use them right away or keep them in a dry place, such as on a wire rack, so that they can breathe. Do not refrigerate or put them in a plastic bag or an airtight container right after skinning, or the water that is still present in the nuts will make them ferment and you will have to throw them out. Allow the almonds to dry completely before storing.

I use another system to skin hazelnuts or filberts. Preheat the oven to 300°F/150°C and place the nuts on a sheet pan lined with parchment paper. Bake the nuts for 15 to 20 minutes. Dump them onto a kitchen towel, fold the towel over the nuts, and rub them together briskly. Most of the skin should come off. If it doesn't, bake them for 5 to 10 more minutes and repeat.

METHOD 2

1 Preheat the oven to 300°F/150°C. Place the nuts on a sheet pan lined with a silpat or parchment paper and bake them for 30 minutes or until brown and toasted all the way through. Remove from the oven and turn it off.

2 Split the vanilla bean lengthwise with a paring knife. Scrape out the seeds and combine the seeds and pod with the water and sugar in a medium saucepan. Place over medium heat. Place the sheet pan with the nuts back in the turned-off oven. The heat of the oven will keep the nuts nice and warm. Let the syrup boil until it has a pale, golden color, then stir slowly while the sugar continues to cook. Watch the color closely. When it is golden brown turn off the heat, add the warm nuts, and stir for 15 seconds.

3 Add the cocoa butter or clarified butter, stir for 15 seconds, and dump the nuts in a pile onto the sheet pan lined with the silpat. Fill the pan immediately with water and place it in your sink. Put on the latex gloves, remove the vanilla bean and set it aside, then separate the nuts as instructed in Method 1 and allow to cool. Store in an airtight container.

All nuts can be roasted and caramelized using this method.

IT'S DONE WHEN IT'S DONE

The finished product should be glossy and have a golden brown color. The nuts will be slightly tacky to the touch because of the cocoa butter, but if they have been properly roasted they will be very crunchy. When you store them in the jar they'll clump together, but don't worry—if you shake the jar or give them a stir they'll come apart immediately and remain perfectly crunchy.

STORAGE

Keep the nuts away from humidity in an airtight container at room temperature together with a couple of packets of silica gel, a strong dessicant. They will stay fresh for 2 weeks. Storing them in the refrigerator would be disastrous, as the caramel will melt and make the nuts soggy and sticky.

WHAT TO DO IF THE CARAMEL SEIZES

If this small amount of caramel seizes, do not panic. Just return the pan to medium-low heat and allow the mixture to heat until it liquefies, without stirring, then begin again.

⊰ NUT ROASTING CHART ⊱

Here is a chart that should help you, but be aware that all ovens bake slightly differently. These values are based on a 300°F/150°C oven with the nuts baked on a parchment paper–lined sheet pan placed on the middle rack.

Almonds, sliced, chopped, or slivered with or without skin	20 to 25 minutes
Almonds, whole with skin	30 to 35 minutes
Almonds, whole without skin	30 minutes
Brazil nut pieces	45 to 50 minutes
Brazil nuts, whole	55 to 60 minutes
Cashew pieces	15 to 20 minutes
Cashews, whole	20 to 25 minutes
Flax seeds	40 to 45 minutes
Hazelnuts, whole	35 to 40 minutes
Macadamia nut pieces	15 to 20 minutes
Macadamia nuts, whole	20 to 25 minutes
Peanut pieces	45 to 50 minutes
Peanuts, whole	55 to 60 minutes
Pecan pieces	17 to 22 minutes
Pecans, whole	20 to 25 minutes
Pine nuts	30 to 35 minutes
Pistachio pieces	10 to 12 minutes
Pistachios, whole	10 to 15 minutes
Pumpkin seeds	20 to 25 minutes
Sesame seeds	40 to 45 minutes
Sunflower seeds	40 to 45 minutes
Walnut pieces	17 to 22 minutes
Walnuts, whole	20 to 25 minutes

WHAT HAPPENS WHEN INGREDIENTS BROWN?

It is crucial to understand the effect of oven heat on your ingredients. Once foods reach a temperature of around 300°F/150°C a browning reaction called the Maillard reaction will take effect if acids are present (if the food does not contain any acids, another reaction, called pyrolysis, occurs). Past 300°F/150°C, provided that a certain amount of moisture has been lost, sugar breaks down and a reaction takes place in which the sugar starts to turn to caramel. If the reaction is controlled so that it doesn't go too far it will result in a very tasty flavor. But if the process is allowed to go too far it will result in an unpleasant burned flavor that cannot be altered. Many savory recipes, like pulled pork or oven-roasted tomatoes, require a very low oven, set between 250°F/120°C and 300°F/150°C. The reason for this is that below 300°F ingredients cannot easily burn; they retain moisture, which prevents their natural sugars from caramelizing. There is a reason why Italian mamas insist that a good tomato sauce must be cooked over the lowest flame possible, so that the tomatoes retain their sweet taste.

→ Caramelized nuts can be used for many applications, such as toppings for ice cream sundaes or baked breads such as brioche. They can also be crushed and folded into a mousse or an ice cream. They go very well with anything chocolate.

→ **$50 TRICK:** Coating the nuts with a little bit of cocoa butter protects them from humidity and keeps them crunchy for a long time.

RECIPES REQUIRING

CARAMELIZED ALMONDS

OR HAZELNUTS

Hazelnut Praline Paste

(PAGE 57, METHOD ONLY; SEE

RECIPE FOR INGREDIENT WEIGHTS)

Croquembouche

(PAGE 109; YOU CAN ALSO USE

JORDAN ALMONDS)

Chocolate and Hazelnut Yule Log

(PAGE 249, USING INGREDIENT

WEIGHTS FOR HAZELNUT PRALINE

PASTE, PAGE 57)

Chocolate Mousse Cake in a Glass

(PAGE 267)

Kougelhof Ice Cream Cake

(PAGE 275)

INGREDIENTS	WEIGHT	MEASURE (APPROXIMATE) OR OUNCE WEIGHT
Hazelnuts, skinned	200 grams	1⅔ cups
Vanilla bean	¼ bean	¼ bean
Water	40 grams	3 tablespoons
Granulated sugar	135 grams	⅔ cup
Cocoa butter, crumbled, or clarified butter	3 grams	1½ teaspoons

Hazelnut praline paste is a sweet, nutty butter made by blending caramelized hazelnuts to a paste. When you make it you'll find the scent absolutely addictive.

The caramelized nuts require more sugar here than in the master recipe on PAGE 51 because the praline paste requires more caramel. I love the way the flavors pair with chocolate, and you'll find this paste in some of the chocolate recipes in this book, such as the Yule Log on PAGE 249, the chocolate-dipped Fours de Lin cookies on PAGE 205 and the Chocolate Mousse Cake in a Glass on PAGE 267. I also use it to add a sweet and nutty flavor to pastry creams, for example the cream I use to fill the Paris-Brest pastries on PAGE 101.

If you blend the caramelized nuts for a long time the paste becomes very smooth, like the hazelnut spreads like Nutella, that your kids love to put on toast. I urge you to make a batch to keep on hand in the refrigerator (it keeps for a month) so that you can quickly make impressive desserts for your guests.

METHOD

Using the ingredients called for above, make a batch of caramelized hazelnuts following the method you prefer on PAGE 51. Once cool, put the nuts in a food processor fitted with the steel blade. Blend for about 1 minute, turn off the machine, remove the blade, and scrape down the sides and bottom of the bowl with a small spatula. Blend until the nuts turn into a smooth paste, 2 to 4 minutes. Transfer the paste to an airtight container and refrigerate if desired.

BEFORE YOU BEGIN

→ Get out the following equipment and allow all of the ingredients to reach room temperature:

Digital scale, set to metric weights
Equipment needed for Caramelized Almonds and Hazelnuts (PAGE 51)
A food processor or mini processor fitted with the steel blade
1 small rubber spatula

→ Read this recipe through twice from start to finish.

UNDERSTANDING INGREDIENTS

This recipe calls for more sugar than the recipe for regular Caramelized Almonds and Hazelnuts (PAGE 51) because the added caramel ensures that when you blend the nuts the mixture will become a semi-liquid paste. If you blend regular caramelized hazelnuts the result will be a much thicker paste.

You can make a praline nut paste with virtually every type of nut that is suitable for caramelizing, but my favorites are almonds, hazelnuts, and peanuts.

It is crucial that you follow the caramelizing instructions on PAGE 51 so that the nuts are properly roasted, in order to extract the true flavor profile of the hazelnuts and caramel.

RECIPES REQUIRING
HAZELNUT PRALINE PASTE

Paris-Brest
(PAGE 101)
Hazelnut and Orange Japonais
(PAGE 121)
Fours de Lin
(PAGE 205)
Chocolate and Hazelnut Yule Log
(PAGE 249)
Chocolate Mousse Cake in a Glass
(PAGE 267)

IT'S DONE WHEN IT'S DONE

The longer you blend the caramelized nuts, the smoother the paste will be. You can blend the caramelized nuts for a shorter time if you want a slightly thicker paste that has some crunchy texture left from the caramel.

STORAGE

You can keep the hazelnut praline paste in an airtight container at room temperature for 2 weeks or for 1 month in the refrigerator. The oil from the nuts might separate and rise to the top. In that case you can mix it with a spoon or fork, or flip the jar over to force the oil to mix back with the rest of the mixture.

JACQUY'S TAKEAWAYS

→ You can add different flavors to praline pastes. I recommend a 1 percent ratio of flavoring to total weight of the praline paste (e.g., 1 gram of flavoring for 100 grams of praline paste). My favorite ones are coffee beans, cardamom seeds, and cinnamon stick. I first roast the spices, adding them to the nuts halfway through their roasting, then grind them together with the rest of the ingredients.

CHOCOLATE NOUGATINE CRISP

YIELD | 166 GRAMS, ENOUGH
TO COVER TWO OF THE 9-INCH
CHOCOLATE TARTS ON PAGE 159

INGREDIENTS	WEIGHT	MEASURE (APPROXIMATE) OR OUNCE WEIGHT
Cocoa powder	5 grams	1 tablespoon
Whole milk (3.5% fat)	15 grams	1 tablespoon plus ¼ teaspoon
Butter (French style, 82% fat)	30 grams	1 ounce
Corn syrup	15 grams	1 tablespoon
Granulated sugar	50 grams	¼ cup
Pectin	1 gram	¼ teaspoon
Sliced almonds	50 grams	Scant ½ cup

This nougatine makes a great crunchy topping for the Chocolate Tart on PAGE 159, but it can also be used as a topping for ice cream and as a decoration for cakes and *verrines* (PAGE 267). It's great to have some on hand for ice cream and other desserts.

METHOD

1 Place the sheet pan in the freezer. Sift the cocoa powder. Place a silpat on your work surface.

2 Combine the milk, butter, and corn syrup in the small saucepan and begin heating over low heat.

3 Mix the granulated sugar with the pectin and very gradually whisk it into the milk mixture. Insert a thermometer and continue to whisk over low heat until the mixture reaches 222°F/106°C. This should take about 2 minutes. Remove from the heat and let cool for 2 minutes. Switch to the rubber spatula, and stir in the sifted cocoa powder and the sliced almonds.

4 Pour the mixture onto a silpat and spread it in a thin, even layer. Place the other silpat on top. Use a rolling pin to roll over it softly to ensure that it is spread in an even layer. Gradually press down harder with the rolling pin until the mixture is as thin as the sliced almonds; you should see the sliced almonds through the silpat. Take the sheet pan out of the freezer and place the silpats on it. Return to the freezer and freeze for 30 minutes.

5 Meanwhile, preheat the oven to 325°F/160°C. Remove the sheet pan from the freezer, peel off the top silpat, and place in the oven. Bake for about 12 to 15 minutes. To ascertain whether or not the nougatine is done, remove a small amount of the crisp with a spatula and place it on your countertop. When you

BEFORE YOU BEGIN

→ Get out the following equipment and allow all of the ingredients to come to room temperature:

Digital scale, set to metric weights
One 12 × 17–inch sheet pan
1 sifter
2 silpats or 2 sheets of parchment paper that will fit on a 12 × 17–inch sheet pan
1 small saucepan
1 medium stainless steel hand whisk
1 digital thermometer
1 medium rubber spatula
1 rolling pin
1 small spatula or knife

→ Read this recipe through twice from start to finish.

RECIPES REQUIRING
CHOCOLATE NOUGATINE CRISP

Chocolate Tart with Nougatine Topping
(PAGE 159)

Chocolate Mousse Cake in a Glass
(PAGE 267)

UNDERSTANDING INGREDIENTS

What makes this recipe so good is the right combination of the different ingredients. The sliced almonds are crucial to the recipe. The reason we use sliced almonds as opposed to other nuts like pecans or hazelnuts is that we roll out the nougatine to the thickness of the nuts. The result with sliced almonds is a very thin and easy-to-eat crisp that works very well as a garnish or special layer in a composed dessert (like the Chocolate Mousse Cake in a Glass on PAGE 267) because you can cut right through it. Another reason why we use almonds is that their flavor is not domineering. When the nougatine crisps are combined with chocolate, for example, the almonds won't interfere with the taste of the chocolate.

The butter is here primarily for taste—no fat can replace the taste of butter. The sugar makes crisps turn crispier, and the cocoa powder offsets the sweetness and adds a wonderful chocolaty dimension.

Pectin is used in this recipe to absorb the liquid in the milk and corn syrup. Pectin is a gelling agent extracted from citrus peel but also from other fruits like apples, apricots, or cherries. When it comes into contact with water it absorbs and retains it. A small amount goes a long way.

Corn syrup prevents the crisp from crystallizing while the water contained in the milk and corn syrup is absorbed by the pectin.

do this, work quickly so that you do not leave the oven door open for too long—scoop up the crisp with a small spatula or knife and immediately close the oven door so that the temperature doesn't drop. Let the crisp cool completely for 1 full minute and then taste it. It should be very crunchy and should not stick to your teeth; if it does, bake for another 3 minutes and test again until it reaches the right consistency.

6 Remove the sheet pan from the oven and allow the crisp to cool completely. This will take at least 15 minutes. Place a piece of parchment paper or a silpat on your work surface and flip the silpat with the crisp over onto it. Slowly peel it off. Break the nougatine into 2-inch pieces and keep them in an airtight container.

IT'S DONE WHEN IT'S DONE

The crisp should be crunchy and shiny and the almonds should be golden brown.

STORAGE

Always keep these in an airtight container; during the humid summer months I recommend that you add a small pouch of silica gel to the container. You probably know silica gel, the small pouches that come with a new pair of shoes or a camera. The pouch is filled with small beads that are clear when they are dry and that turn pink or blue when they are humid. Once humid, they can be re-dried in a 150°F oven for about 20 to 30 minutes until they turn clear again and can be reused. See PAGE XXXI for a silica gel supplier.

JACQUY'S TAKEAWAYS

→ You can vary the flavor of this nougatine with other ingredients such as spices, vanilla, coffee, or tea. You would use 2 percent of the total weight of the ingredients, about 3 grams, in powdered or extract form.

ITALIAN MERINGUE BUTTER CREAM

YIELD | ABOUT 550 GRAMS (1 QUART)

INGREDIENTS	WEIGHT	MEASURE (APPROXIMATE) OR OUNCE WEIGHT
Butter (French style, 82% fat)	300 grams	10½ ounces
Vanilla extract	5 grams	1 teaspoon
Egg white	105 grams	3 whites, less a scant tablespoon
Sea salt	1 gram	Pinch
Water	50 grams	¼ cup
Granulated sugar	210 grams	1 cup plus 1 teaspoon
Corn syrup	10 grams	2 teaspoons

Butter cream is a rich frosting made with butter and eggs. This one utilizes Italian meringue. Years ago butter cream was king in pastry, but nowadays we use it less often because we're not so enamored with icings that have such a high fat content. I use it here and there, as a filling or as a component of another recipe such as a *mousseline*, in which it's combined with pastry cream (a *mousseline* can also refer to a mixture of pastry cream and butter only). Even though it's not in vogue today, butter cream is an essential basic French pastry recipe.

There are three different types of butter cream, each involving a different method. Classic or French butter cream calls for a syrup made with sugar, corn syrup, and water that is heated to 244°F/118°C and then slowly poured over a mixture of whole eggs and egg yolks as they are beaten. The hot syrup pasteurizes and coagulates the eggs, making them safe for consumption. The mix is then whipped until it cools, at which point soft butter is whipped in. This type of butter cream is usually used for fillings but not for frostings, because of its off-white color.

The second type, Italian butter cream, is essentially an Italian meringue with butter whipped into it. The method is the same as the one used in French butter cream, but only egg whites are used. A hot syrup is cooked to 244°F/118°C and slowly whipped into the egg whites. The mixture is then beaten until it cools, at which point soft butter is whipped in. Italian butter cream can be used for filling or for frosting because it is pure white. It is also the safest in terms of bacterial content and the most versatile; it can be used for all applications in pastry, which is why it's the version I use most often and the recipe I am giving you here.

BEFORE YOU BEGIN

→ Get out the following equipment and allow all of the ingredients to come to room temperature:

Digital scale, set to metric weights
KitchenAid or stand mixer fitted with the whisk and paddle attachments
1 medium mixing bowl
1 medium stainless steel hand whisk
1 small saucepan, preferably one with a lip
1 high-heat rubber spatula
1 pastry brush
1 digital thermometer

→ Read this recipe through twice from start to finish.

FRENCH PASTRY FUNDAMENTALS | 61

For Italian butter cream we use corn syrup to prevent the mixture from crystallizing and becoming unusable. Corn syrup is an inverted sugar that has had water and acid added to it. The acid prevents the sugar crystals from fusing together, so the corn syrup will never set hard in crystal form. The presence of corn syrup will have the same effect on the sugar in the syrup, preventing it from crystallizing.

The butter has to contain 82 percent fat so that the butter cream can hold its shape. If it has a lower fat content it will contain more water, taste blander, and make the butter cream too soft.

The third type of butter cream is made by incorporating butter into a vanilla sauce (such as the one on PAGE 35). This type is only used for fillings. It's too soft to use for frosting because of the liquid vanilla sauce.

Butter creams are usually flavored with vanilla, chocolate, coffee, caramel, spices, or alcohols. I am not a fan of mixing them with fruity flavors, as the butter and eggs overpower the tangy flavors of the fruit.

METHOD

To succeed with this recipe it's very important that you follow this sequence of instructions exactly.

1 Make sure that the butter is soft. If it is not, microwave it for 5 seconds only. Do not allow it to melt.

2 Place the butter in the bowl of your standing mixer and add the vanilla extract. Insert the paddle and mix for 5 minutes on medium speed, until the butter is airy and pale light yellow. Transfer to a medium mixing bowl and set it aside. Wash the bowl of your standing mixer thoroughly with hot water and soap, and dry with a clean kitchen towel. It is crucial to wash the bowl well, as any fat residue will prevent the egg whites from setting up.

3 Begin whipping the egg whites with the pinch of sea salt in the mixer on the lowest speed. Double-check the temperature of the egg whites by feeling the bottom of the bowl. If it is at all cold, fill a sink with 1 inch of hot water. Stop the machine, unlock the bowl, and place it in the hot water for 1 full minute while mixing by hand with the KitchenAid whisk or a hand whisk. Remove the bowl from the water and wipe dry. Feel the bottom of the bowl with your hand; it should feel neither cold nor hot. Return the bowl to the mixer and resume whipping on low speed.

4 Meanwhile, place the 50 grams of water in the saucepan and pour the sugar into the center of the pan. With a rubber spatula, stir very slowly to mix the sugar and water together, being careful not to wipe or splash the mixture onto the sides of the saucepan. If you do, sugar crystals will adhere to the sides, and once you begin to heat the pan and the sides get hot, the sugar crystals will fall back into the syrup and make the entire mixture crystallize and become unusable. Add the corn syrup. Examine the saucepan closely, and if you see sugar on the sides, wash them down with a clean, wet pastry brush, using the brush to push the sugar adhering to the sides of the pan back into the mixture. Use a lot of water on the brush when you wash down the sides of the pan; you don't have to worry about adding excess water to the recipe; once the syrup reaches 244°F/118°C it will have the same consistency no matter how much water was added. The excess water will just make the cooking process take longer. Once the syrup comes to a boil do not stir or it will crystallize. Insert a digital thermometer and cook the syrup to 244°F/118°C.

5 Keep an eye on your egg whites while you are heating the syrup. When the syrup is at 230°F/110°C your egg whites should be slightly foamy. If they are not, increase the speed slightly. At 239°F/115°C the syrup is just about ready to be poured into the egg whites. Check the bottom of the mixing bowl for unbeaten egg whites and if necessary, tilt the bowl very slightly so that the egg whites at the bottom of the bowl are also beaten until foamy.

6 Turn the mixer on to its highest speed. When the syrup reaches 244°F/118°C remove from the heat and very gradually stream it into the egg whites, taking great care to pour the syrup right between the whisk and the sides of the bowl. This is crucial, because if the hot syrup engages with the whisk before it hits the egg whites, all of it will splatter onto the sides of the bowl instead of going into the egg whites (it also could splatter on your hands and burn you). Once this happens you cannot undo it; you will have to scale a new recipe and begin again. If you pour the hot syrup between the whisk and the sides of the bowl as instructed, most of it will go into the egg whites and the recipe will work. No matter how careful you are, though, there will always be a small amount of syrup that splashes onto the bowl, so that you will have a thin candy-like ring of sugar around the inside of the bowl above the meringue.

7 Once all of the syrup has been added, whip on high speed for 2 minutes, then reduce to medium and whip for another 5 minutes. The meringue should have cooled to lukewarm or room temperature. Feel the bottom of the bowl to check the temperature.

8 Stop the mixer and add the soft butter to the meringue. Mix first on low speed for 30 seconds, then turn to medium speed and mix for another 30 seconds. At this point the mixture will not yet be homogenized. The butter and meringue have a difficult time combining because they are opposites: butter is all fat, and meringue is water based. Turn the mixer up to the highest speed and mix for 3 seconds only. You should see the butter cream come together into a shiny, smooth mixture. If this doesn't happen, mix on the highest speed for another couple of seconds. Do not over-mix or you will completely deflate the meringue. If your butter was too cold it will not mix with the meringue and the recipe will fail; if the butter was too soft or melted, it will mix but make a greasy-tasting butter cream.

IT'S DONE WHEN IT'S DONE

The finished butter cream should look shiny and smooth. Most fatty creams and sauces should look shiny. This indicates that the fat and water have successfully emulsified.

STORAGE

I like to use butter cream right away after making it, as it is at its lightest and has the best texture when freshly made. However, it can be refrigerated for a couple of days, and it can be frozen. The best way to defrost it is to take it out of the freezer and let it sit on the counter overnight. The next day the butter cream will be at room temperature and ready to use. You can also defrost it by removing it from the freezer and allowing it to sit on the counter for 2 hours, then warming it very gently in a double boiler for 30 seconds and whisking quickly by hand for about 5 seconds, until it comes together nicely. Unfortunately, this method always makes it deflate slightly.

JACQUY'S TAKEAWAYS

→ **$50 TRICK:** It is difficult to pour the hot syrup into the exact spot between the side of the KitchenAid bowl and the whisk, as there is only ¼ inch of space. One is always drawn toward the center of the bowl because of the whip's rotation. I recommend that you use a saucepan that has a lip so that you can rest the lip right on the edge of the mixing bowl and never be tempted to pour it closer to the center.

FRENCH MERINGUE

INGREDIENTS	WEIGHT	MEASURE (APPROXIMATE) OR OUNCE WEIGHT
Confectioners' sugar, sifted	50 grams	½ cup
Granulated sugar	150 grams	Scant ¾ cup
Egg white	100 grams	About 3 whites
Sea salt	Pinch	Pinch
Vanilla extract	5 grams	1 teaspoon
Toasted sliced almonds	25 to 50 grams, or as needed	¼ to ½ cup, or as needed
Confectioners' sugar, for dusting	As needed	As needed

French meringues have long been a classic of French pastry. They're dry cookies or shells that are very sweet—pure sugar—but they usually don't stand alone. In this book you'll use meringues to decorate the Lemon Cream Tart with Meringue Teardrops (PAGE 163) and to enclose layers of mango puree, pineapple sorbet, and banana ice cream in Vacherin Glacé (PAGE 281). In both of these desserts the acid from the fruit offsets the sweetness of the meringues.

I have an effective system (I love systems!) for whipping together the sugar and egg whites for French meringues that I created over the years in order to help my students make this recipe successfully. I divide the sugar into 3 equal portions rather than adding all of the sugar in a slow stream; the results are more consistent. It requires patience—but what is there in pastry that does not?

BEFORE YOU BEGIN

→ Get out the following equipment and allow all of the ingredients to come to room temperature:

Digital scale, set to metric weights
1 sifter
KitchenAid or stand mixer fitted with the whisk attachment
1 timer
1 bowl scraper
1 large mixing bowl
1 large rubber spatula
1 large pastry bag fitted with a ½-inch round tip
2 sheet pans lined with parchment paper

→ Read this recipe through twice from start to finish.

·⊰ ABOUT MERINGUE ⊱·

When you make a meringue you are whipping air into egg whites while mixing in sugar. As you whip air into the egg whites the albumen (the clear liquid that is the egg white) wraps itself around each air bubble, creating a foam. The amount of sugar and water in the recipe will determine the firmness of the final meringue. In French pastry we refer to any whipped egg white and sugar combination as meringue. You will see the term when you make cakes such as Sponge Cake (Génoise) (PAGE 237) and Flourless Chocolate Sponge (PAGE 246), where the meringue is folded into other ingredients in a cake batter.

There are 3 different techniques for meringue: French, Italian, and Swiss.

FRENCH MERINGUE

French meringue, made with 2 parts sugar to 1 part egg white, is usually used for hard-shelled meringues. This might seem like a lot of sugar, but it is required to produce a hard shell. Reducing the amount of sugar results in a softer, gooey texture. French meringue can be flavored, usually with dry ingredients such as chocolate, coffee powder, spices, or ground nuts. Baked French meringues are always stored at room temperature in an airtight container. Since they are free of water and loaded with sugar, they basically cannot spoil. If stored in the refrigerator or freezer they will become soggy over time, because they're very porous and will absorb the humidity in the air.

ITALIAN MERINGUE

Italian meringue is much softer than French meringue. It is never used to make hard shells. Rather, it is usually a component of another recipe like butter cream or a mousse, added to create a lighter texture. It can also be used to frost pastries such as baked Alaska, or to top a tart such as a lemon meringue pie.

SWISS MERINGUE

The proportions of sugar and egg whites in Swiss meringue, also used for hard-shell recipes, are the same as in French meringue, 1 part egg whites to 2 parts sugar, but the method is different. The egg whites and sugar are combined in the bowl of your mixer and are first whipped together by hand over a bain-marie (double boiler) of hot water until the mixture reaches 149°F/65°C. At this temperature the egg whites coagulate and are more stable. After this step, the hot foam is whipped in the mixer until it reaches room temperature. Like the French meringue, Swiss meringue is used for hard-shell meringue recipes, but some chefs also use it in butter cream because of its stability. I find hard-shell meringues made using the Swiss meringue method to be a little chalky, and prefer to use the French meringue technique for that.

No matter what kind of meringue you are making, you must be sure that the egg whites are free of fat. Fat prevents the albumen from wrapping itself around the air bubbles. The fat can come from the smallest trace of egg yolk or a greasy mixing bowl or whisk. If you see that your egg whites are not expanding into a foam after 2 minutes, do not bother to continue whipping them, as they will not increase in volume even if you beat them for hours; just throw them out, wash and dry all your equipment thoroughly, and scale out a new batch.

The sugar used for meringue is granulated sugar or superfine sugar. Other types like brown sugar are not used as the impurities would make the meringue and the syrup for Italian meringue crystallize. Often you will see a type of acid added to the egg whites. It could be a drop of lemon juice, a pinch of cream of tartar, or sea salt. The acid helps with the coagulation by strengthening the egg whites and allowing them to hold more air.

METHOD

1 Preheat the oven to 250°F/120°C with the rack positioned in the center. Sift the confectioners' sugar and set aside.

2 Divide the granulated sugar into three 50-gram portions.

3 Carefully wash and dry the bowl and whisk of your standing mixer. Place the egg whites and sea salt in the bowl and whip on medium speed for 30 seconds.

4 Add the first 50-gram portion of sugar to the lightly mixed egg whites and whip for 2 minutes at the highest speed. Don't forget to set a timer. You need to whip for the full 2 minutes to incorporate enough air.

5 Lower the speed, add another 50 grams of sugar, then turn the speed back up to high and whip for another 2 minutes. Turn the speed down again, add the last 50 grams of sugar, turn the speed up to high, and mix for another 2 minutes. The total mixing time should be 6 minutes.

6 After the 6 minutes of mixing you should have a stiff, shiny meringue. Take the bowl off the mixer. Remove the whisk and carefully scrape the meringue into a large wide bowl, which will be more suitable for folding. Add all of

WHY I ADD THE SUGAR IN THREE SEPARATE ADDITIONS

The albumen of the egg whites does its best job at wrapping itself around air bubbles when the sugar is added gradually. Egg whites are made of 85 percent water, and if you add all of the sugar at once, the water in the egg whites and the sugar will turn into syrup, which will get in between the albumen and the air bubbles. The result will be a mixture that won't expand well.

the sifted confectioners' sugar and the vanilla extract to the meringue, then fold it in with a large rubber spatula, turning the bowl counterclockwise with one hand each time you fold. The more efficient you are when you fold, the less the meringue will collapse. Since the dry ingredients always end up on the bottom of the bowl, you must be careful to scrape the bottom each time you scoop up the meringue and fold. But be careful not to over-fold or your meringue will be like soup, and you cannot undo that. When you fold, always keep the bowl on the table, never fold with the bowl under your arm. Holding the bowl is not practical or efficient.

7 Now fill a pastry bag fitted with a ½-inch round tip and pipe teardrop shapes onto 2 parchment paper–covered sheet pans. To pipe teardrops, pipe a round shape with the tip pointed straight down, then stop pressing on the pastry bag as you pull up and away (see the piping directions on **PAGES 15-20**). Sprinkle with the toasted sliced almonds and confectioners' sugar.

8 Bake 1 pan at a time in the preheated oven for 1 hour, until crisp. Usually I do not like to bake 2 sheet pans at the same time because the results can be uneven. But if you must, rotate the pans after 30 minutes of baking, switching the upper pan with the lower one.

IT'S DONE WHEN IT'S DONE

The baked meringues should have an off-white color on the surface. When you crack one open, it should be a creamy, light-brown color. They will have a slight caramel flavor and will not taste as sweet as unbaked meringue. If they are still completely white and feel wet, bake them for another 15 minutes. Sometimes meringues crack during baking. This can be a result of over-folding after adding the confectioners' sugar. American confectioners' sugar contains 3 to 5 percent cornstarch (to prevent goods from caking), and over-folding the meringue mix after you add it creates a tight mixture that can crack during baking. Cracking can also occur if the oven heat is too high. Remember, egg whites are full of water, and too much heat will make that water sizzle and evaporate quickly, breaking the shell open. Sometimes the evaporating water—which is sugar water—will form droplets on the surface of the meringue and solidify in round caramelized spheres.

STORAGE

After baking, allow the meringues to cool completely and use them right away, or store them at room temperature in an airtight container along with a packet or two of silica gel. They will keep for weeks or even months. Do not keep in the refrigerator or freezer or they will become soggy and melt.

> ### *JACQUY'S TAKEAWAYS*
>
> → You can flavor meringues by folding chocolate shavings, toasted or raw coconut flakes, toasted nut flour, or chopped toasted nuts into the meringue. My rule of thumb is to add no more of these ingredients than the weight of egg white; for this recipe, for example, you would not add more than 100 grams. They are always added and folded in together with the confectioners' sugar. You can also flavor the meringues with cocoa powder or coffee extract. Begin by folding in 5 grams and check for taste; add 5 more grams if desired.

SOFT, MEDIUM, AND STIFF MERINGUE: THE 11-STEP PROGRAM

We talk in pastry about soft, medium, and stiff meringue. On the following pages you will see my Meringue Experiment, which illustrates the different stages of whipping. It is done with 100 grams of egg white, a pinch of sea salt, and 50 grams of sugar to show you what meringue looks like at each of its stages, including the stage at which you've over-whipped it and it is no longer usable.

When you make meringue you are forcing the albumen in the egg whites to create a membrane around each air bubble. The more air you whip in, the more the membrane is stretched thin. Once there is too much air for the amount of albumen, the membrane structure collapses and the meringue becomes grainy. This is why we use the pinch of sea salt to strengthen the albumen. The sea salt provides acid that strengthens the albumen so that it can hold more air. Cream of tartar will do the same thing.

PHOTO 1 I start my meringue by whipping the room-temperature egg whites on medium speed with a pinch of sea salt or cream of tartar. After whisking them for 10 seconds on medium the bubbles are starting to make the egg whites foamy. From now on I will whisk on high.

PHOTO 2 After adding sugar and whipping on high for 1 minute the meringue is starting to foam but is too liquid to make a "beak." We never use meringue that is this soft in pastry.

PHOTO 3 Loose peaks: After 1 more minute on high, the meringue is getting thicker; the albumen has wrapped itself around more air bubbles, but the beak is still very soft and loose.

PHOTO 4 Very soft peaks: More whipping on high indicates that more air is being contained inside the albumen membranes. A "beak" is starting to form.

PHOTO 5 Soft peaks: More whipping stiffens the meringue. The beak has now formed but it has a "tail" at the end.

PHOTO 6 Semi-stiff peaks: The meringue has now incorporated enough air for the beak to look like a beak.

1

2

3

4

5

6

7

8

9

10

11

PHOTO 7 Stiff peaks: The whisk can be held right side up and the beak does not collapse.

PHOTO 8 Very stiff peaks: The egg whites are struggling to be able to hold more air and signs of graininess appear on the edges.

PHOTO 9 Grainy or broken meringue: The albumen has given up and its structure has collapsed. The meringue is unusable.

PHOTO 10 I let the meringue sit on the counter for 1 hour. The bubbles have popped open and the meringue is very grainy on top and liquid on the bottom. It is still unusable.

PHOTO 11 I whipped the meringue again for 5 minutes and—*ta-da!*—it is semi-stiff again. This is a way to save over-whipped meringue. Technically it is usable, but it will never be the same as freshly whipped egg white. You can see that it is grainy.

GANACHE

INGREDIENTS	WEIGHT	MEASURE (APPROXIMATE)
Dark chocolate couverture (64%)	300 grams	10½ ounces
Butter (French style, 82% fat)	50 grams	1¾ ounces or 3½ tablespoons
Clover honey	20 grams	1 scant tablespoon
Vanilla bean	½ bean	½ bean
Heavy cream (35% fat)	275 grams	1¼ cups

BEFORE YOU BEGIN

→ Get out the following equipment and allow all of the ingredients to come to room temperature:

Digital scale, set to metric weights
1 large chef's knife
1 small microwave-safe bowl or ramekin
1 small rubber spatula
1 medium microwave-safe bowl
1 paring knife
1 medium saucepan
Plastic wrap
1 medium rubber spatula
1 digital thermometer
1 small stainless steel hand whisk
1 immersion blender

→ Read this recipe through twice from start to finish.

NOTE: For this small amount of ganache I like to use a rubber spatula. For anything larger a whisk is your tool of choice.

Ganache is a chocolate filling used in pastry and especially in chocolate candies (think truffles and filled chocolates), usually made of dark, milk, or white chocolate, heavy cream, butter with a fat content of 82 percent, and a flavor like vanilla or coffee. It is fairly simple to make, but without some basic understanding of the ingredients and the process, things can go wrong. Ask my students—they sometimes experience anger and frustration when they are learning to make ganache. But ganache is so delicious that it should never be the cause of stress. Follow these instructions and you should not have any problems.

METHOD

1 If you purchased your chocolate in a block form, place it on a cutting board. Using the largest chef's knife you own, shave the chocolate off the side of the block from the top down; the tip of the knife should never leave the cutting board while the middle of the knife goes up and down. Once you have shaved off 300 grams of chocolate, chop the shavings into ¼-inch pieces. It's important to have uniform pieces so that they will melt evenly. If you are using coins there is no need to chop them.

2 In a small microwave-safe bowl, soften the butter by creaming it with the honey, using a small rubber spatula. Microwave it for 5 seconds if it is too firm, but do *not* melt it. If the fat crystals are melted they'll make the ganache feel greasy.

3 Place the chopped shaved chocolate or coins in a medium microwave-safe bowl. Microwave the chocolate for 30 seconds at 50 percent power. *Melting at 50 percent power is crucial*: since chocolate does not contain any water, high heat will make it go straight from melting to burning. The chocolate should just be semi-melted—stir for 5 seconds and you should see some of it beginning to melt. Repeat this process if you don't; the key is to have some melted chocolate and some that is still hard.

4   Split the vanilla bean in half lengthwise and scrape the seeds out with a paring knife. Place the cream in a medium saucepan with the vanilla bean and seeds. Bring it to a boil, remove from the heat, and remove the vanilla bean.

5   Immediately pour the hot cream mixture over the half-melted chocolate; *do not wait* or the cream will cool down and will not melt the chocolate properly. Waiting also allows steam to escape from the hot cream. Steam equals water, so if the steam escapes, water escapes, and your ganache will be dry. Cover the bowl tightly with plastic wrap and let the mixture stand for 60 seconds before mixing. Remove the plastic wrap and shake off the condensation clinging to it into the ganache. Using a rubber spatula, stir the mixture by making very small circles beginning in the very center, to homogenize. You will see the mixture begin to emulsify—the fat and water becoming one—in the center of the bowl. Once you see this beginning to happen (and not before), you can gradually stir from the center to the edges of the bowl by making wider and wider circles, until the cream and chocolate are completely homogenized into a thick, smooth mixture.

6   It is now time to add the butter. But you cannot just add it without measuring the temperature of the ganache. The optimal temperature for the ganache before adding the butter should be between 100.4°F/38°C and 104°F/40°C. A ganache that is too hot will instantly melt the butter, causing it to lose its creamy texture. If you try to mix the butter into a ganache that is too cold, at room temperature it will become so cold that it will trigger the crystallization of the cocoa butter and butter fat crystals—both of which begin to crystallize at around 90°F/32°C—making them separate from the water in the ganache. In cooking, when a fatty sauce gets too cold and the fat separates out we call this a broken sauce; it's a common occurrence. With ganache we call it a broken ganache. If your ganache does break, you can fix it (see my $100 trick on PAGE 77), but if you use a thermometer before you add the butter your ganache won't break. To bring the temperature down, just simply wait; do not stir too much or the ganache will be full of air bubbles and it won't be as appealing to the eye. Once the ganache has reached the right temperature, add the butter. Mix it first with a small whisk and immediately finish the mixing with an immersion blender for about 30 seconds, until the ganache is smooth and shiny. Use as needed.

IT'S DONE WHEN IT'S DONE

Your finished ganache should be silky and very shiny. This means that the emulsion has been perfectly achieved. It should also taste creamy because the fat has been broken down into the finest crystals possible. These are the characteristics of creams and sauces that involve an emulsion of water and fat.

STORAGE

Ganache can be used as soon as it's made or it can be tightly covered and refrigerated for up to 1 week, or frozen for up to 1 month. Lay a sheet of plastic wrap directly on top of the ganache, then cover the bowl with another sheet. The best way to use it after it has been refrigerated is to let it sit on the counter for 3 hours so that it has a chance to come to room temperature; frozen ganache should be allowed to come to room temperature overnight on the counter.

VARIATIONS

FLAVORED GANACHES: Ganache can be flavored with a variety of ingredients, such as spices, flowers, coffee, citrus, or herbs. The flavorings are infused in the cream. For best results, add your flavoring to the cream a day ahead and let it infuse overnight. Flavored ganaches fall into two categories: those flavored with spices, and those flavored with other ingredients such as coffee, citrus, or herbs.

For a spice-flavored ganache, always use whole or crushed spices. Crushed spices release more flavor. Do not use ground spices because they leave a grainy feel on the tongue. As a general rule, the amount of spice you add should equal 0.2 percent of the total weight of the ganache. So for this recipe you would add about 1 gram of spice, the equivalent of ½ cinnamon stick, 15 peppercorns, or ½ vanilla bean. For strong spices such as cloves or nutmeg you would use less, or they will overpower the flavor of the chocolate. Let your palate be your guide. If adding an acidic spice like ginger, use the candied form, as fresh ginger will curdle the cream in a split second. Bear this in mind also when using other acidic ingredients such as lemon and orange.

When flavoring ganache with other flavors such as coffee, tea, or herbs, use 2 percent of the total weight. For this recipe, that would be about 12 grams. If using coffee beans, crush the beans, as they will release more flavor than whole; do not use ground coffee. As with spices, infuse the ingredient in the cream overnight for the best results.

One last bit of advice: beware of flavors like rose or lavender, which are extremely strong and must be used sparingly, as they can make your ganache taste like cheap soap.

JACQUY'S TAKEAWAYS

→ **$50 TRICK:** Place the vanilla bean and seeds in the heavy cream the day before making the ganache. Let it infuse overnight in the refrigerator before heating the cream and making the ganache the next day. This will make a much more flavorful ganache.

Dark chocolate contains cocoa solids, cocoa butter, sugar, and vanilla. Milk chocolate is similar but it also has milk powder, which gives it its creamy/milky flavor. White chocolate does not contain any cocoa solids other than cocoa butter fat solids; it has no chocolate flavor at all and is very sweet. When we make pastries with white chocolate at the French Pastry School we always try to combine some acidic, bitter, or sour flavors with the white chocolate to offset its sweetness. You will very rarely see me use white chocolate because it's so sweet.

Chocolate does not contain any water, which is why it doesn't easily spoil. You can buy it in a block or in the form of coins or chips. I recommend that you always use chocolate that has the "couverture" appellation on the package: this guarantees that the chocolate contains at least 31 percent cocoa butter by weight and will ensure that it will melt in your mouth and turn to liquid when you melt it. Chocolate that is not designated as couverture is simply labeled chocolate, or coating chocolate. It has more sugar and contains some fats other than cocoa butter, such as vegetable fats and oils like palm kernel, soybean, or a mix of similar types that do not have the flavor or properties of cocoa butter. Cocoa butter is a very complex fat that contains more than 10 different types of fat crystals that melt and crystallize at different temperatures. Because of its complexity it can't be manufactured.

Since this recipe is for a dark chocolate ganache I recommend using a 60 percent to 70 percent dark chocolate couverture. When you buy chocolate you will notice a cocoa (or cacao) percentage number on the package. The percentage on the package indicates the cocoa content in the chocolate—the cocoa butter and cocoa solids combined. In couverture, the rest will be sugar. So, for example, a 60 percent couverture will contain at least 31 percent cocoa butter, 29 percent cocoa solids, and 40 percent sugar. The higher the percentage on the package, the less sugar in the chocolate and the stronger the chocolate taste. Be careful though, as stronger does not always mean better.

The tasting and appreciation of chocolate is very similar to wine tasting. Learn to appreciate chocolates from different cocoa beans and regions of the world, as they are unique and their flavors vary tremendously. They can be acidic, sweet, smoky, earthy, or just simply bitter. Some 70 percent chocolates are surprisingly sweet to the taste while some 60 percent chocolates are bitter. These characteristics are important to consider when you are making a ganache. For example, it would be a mistake to make a lemon ganache with an acidic chocolate, or a coffee ganache with a bitter one. The flavor of the chocolate has to balance nicely with the flavor added to the ganache. When we hold creative workshops with our students they tend to combine bold flavors such as ginger, clove, cinnamon, or nutmeg with bold and acidic chocolates to obtain an instant strong flavor in the mouth at the moment when the candy is first tasted. But what one needs to know is that the last taste in your mouth should be chocolate. In this way it's comparable to wine: some wines are very strong at the first sip but then the taste fades in the mouth. A good chocolate candy, like a good wine, needs to be subtle at first and then get better and better as you taste it.

The heavy cream that I usually use is 35 percent fat. Some chefs use 30 percent or 40 percent fat, but I like 35 percent because it's right in the middle and gives me a consistent product. Thirty percent cream contains less fat and therefore fewer solids, which could make your ganache runnier; a 40 percent cream contains so much fat that it might cause your ganache to separate, or "break." (I'll explain later how to fix a broken ganache.)

The butter in a ganache is optional. I like to add it because it contributes a nice creamy texture.

I like to add a little bit of honey in recipes that are high in fat since the intense sweetness of the honey will break down the droplets of fat into smaller ones and therefore increase the chances of a great emulsion.

Fixing a Broken Ganache

$100 TRICK: You will know right away if your ganache breaks, as it will look completely separated. There's no need to cry over a broken ganache; here's a trick to fix it. It's a two-person job, so grab somebody to help. Since a cold temperature is what makes cocoa butter and butter fat crystallize, the first thing we need to do is to microwave the broken ganache at 50 percent for a few seconds, until it reaches 104°F/40°C. Then place 1 tablespoon of heavy cream in a medium bowl and microwave for 5 seconds only. Tilt the bowl with the cream to the side and get ready with a very small whisk. Have someone pour the broken ganache slowly and gradually into the bowl while you stir it into the cream. This has to be a continuous process and the broken ganache cannot be poured faster than you can incorporate it with the whisk. Once the process is completed your ganache will be fixed and you will be able to use it as before.

Emulsion and especially fat in water have always intrigued chefs. The French hot-food chefs have mastered the art of hiding fat in their sauces, and we thank them for that. A ganache is similar to many savory sauces, as it is a fat-in-water emulsion, which means that the fat crystals are surrounded with water (SEE DRAWING ON THE LEFT). Once the ganache breaks, the fat molecules separate from the water molecules and wrap themselves around them (SEE DRAWING ON THE RIGHT). The reason why we fix a ganache with cream is because cream is a fat-in-water emulsion itself, and if you mix it properly it will convert the broken ganache back into a proper emulsion. The amazing thing is that one can fix a bathtub full of broken ganache with a single tablespoon of heavy cream.

RECIPES REQUIRING
GANACHE

Chocolate Mousse
(PAGE 78)
Chocolate and Hazelnut Yule Log
(PAGE 249)
Black Forest Cake
(PAGE 259)
Chocolate Mousse Cake in a Glass
(PAGE 267)

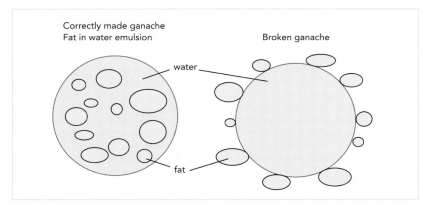

Correctly made ganache
Fat in water emulsion

Broken ganache

water

fat

CHOCOLATE MOUSSE

INGREDIENTS	WEIGHT	MEASURE (APPROXIMATE) OR OUNCE WEIGHT
Dark chocolate couverture (64%)	105 grams	3⁷⁄₁₀ ounces
Heavy cream (35% fat)	260 grams	1 cup plus 3 tablespoons
Corn syrup	22 grams	1 scant tablespoon
Clover honey	22 grams	1 scant tablespoon

BEFORE YOU BEGIN

→ Get out the following equipment and allow all of the ingredients to come to room temperature:

Digital scale, set to metric weights
1 large chef's knife
1 medium mixing bowl
1 small saucepan
1 stainless steel hand whisk
Plastic wrap
KitchenAid or stand mixer fitted with the whip attachment or a handheld electric mixer

→ Read this recipe through twice from start to finish.

RECIPES REQUIRING
CHOCOLATE MOUSSE

∿

Black Forest Cake
(PAGE 259)
Chocolate Mousse Cake in a Glass
(PAGE 267)

∿

Pastry and cooking in general would be boring if there were only one way to make a dish. My students sometimes resist this notion; they like to believe that there is just one way to make a recipe. But when it comes to making chocolate mousse, one of the most beloved recipes that French pastry has to offer, there are many versions. In French, as in English, we liked to say *"Tous les chemins mènent à Rome"*—All roads lead to Rome—and this certainly applies to chocolate mousse.

This chocolate mousse is made by making a ganache with a large proportion of cream in relation to chocolate and no butter, letting the mixture rest overnight in the refrigerator, and whipping it the next day. It's like a rich chocolate whipped cream. I use it to fill cakes (see the Black Forest Cake on PAGE 259) and for any dessert requiring chocolate mousse, such as the beautiful *verrines* on PAGE 267.

METHOD

DAY 1

1 Finely chop the chocolate on a cutting board using a large chef's knife (if you are using coins, you do not need to chop them). Place in a medium mixing bowl.

2 Combine the heavy cream, corn syrup, and honey in a small saucepan; bring to a boil and pour half the mixture over the chocolate. Immediately cover the bowl with plastic wrap and let sit for 1 minute. Remove the plastic wrap and shake all the water created by the steam back into the bowl; mix with a rubber spatula or whisk, starting from the middle and making wider circles as the emulsion is taking place. When the ganache is emulsified add the remaining cream and repeat the whisking until it is completely emulsified. Place a sheet of plastic wrap directly on top of the mixture, then cover the bowl and refrigerate overnight.

DAY 2

Place the ganache in the bowl of your mixer and fit with the whisk attachment, or use a handheld electric mixer. Whip for 1 minute on high speed. Scrape down the sides of the bowl and whip on high speed until the ganache is transformed into a mousse, about 1 minute. Stay by the mixer and observe it very carefully to make sure that you don't over-whip; if you do, your mousse will be grainy. Transfer to a bowl, cover, and refrigerate until ready to use.

IT'S DONE WHEN IT'S DONE

The mousse should be glossy and smooth, with no hint of graininess. Like many mousses or sauces, when they are made well they should look shiny, which signifies a properly made emulsion.

STORAGE

This mousse will easily last 2 to 3 days in the refrigerator. It can also be frozen for up to 1 month.

> ### JACQUY'S TAKEAWAYS
>
> → You can easily make a dessert with this mousse by serving it in 8 ramekins.
> → You can also substitute milk chocolate or white chocolate for the dark chocolate without changing the proportions.

UNDERSTANDING INGREDIENTS

Chocolate mousse is very easy to make, but you must follow the instructions to a T. If your ganache is not completely emulsified to begin with, your mousse will be grainy. You must bring the cream to a boil with the honey and corn syrup and pour the mixture over the finely chopped chocolate. Because there is more cream in proportion to chocolate, it's much easier to emulsify the chocolate if you first pour half of the boiled cream over the chocolate and mix it together, as you do when you make Ganache (PAGE 72). Here it is easier to use a whisk than a rubber spatula to emulsify the two. Whisk until it is smooth and shiny, then whisk in the remaining hot cream. Once mixed together, it will look like a ganache and the heat will have allowed all the fat crystals from the heavy cream and the cocoa butter fat to melt together.

The honey is a great natural emulsifier due to its very high sweetening power; it will break down the droplets of fat into smaller ones. The corn syrup will help the cream bind together and prevent crystals from forming. You have to let the ganache cool completely overnight in the refrigerator to allow all the fat crystals to harden. Then the next day you will whip the cream to obtain a very smooth and creamy mousse. When you do this it is very important not to over-whip the cream, as the fat in the cream will separate out and make the mixture grainy.

RASPBERRY JAM

INGREDIENTS	WEIGHT	MEASURE (APPROXIMATE) OR OUNCE WEIGHT
Fresh ripe or frozen raspberries	1200 grams	2 pounds 10 ounces or about 10½ cups
Granulated sugar	480 grams	About 2½ cups
Granulated sugar	480 grams	About 2½ cups
Lemon juice, freshly squeezed and strained	60 grams	5 tablespoons

BEFORE YOU BEGIN

→ Get out the following equipment and allow all of the ingredients to come to room temperature:

Digital scale, set to metric weights

1 large mixing bowl

Plastic wrap

1 stainless steel saucepan that is less than double the volume of the fruit and sugar

1 high-heat rubber spatula or wooden spoon

Scissors

1 paper drinking cup with a bottom that will fit inside the rim of your jam jars

1 small plate

Six 4-ounce jam jars

1 small bowl

1 skimmer

Heat-resistant gloves

1 sheet pan

1 small ladle

→ Read this recipe through twice from start to finish.

Raspberry jam is my favorite jam of all. With its perfect balance of sweetness and tartness it's suitable to use in many desserts, as well as to spread on your morning brioche. I particularly like it as a filling for Beignets (PAGE 323).

There is something romantic and evocative about jam making, as basic and simple a procedure as it is. Making it always brings back joyful memories. I can remember working alongside my mother as a child every summer when she made jam. As busy as she was running the front of my father's bakery and raising her four children, she would always find the time to make *confitures* in the summer when the fruit was at its best. From the time I was about nine years old she would send me out to get 30 to 40 pounds of the small yellow plums called *mirabelles* from the neighboring farm. We kids would help remove the stems and pits, then my tiny mom would cook the fruit in a huge copper pot with sugar and a little bit of lemon juice. As we watched her work she'd give us lots of advice about jam making. One of her tips was to fill the jars with the hot jam, then top the surface with a round piece of cellophane and a splash of *mirabelle eau de vie*—plum schnapps. This would not only contribute a fantastic flavor, it would also pasteurize the small gap of air between the lid and jam. We would store the finished jars in a kitchen cabinet and enjoy the jam throughout the year. Little did I know that decades later I would be passing on her tips to hundreds of students.

UNDERSTANDING INGREDIENTS

As a general rule it's best to make jam when the fruit is in season and just ripe. Good ripe fruit makes good jam. The process of jam making involves cooking fruit with sugar until enough water from the fruit has evaporated and the fruit is candied. This process is a slow one and cannot be rushed. You begin by mixing the fruit with half of the sugar, which starts the candying process. What causes the mixture to gel is an ingredient in the fruit called pectin. Pectin is present in fruit naturally and is at its strongest when the fruit is ripe. Unripe fruit will not have a good flavor and does not contain enough natural pectin. But overripe fruit can bring an unpleasant flavor to the jam and will have lost its pectin. When I make raspberry jam I like to keep the seeds in the jam because this is where the natural pectin is. Use frozen raspberries if you need to make this jam out of season, as frozen fruit is always picked at its ripest.

If you have the chance to pick the fruit yourself, begin by working your way around the outside of the tree or bush, as this is the area that gets the most sun and where the fruit will be ready first. The fruit in the center takes longer to ripen because it's in the shade. Whether it's a stone fruit or a berry, ripe fruit should be easy to pluck.

Pectin requires sugar and an acid (in this case, lemon juice) to set. Lemon juice is added here to bring a nice tangy flavor; the acid will extend the shelf life of the jam as well as help extract the natural pectin in the fruit and set it up.

⊹ ORGANIZING YOUR TIME ⊱

Jam making is a 2-day process. The first day you macerate the fruit with half the sugar for an hour, then bring the mixture to a boil, let it cool, and refrigerate it overnight. The next day you add the remaining sugar and the lemon juice and finish cooking the jam. There's no need to squeeze the lemon juice until the second day.

METHOD

DAY 1

1 If using fresh raspberries, remove all the stems and leaves. Wash the fruit only if you must; I prefer to work with organic fruit that does not require any washing. Washing the fruit will add water to the mix and the jam will have to be boiled for a longer time.

2 Mix the fruit with 480 grams of sugar in a large mixing bowl. Cover with plastic wrap and refrigerate for 1 hour.

3 Place the mixture in a stainless steel saucepan with a wide, flat bottom. The fruit and sugar should cover more than half and up to three-quarters of the volume of the pan. If the pan is too large, too much water will evaporate during the jam making and the jam will be too stiff. Over medium heat, bring the mixture to a full boil while stirring with a spatula. Once the mixture comes to a boil, scrape it back into the mixing bowl. Cover with plastic wrap, allow to cool, and refrigerate overnight.

DAY 2

1 The next day, cut the bottom away from the paper cup. You will use it later as your "MacGyver funnel" for neatly funneling the jam into your jars. Place a small plate in the refrigerator and put the oven on its lowest setting. Place the jars in the preheated oven to warm them for 5 to 10 minutes, but do not place the lids in the oven as they may have a rubber seal that will burn.

2 Remove the plastic wrap from the bowl and scrape the berry mixture into the saucepan. Fill a small bowl with water and place it next to the saucepan with the skimmer. Bring the jam to a boil over medium heat, stirring. Stir in the remaining 480 grams of sugar and the lemon juice. Boil, stirring all the while, until the jam looks thick but not too concentrated, 5 to 10 minutes (depending on the size of your pan). Skim off any white foam that rises to the surface; these are impurities that you do not want in your jam as they might make it spoil or crystallize. To see if the jam is ready, remove the cold plate from the refrigerator and place a drop of jam on the plate. Let it cool for 10 seconds and hold the plate at an angle to see if the jam is still runny or if it sets. If the jam is still runny, boil it for a few more minutes, until it sets on the plate. Once it sets, remove it from the heat.

3 The jars are now ready to be filled. Take the jam off the heat. Remove the hot jars from the oven (use latex or heat-resistant gloves or oven mitts), place them on a sheet pan, and place the paper cup/funnel over one of the hot jars. Fill the jar with hot jam all the way to the rim. Immediately seal the jar with the lid and flip the jar over. Use heat-resistant gloves, oven mitts, or kitchen towels to hold on to the hot jar when you seal it. Repeat the process until all the jars are filled. Let cool for 3 hours or overnight.

4 When the jam has cooled, rinse the jars with water to make sure they are not sticky. (Do not rinse the jars while they are still hot, as they will crack.) Dry thoroughly and place stickers on the jars if you wish. Keep in a cupboard or in a pantry away from the light. Once opened, refrigerate.

IT'S DONE WHEN IT'S DONE

The jam should have a vibrant color and the fruit should still have some acidity. It should not be too stiff—this means you cooked it too long or you added too much pectin. The longer you cook the jam, the sweeter it gets, but also the more liquid evaporates. It's important to use a flame that is neither too low nor too high. If it's too high you can burn the jam.

STORAGE

This jam does not need to be refrigerated until you open the jar. You can keep it in a cupboard out of the light for at least 1 year. At my house it never lasts that long, as my kids are addicted to it.

Pectin in Fruit

This recipe can be used for many different types of fruit, but each one will behave slightly differently. Certain fruits, such as black currants, do not contain enough natural pectin to set and require the addition of a small amount of pectin mixed with the granulated sugar. Pectin absorbs and retains water; it usually comes in a powder form and is always mixed with the sugar so that it does not create lumps. I recommend starting with 1 percent pectin and 99 percent fruit, and seeing if the jam sets enough. For this recipe I would add 12 grams of pectin if I found that my jam was not setting up. The ripeness of the fruit will also affect its behavior. Raspberries, for example, are not high in pectin but when they are perfectly ripe they will not require the addition of pectin.

Another way to make jam with fruit that lacks pectin is to mix the fruit with another fruit that is high in pectin, such as apples. This way you will not have to add pectin to the jam.

HIGH PECTIN CONTENT: apples, blackberries, cranberries, currants, gooseberries, concord grapes, plums, quinces.

MEDIUM CONTENT: (fruit that would need an addition of 1 percent pectin): cherries, elderberries, grapefruit, loquats, oranges, black currants, red currants.

LOW PECTIN CONTENT: (fruit that would need an addition of 2 percent pectin): apricots, blueberries, figs, guavas, peaches, pears, raspberries, strawberries.

NOTE: In the case of this raspberry jam, if the raspberries are perfectly ripe they will not need the addition of pectin.

JACQUY'S TAKEAWAYS

→ Jam making is fun, but it takes practice to know when you've reduced enough water without burning the fruit or if you overcooked it, making the jam too stiff. If you fail to reduce the liquid enough, the jam will mold in the jar. If you make jam that is too stiff but has not burned you can rectify it by making a smaller runny batch, and heating the stiff batch with the runny batch. Test the combined batches on the cold plate as instructed in the recipe.

→ For jam aficionados, I recommend the purchase of a 0–80° B (B stands for Brix degree) refractometer, a tool that measures the solid content of a product, which is measured in Brix degrees. I recommend that you cook your jam to 60 Brix. This means that it will have 60 percent solids and 40 percent water.

→ Never use an aluminum pot when making jam; the acid in the fruit will react with the metal and leave a very bad metallic aftertaste. In a perfect world you would make your jam in a *confiturier*, a copper pot that has a flat bottom, which allows efficient and even water evaporation. Also, copper releases an acid when mixtures are cooked in it, and in this case it helps the pectin to set. Copper oxidizes after it is left in the air for a day; the way to cook safely in it is to make a mixture of 2 parts vinegar, 1 part sea salt, and 1 part flour. Place the copper pot in the sink, put on some latex gloves, and rub the mixture over the entire surface of the pot. You will see that all the oxidization will disappear instantly. Then rinse thoroughly with water, dry it well with a paper towel, and *voilà*! Your copper pot is ready for use for the entire day. Some copper pots are sold for decoration only; these are very light. When choosing make sure that the pot is very heavy. A good copper pot will last generations and it is a wonderful tool to pass on to your children.

→ **$50 TRICK:** Flipping over the jam jars after they are filled will force the air bubble left between the top of the jam and the lid to flow through the hot jam and be pasteurized.

ANOTHER FAVORITE JAM-MAKING MEMORY is of working on a project in Alsace with the French pastry chef Christine Ferber when I was competing in the finals of the Meilleurs Ouvriers de France (MOF) competition. Christine is the absolute queen of jam making. She makes close to 300,000 jars of handmade jam a year, following artisan methods and using the best fruit. Her pâtisserie is in Niedermorschwihr, a very small and charming fifteenth-century village nestled in the Alsatian vineyards. People from all over the world come to this full-blown pastry shop for Christine's wonderful jams.

Christine's success did not come easily. When she was young she had great difficulty making a name for herself as a pastry person, because at that time women were not accepted in professional kitchens. After her apprenticeship and a number of jobs in several pastry shops, she returned to work with her father at their family pâtisserie. There she gradually developed a passion for jam making, but Monsieur Ferber, a very tough man who ran his operation with an iron fist, insisted that "pastry chefs don't make jam, they buy it at the supermarket." However, Christine was determined. She tricked her dad into letting her put her jars of jam in the display window "just as a decoration." She knew that soon enough customers would ask to buy them.

For the MOF competition I was required to make a jam combining a fruit and a flower. I went to Niedermorschwihr and with Christine's help I developed a muscat grape jam flavored with rose petals. For my MOF project, she and her assistants seeded 10 pounds of Alsatian Muscat grapes, checking each one in the light to make sure that no seeds were left. With her help and guidance we came up with a magical result. I will never forget that moment in my career and will always be grateful for her precious help.

CANDIED PEEL

YIELD | 80 PEELS (FROM 20 PIECES OF FRUIT)

10-DAY RECIPE

INGREDIENTS	WEIGHT	MEASURE (APPROXIMATE) OR OUNCE WEIGHT
Citrus (orange, limes, lemons)	20 pieces	20 pieces
Sea salt	10 grams	1½ teaspoons
Water	1000 grams	1 quart plus 3 tablespoons
Granulated sugar	1550 grams	3⅖ pounds or 7⅓ cups
Corn syrup	50 grams	3 tablespoons

Candying citrus peel is a great way to use peels that you would otherwise throw away. Once they are candied they last forever in your refrigerator, as bacteria cannot grow in a product saturated with sugar. It's best to use organic and untreated fruit that is ripe but not overripe. Since candying peel is a long process, make a large batch so that you will have it for a long time.

The process involves replacing the natural water in the fruit with sugar syrup. Every day the sugar concentration is increased until all the water has been replaced and the fruit is completely stable. The shortest recipe, which I am giving you here, takes 10 days. Whole fruit can take as long as 4 months. Practically any fruit can be candied, but the most common are oranges, mandarins, lemons, limes, cherries, pears, melons, and figs.

Candied fruit has many uses. It makes a beautiful garnish or flourish on desserts, like the Lemon Cream Tart with Meringue Teardrops on PAGE 163. Strips of candied orange peel dipped in chocolate are absolutely addictive treats. Chopped candied peel brings great flavor to cakes and breads, such as Brioche or Stollen (PAGES 21 AND 303) and Pain d'Épices (PAGE 335), which absorb its wonderful candied aroma. And let's not forget fruitcake, which probably plays the greatest part in keeping the candied fruit industry strong. No matter how you use it, it is fascinating to learn how to conserve and completely stabilize fruit with this easy technique.

BEFORE YOU BEGIN

→ Get out the following equipment and allow all of the ingredients to come to room temperature:

Digital scale, set to metric weights
1 vegetable brush
1 paring knife
1 soup spoon
1 tall stainless steel pot large enough to accommodate all the peels but not too wide
1 spider
1 large strainer or colander
1 medium stainless steel pot
1 plate that fits snugly in the tall pot
Plastic wrap

→ Read this recipe through twice from start to finish.

METHOD

1 Let's take the example of candying orange peels. Scrub the oranges under water with a small vegetable brush. Score the orange skin once around the circumference laterally with a paring knife and then repeat horizontally so that

UNDERSTANDING INGREDIENTS

There are many ways to preserve fruit, and candying is one of them. Fruit consists mainly of water, a place where bacteria likes to grow and will eventually cause the fruit to rot. But if the fruit is candied the water located in the cells is replaced by sugar, and bacteria cannot grow. If it is done properly the water in the cells will gradually be extracted and replaced by sugar, and the fruit will be preserved with its tangy flavor intact. Like wine making and many other good things, the process of candying fruit is a gradual one; it cannot be done quickly.

The first step—cooking the peels in hot water, a process called blanching—is crucial. You blanch the peels to remove all of the waxes on the skin. Then you rinse the peels well and cook them in boiling salted water, which removes the bitterness and opens up the cells so that the sugar will have a way in. The peels will then be cooked briefly once a day for 10 days in sugar syrup that is low in sugar at first and that becomes sweeter each day as a small amount of sugar is added to it. Little by little the sugar will replace the water in the citrus skin's cells and make them safe from bacteria. The last boil will include an addition of corn syrup; corn syrup prevents the sugar mixture from crystallizing.

you obtain nice quarters. Slide a soup spoon between the skin and the flesh and carefully remove each quarter of peel. (Store the fruit in the refrigerator for another use.) You can also quarter the skin longitudinally and peel it off, or quarter the whole fruit and peel off the skins. Fill a tall stainless steel pot (large enough to hold all of the peels but not too wide or large) with water and bring it to a boil. Plunge the orange peel quarters into the boiling water, turn the heat down to medium, and leave the peels for 2 minutes. The water does not need to come back to a boil. Using a spider, fish out all the peels and transfer them to a strainer or colander; rinse them thoroughly with cold water. Drain the hot water and scrub the pot well, as the waxes on the orange peels will leave a film on the sides of the pan.

2 Pour 2 quarts of water into the cleaned pot, add the 10 grams of sea salt (increase these quantities if you are making a larger batch), and bring it to a boil. Reduce the heat to medium and add the orange peels. Keep them in the simmering salted water for 20 minutes; they should feel slightly mushy. If they still feel hard, keep them in the hot water for another 10 minutes.

3 Fish the peels out of the pot with the spider and transfer them to the strainer or colander. Rinse them well with cold water. Clean the pot again and return to the stove.

4 Arrange the peels very tightly next to each other in the tall stainless steel pot in concentric circles. It is important that they are not loose or they will rise up and float in the syrup. It is also important that you use the right size stainless steel pot for the right quantity of peels; you should have 2 inches of room between the top of the peels and the top edge of the pot. Do not use a wide, shallow pot, as you would have to make a huge quantity of syrup. You can definitely stack the rows of peels if you wish.

5 Cover the peels with a plate that fits perfectly in the pot. The plate will prevent the peels from floating in the syrup.

6 In the medium pot make a syrup with 1000 grams (1 quart plus 3 tablespoons) of water and 550 grams (about 2¾ cups plus 1 teaspoon) of the sugar. Once the sugar is completely dissolved in the water, pour the syrup into the pot with the citrus peels. The peels and the plate should be covered with at least ½ inch of syrup. Bring the syrup just to a boil and turn off the heat. Cover the pot with plastic wrap and tie a long strip of plastic wrap around the rim. The steam will first push the plastic up like a balloon, then pull it down to create a vacuum.

7 Leave on the stove at room temperature overnight. (If you are making this in the summer and you are afraid of attracting flies and bees, let it cool at room temperature for 1 hour and then store the pot in the refrigerator.) The next day, remove the plate and sprinkle 100 grams of granulated sugar (about ½ cup) into the syrup. Place the plate back on the peels and bring just to a boil. Turn off the heat, cover the pot with plastic wrap, and tie a long strip of plastic wrap around the rim to create a vacuum. Repeat this every day for 10 days. On the tenth day, after you've used up the last of the sugar, add 50 grams of corn syrup, bring the syrup just to a boil, and turn off the heat. Cover the pot with plastic wrap and tie a long strip of plastic wrap around the rim to create a vacuum. Allow the mixture to cool for 1 hour, then store the pot in the refrigerator overnight.

The peels are now candied and are ready to be used. Transfer to a container, cover the peels with their syrup, and store indefinitely in the refrigerator.

The candied fruit industry is very famous in the south of France, especially in the city of Apt in the Luberon area of Provence, which claims to be the world capital of candied fruit. The area is a great fruit-growing region; the industry grew there out of a need to conserve the abundant harvests.

IT'S DONE WHEN IT'S DONE

The finished peels look glossy and translucent. If they do not look translucent, bring them back to a boil one more time and leave for an extra day.

STORAGE

I like to keep my candied peels in their syrup in the refrigerator. They could be kept at room temperature, but you would attract every fly and bee in the neighborhood.

RECIPES REQUIRING
CANDIED PEEL

Lemon Mirrors
(PAGE 201)
Lemon Cream Tart with Meringue Teardrops
(PAGE 163)
Stollen
(PAGE 303)
Pain d'Épices
(PAGE 335)

JACQUY'S TAKEAWAYS

→ Never use an aluminum pot, as it would react with the acidity of the peels.

→ You cannot candy the peels in one cooking session of a few hours with 1000 grams of water and 1400 grams of sugar, as the high amount of sugar would first crystallize and then slowly caramelize, making the peels taste bitter.

→ Keep the weighed-out sugar in a container next to your stove, then follow the instructions in Step 7 every day until you run out. Then you won't lose track of what day you are on.

CHOCOLATE CROISSANTS
(SEE PAGE 127 FOR RECIPE)

*O*ver the centuries chefs and pastry chefs have strived to come up with new creations. They invented them for kings and queens, movie stars and opera singers. The royal chefs worked especially hard, because European kings and queens were always trying to outdo each other both on the battlefield and in the feast hall. Whenever there was an important occasion the chefs were ordered to wow guests with a new dish, a new cake or pastry that would prove the king superior. It took lots of sweat and sometimes blood—Louis XIV's maître d'hôtel François Vatel committed suicide after he was late delivering an extravagant dinner for 2,000 royal guests—to achieve the perfect result. Some creations came out of intensive research and experimentation; others were the results of mistakes that changed history. The recipes in this chapter are the successes, the pastries that proved to be universally popular and have remained so through the ages.

Many of these French pastries are international in their appeal. Who has never heard of a flaky, buttery Croissant (PAGE 127), a Chocolate Éclair (PAGE 97), or a Napoléon (PAGE 116; in France we call it a *mille-feuille*)? What child does not love *pains au chocolat* (PAGE 127), the world's best excuse to start the day with chocolate? When these pastries are made well, everybody likes them. That is what makes them classics.

Some of the recipes in this chapter are better known in France than internationally. They include delicious pastries made with *pâte à choux*, such as the Salambos on PAGE 93, cream puffs that are filled with pastry cream, glazed with caramel, and studded with a toasted almond. When you build a tower with caramel-glazed cream puffs you end up with France's most classic wedding cake, the Croquembouche (PAGE 109). Other popular *pâte à choux* pastries are the Religieuse (PAGE 104), made by stacking two cream puffs filled with coffee pastry cream and glazed with fondant, and the Paris-Brest (PAGE 101), shaped like a bicycle wheel and filled with a scrumptious hazelnut cream.

If you travel around France you will find regional pastries made with local ingredients, interesting and delicious products that come with a little piece of history and speak of the *terroir*. In Alsace, for example, we love Hazelnut and Orange Japonais (PAGE 121), a sort of cake made with two crunchy hazelnut meringues filled with an orange butter cream that is very closely related to two other French pastries from other French regions, the *succès* and the *dacquoise*.

The recipes in this chapter represent the mere tip of the classics iceberg. In addition to these recipes, you can find classics like Elephant Ears/Palmiers (PAGE 227) and Macarons (PAGE 221) in the cookie chapter, where they belong. But they too are the pillars of French pastry, visited and revisited, constructed and deconstructed, year after year. Some may fade away momentarily only to reappear, like today's fashionable *macarons*, but they are all here to stay.

SALAMBOS

YIELD | ABOUT 4½ DOZEN
1½-INCH-LONG *SALAMBOS*

INGREDIENTS	WEIGHT	MEASURE (APPROXIMATE) OR OUNCE WEIGHT
Pâte à Choux (PAGE 11)	1 recipe	1 recipe
PASTRY CREAM		
Whole milk (3.5% fat)	375 grams	1½ cups
Butter (French style, 82% fat)	37.5 grams	1½ ounces or 3 tablespoons
Granulated sugar	45 grams	¼ cup less 1 teaspoon
Vanilla bean	¾ bean	¾ bean
Cornstarch	15 grams	1½ tablespoons
Cake flour	15 grams	1½ tablespoons
Granulated sugar	45 grams	¼ cup less 1 teaspoon
Egg yolks	90 grams	About 6 yolks, depending on the size of the eggs
Kirschwasser or rum, optional	12.5 grams	1 tablespoon
Caramel (PAGE 47)	1 recipe	1 recipe
Sliced almonds	25 to 50 grams	¼ to ½ cup

Salambos, oval-shaped *choux* pastries filled with pastry cream and glazed with caramel, are among my favorite French pastries. I love the simple flavors and the three complementary textures—a crunchy caramel coating, a creamy filling, and a crisp *choux* pastry shell. The pastry cream in traditional *salambos* is flavored with kirschwasser or rum. I have made this ingredient optional, but I recommend it. If you are making more or less than this recipe yields, calculate 2 percent of the weight of the pastry cream to figure out how much kirschwasser or rum you will need.

Making *salambos* always reminds me of the first time I made caramel when I was an apprentice (PAGE 50). My boss put me in charge of glazing the *salambos* that day and I had to make the caramel, which I'd never done before. I stirred it too quickly and ended up with a horrible burn on my arm that took months to heal. I have never stirred caramel quickly since that day.

BEFORE YOU BEGIN

→ Get out the following equipment and allow all of the ingredients to come to room temperature:

Digital scale, set to metric weights
Equipment for Pâte à Choux (PAGE 11)
Equipment for Pastry Cream (PAGE 39)
Equipment for Caramel (PAGE 47)
1 pastry bag fitted with a ⅜-inch round tip
1 sheet pan lined with plastic wrap
Plastic wrap
1 paring knife
1 pastry bag fitted with a ¼-inch round tip
1 medium mixing bowl
1 rubber spatula
1 stainless steel hand whisk
1 or 2 sheet pans lined with parchment paper
1 pie tin
1 heating pad or warming tray
One 3 × 3-inch square of aluminum foil
Latex gloves

→ Read this recipe through twice from start to finish.

FRENCH PASTRY CLASSICS | 93

METHOD

1 Preheat the oven to 400°F/200°C and line sheet pans with parchment paper. Make the *choux* pastry following the instructions in the master recipe on PAGE 11. Using a pastry bag fitted with a ⅜-inch round tip, pipe 1½-inch ovals onto sheet pans lined with parchment paper (see PAGES 15-20 for piping instructions) and bake as directed in the master recipe, reducing the oven heat to 325°F/160°C after the first 15 minutes. When done, remove from the oven and allow to cool. Turn the oven down to 300°F/150°C.

2 Make the pastry cream using the quantities listed above and following the method in the master recipe on PAGE 39. If desired, add the kirschwasser or rum to the finished pastry cream and whisk until smooth. Transfer to a sheet pan lined with plastic wrap, cover airtight with additional plastic wrap, and cool in the freezer for 15 minutes. If you are not using right away, transfer to the refrigerator.

3 Using the tip of a paring knife or a round ¼-inch pastry tip, make a small hole in the top of each *salambo*, right in the center. Fit a pastry bag with a ¼-inch tip. Remove the pastry cream from the freezer or refrigerator and transfer to a medium bowl. Using a rubber spatula, mix for 1 minute to loosen it up. At the end of mixing it should be smooth and shiny. If it still looks lumpy, switch to a whisk and beat some more until smooth. Fill the pastry bag, following the instructions on PAGE 15. Insert the piping tip into the little hole in each *salambo* and fill the shells with the pastry cream. Gently apply pressure to the pastry bag until you see the cream just beginning to ooze out of the hole. Stop applying pressure and remove the tip. Wipe away any pastry cream from the opening.

4 Place the almonds on a sheet pan lined with parchment paper and bake in the 300°F/150°C oven for 15 to 20 minutes, until golden brown. Remove from the oven and set aside to cool.

5 Make the caramel following the directions on PAGE 47. Once it is ready you must dip your *salambos*. Keep the caramel warm by placing it on an upside-down pie tin placed over a heating pad or a warming tray. This will prevent the caramel from seizing up too quickly. Alternatively you can reheat the caramel on the stove from time to time, but take care not to let it become darker. Wrap the 3 × 3–inch piece of aluminum foil on the edge of the pan to facilitate wiping the puffs.

6 Put on latex gloves to make sure that this next step is done safely. Place a sheet pan lined with parchment paper, if desired, next to the caramel and the toasted almonds at arm's reach. Hold the bottom of the first *salambo* in one hand and briefly dip the top of it into the liquid caramel. The caramel coating should be light. Scrape off any excess caramel dripping down the sides of the *salambo* on the aluminum-wrapped edge of the pan and place the glazed *salambo* on the sheet pan. Immediately place 1 toasted sliced almond in the middle over the piping hole. The almond decorates the puff and covers the hole. Continue until all of the *salambos* are glazed and decorated. They are now ready to be eaten.

IT'S DONE WHEN IT'S DONE

The *pâte à choux* should look golden brown and the caramel a little bit darker. The caramel layer should be thin. If it is thick the *salambos* will be difficult to eat. A thin layer of caramel goes a long way.

STORAGE

Salambos can be stored, uncovered, in a refrigerator for up to 12 hours at the most. After that the caramel will melt and become sticky.

CHOCOLATE ÉCLAIRS

INGREDIENTS	WEIGHT	MEASURE (APPROXIMATE) OR OUNCE WEIGHT
Pâte à Choux (PAGE 11)	½ recipe	½ recipe
Egg Wash (PAGE 7)	1 recipe	1 recipe
CHOCOLATE PASTRY CREAM		
Dark chocolate couverture (70%)	43 grams	1⅜ ounces (about ¼ cup coins)
Whole milk (3.5% fat)	320 grams	1⅓ cups
Granulated sugar	30 grams	2 rounded tablespoons
Vanilla extract	5 grams	1 teaspoon
Cornstarch	8 grams	2½ teaspoons
All-purpose flour	4 grams	1 rounded teaspoon
Granulated sugar	30 grams	2 rounded tablespoons
Egg yolks	40 grams	About 2½ yolks
GLAZE		
Unsweetened chocolate	36 grams	1¼ ounces
Simple Syrup (PAGE 6)	40 grams (more as needed)	2 tablespoons (more as needed)
Fondant	125 grams	⅓ cup

Nothing can compare with the simplicity and perfect balance of an oblong cream puff filled with chocolate pastry cream and coated with chocolate fondant. Chocolate éclairs are sweet heaven to me.

When I first landed in San Francisco in 1986, fresh from a job in Saudi Arabia, I was appalled when I saw 18-inch-long pastries that were labeled "éclairs" in a Sam's Club. I was sure that it must be a mistake. What had they done to this wonderful French classic? There would be much too much cream in the center, it would gush out when you took the first bite, and these monstrosities were covered with a disgusting frosting that was nothing like fondant. I was so horrified (and naive) that I looked around for a manager. I spoke very little English but thought it imperative to alert the Sam's Club people to their mistake. I went up to a man who was restocking the shelves and in my broken English earnestly made my case. I told him it was important that he remove these éclairs from the shelves right away so that customers wouldn't buy them, as they were not the right size. Needless to say, he laughed and walked away shaking his head.

BEFORE YOU BEGIN

→ Get out the following equipment and allow all of the ingredients to come to room temperature:

Digital scale, set to metric weights
Equipment for Pâte à Choux (PAGE 11)
Equipment for Pastry Cream (PAGE 39)
1 pastry bag fitted with a ½-inch round tip
1 pastry brush
1 serrated knife
1 large chef's knife
1 pastry bag fitted with a ⅜-inch round tip
1 small microwave-safe bowl
1 rubber spatula
1 wooden spoon or spatula
1 digital thermometer
Latex gloves

→ Read this recipe through twice from start to finish.

The chocolate in this pastry cream not only defines its flavor but also contributes to its smooth, creamy texture. All pastry creams are made with whole milk, and some also contain heavy cream or butter, which add a nice and creamy texture and also introduce solids that make the cream set and prevent it from becoming soupy. In this recipe the creamy feel comes from the cocoa butter and solids in the chocolate.

The traditional way to glaze the top of an éclair is with fondant, which is made with hot syrup that is left to cool for a while and then mixed together until it crystallizes into a white sugar paste. This type of fondant is only used to glaze pastries and you should not mistake it with the "rolled fondant" that is used to cover wedding cakes. Nobody makes his own fondant anymore. You can buy it from specialty pastry suppliers, such as **www.lepicerie.com**, and in powdered form from **www.chefrubber.com**. The fondant in this recipe is mixed with unsweetened chocolate for taste and to offset its sweetness. Simple syrup is added to the fondant to thin it and make it usable for glazing. The three are heated together and then used to glaze the top of the éclairs. The very important thing to remember is to check the temperature of the mixture while heating and not allow it to go higher than 87.8°F/31°C. If it goes beyond this it will crystallize and lose its shine once it cools.

But the sin with those éclairs went beyond portion control. If you do not make éclairs the right size you cannot achieve the balance of crust and cream that makes éclairs such perfect pastries. A 3- to 4-inch-long *choux* pastry like the ones in our recipe is just the right size for achieving this. Mini éclairs that are only 1½ or 2 inches long will also work, but they are almost too much crust in proportion to cream.

METHOD

FOR THE *PATE À CHOUX*

1 Make a whole batch of the *pâte à choux* recipe on PAGE 11. Weigh out half the batch for the éclairs and spoon it into a pastry bag fitted with a ½-inch round tip. Use the rest for another purpose. Read my piping directions on PAGES 15–20 and pipe twelve 3- to 3 ½-inch éclairs onto a sheet pan lined with parchment paper, taking care to leave at least ¾ inch of space between them and to stagger the rows.

2 Preheat the oven to 400°F/200°C. Brush the tops of the éclairs with egg wash. Dip the end of a fork in the egg wash and run the tines down the surface of the dough. The lines will ensure that the éclairs will expand in the oven in a uniform way.

3 Bake in the preheated oven for 10 to 15 minutes, until the éclairs rise. Then turn down the oven to 325°F/160°C and bake for another 35 to 40 minutes, until they are golden brown. Do not interrupt the baking by opening the oven door multiple times, as this can cause the éclairs to collapse and they may never rise again.

4 Remove the éclairs from the oven and allow to cool. Once they have cooled, cut them laterally with a serrated knife—but do not cut all the way through. The top and bottom should still be attached along one long side.

FOR THE CHOCOLATE PASTRY CREAM

1 Finely chop the chocolate on a cutting board with a large chef's knife and set aside (this isn't necessary if you are using chocolate coins). In a medium saucepan combine all but ¼ cup of the milk with the first 30 grams of sugar, and the vanilla. Stir with a whisk and place over medium heat.

2 Meanwhile, in a medium bowl whisk the cornstarch and the flour together with the remaining 30 grams of sugar. Add the ¼ cup of milk you set aside and whisk in the egg yolks.

3 When the milk mixture comes to a boil, turn off the heat. Whisk half of the hot milk mixture into the egg yolk mixture. Strain the egg yolk mixture back into the saucepan.

4 Turn the heat back to medium and whisk, making sure to whisk everywhere—bottom and sides and bottom edges of the pan—so that the mixture does not scorch. As soon as you feel that the mixture is becoming slightly thick on the bottom of the pan, remove it from the heat and whisk until the entire mixture is thick and thoroughly uniform. This will allow a slow and even coagulation of the eggs and result in a nice, creamy pastry cream. Return to the heat and bring back to a boil, whisking constantly. Cook, whisking, for 1 minute to cook out the starch flavor.

5 Immediately remove from the heat and whisk in the finely chopped chocolate. Whisk until the chocolate has melted and the mixture is uniform. Transfer to the plastic-lined sheet pan. Spread in an even layer and place another sheet of plastic wrap directly on top of the cream so that the pastry cream is not in contact with the air. This will prevent the pastry cream from developing a dry skin. Place the sheet pan in the freezer to cool the cream rapidly and stop the growth of bacteria. This should only take 15 to 20 minutes. Scrape into a bowl, cover with plastic wrap, and store in the refrigerator for up to 1 day or proceed with the recipe.

ASSEMBLING AND FINISHING THE ÉCLAIRS

1 Whisk the pastry cream vigorously for 15 seconds, either by hand or in the stand mixer fitted with the whip. Scrape the cream into a pastry bag fitted with a ⅜-inch round tip.

2 Open up the éclairs, fill them with the pastry cream, and close them back up. Set aside.

3 Place the unsweetened chocolate on a cutting board and chop fine with a large chef's knife (no need to chop if you are using chocolate coins). Place half of the simple syrup in a small microwave-safe bowl. Microwave at 50 percent power for 1 minute.

4 Add the chopped chocolate to the warm syrup and stir for 10 seconds. Microwave the mix for 1 more minute at 50 percent power and stir together with a rubber spatula until the mixture is homogenous. If it does not come together, repeat the microwaving for 1 minute. Work the fondant in your hands for a minute just as if you were kneading dough. Add it to the chocolate and syrup mixture and stir with a wooden spatula or spoon for 2 minutes. It will be very hard to stir this mixture at first, but then it will come together. You can slowly thin it down with the remaining syrup heated up at 50 percent power for 1 minute. The mixture should have a soft feel, and when you lift the spatula up and hold it straight the fondant should form a ribbon as it falls back into the bowl. If the fondant seems too thick, add a little more syrup; if it feels

→ Fondant is always thinned down with simple syrup. Vanilla éclairs are usually dipped in plain fondant while coffee éclairs are dipped in fondant mixed with 3 percent coffee extract.

→ If you are using fondant powder, which is very convenient, add the chocolate syrup and 25 grams of warm water to 150 grams of powder, mix together, and heat to 87.8°F/31°C as directed. Adjust the consistency with a tablespoon of warm water if necessary. This method works well and is very convenient.

→ I have seen éclairs dipped in chocolate couverture. It is not the classic way to go, and it is not to my taste, but technically it works.

→ Don't forget to put on latex gloves before you begin the dipping procedure.

too soft, add a small amount of fondant. If it cools and thickens too much adjust the temperature by heating it in very short bursts in the microwave at 50 percent power. But be very careful that it does not exceed 87.8°F/31°C or it will not be shiny again. The fondant is now ready to be used.

5 Put on the latex gloves. With your left hand hold an éclair by the base and flip it over so that the top is now sitting on the surface of the fondant. Also with your left hand, lift the éclair from the fondant and hold it straight up over the fondant. With your right index finger wipe off the excess fondant, leaving enough of a layer to cover the surface. Scrape your index finger on the side of the bowl to remove the glaze and slide it around the glazed area of the éclair so that it is nice and smooth. Set the éclair on a tray and repeat with the other éclairs. Once they are all glazed, place them in the refrigerator. Serve them at once or store them in the refrigerator for up to 1 day.

IT'S DONE WHEN IT'S DONE

Freshly glazed éclairs always have a shiny glaze. If you have overheated the fondant, however, the shine will be gone when you pull the éclairs out of the refrigerator.

STORAGE

Always keep éclairs in the refrigerator. They should be good for 24 hours. After that they will still be good for a day but the *pâte à choux* will be soggier.

INGREDIENTS	WEIGHT	MEASURE (APPROXIMATE) OR OUNCE WEIGHT
Pâte à Choux (PAGE 11)	½ recipe	½ recipe
Egg Wash (PAGE 7)	15 grams	About 1 tablespoon
Sliced almonds	25 grams	2½ tablespoons
PASTRY CREAM		
Whole milk (3.5% fat)	225 grams	1 cup
Butter (French style, 82% fat)	23 grams	⅘ ounce
Granulated sugar	33 grams	2 tablespoons plus 2 teaspoons
Vanilla beans or extract	1 bean or 5 grams extract	1 bean or 1 teaspoon extract
Cornstarch	12 grams	1 tablespoon plus ¾ teaspoon
All-purpose flour	6 grams	2 teaspoons
Granulated sugar	33 grams	2 tablespoons plus 2 teaspoons
Egg yolks	54 grams	About 3 yolks
HAZELNUT *MOUSSELINE*		
Butter (French style, 82% fat)	90 grams	3 ounces
Hazelnut Praline Paste (PAGE 57)	80 grams	¼ cup

Over the centuries many French pastries have been conceived in shapes that represent events in history. The Paris-Brest—a pastry made with *choux* paste piped in a ring shape and baked, then filled with a hazelnut *mousseline*, a mix of pastry cream, butter, and hazelnut paste—is one of them. Paris–Brest was a race created in France in 1891 by Pierre Giffard, the editor of a newspaper called *Le Petit Journal*, to promote the use of bicycles. The cyclists had to race from Paris to the city of Brest, on the coast of Brittany, and back in a single stretch, a distance of 1,200 kilometers, or 720 miles. The first winner rode for 71 hours and 22 minutes without sleeping. The grueling race took place every 10 years. After the first race Giffard decided that the city of Brest needed to be showcased more, so in 1910, to create awareness, he asked Louis Durand, a pastry chef located in Maisons-Laffitte, near Paris, to create a pastry shaped like a bicycle wheel that would be named for the race. Some say that the ring shape also represents the head wreath that Greek athletes wore after a victory.

BEFORE YOU BEGIN

→ Get out the following equipment and allow all of the ingredients to come to room temperature:

Digital scale, set to metric weights
Equipment for Pâte à Choux, PAGE 11
Equipment for Pastry Cream, PAGE 39
1 pastry bag fitted with a ½-inch star tip
1 pastry brush
KitchenAid or stand mixer fitted with the whisk attachment
1 rubber spatula
1 serrated knife

→ Read this recipe through twice from start to finish.

UNDERSTANDING INGREDIENTS

Because of its ring shape, the Paris-Brest does not crack open during baking. The shape allows the water in the *pâte à choux* to evaporate in all directions when the piped rings are placed in the hot oven, and this helps the pastry maintain its shape and look. By contrast, a cream puff is piped in a dome shape, which means that there is a concentration of an inch or more of *pâte à choux* in one place. When cream puffs bake, a lot of water will evaporate from the same place and cause the puffs to crack open.

The pastry cream is enriched with butter and hazelnut praline paste. It is very important that the butter be soft when you add it to the pastry cream so that it will mix in properly. Otherwise there will be lumps. You can remove it from the refrigerator the day before to give it time to soften.

METHOD

FOR THE *PÂTE À CHOUX*

1   Preheat the oven to 400° F/200°C with the rack positioned in the middle. Make the *pâte à choux* following the recipe on PAGE 11. Transfer half the *pâte à choux* dough to a pastry bag fitted with a ½-inch star tip. Pipe fifteen 2-inch rings on sheet pans lined with parchment paper. (With the remaining *choux* pastry you can make other shapes, or pipe 30 rings and freeze half of them—this recipe only uses half the dough.) Brush lightly with egg wash and decorate with the sliced almonds.

2   Bake 1 sheet pan at a time at 400°F/200°C for 10 to 15 minutes, until the Paris-Brest rise. Then turn down the oven to 325°F/160°C and bake for another 35 to 40 minutes, until they are golden brown. Do not interrupt the baking by opening the oven door multiple times, as they might collapse and never rise again. Remove them from the oven and allow them to cool on a rack.

FOR THE HAZELNUT *MOUSSELINE*

1   Make the pastry cream using the quantities listed above and following the method in the master recipe on PAGE 39. When it is done immediately remove it from the heat and transfer to a plastic-lined sheet pan. Spread in an even layer and place another sheet of plastic wrap directly on top of the cream so that it is not in contact with the air. Place the sheet pan in the freezer to cool the cream rapidly and stop the growth of bacteria. This should only take 15 to 20 minutes.

2   Make sure that your butter is soft. Once your pastry cream is very cold to the touch (about 42°F/5°C), place it in the bowl of your mixer fitted with the whisk attachment. Whisk on high speed for 30 seconds. Scrape down the sides of the bowl with a rubber spatula and whisk on high for another 30 seconds. Add the soft butter and praline paste and whisk for 1 minute on medium high. Scrape down the sides of the bowl and whisk for another minute on high, until you get a nice and light emulsion.

ASSEMBLING THE PARIS-BREST

Place each Paris-Brest on a cutting board and cut in half horizontally with a serrated knife. Place each bottom and top on a sheet pan. Transfer the cream to the pastry bag fitted with a ½-inch star tip and pipe small swirls onto the Paris-Brest bottoms. Place the tops over the filling and dust with confectioners' sugar. Refrigerate for 1 hour. You can now serve them to your guests.

IT'S DONE WHEN IT'S DONE

The Paris-Brest shells should be golden brown and, like all *pâte à choux* shells, should be thoroughly baked so that the pastry cream filling does not cause them to become soggy after a few hours.

The cream should look shiny and semi-stiff, stiff enough for it to be piped. If it looks soupy, the pastry cream was probably not cold enough. If that is the case you can remedy it by whisking the mixture for 2 to 3 minutes, which cools it by incorporating cold air. If it still looks too soft, place the entire bowl in the refrigerator for 30 minutes, then place it over a bowl filled with ice for 10 minutes and mix every 2 minutes. Return to the mixer and whip again. It should now be firm enough to pipe. If the mixture looks a little grainy, that means that it is slightly too cold. Bring the bowl out of the mixture and place it in a sink filled with 2 inches of hot water for 30 seconds. Whisk again in the mixer and you should see it turn smooth and shiny.

STORAGE

Paris-Brest can be refrigerated for 24 hours and can be frozen for up to 1 month.

JACQUY'S TAKEAWAYS

→ This is the kind of dessert that is so rich but also so good. It combines the creamy feel of a pastry cream and butter with the nutty flavor profile of the praline paste.

→ You can always sprinkle some crushed caramelized nuts onto the piped swirls of cream and enhance them with chocolate decorations; this will add a wonderful additional texture.

COFFEE RELIGIEUSES / RELIGIEUSES AU CAFÉ

INGREDIENTS	WEIGHT	MEASURE (APPROXIMATE)
Pâte à Choux (PAGE 11)	1 recipe	1 recipe
Egg Wash (PAGE 7)	1 recipe	1 recipe
COFFEE PASTRY CREAM		
Whole milk (3.5% fat)	650 grams	2⅔ cups
Coffee extract, such as Trablit	35 grams	2 tablespoons
Butter (French style, 82% fat)	65 grams	2³⁄₁₀ ounces
Granulated sugar	81 grams	6 tablespoons plus 1⅞ teaspoons
Vanilla beans	1½ beans	1½ beans
Cornstarch	31 grams	3 tablespoons
All-purpose flour	15 grams	1½ tablespoons
Granulated sugar	81 grams	6 tablespoons plus 1⅞ teaspoons
Egg yolks	156 grams	About 8½ yolks
GLAZE		
Simple Syrup (PAGE 6)	125 grams	⅓ cup
Coffee extract, such as Trablit	25 grams	1½ tablespoons
Fondant	450 grams	1 pound
DECORATION		
Coffee Pastry Cream, above	70 grams	2½ ounces
Butter, softened	20 grams	⁷⁄₁₀ ounce

BEFORE YOU BEGIN

→ Get out the following equipment and allow all of the ingredients to come to room temperature:

Digital scale, set to metric weights
Equipment for Pâte à Choux (PAGE 11)
Equipment for Pastry Cream (PAGE 39)
2 sheet pans lined with parchment paper
1 pastry bag fitted with a ½-inch
    round tip
1 pastry brush
1 fork
1 paring knife
1 pastry bag fitted with a ¼-inch
    round tip
1 medium mixing bowl
1 rubber spatula
1 stainless steel hand whisk or handheld
    electric mixer
1 small microwave-safe bowl
Latex gloves
1 digital thermometer
1 small pastry bag fitted with a ¼-inch
    star tip

→ Read this recipe through twice from start to finish.

Religieuses are cream puffs filled with pastry cream and glazed with fondant, like an éclair. But what's really special is that there are two cream puffs, a large one and a small bonus puff that sits on top. Fondant and piped teardrops of butter cream or pastry cream enriched with butter (*mousseline*) hold the two together. The resulting pastry is very attractive, almost like a small wedding cake. This recipe will yield 30 *religieuses*. If you don't want to make that many, cut the quantities for the pastry cream and fondant in half. Make a full recipe of *choux* pastry but pipe and freeze other shapes with half of it. Although you can do this recipe in 1 day, you can also make the cream puff shells the day before, which will lighten your workload when you assemble the *religieuses*. Make sure to bake the cream puffs long enough so that they dry out completely. Otherwise they will get soggy as soon as they are filled with cream.

The pastry cream and the fondant glaze for these *religieuses* are both flavored with coffee extract, which balances nicely with the sweetness of the fondant glaze. Coffee extracts come in different forms. Some are alcohol based, like vanilla extract, while others are more syrupy. Taste your pastry cream, and if you desire a more intense coffee flavor you can add a little more. The quantity here is based on a coffee extract called Trablit, which is available in baking-supply stores and specialty markets.

As with the Éclairs on PAGE 97, fondant is used to decorate the top of the *religieuses.* It is mixed with simple syrup and coffee extract and requires heating, but should not get hotter than 87.8°F/31°C; otherwise the fondant will start to crystallize and lose its shine. If this happens, you can only remedy it by adding more fondant to the overheated batch.

METHOD

FOR THE *PÂTE À CHOUX*

1 Preheat the oven to 400°F/200°C. Make the *pâte à choux* following the directions on PAGE 11. Using a pastry bag fitted with a ½-inch round tip, pipe thirty 1⅞-inch-wide × ⅜-inch-high rounds onto 2 sheet pans lined with parchment paper, making sure to stagger the rows and leave at least ½ inch between each round. Pipe thirty 1-inch-wide by ½-inch-high rounds onto 2 other sheet pans. If it helps, draw the circles onto the parchment paper before piping—but be sure to flip the parchment paper over so that the pencil marks do not bake onto the pastries.

2 Make a recipe of egg wash and glaze the top of each puff using a pastry brush, then cross-hatch the top with the tines of a fork, to ensure that the dough rises evenly in the oven.

3 Bake the puffs at 400°F/200°C for 10 to 15 minutes, until they rise. Then turn down the oven to 325°F/160°C and bake for another 25 minutes for the small ones, until they are golden brown, and an additional 35 to 40 minutes for the large ones. Do not interrupt the baking by opening the oven door multiple times, as this might cause the puffs to collapse, and if they collapse they will not rise again. Remove from the oven and allow to cool completely.

FOR THE PASTRY CREAM

1 While the puffs are baking, make the coffee pastry cream. Line a sheet pan with plastic wrap. In a medium stainless steel saucepan combine all but ¼ cup of the milk, the coffee extract, butter, 81 grams of sugar, and the vanilla bean seeds and pod. Stir with a whisk and place over medium heat.

2 Meanwhile, in a medium bowl whisk the cornstarch and the flour together with the remaining 81 grams of sugar. Add the ¼ cup of milk you set aside and whisk in the egg yolks.

3 Make a pastry cream using these ingredients following the instructions on PAGE 39. When the pastry cream is ready, pour onto the sheet pan lined with plastic wrap, spread evenly, and cover with another sheet of plastic wrap. Place in the freezer for 15 minutes, then transfer to the refrigerator for 15 more minutes.

FILLING THE CREAM PUFFS AND ASSEMBLING THE *RELIGIEUSES*

1 Make sure that the puffs are completely cooled. Using the tip of a paring knife or a ¼-inch round pastry tip, make a small hole in the top of each large puff, right in the center, and on the bottom of each small puff, right in the center. Fit a pastry bag with a ¼-inch round tip.

2 Remove the coffee pastry cream from the refrigerator and transfer to a bowl. Using a rubber spatula, mix for 1 minute to loosen it up. At the end of the mixing it should be smooth and shiny. If it still looks lumpy, switch to a hand whisk or handheld electric mixer and continue to beat until smooth. Set aside 70 grams (2½ ounces) of the pastry cream and fill the pastry bag with the remaining cream. Insert the tip into the little hole in each puff and fill all of the shells with the pastry cream.

HEATING UP THE FONDANT

1 Place half of the simple syrup and the coffee extract in a small microwave-safe bowl. Microwave at 50 percent power for 1 minute and

JACQUY'S TAKEAWAYS

→ You can be creative and fill a *religieuse* with different types of pastry cream. The top is usually glazed with fondant but you can also use caramel, just like for Salambos (PAGE 93). Ganache or butter cream can be used for the teardrop piping.

→ If you are using fondant powder, add the extract and 25 grams of warm water to 150 grams of powder, mix together, and heat to 87.8°F/31°C as directed. Adjust the consistency with a tablespoon of warm water if necessary.

then stir for 10 seconds. Wear latex gloves and work the fondant in your hands for a minute just as if you were kneading dough. Add it to the coffee syrup mixture and stir with a wooden spoon or spatula for 2 minutes. It will be very hard to mix at first, but then it will come together. Heat the remaining syrup at 50 percent power for 1 minute and slowly add to the fondant to thin it down until the fondant is soft and makes a ribbon when you lift it on the spatula or spoon above the bowl. If the fondant seems too thick, add a little more syrup; if it feels too soft, add a small amount of fondant. If the fondant cools and stiffens, adjust the temperature by microwaving it at 50 percent power for no more than 10 seconds at a time. After heating, check the temperature; it should never exceed 87.8°F/31°C, or the *religieuses* will not shine when you remove them from the refrigerator. The fondant is now ready to be used.

2 Make sure you are wearing latex gloves. With your left hand hold a small puff by the base and flip it over so that the top is now sitting on the surface of the fondant. With your left hand lift the puff up and hold it straight over the fondant. With your right index finger, scrape off the excess fondant, leaving enough of it to cover the surface. Scrape your index finger on the side of the bowl to remove the glaze and slide it around the glazed area so that it is nice and smooth. Place the glazed puff back on the sheet pan. Repeat with all the other small puffs and then move on to the large puffs. Glaze 1 large puff and set it on the sheet pan. Take 1 small puff and stick it right on top of the large puff while the fondant is still soft. Repeat with all the other puffs.

3 Make sure that your 20 grams of butter for the decoration is soft. Once the puffs are all glazed and the *religieuses* assembled, place the 70 grams of pastry cream you set aside and the 20 grams of soft butter in a small bowl and whip until smooth, using a hand whisk or handheld electric mixer. Transfer to a pastry bag fitted with a ¼-inch star tip and pipe small teardrops at the neck of the *religieuses*, going upward where the 2 puffs meet. Pipe a small rosette on the top of the small puff. The *religieuses* are now ready to be served.

IT'S DONE WHEN IT'S DONE

Freshly glazed *religieuses* should have a shiny glaze, but they will lose their shine within minutes if you have overheated the fondant.

STORAGE

Keep the *religieuses* in the refrigerator until you serve them. They will be good for 24 hours. After that they will still keep for a day, but the *pâte à choux* will be soggier.

TO PIPE A ROSETTE

Hold the pastry bag with the tip pointing straight down. Start piping—this will be the center of your rosette. Come off the center at 9 o'clock and go around the center clockwise until you come back to 9 o'clock. While still rotating, stop pressing on the bag and come off the center as if you were going to go around again. Do this in one fast motion.

CROQUEMBOUCHE

YIELD | ONE 14-INCH-TALL CROQUEMBOUCHE, SERVING 12 PEOPLE (ABOUT 9 SMALL PUFFS PER SERVING)

INGREDIENTS	WEIGHT	MEASURE (APPROXIMATE) OR OUNCE WEIGHT
Pâte à Choux (PAGE 11)	1 recipe	1 recipe
PASTRY CREAM		
Whole milk (3.5% fat)	450 grams	2 cups
Heavy cream (35% fat)	45 grams	3 tablespoons
Butter (French style, 82% fat)	70 grams	2½ ounces or 5 tablespoons
Granulated sugar	45 grams	3 tablespoons plus 1 teaspoon
Vanilla bean	1 bean	1 bean
Cornstarch	27 grams	3 tablespoons
All-purpose flour	14 grams	1 tablespoon plus 1 teaspoon
Granulated sugar	45 grams	3 tablespoons plus 1 teaspoon
Egg yolks	90 grams	5 yolks
CRÈME DIPLOMATE		
Pastry Cream, above	As needed	As needed
Heavy cream (35% fat)	105 grams	½ cup
Caramel (PAGE 47)	Double recipe	Double recipe
Vegetable, canola, or grapeseed oil, for the foil-covered cone	As needed	As needed
Jordan Almonds or Caramelized Almonds (PAGE 51)	As needed	As needed

Croquembouche, a cake made out of cream puffs coated with and held together by caramel, is *the* celebration cake in France. It's the country's best-known wedding cake, but it is also served for all sorts of other occasions, from baptisms to anniversaries to engagements. *Croque-en-bouche* means "crunch in the mouth," which is exactly what these caramel-covered cream puffs do when you eat them.

The classic croquembouche has a conical shape: the puffs are dipped in caramel and then stuck to each other around a cone. France has had a tradition of stacked or pyramidical desserts that goes back to the Middle Ages, when wedding cakes were often made of flat breads stacked on top of each other, from a large one on the bottom to a small one on the top. Nougatine—hot caramel mixed with toasted sliced almonds—was used to support and decorate the structures: it would be rolled out on an oiled

BEFORE YOU BEGIN

→ Get out the following equipment and allow all of the ingredients to come to room temperature:

Digital scale, set to metric weights
Equipment for Pâte à Choux (PAGE 11)
Equipment for Pastry Cream (PAGE 39)
Equipment for Caramel (PAGE 47)
Equipment for Caramelized Almonds (PAGE 51), if desired
KitchenAid or stand mixer fitted with the whisk attachment, a stainless steel hand whisk, or a handheld electric mixer
1 large bowl
Plastic wrap
1 rubber spatula
1 pastry bag fitted with a ¼-inch round tip
1 sheet pan lined with plastic wrap
Aluminum foil or parchment paper
One Styrofoam cone, 12 inches tall by 3½ inches wide (available in craft-supply shops)
1 silpat, platter, or plate wrapped in aluminum foil
1 pie tin
1 heating pad or warming tray
One 3 × 3-inch piece of aluminum foil
Latex gloves

→ Read this recipe through twice from start to finish.

The pastry cream used to fill the cream puffs is a pastry cream enriched with extra butter and a little whipped cream, which we call *crème diplomate*. The fat in the butter and cream not only make the pastry cream taste richer but also make it stiffer and less likely to make the cream puffs soggy, since fat crystallizes when it is cool.

When you make the caramel you will have to keep it warm so that it is easy to dip the cream puffs and coat them with a thin layer of caramel, without letting it get too dark. As caramel cools, it thickens. One way to keep it warm without cooking it is to keep the pot on a towel-covered heating pad or on a warming plate. You can also keep reheating it on the stove, but be careful not to let it cook when you reheat it.

slab of marble or granite and cut into the desired shapes while it was still warm. In the old days the cakes usually represented religious buildings such as churches, but then chefs began to get more creative and make replicas of monuments. Over the centuries pastry chefs perfected the art of cone-shaped celebration cakes, and by the turn of the last century they were using cream puffs to build other elaborate structures, like a baby's cradle for a baptism or a wishing well or fountain of love for a marriage.

No matter what the shape, a cream puff filled with buttery, creamy, vanilla-scented pastry cream and coated in caramel is pretty hard to resist. When I was testing this recipe and brought it home to my family we almost ate the whole thing in one night—and probably would have if we hadn't taken some of it to our neighbors.

Making croquembouche is a time-consuming project, as it involves making and filling about 110 cream puffs, then dipping them in hot caramel (you will be wearing latex gloves for this, don't worry) and attaching them to an oiled foil-covered Styrofoam cone and to each other. You can get ahead by making the puffs and the pastry cream the day before. It is a project that will be well worth your time!

METHOD

1 Make a batch of *pâte à choux* following the recipe on PAGE 11. Fill a pastry bag fitted with a ⅜-inch round tip and pipe 1-inch rounds onto parchment paper–lined sheet pans, taking care to leave at least ½ inch between each round and to stagger the rows. Bake as directed and allow to cool.

2 Make the pastry cream using the ingredients above and following the directions on PAGE 39. When it is done immediately remove from the heat and transfer to a plastic-lined sheet pan. Spread in an even layer and place another sheet of plastic wrap directly on top so that the pastry cream is not in contact with the air. This will prevent the cream from developing a dry skin. Place the sheet pan in the freezer to cool the cream rapidly and stop the growth of bacteria. This should only take 15 minutes. Refrigerate until needed.

MAKE THE *CRÈME DIPLOMATE*

1 Whip the cold heavy cream in the stand mixer on high speed until it becomes stiff but not grainy (see photo on PAGE 71). Transfer to a large bowl, cover with plastic wrap, and refrigerate.

2 Transfer the pastry cream to the mixer and whip on high speed for 1 minute, until smooth and shiny. Transfer the pastry cream to the bowl with the whipped cream and fold the mixture together very gently with a large rubber spatula until the cream is well incorporated. Transfer to a pastry bag fitted with a ¼-inch round tip.

3 Poke a small hole in the bottom of each puff and fill with the *crème diplomate*. Place on a plastic-lined sheet pan. Go on to the next step right away so that your puffs do not become soggy.

ASSEMBLING THE CROQUEMBOUCHE

1 Line your work surface with aluminum foil or parchment paper so the caramel drips on the paper instead of on the counter. Wrap the Styrofoam cone with an 18 × 18–inch piece of aluminum foil and rub the foil with a small amount of oil. Place the cone on a silpat or a flat plate wrapped in oiled foil.

2 Make a double recipe of caramel using the recipe on PAGE 47. Keep the caramel warm by placing it on an upside-down pie tin placed over a heating pad or a warming tray. This will prevent the caramel from seizing up too quickly. Alternatively you can reheat the caramel on the stove from time to time, but take care not to let it become darker. Fold a 3 × 3–inch piece of foil over the edge of the pan to facilitate wiping the caramel drippings off the puffs.

3 Put on a pair of latex gloves before you begin to dip the puffs. Hold the bottom of a puff in one hand and briefly dip the top of it in the liquid caramel. The caramel coating should be light. Scrape off any excess caramel that runs down the sides of the puff on the foil-covered edge of the pan and place the glazed puff on the plastic-lined sheet pan. Repeat until all of the puffs are coated with caramel.

4 Take 1 puff and dip the *bottom* of it into the caramel, then place it against the cone at the bottom of the cone. Take another puff, glaze a *side* of it with soft caramel, and stick it next to the first puff. Repeat until you are 1 puff away from completing the circle. The last puff that completes the circle should be glazed on both the right and the left sides to make sure that all of them are glued together (SEE ILLUSTRATION).

5 You are now ready to build your second row of puffs. It is very important to stagger the puffs so that the second round of puffs will be glued into the spaces between the puffs of the bottom row. Take another puff, glaze it both on the sides *and* on the bottom, and glue it on top, between 2 puffs from the first round. As you glue in the puffs you need to force them tightly into place against each other to make sure that you are creating a wall of puffs that is free of holes. You will sometimes need to look at all the available puffs on the sheet pan and find the perfect puff for the perfect fit. Continue until you have completed a second round; the last puff will be glazed on the *left*, *right*, and

IMPROPER WAY OF GLUING THE CROQUEMBOUCHE

The puffs are not staggered, leaving gaps that will create weak spots. The croquembouche will eventually collapse.

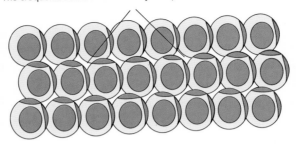

ASSEMBLING THE CROQUEMBOUCHE

The puffs in the first row are glued together at the sides. The last puff that completes the circle should be glazed on the right and the left sides to make sure that all of them are glued together.

puff   caramel

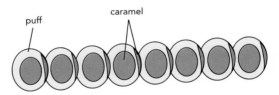

The subsequent rows are glued together on the sides and to the puffs below them on the bottom.

The puffs are tightly packed and the rows are staggered.

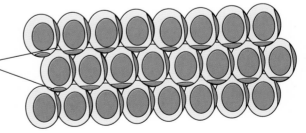

bottom to make sure that all the puffs are connected. If the caramel gets too cold, reheat it slightly and stir with a spoon or spatula until it becomes liquid again, but do not let it cook or it will become very dark and bitter. It's important to keep the caramel thin so that the coating on the puffs isn't too thick; otherwise the puffs will be difficult to break apart when you serve the cake. Continue building the croquembouche until you arrive at the top, making sure with each row that the puffs are very tightly glued together (SEE ILLUSTRATION). It is difficult to avoid having some holes, which is why we have Jordan Almonds or caramelized almonds to fill in the spaces where you can see the foil. Dip them into the caramel and fill where necessary.

6 Make room in your refrigerator and refrigerate, or place in a cool room until ready to serve, but for no longer than 8 hours.

7 When it is time to serve the cake, I usually serve 5 puffs per person to start with. The best way to dish it up is to take a pair of scissors or shellfish shears, insert them in an opening between the puffs, and cut off a 5-puff cluster close to the top. I like to do it in front of the guests, as it looks like the cake is being demolished, which is always great for conversation. Once the first 5 puffs are detached it is easy to continue with the remaining servings.

IT'S DONE WHEN IT'S DONE

The croquembouche tower should be free of large holes.

STORAGE

After the croquembouche is built you should refrigerate it or put in a very cold room before serving, because the puffs are filled with pastry cream and need to be kept at a safe and cool temperature. It will hold for up to 8 hours.

JACQUY'S TAKEAWAYS

→ When you build a croquembouche you need to make sure that the puffs are small and well baked. As soon as puffs are filled with cream they are on their way to becoming soggy. A larger puff will have a bigger cream-to-pastry ratio, and the puff will get soft very quickly. This will cause the croquembouche to collapse or, at best, lean over to one side.

→ The puffs should always be filled with a type of pastry cream, but the flavors can be varied. Try coffee, caramel, hazelnut, or chocolate.

Like egg whites, whipped cream goes through different stages. When you whip heavy cream you are incorporating air into it. As you whip, the fat in the cream creates a network of bonds that wraps around each air bubble. In order to get the fat to hold the air the cream must have a fat content of at least 30 percent. I prefer to use regular heavy cream, which is about 35 percent fat. I would not advise you to use 40 percent cream because it separates very easily. Don't try with half-and-half, as that contains between 10 and 12 percent fat and will never develop as a foam.

The colder fat is, the harder it is, thus the stronger its structure. Since fat is the key to holding the air bubbles in whipped cream, the colder the cream is, the more able it will be to hold air when you whip it. Warm cream would just create a very loose network around the air bubbles and would collapse easily. Therefore it is crucial that your heavy cream be stone cold, and even better if your bowl and beater are as well. But don't freeze it. Cream won't whip once frozen. The reason is that heavy cream is processed and homogenized into a water-in-fat emulsion; the fat encapsulates the water. When the cream is frozen, the water in the "fat capsules" turns into crystals and breaks through them, making the emulsion collapse; defrosted cream will still be usable for ganaches or sauces, but cannot be made into whipped cream.

I run some ice cubes in the bowl for 10 seconds, then I dry the bowl. You could also chill your bowl in the freezer.

Cream should always be whipped quickly because you need to incorporate air into it as fast as possible so that the cream stays cold and holds the air well. Imagine, for instance, that you are working in a warm kitchen and whipping heavy cream on medium: the warm air in the kitchen will quickly soften the butterfat in the cream and make the foam collapse. Always use enough cream so that the whisk makes contact with all of the liquid. Otherwise it will not be efficient and will take forever to make a foam. Since I want you to whip quickly, my advice is to wrap a large piece of plastic wrap around the top of the bowl and around the mixer so that it doesn't splatter everywhere. Don't walk away from the mixer, as the cream whips very quickly.

1

2

3

5

6

PHOTO 1 After 30 seconds of whipping on high, the cream is starting to get foamy. It is still at the runny stage and cannot be used yet.

PHOTO 2 Soft peaks: After 20 more seconds of whipping on high the cream is now at the soft peaks stage. When cream is at this stage its texture is very good for mousse making because it folds well with other mixtures. Should you want to sweeten or flavor your cream, this is when you would do it. Sweetened whipped cream is called *crème chantilly.*

PHOTO 3 Stiff peaks: After 10 more seconds of whipping on high, the cream is at the stiff stage. Stiff whipped cream is good for piping.

PHOTO 4 After 10 more seconds of whipping on high we can see that the cream is starting to be over-whipped and is separating. The only way to salvage it at this point is to add a little more liquid cream and whip it for 5 seconds to obtain a creamy texture again.

PHOTO 5 Whipping for another 15 seconds on high causes the foam to collapse. The butter and buttermilk in it begin to separate.

PHOTO 6 Now the butter and the water are completely separated. The only thing you can do is to strain the butter and use it as butter. It can never be turned back into cream again.

3-DAY RECIPE

MILLE-FEUILLE / NAPOLÉON

INGREDIENTS	WEIGHT	MEASURE (APPROXIMATE) OR OUNCE WEIGHT -
Puff Pastry (PAGE 28)	½ batch	½ batch
MOUSSELINE		
Whole milk (3.5% fat)	225 grams	1 cup
Granulated sugar	33 grams	2 tablespoons plus 2 teaspoons
Vanilla bean	1 bean	1 bean
Cornstarch	12 grams	1 tablespoon plus 1 teaspoon
All-purpose flour	6 grams	2 teaspoons
Granulated sugar	33 grams	2 tablespoons plus 2 teaspoons
Egg yolks	54 grams	3 yolks
Butter (French style, 82% fat), softened	73 grams	3²⁄₅ ounces
Confectioners' sugar, for dusting	As needed	As needed

BEFORE YOU BEGIN

→ Get out the following equipment and allow all of the ingredients to come to room temperature (this is particularly important for the butter used for the puff pastry butter block and for the *mousseline* filling):

Digital scale, set to metric weights
Equipment needed for Puff Pastry (PAGE 28)
Equipment needed for Pastry Cream (PAGE 39)
Two 12 × 17-inch sheet pans lined with parchment paper
1 dough docker or fork
Plastic wrap
1 digital thermometer
KitchenAid or stand mixer fitted with the whisk attachment
1 rubber spatula
1 wire rack
1 pastry bag fitted with a ½-inch round tip
1 ruler
1 long serrated knife or electric serrated knife
Paper

→ Read this recipe through twice from start to finish.

Once you have mastered two basic recipes, Puff Pastry (PAGE 28) and Pastry Cream (PAGE 39), you will be able to make a mille-feuille, also known as a Napoléon, one of the wonders of French pastry. A mille-feuille is made simply by layering the two, often along with fruit, most often strawberries and raspberries. This is one of the best pastries ever invented. The flaky puff pastry marries perfectly with the creamy pastry cream, while the top is usually covered with some kind of sugar coating. It's simple and it's delectable.

In French *mille-feuille* means a thousand leaves, which describes the multiple layers of flaky dough in the laminated pastry. In the United States and many other countries this dessert goes by the name Napoléon, which could be a reference to the Italian city of Naples, known for its own baroque desserts, or to Napoléon Bonaparte, the fearless French emperor and dictator. References to the mille-feuille date back as far as 1651, which again proves that a great classic pastry will live for centuries.

I am giving you a recipe that uses a half batch of puff pastry, making enough to yield six 2 × 3–inch Napoléons. Once you get the hang of them you might want to double the pastry cream and make a full batch of 12 Napoléons.

Although assembling the mille-feuille is straightforward and you could do this process in 2 days, ideally you should leave the rolled-out puff pastry dough in the refrigerator overnight to dry out slightly so that it won't puff too high when you bake it, which makes the three-layered mille-feuille very high. You can make the filling—the *mousseline*—a day ahead or on the day you are assembling the pastries.

METHOD

DAY 1 AND DAY 2

Make the puff pastry dough 1 or 2 days ahead of time following the recipe on PAGE 28. If you make a full batch, which I recommend (it's always a good idea to have some puff in your freezer), once you have completed the 6 turns, cut the dough in half, cutting parallel to the open ends. Line 2 sheet pans with parchment paper. Roll out each piece of dough into a thin rectangle that fits the sheet pan, 12 × 17 inches. Place the dough on the parchment paper–lined pans. Using a dough docker or a fork, poke holes in the dough every ¾ inch. Wrap and freeze one of the sheet pans; once the pastry is frozen, remove it from the pan and wrap it airtight in plastic, label it, and return it to the freezer. Refrigerate the other half, uncovered, for at least 2 hours and preferably overnight.

DAY 2 OR DAY 3

MAKING THE *MOUSSELINE*

1 Line a small sheet pan with plastic wrap. In a medium stainless steel sauce-pan combine all but ¼ cup of the milk, 33 grams of the sugar, and the vanilla bean seeds and pod. Stir with a whisk and place over medium heat.

2 In a medium bowl whisk the cornstarch and the flour together with the remaining 33 grams of sugar. Add the ¼ cup of milk you set aside and whisk in the egg yolks. Using these ingredients, continue to make the pastry cream, following the instructions on PAGE 39.

3 When the pastry cream is ready, immediately remove it from the heat and transfer it to a plastic-lined sheet pan. Spread in an even layer and place another sheet of plastic wrap directly on top so that the pastry cream is not in contact with the air. This will prevent the pastry cream from developing a dry skin. Place the sheet pan in the freezer to cool the cream rapidly and stop the growth of bacteria. This should only take 15 minutes. Once cool, transfer to the refrigerator and chill for 30 minutes.

4 To finish the *mousseline*, remove your pastry cream from the refrigerator and bring it to room temperature so that it is not too cold. Make sure that your butter is nice and soft. Both components should be around 60°F/16°C.

UNDERSTANDING INGREDIENTS

The cream used to fill these Napoléons is called *mousseline*, a pastry cream enriched with butter. Pastry cream will always stiffen up once it is chilled, but in order to be firm enough to hold its shape once piped, it needs additional fat. Fat is a solid and crystallizes once it cools, so the more of it you add to the pastry cream, the firmer your cream will become once it cools. If you didn't add a fat you would need to incorporate gelatin into the pastry cream as a gelling agent. It is important that the butter be soft when you add it to the pastry cream, and that the pastry cream not be too cold, or the butter will crystallize into little lumps instead of being homogenized with the cream. Because we need to add a good quantity of butter to the pastry cream so it will be sufficiently stiff, we do not melt butter with the milk as we do in other pastry cream recipes in this book.

Before assembling the mille-feuille we dust the top of the baked puff pastry with confectioners' sugar and run it under the broiler briefly so that the sugar caramelizes. In addition to looking and tasting very nice, this creates a barrier between the pastry and the cream so that the pastry will remain crisp for a longer time.

Place the pastry cream in the mixer fitted with the whisk attachment and whisk on high speed for 1 minute. Scrape down the sides of the bowl with a rubber spatula and whip for another minute on high. Add the soft butter and whip until the butter is homogenized and the mixture is glossy. If the cream is grainy this indicates that the butter or the pastry cream is too cold. To remedy this, place the mixing bowl in a bowl of hot water for 15 seconds, then return to the mixer and whip again for 15 seconds. Repeat until the cream is very shiny. Refrigerate for an hour or two, until ready to use.

BAKING THE PUFF PASTRY AND ASSEMBLING THE MILLE-FEUILLE

1 Preheat the oven to 400°F/200°C with the rack positioned in the middle. Place a wire rack on top of the puff pastry with the legs down; the rack should be ½ inch above the dough. It's okay if the legs have to sit on the dough; they will cause indentations, but these won't matter. Place the sheet pan in the hot oven and bake for 20 minutes. Open the oven quickly and remove the wire rack. Reduce the oven temperature to 300°F/150°C and bake for another 35 to 40 minutes, until the puff pastry is a rich brown color all the way through. Remove from the oven and turn on the broiler.

2 Flip the puff pastry over so that the top is now even and flat, and dust with confectioners' sugar. Place under the broiler, about 3 inches away from the heat, and watch carefully as the top caramelizes. This should not take more than a minute or two. Do not move away from the oven, as once the sugar begins to caramelize it will rapidly burn, and there goes your puff pastry. As soon as you see the sugar caramelize remove the puff from the oven and allow it to cool completely.

3 Transfer the *mousseline* to a pastry bag fitted with a ½-inch round tip.

4 Place the baked puff pastry on a cutting board and trim the sides so that you have a perfect rectangle. Measure the puff, and, using a long serrated knife, carefully cut lengthwise into 3 evenly sized rectangles. They should be approximately 3 inches wide by 12 inches long. You will be cutting the assembled mille-feuille into 6 portions that should each measure approximately 2 × 3 inches.

5 Place a long strip of puff pastry on your work surface with the caramelized side facing up. Pipe rows of round ½-inch balls of *mousseline* onto the rectangle. Place the second rectangle of puff on top and press down lightly just to make sure that the top sheet is stuck to the pastry cream. Do not press too hard or the cream will squish out. Repeat with the rest of the cream and top with the last piece of puff pastry, making sure that the caramelized part is facing up (SEE ILLUSTRATION).

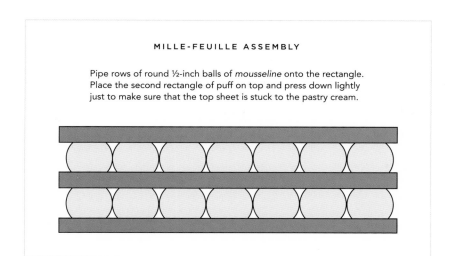

MILLE-FEUILLE ASSEMBLY

Pipe rows of round ½-inch balls of *mousseline* onto the rectangle. Place the second rectangle of puff on top and press down lightly just to make sure that the top sheet is stuck to the pastry cream.

6 Cut ¾-inch-wide strips of paper and set them diagonally on top of the mille-feuille. Dust the tops with confectioners' sugar and carefully remove the paper strips 1 at a time. Keep refrigerated until you serve it, but keep in mind that after 3 or 4 hours it will begin to get soggy. Cut into 2 × 3-inch pieces. I recommend an electric serrated knife for this task.

IT'S DONE WHEN IT'S DONE

The finished cream should be smooth, shiny, and creamy and hold it shape after it is piped. After baking, the puff pastry's surface should be slightly caramelized and the inside should have an even light brown color. The assembled mille-feuille should be tall but not oversized; I recommend a maximum height of 2 inches.

STORAGE

Keep the mille-feuille refrigerated for 3 to 4 hours; after that the cream will start to make it soggy.

VARIATION

MILLE-FEUILLE WITH BERRIES: You can add strawberries or raspberries to your mille-feuille. Place the berries between the rounds of *mousseline*, or on top of the mille-feuille, or both. I like to spread a thin layer of raspberry jam on the pastry before topping when I use fruit.

JACQUY'S TAKEAWAYS

→ Mille-feuille is best served when it is freshly made. The caramelized sugar on the surface creates a natural moisture barrier for 3 to 4 hours, but after that the cream will begin to penetrate the puff and make it soggy. A trick would be to cut the baked puff pastry into small individual pieces and fill them just before serving them to your guests. This will ensure a flaky puff.

→ **$50 TRICK:** Combine the milk with the vanilla seeds and bean the day before and refrigerate overnight for a more intense vanilla flavor.

→ For cutting the assembled mille-feuille, nothing beats an electric serrated knife.

HAZELNUT AND ORANGE JAPONAIS / JAPONAIS AUX NOISETTES ET À L'ORANGE

YIELD | ONE 8-INCH CAKE
2-DAY RECIPE

INGREDIENTS	WEIGHT	MEASURE (APPROXIMATE) OR OUNCE WEIGHT
ORANGE MARMALADE		
Fresh orange, preferably thin-skinned	1 orange (about 250 grams)	1 orange (about 8⅘ ounces)
Water	2000 grams	2 quarts
Water	2000 grams	2 quarts
Sea salt	20 grams	1 tablespoon
Granulated sugar	157 grams	¾ cup
JAPONAIS DISKS		
Hazelnuts	44 grams	5 tablespoons
Confectioners' sugar	94 grams	⅞ cup
All-purpose flour	9 grams	2½ teaspoons
Hazelnut flour	94 grams	1¼ cups, tightly packed
Egg whites	119 grams	About 4 whites
Cream of tartar	Pinch	Pinch
Sea salt	Pinch	Pinch
Granulated sugar	22 grams	2 tablespoons less ½ teaspoon
Additional confectioners' sugar, for dusting	As needed	As needed
PASTRY CREAM		
Whole milk (3.5% fat)	125 grams	½ cup
Butter (French style, 82% fat)	12.5 grams	½ ounce or 1 tablespoon
Granulated sugar	16 grams	1 tablespoon plus ¾ teaspoon
Vanilla bean	¼ bean	¼ bean
Cornstarch	5 grams	1½ teaspoons
Cake flour	5 grams	1½ teaspoons
Granulated sugar	16 grams	1 tablespoon plus ¾ teaspoon
Egg yolks	30 grams	1½ to 2 yolks, depending on the size of the eggs
HAZELNUT *MOUSSELINE*		
Hazelnut Praline Paste (PAGE 57)	70 grams	About ¼ cup
Butter (French style, 82% fat), softened	40 grams	1⅖ ounces or scant 3 tablespoons

BEFORE YOU BEGIN

→ Get out the following equipment and allow all of the ingredients to come to room temperature:

Digital scale, set to metric weights
1 vegetable brush
1 tall medium-sized stainless steel pot
1 spider
1 chef's knife
1 food processor fitted with the steel blade
1 small stainless steel saucepan
1 large rubber spatula
1 small mixing bowl
Plastic wrap
1 pastry bag in which to crush the hazelnuts
1 rolling pin
1 sheet pan lined with parchment paper
1 sifter
One 8-inch round plate or tart pan insert
Parchment paper
KitchenAid or stand mixer fitted with the whisk attachment
1 large mixing bowl
1 pastry bag fitted with a ½-inch round piping tip
1 pastry bag fitted with a ⅜-inch round piping tip
1 pastry bag fitted with a ¼-inch round piping tip

→ Read this recipe through twice from start to finish.

UNDERSTANDING INGREDIENTS

Japonais is a nutty meringue that is a cross between a sponge and a hard meringue. It has a hard and crunchy texture on the outside and, after it has been in contact with the cream filling for a while, a moist texture in the center. The crunch is due to the high amount of sugar in the mixture. Interestingly, it is also the sugar that helps the *japonais* become moist again, because sugar is hygroscopic, meaning that it absorbs and retains humidity. As for any meringue, it is preferable to let the egg whites air dry overnight in order to allow water to evaporate so the albumen will be more concentrated and hold the air bubbles in the meringue better.

Since *japonais* does not contain any fat other than the oil of the nuts, it is appropriate to use a rich buttery cream for the filling. Because the *japonais* is a porous meringue, too much moisture would make it soggy very quickly. It can only stand up to a filling that does not contain a lot of water and contains a decent amount of fat, as fat blocks water. A *mousseline* is a good candidate because it contains fat from the added

Japonais is one of my favorite desserts because of its unique combination of textures and flavors. The layers of this cake are made of nutty hazelnut meringue filled with a rich, nutty hazelnut pastry cream and a layer of homemade orange marmalade. The recipe is based on the traditional one that I used to make during my apprenticeship, but I've added the marmalade to the mix. The slight bitterness and acidity of the preserve provides a delicious contrast to the sweet meringue shells. The sweet meringue, the nutty hazelnut cream, and the tart marmalade is a winning combination.

Dacquoise, *succès*, and *japonais* are all terms used to describe meringues with nuts. More or less, they all follow the same technique, but they can differ depending on the type of nut that is used. For some reason *dacquoise*, from the city of Dax in southwestern France, is the best known nowadays. *Dacquoise* mixtures are usually softer than *japonais*, closer to a sponge.

⊰ ORGANIZING YOUR TIME ⊱

You will have to make the marmalade the day before you make the cake. You can also make the pastry cream and the hazelnut praline paste a day ahead. Once the cake is assembled it will need 4 hours in the refrigerator before it is ready to serve.

METHOD

DAY 1

MAKING THE MARMALADE

1 Using a vegetable brush, scrub the orange under cold running water. Bring 2000 grams of water (about 2 quarts) to a boil in a medium-sized pot that is tall enough so that the water will cover the orange completely (you may have to place a spider over the orange to keep it submerged). Place the orange in the boiling water and once the water comes back to a boil, boil for 2 full minutes. Using a spider, remove the orange from the pot and rinse under cold water. Drain the water from the pot and scrub and rinse thoroughly, taking care especially to clean the sides where all the waxes and impurities have stuck. Fill the pot with another 2000 grams of water, add 20 grams of sea salt, and bring to a boil.

2 Add the orange to the salted boiling water, turn the heat to low, and boil slowly for 10 minutes. Drain and rinse the orange under cold water.

3 Cut the orange in half and remove and discard the pithy part in the center and seeds. Cut the orange in 1-inch chunks and scale them together. You should have about 175 grams. If the weight is not 175 grams, adjust the weight of the sugar you will use. The weight of the sugar should be 90 percent of the weight of the orange pieces. For example, if you end up with 160 grams of orange, you should use 144 grams of sugar. Place the orange pieces and sugar in a food processor and pulse until you have ⅛-inch pieces; they need to be small enough to be piped through a ¼-inch tip.

4 Transfer the pureed orange from the food processor to a small stainless steel saucepan and bring to a boil over low heat. Boil over low heat for 3 full minutes, stirring all the while with a rubber spatula.

5 Transfer to a small mixing bowl and cover with plastic wrap. Refrigerate overnight.

DAY 2

The next day return the orange puree to the small saucepan, bring to a boil, and boil for 5 more minutes over medium-low heat while stirring. The finished jam should be translucent. Transfer to a jar or small bowl, cover with a lid or plastic wrap, and set aside.

MAKING THE *JAPONAIS* DISKS

1 Preheat the oven to 300°F/150°C. Place the whole hazelnuts in a disposable pastry bag, hold the open end shut, and crush them in half by rolling over the nuts gently with a rolling pin. Spread the halved nuts on a sheet pan lined with parchment paper and bake them for 15 minutes. Let them cool and increase the oven temperature to 350°F/180°C.

2 Sift the confectioners' sugar and all-purpose flour together. Sift the nut flour and add to the confectioners' sugar and all-purpose flour. Set aside in a bowl or on a sheet of parchment paper.

3 Using a pencil and an 8-inch round plate or tart pan insert, draw two 8-inch circles as far apart as you can get them on a sheet pan–sized piece of parchment paper. Flip the paper over so that the pencil marking is underneath; otherwise it will bleed onto the *japonais* mixture when you pipe it onto the parchment paper and bake it.

4 Place the egg whites, cream of tartar, and sea salt in the bowl of your stand mixer fitted with the whisk attachment. Whisk for 10 seconds on medium. Add the sugar and whip on high until the mixture forms a stiff but not dry meringue, about 1½ minutes. Watch carefully, because if the meringue gets too dry it will fall apart when you fold in the other ingredients. Transfer the meringue to a large mixing bowl, add the sifted dry ingredients, and gently fold them in using a large rubber spatula.

butter and in this case also contains fat from the hazelnut praline. You could also fill the cake with a straight butter cream, which is what we used when I learned to make *japonais* during my apprenticeship.

I had to include an orange marmalade in this book because it is so delicious and easy to make. First, the whole fruit is boiled in hot water in order to open the pores of the skin and remove any impurities and waxes on the skin's surface. Then the fruit is boiled in salted water, which might sound very surprising but it actually removes some of the fruit's bitterness. Then the orange is combined with sugar and blended to a mush. This mixture is brought to a first boil and left to rest in a bowl in order to allow the sugar to candy the fruit: it enters the flesh of the fruit through the pores opened up by the boiling process. For this kind of citrus jam I like to use thin-skinned oranges because the bitterness resides in the white pith; the thicker the skin, the more bitter the final product will be. The best is to use organic oranges; regular oranges will work but you will have to scrub the chemicals and waxes off before you begin.

5 Scrape the mixture into a pastry bag fitted with a ½-inch round piping tip. Hold the bag vertically over the sheet pan with the tip 1 inch above the center of one of the two circles. Pipe a tight spiral from the center out to the edge of the drawn circle. Make a second spiral on the other circle with the rest of the mixture. Sprinkle the crushed hazelnuts on one of the spirals only, dust both of them with confectioners' sugar, and let sit for 5 minutes. Dust with confectioners' sugar a second time. Bake at 350°F/180°C for 5 minutes, then lower the oven to 300°F/150°C and bake for another 30 minutes, until the tops of the meringues are golden brown. Let cool completely. Keep at room temperature.

MAKING THE HAZELNUT *MOUSSELINE*

1 Make sure to bring your ingredients to room temperature, especially the 40 grams of butter that you will be adding to the pastry cream after it has cooled. Refer to the instructions for making pastry cream on PAGE 39 and make a pastry cream using the ingredients listed above, which is a half batch. Once made, transfer to a small sheet pan or plate covered with plastic wrap. Place another piece of plastic wrap directly on top and set the pan in the freezer to cool the cream rapidly and stop the growth of bacteria. This should only take 15 minutes.

2 Once the pastry cream has cooled, place it in the bowl of your stand mixer and whip on high speed for 30 seconds. Make sure the butter is soft and add it to the pastry cream. Whip for 2 minutes on high speed. Add the hazelnut praline paste and whip until incorporated (you can also use a handheld electric mixer for this). Transfer the cream to a pastry bag fitted with a ⅜-inch round tip.

ASSEMBLING THE CAKE

1 Gently flip one of the *japonais* disks over, holding the parchment paper on each side. Carefully peel the parchment paper off the meringue and flip the *japonais* back over so the flat side is down. Repeat with the other disk. Place the disk that is not sprinkled with the nuts on a platter, the sugared side facing up. Pipe a hazelnut cream spiral on the disk, beginning in the center and stopping ¼ inch away from the edge.

2 Fill a pastry bag fitted with a ¼-inch round tip with the orange marmalade and pipe a spiral onto the hazelnut cream beginning in the center and stopping ¼ inch from the edge of the *japonais*.

3 Top with the other *japonais* disk, with the nut-covered side up. Press down gently to make sure that the top layer is in contact with the filling. Refrigerate the cake for 4 hours and serve.

IT'S DONE WHEN IT'S DONE

The crushed nuts and the *japonais* should be golden brown. The cream should look glossy.

STORAGE

The cake can be refrigerated for 48 hours or frozen for up to 1 month.

CROISSANTS AND CHOCOLATE CROISSANTS

YIELD | 10 REGULAR OR CHOCOLATE CROISSANTS

2-DAY RECIPE

BASE TEMPERATURE | 54°C

INGREDIENTS	WEIGHT	MEASURE (APPROXIMATE) OR OUNCE WEIGHT
POOLISH		
All-purpose flour	100 grams	¾ cup
Water	100 grams	½ cup less 1 teaspoon
Dry yeast	5 grams	1¾ teaspoon
DOUGH		
Bread flour	200 grams	1¾ cup plus 1 tablespoon
Granulated sugar	38 grams	2½ tablespoons
Butter (French style, 82% fat), softened	15 grams	½ ounce
Water	45 grams	¼ cup less 1 teaspoon
Whole eggs	30 grams	About 1½ eggs or 2½ tablespoons beaten
Sea salt	7 grams	1 teaspoon
Butter (French style, 82% fat), for butter block	150 grams	5³⁄₁₀ ounces
Egg Wash (PAGE 7)	As needed	As needed
Chocolate coins, or bars (for *pains au chocolat* only)	20 bars or 40 coins	20 bars or 40 coins

For my last supper, I would definitely like to have fresh croissants. They combine the pleasures of puff pastry—layers of butter and dough—with that of yeasted bread. The result of this combination is the incredible breakfast pastry that everybody loves: flaky on the outside, moist on the inside. Even though you know you're eating a lot of butter when you eat a croissant, you cannot resist. It is a good kind of evil.

Making croissant dough is a lot like making puff pastry, except the base dough, called *détrempe,* is yeasted, this version contains a little egg (so technically speaking it is Danish dough), and the dough only requires 3 turns before you shape the croissants. Because the dough is yeasted it shrinks back more than puff pastry dough when you are wrapping the butter block and making the turns. You may find it challenging to make croissants the first few times, but if you are patient and follow this recipe carefully you should not have a problem. I became comfortable with making croissants when I had a job at Boulangerie Paul, a big bakery chain in France. My job was making 3,000 croissants a day. It was boring, but

BEFORE YOU BEGIN

→ Get out the following equipment and allow all of the ingredients to come to room temperature:

Digital scale, set to metric weights
1 digital thermometer
KitchenAid or stand mixer fitted with the hook attachment
1 small rubber spatula
1 medium mixing bowl
Plastic wrap
1 medium saucepan
1 rolling pin
1 full-sized silpat
1 ruler
1 chef's knife
2 sheet pans lined with parchment paper
1 pastry brush

→ Read this recipe through twice from start to finish.

NOTE: To scale 150 grams of butter you should cut a block of butter lengthwise into 3 pieces and you will see that each piece will probably read very close to 150 grams, since all blocks of butter are 454 grams.

UNDERSTANDING INGREDIENTS

I use all-purpose flour for the *poolish*, the liquid fermentation that kick-starts the action of the yeast and brings character to the flavor profile of the dough. I use bread flour, which has more gluten, for the rest of the *détrempe*, the base dough. I don't use all bread flour, because that would introduce too much gluten and the dough would be difficult to manipulate when it's being rolled out, turned, and shaped. I also like to add a small amount of egg to the dough for flavor.

The choice of butter is crucial; you need a butter that contains at least 82 percent fat. If butter contains less fat, it contains more water, and your dough will be sticky and difficult to roll. More water also causes the croissants to rise tremendously during the baking process, as it evaporates in the oven, but because there are fewer solids in the butter and therefore in the dough, the croissants will collapse soon after rising.

if you make a few thousand croissants every day your hands will eventually know how the dough should feel and how to shape the croissants and *pains au chocolat*. This recipe will give you a good start, and soon you will be making croissants with ease.

METHOD

DAY 1

1 Make the *poolish* with a base temperature of 54°C. Take the temperature of the flour and the room (convert to Celsius) and add them together. Then adjust your water temperature (Celsius) so that the sum of the three ingredients is 54°C. If you wish, you can now convert the result into Fahrenheit. Place the 100 grams of water in the bowl of your stand mixer and add the yeast. Stir together. Sprinkle the all-purpose flour over the top; let sit in a warm area undisturbed for 15 minutes, until cracks form on the surface of the flour. This signifies that the yeast is active and fermenting.

2 Once the yeast has been activated it is time to mix the dough. Adjust the water temperature to the same temperature as the water you used for the *poolish*. Add the bread flour, sugar, 15 grams of softened butter, 45 grams water, and finally the eggs and sea salt. Mix with the hook for about 1½ minutes on medium speed, until the dough comes together. Stop the mixer and verify with a rubber spatula that there is no residue of unmixed dry ingredients on the bottom of the mixing bowl. If there is, scrape it into the dough and mix on medium speed for another 20 seconds. The dough should come together and feel and look rough, but it should not feel dry; if it does feel dry add 1 to 2 tablespoons of water and gently work it in. At the end of the mixing you should not see traces of dry unmixed ingredients and the dough should not feel lumpy.

3 Place the dough in a medium bowl, dust the surface with a small amount of all-purpose flour, and cover the bowl with plastic wrap or a towel. Let the dough rest at room temperature or in a warm place that is not hotter than 80.6°F/27°C until it doubles in volume. This can take 1 to 1½ hours depending on the temperature of the room. You can create an ideal environment for rising in your oven if it doesn't have a pilot light. Fill a medium saucepan halfway with boiling water and place in the cold oven. Set the dough in the oven along with the pan of steaming water and close the door. The hot water will provide heat and humidity. This system works very well, as it will keep the dough away from drafts. Just make sure that the temperature stays below 80.6°F/27°C or the butter will melt out.

4 Dust the counter with flour, place the dough on it, and shape it into a ball. This should only take a few seconds. Do not knead the dough, otherwise you will activate the gluten and make it difficult to roll out the dough. Flatten the ball into a 1-inch-thick disk. Wrap in plastic and place in the refrigerator for 1 hour.

5 Meanwhile, take your 150 grams of butter out of the refrigerator and let it soften, or tap the top surface for about 10 seconds with a rolling pin so that it is easy to shape. On a piece of plastic wrap, use a marker to draw an 8 × 6–inch rectangle. Place your butter on another piece of plastic wrap or on a silpat, place the marked plastic wrap on top, and, using the rectangle as your guide, roll the butter out to an 8 × 6–inch rectangle. Wrap in the plastic and place in the refrigerator for 45 minutes.

6 Check that your dough and butter are cold. If they are not, return them to the refrigerator for another 20 to 30 minutes. Dust the counter or a large silpat with flour and bring out the dough. Using your rolling pin, roll the dough out to a 16 × 8–inch rectangle. Remove the butter from the refrigerator, place it on the counter, and tap the top surface again with the rolling pin for 10 seconds to soften it slightly. Place the butter on one half of the dough and fold the dough over it so that it is completely trapped.

7 Now you are ready to roll out the dough and make the first "turn." The absolute key to this procedure is to make sure that the dough and the butter are cold yet still pliable and that you work quickly so that the dough and the butter don't become too soft. If the butter becomes too soft it will ooze out from the dough; if it is too hard it will crack and break into small lumps during the rolling process (which is why you should never chill the butter in the freezer). Dust your silpat or rolling area generously with flour, place the dough on it, and dust the surface of the dough as well. Slide the dough back and forth a few times so that it is nicely floured. Start rolling out the dough gently and evenly. It is important not to apply too much pressure to any particular area of the dough, as this will result in uneven layers of dough and butter, causing them to rise and bake unevenly. Roll in long continuous strokes over the entire dough and make sure to roll over the ends. Another crucial thing is to roll the dough for 10 seconds only at a time, then stop and check to make sure that the dough isn't sticking to the silpat or table. If the dough does not slide, stop rolling at once and dust more flour underneath to ensure that it will (this principle is the same for all rolled doughs). Also, if the rolling pin gets sticky, stop rolling and dust it and the top of the dough lightly with flour. If the butter feels soft during the rolling and oozes out of the dough, it has become

too warm. Stop rolling immediately and place the dough-and-butter "book" in the refrigerator for 30 minutes. If the butter breaks apart and looks like a cracked desert floor, it is too cold or was not tapped enough to make it pliable. In this case, stop rolling at once and leave the book on the work surface for 5 minutes, flipping it over every 2 minutes so that it will warm up evenly, then continue rolling out.

8 Once the dough is rolled out to about 20 inches long, turn the rectangle sideways so that the long edge is closest to you, and brush off the surface with a dry pastry brush. Fold the dough like a business letter—fold the right third of the rectangle over the center third and the left third over the center. This is the first of 3 turns. Using your thumb or a finger, make a slight indent on the dough's surface to register the first book fold. Wrap tightly in plastic and refrigerate for 30 minutes.

9 Flour your work surface and place the folded dough on top vertically, with the open ends facing you and the folded edges to your right and left. Repeat the same procedure; your dough should now have 2 turns. Make 2 indents with your finger to mark the 2 turns. Wrap the dough in plastic wrap and refrigerate it overnight (you can also mark the plastic wrap).

DAY 2

1 The next day, dust the rolling surface with flour and place the folded dough on top vertically, with the open ends facing you and the folded edges to your right and left. Roll out the dough following the same procedure as before and fold the dough to give it its last turn. Wrap in plastic and refrigerate for 30 minutes.

2 Flour your work surface and place the folded dough on top vertically, with the open ends facing you and the folded edges to your right and left. Roll out the dough to a long rectangle, 20 × 7 inches. Because there will be some shrinkage, roll it a little longer and wider at first—the rectangle you cut into croissants should be 20 inches long by 7 inches wide. At this point, if you are using a silpat, transfer the dough to a floured work surface, because you will be cutting it with a chef's knife and you don't want to cut the silpat. Turn the dough so that the long edge is closest to you.

SHAPING CROISSANTS

1 Mark one of the long edges of the dough every 3½ inches and, using a large chef's knife, cut 9 triangles, each 3½ inches wide by 7 inches long. There will be a half triangle on each end, and you will make the tenth croissant by pressing together these 2 end pieces (SEE ILLUSTRATION).

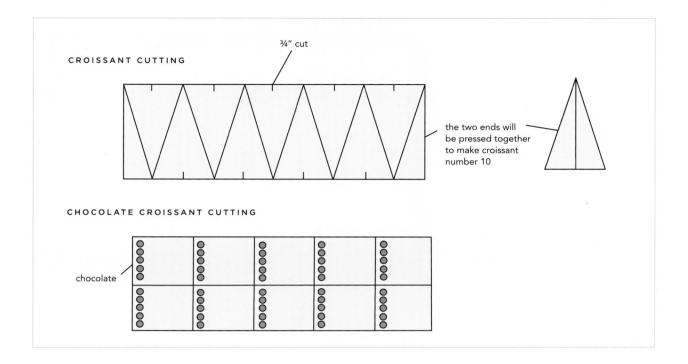

CROISSANT CUTTING

¾" cut

the two ends will be pressed together to make croissant number 10

CHOCOLATE CROISSANT CUTTING

chocolate

2 Place a triangle in front of you, the wide end facing you and the tip pointing away from you. Make a ¾-inch incision in the middle of the wide end. With
your fingers, take up the 2 sides of the incision and fold out toward the sides
of the triangle, to make 2 small dog-ear flaps (SEE ILLUSTRATION AND PHOTO).
Place your fingers on the fold and start rolling forward, forcing the croissant
to curl and roll up (SEE PHOTO). Place on a parchment paper–lined sheet pan.
Repeat with the other triangles, using 2 sheet pans and leaving 1 inch of
space between each croissant. Brush the croissants with egg wash.

SHAPING *PAINS AU CHOCOLAT*

Cut the 20 × 7–inch rectangle in half lengthwise into two 10 × 3½–inch strips.
Cut each strip into five 4 × 3½–inch rectangles. Lay a rectangle in front of you
with the longer edge facing you and place 2 bars or 4 or 5 coins of chocolate
along the left edge (SEE ILLUSTRATION). With your fingers, fold the left edge
of the rectangle over the chocolate. Place your fingers over the fold and
roll up the dough tightly. Place with the seam side down on the parchment
paper–covered sheet pan. Repeat with the other rectangles, making sure to
leave 1 inch between each *pain au chocolat*. Press down on each roll to flatten
slightly and brush with egg wash.

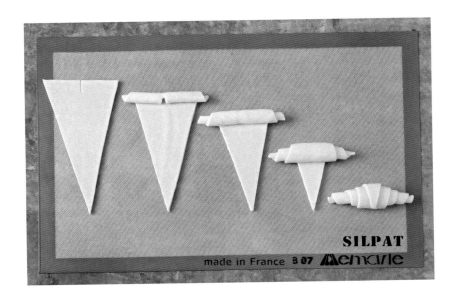

RISING AND BAKING

1 Set the croissants in a warm place to rise, taking care that the temperature does not exceed 80.6°F/27°C. If they get too warm the butter will ooze out of them, and this cannot be fixed. Let them rise for 1 to 1½ hours, until doubled in volume but not in size. To check if they have risen enough, poke one of them with your finger and see how it bounces back; if the dough still seems very tight and bounces back rapidly, the croissant will probably need another 20 to 30 minutes of rising. If after you poke it the dough barely bounces back and you can see a slight mark left by your finger, then the croissant has risen enough.

2 Preheat the oven to 375°F/190°C. Gently brush the croissants with egg wash a second time, being very careful not to deflate them, as they are very fragile at this point. If you poke them by mistake with your brush they might deflate for good. If the bristles of your brush are nice and soft, you will avoid this. Bake them 1 sheet pan at a time for 18 to 20 minutes, until golden brown. Remove from the heat and allow to cool for 30 minutes before serving.

IT'S DONE WHEN IT'S DONE

The baked croissants should be golden brown on the top and bottom. The inside should be moist but not doughy.

STORAGE

I prefer to eat these when they are freshly baked. The raw croissants can be frozen right away once shaped, though I do not recommend freezing them for longer than 1 month. To defrost them, place them on a sheet pan and let them defrost at room temperature for a full hour and a half. Then brush them with egg wash and place them in a warm place until they rise and double in volume.

The baked croissants can be frozen for 1 month as well. To defrost them, place them on a sheet pan and let them fully defrost. This should take about 2 hours. Bake them for 1 minute at 450°F/230°C just to crisp them up again.

JACQUY'S TAKEAWAYS

→ Croissants should not be the huge puffed, doughy pastries that go by the name of croissants in most American coffee shops. Nothing disgusts me more than the oversized and soggy croissants you can find in plastic bags in some supermarkets. These horrible imitations are just a good reminder that croissants are possibly the best breakfast pastry invented by man, but that whenever they are made, quality ingredients must be used and care must be taken with technique. I always tell my students, "You are only as good as your last croissant."

PLUM TART
(SEE PAGE 156 FOR RECIPE)

• CHAPTER 3 •

TARTS

fter years of making pastry at the highest level my answer to the question "What is your favorite dessert" is still a nice warm tart. It goes back to my childhood. We had wonderful fruit in Alsace, and whenever anybody made a dinner for family or friends a fruit tart would be the standard dessert. In the summer we would spend many afternoons picking blueberries in the forest or *mirabelles* from my grandmother's trees, and the fruit would inevitably end up baked inside a flaky pastry shell, needing little more than a bit of sugar to showcase its superb flavor.

I like a good mousse cake just as much as the next person, but I am very interested in textures in desserts, and those I appreciate most are the crusty and crunchy textures you find in many tarts, such as the Apple Nougat Tart (PAGE 149) or the Rhubarb Tart with Hazelnut Crumble (PAGE 179) in this chapter. I also love the fact that you can enjoy tarts warm. We love warm pastries because our taste buds can perceive their flavors and aromas so quickly. Warm tarts are nurturing and comforting. All of their elements, especially the fats, melt in your mouth.

You'll find several types of tart here. My Alsatian Sour Cream and Berry Tart (PAGE 166) is like a soufflé in a pastry shell. The fruit in the Raspberry and Hazelnut Tart (PAGE 169) is baked on top of a hazelnut cream—the juices from the fruit are captured by the nut flour in the cream. Some, like the Plum Tart and the Wild Blueberry Tart (PAGES 156 AND 153), highlight the fruit itself. I don't add much, as it would be unfair to mess with the ripe flavors of the fruit. You'll also find classics like the Chocolate Tart (PAGE 159), topped with beautiful, crunchy nougatine crisp, which is my family's favorite, and the Lemon Cream Tart with Meringue Teardrops (PAGE 163), which showcases the richness of lemon curd and how its tart flavor is best shown off against the sweet meringues that top the pie. And, good Alsatian that I am, I could never leave out the amazing raspberry jam and spiced hazelnut Linzer tart (Tarte de Linz Ma Façon/Linzer Tart My Way, PAGE 173), with its wonderful flavors and textures. You'll appreciate my version, because the new technical twist I've introduced will make this delicious tart easy for everybody to make.

PASTRY DOUGHS

These recipes could have just as appropriately been placed in Chapter 1, Pastry Fundamentals, as they are fundamental pastry recipes that you must master before you can go on to make successful tarts. I advise you to make all three of the doughs several times before going on to the other recipes in this chapter (you can store them in the freezer), so that you develop a strong "hand memory" of how each one should feel and the most efficient way to roll them out and line pastry rings or tart pans. This is one of the most important basic skills in pastry, one that every apprentice must master if he wants to go on to practice the craft.

We Pastry Chefs are Geeks

Pastry is a science; everything that happens can be explained chemically. If you wanted to, you could dissect and chart the ingredients in most recipes and compare their properties. Then if you were more courageous and math inclined, you could do what we professional pastry chefs do and break down the fat, sugar, solids, and water content of each ingredient. We do that when we are comparing recipes for the same type of product, to control the outcome but also to cost out each ingredient and the entire recipe.

For example, you can break down the ingredients in the two sweet dough recipes that follow, *pâte sucrée* and *pâte sablée*, and make a chart where the amounts of butter, sugar, egg, and flour are placed side by side. Then you can compare their differences. You would see that one recipe has more butter than the other and therefore will taste more buttery but will be softer to roll out; it will also become flakier and more delicate when you bake it. Another might contain comparatively more sugar, which will make it brown faster in the oven due to the sugar turning into caramel. This recipe will result in a crust that tastes sweeter and is harder, thus sturdier, after baking.

This is the way pastry chefs operate, as opposed to hot-food chefs, who have to deal with ingredients that are much less stable. Hot-food chefs have to think on their feet. They don't have much time to be creative because the products they work with—fish, meat, produce—are alive and moving quickly in the opposite direction once they are delivered; and sometimes the chefs don't know how long those products have been around before they were delivered. So they're under the gun to come up with something wonderful before their products die. Their job is difficult in that sense, compared to ours.

Pastry chefs don't have any excuses. The only products that we can't control are fruits. We deal with so many things that we can control, like chocolate, nut flours, flour, butter, and sugar. Our basic ingredients have long shelf lives and we understand their properties.

SWEET DOUGH / PÂTE SUCRÉE

INGREDIENTS	WEIGHT	MEASURE (APPROXIMATE) OR OUNCE WEIGHT
Butter (French style, 82% fat)	168 grams	6 ounces
Sea salt	1.4 grams	¼ teaspoon
Confectioners' sugar	112 grams	1 cup
Almond flour, skinless	39 grams	Rounded ⅓ cup
Vanilla extract	7 grams	1½ teaspoons
Whole eggs	63 grams	1 extra-large egg plus 1 to 2 teaspoons
Cake flour, sifted	315 grams	2⅞ cups

BEFORE YOU BEGIN

→ Get out the following equipment and allow all of the ingredients to come to room temperature:

Digital scale, set to metric weights
1 sifter
3 small mixing bowls
KitchenAid or stand mixer fitted with the
    paddle attachment, or a large bowl
    and a rubber spatula
1 rubber spatula
1 dough scraper
Plastic wrap
1 rolling pin
Two 9-inch tart pans or rings
1 fork or dough docker
Pie weights

NOTE: Sift the confectioners' sugar, almond flour, and cake flour into separate bowls.

→ Read this recipe through twice from start to finish.

Sweet dough, or *pâte sucrée,* is a good dough to use for fresh fruit tarts, both baked and unbaked, and for tarts with creamy fillings like lemon curd or chocolate. It's sturdier than the more crumbly *sablée* dough (PAGE 144) because it contains less butter in proportion to flour. Pastry chefs have been working with pie doughs for decades, and there are many formulas for *pâte sucrée.* The version we teach at the French Pastry School calls for confectioners' sugar (as opposed to granulated), butter, cake flour, almond flour, and egg. It's easy to work with and makes a sturdy, flavorful crust that won't become soggy. We use almond flour because it contributes a lot of flavor to the crust; if you can't get hold of it you can substitute the same weight of cake flour, but don't substitute another type of nut flour, which would be too fatty.

It's important to begin this a day or even 2 days ahead. Once mixed, pie dough needs time to rest in the refrigerator—overnight is ideal—so that the gluten developed during mixing can relax and the starch in the flour can absorb liquid. Make sure that your ingredients are at room temperature before you begin to mix, and that the dough is well chilled before you roll it out. Once you roll it out, it will perform best if you give it several hours or overnight to dry out in the refrigerator.

METHOD

DAY 1

1 In a KitchenAid or stand mixer fitted with the paddle attachment, or in a bowl with a rubber spatula, cream the butter and sea salt on medium speed for about 60 seconds. DO NOT WHIP—this would incorporate too much air into the butter. Air bubbles make the final dough puff when you bake it. They also make the dough porous, which would allow moisture from the filling to get through the dough and make your tart soggy. There's nothing worse than a tart or pie with a soggy crust.

2 Scrape down the sides of the bowl and the paddle with a rubber spatula and add the confectioners' sugar. Combine with the butter at low speed. Scrape down the sides of the bowl and the paddle.

3 Add the almond flour and vanilla and combine at low speed.

4 Gradually add the eggs and one-quarter (55 grams or ½ cup) of the cake flour. Beat at low speed until just incorporated. Stop the machine and scrape down the bowl and the paddle.

5 Gradually add the remaining flour and mix just until the dough comes together. It will feel soft to the touch but it won't be sticky. DO NOT OVER-MIX. Over-mixing instantly activates the gluten in the flour, which results in a rubbery dough that shrinks during baking. From time to time stop the machine, scrape the sides and bottom of the bowl, then restart the machine to incorporate the crumbly mixture that separates from the dough and settles at the bottom.

6 Scrape the dough out of the bowl and press it into a ½-inch-thick rectangular block. Wrap airtight in plastic wrap and refrigerate overnight or for at least 2 to 3 hours (this is called "letting the dough rest"). After the dough is chilled it will be firm but it should still be pliable.

DAY 2

1 For a 9-inch crust, remove the dough from the refrigerator, weigh it (you should have approximately 700 grams of dough), and cut it into 2 equal portions. Return 1 portion to the refrigerator. Following the instructions on PAGE 144, roll the dough into a ¼-inch-thick circle and line a 9-inch tart pan or ring. Using a fork, perforate the bottom of the shell, making rows of little holes up and down the bottom of the dough with the tines of your fork. This step, called "docking," is important, as it will allow steam to escape evenly during baking. Professional bakers use a tool called a dough docker but a fork will do just fine if there is no docker in the room. Refrigerate uncovered for at least 1 hour, or overnight if possible.

UNDERSTANDING INGREDIENTS

Powdered sugar melts fast and combines quickly with the other ingredients. This will allow you to whip the mixture less, thus avoiding the development of air bubbles and gluten.

All wheat flours naturally contain a protein called gluten. Gluten creates elasticity in dough, which is the last thing you want in a pie crust because elasticity will cause it to shrink during baking. Think of the flour as a bunch of powdered rubber bands whose consistency can change from powder to rubber if the powder is activated. Two things will activate the powder and turn it to rubber: moisture and heat. All doughs require some moisture, in the form of wet ingredients. The friction of mixing creates the heat. The more you mix the dough, the more rubber bands you create and the stronger they get. This is what you want when you make bread dough, as the activated gluten makes it possible for the dough to be shaped and the final product to hold its shape. But you don't want to activate the gluten too much when you make other types of pastry, so it is important to keep the mixing slow and at a minimum. Cake flour has the least amount of gluten of all the wheat flours, which is why we use it here.

The butter is at room temperature so that it will mix together fully with the other ingredients. If you use cold butter it might not incorporate evenly or completely, and the resulting dough will have patches of butter in it. This will create problems when you roll out and bake the crust.

Almond flour adds flavor to the dough. It absorbs moisture better than other nut flours because it is not as fatty.

Egg is necessary in a sweet dough designed for a tart shell. It binds the ingredients and allows the dough to be rolled and to hold its shape.

2 To pre-bake the dough (bakers call this "blind-baking"), preheat the oven to 325°F/160°C with the rack positioned in the middle of the oven (if you pre-bake the pastry on the lower setting the bottom will bake faster than the top). I recommend that you use pie weights to blind-bake your tart shell if you are not a seasoned tart shell lining pro. When I do this, I make a purse out of a piece of cheesecloth and dry rice. It's a cheap way to do the job and it works very well. When the pie is blind-baked then you just need to lift the purse out of the pie. Otherwise, I recommend that you use parchment paper. You can make it into a pouch for the rice to facilitate lifting out of the crust. Fill the lining all the way to the edges of the tart with rice or beans. Bake with this "faux filling" for 15 minutes, then remove the faux filling and return the tart shell to the oven. Bake until golden brown and evenly colored, another 5 minutes in a convection oven, 15 minutes in a regular oven. Remove from the oven and allow to cool completely before filling.

NOTE: At the French Pastry School we don't use pie weights. Our sweet and *sablée* doughs are so well formulated that they don't collapse in our convection ovens. They have just the right proportions of butter and flour, which means that there is no excess fat to melt out and cause the dough to slide down the sides of the ring. But I advise you to use pie weights at first. Always make sure that there is no space between the dough and the bottom of the ring where the bottom and sides meet (see illustration on PAGE 142), and remember to dock the dough thoroughly.

ROLLING OUT DOUGH AND LINING RINGS OR TART PANS

When students at the French Pastry School begin learning about crusts, initially they have a hard time rolling out dough. This is mostly because they think that rolling out pie dough is about strength, when it actually requires smooth, even gentle action.

PREPARING THE DOUGH

- If you are going to roll out your dough on a cutting board, place the cutting board in the refrigerator for about 30 minutes. Do not use a cutting board if it is at all warped.
- Butter your pans or rings *very lightly* and evenly with softened butter. DO NOT USE OIL OR PAN SPRAY. Use just enough butter to prevent

the dough from sticking to the ring; if you use too much, the dough will slide down the ring when you bake it. If you can see the butter, you have used too much. If using a ring (as opposed to a tart pan with a removable bottom), place it on a sheet pan lined with parchment paper or a silpat. Set it aside while you roll out the dough.

· Pull out only enough dough needed for 1 tart shell.

· Place a piece of parchment paper or a silpat on the refrigerated cutting board or on your work surface if using a countertop or table, and dust it evenly but lightly with flour. It's easier to deal with the dough if it sticks to parchment paper or a silpat than if it sticks to your countertop. Once you gain more experience you'll be able to roll dough directly on the countertop.

· If you are using bars to ensure an even thickness, place 1 bar on each side of the cutting board or work surface, a rolling pin's width apart.

· Tap on the dough lightly with the rolling pin to make it pliable.

· Begin rolling gently, to stretch out the dough. The key to rolling dough evenly and successfully is to roll gently, 3 times in one direction, from the edge nearest to you to the far edge, then check to see if the dough has stuck to the parchment paper or silpat. You must always be able to slide the dough on the rolling surface during the rolling process. If it is sticking, run an offset spatula underneath to loosen it, then gently lift it off and lightly dust underneath with flour. Rotate the dough a quarter turn clockwise, make sure that there is still enough flour underneath that it doesn't stick, and roll 3 more times. Never apply too much pressure to the dough; this will make it stick to the board or to the rolling pin. Continue to rotate the dough, check the flour, and roll 3 times, until it has reached the desired thickness, about ¼ inch (a little more than ½ centimeter). Each time you turn the dough imagine that you are a human pasta roller rolling the dough at a thinner setting, evenly and all over. Roll briskly so that the dough doesn't have time to warm up and become sticky.

⊱ LINING THE RING OR TART PAN ⊰

· After you have rolled out the dough, cut a circle that is 1½ inches larger in diameter than your tart pan or ring. An easy way to do this is to use a larger pan or ring as a guide; set it on top of the dough and cut your round of dough. Refrigerate the excess dough.

· Very lightly dust the dough—not too much, or it won't stick to your

→ First get out all the equipment required for rolling out the dough and lining the pan:

1 silpat or parchment paper: I recommend that you acquire a large silpat for rolling out dough, as it makes it very easy to prevent the dough from sticking

Tart pans or rings: Use rings or pans made of steel or galvanized metal, as they are the best heat conductors; glass and ceramic do not conduct heat very well

If you are using a ring, you'll need a sheet pan lined with a silpat or parchment paper that the ring or pan can sit on top of

A ring, plate, or pan that has a diameter that is 1½ inches larger than your tart pan or ring

Flour, for dusting

Rolling pin

At the school we also use plastic or aluminum bars (available in hardware stores) that are the desired thickness of the dough; we set them on either side of our boards, and as the dough flattens out the rolling pin eventually rests on the bars and the dough will be rolled out to an even thickness

→ Read this recipe through twice from start to finish.

→ Adding the flour in 2 steps will ensure that you will not have lumps of it in the dough.

→ Letting dough "rest" does not mean that it is tired and needs a nap. What it means is that some of the gluten was activated during the mixing, so the dough needs to rest to allow the gluten to relax and get weaker. The resting will also allow the starch in the flour to act like a dry sponge. It has the power to absorb and retain moisture so that dough can come together and hold its shape. But it needs time. Let any dough made with flour rest for even an hour after mixing and, even if it's a sticky whole wheat dough, you will see that it comes together.

→ A low oven temperature allows the crust to bake long enough to chase out all of the moisture without browning the crust. A perfectly baked crust will be golden and evenly colored.

→ If you want to make a nut-free sweet dough, replace the almond flour with cake flour.

pan. Use a pastry brush to remove excess flour. Wrap the dough loosely around your rolling pin to lift it from your work surface, then immediately unroll it onto your tart pan or ring. Be careful to position the dough evenly over your ring or pan so that there's an equal amount on all sides. Gently guide the dough down the sides of the ring, working quickly, until it hits the bottom of the sheet pan (if using a ring) or the bottom of the tart pan. Make sure that the dough leaves no gap between the bottom edge of the ring and the sheet pan or tart pan bottom (SEE ILLUSTRATION).

· This is key: if the dough does not extend all the way down the sides of the ring to the surface of the sheet pan or tart pan and leaves a gap at the corners, it will slide down the ring during baking and will not be a uniform height all around. If you do the job right you will see a line where the sheet pan or tart pan bottom meets the ring. But it's also important not to press the dough into that seam, because you'll make it thinner than the rest of the dough if you press; ease it in and put just enough pressure on it to be sure that it has left no gap.

· Using a paring knife, trim away the excess dough that is overhanging the edges. Refrigerate the tart shell (do not cover) for at least 1 hour and preferably overnight before pre-baking.

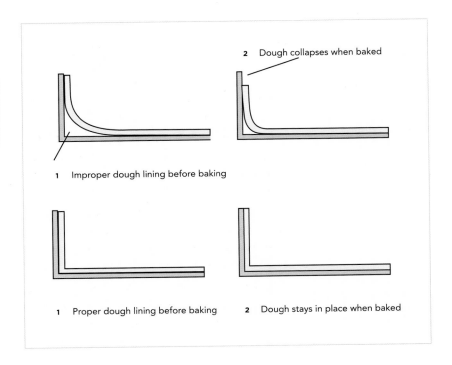

2 Dough collapses when baked

1 Improper dough lining before baking

1 Proper dough lining before baking

2 Dough stays in place when baked

THE FIRST DAY OF MY *certificat d'aptitude professionelle*, the rigorous final exam that all apprentices must take in order to work in their field, was a sunny day in July 1978, at the end of my grueling two-year apprenticeship with Jean Clauss. I had been practicing my pastry skills every night after work for weeks in preparation for the exam. The knowledge that I would have to repeat another year with Jean Clauss if I failed my CAP was motivation enough for me to make sure that I had mastered every skill the judges might ask to see. We didn't know ahead of time which tasks we would be asked to perform.

The two-day exam took place at a cooking school in Illkirch-Graffenstaden, a suburb of Strasbourg. Each candidate had his own station. As soon as I arrived I got to work setting up my table. A judge smiled at me and said, "You're one of Jean Clauss's apprentices." I asked him how he knew, and he just smiled again and walked away. Then another judge came by and asked, "Are you an apprentice of Jean Clauss?"

"Yes, how did you know?"

"Because you have a black eye."

The night before, Jean Clauss, in one of his typical alcoholic rages, had hit me. It had come from out of nowhere, while I was practicing lining tart shells. The other apprentice I worked with had angered him and had been sent away, leaving me alone with the unpredictable master. Did Jean Clauss routinely send his apprentices to their exams with black eyes as well as impeccable skills?

The judges asked me to do a number of pastry items, including pie dough. They told me to mix up the dough and let it rest overnight. The next day they asked me to bring the dough and the ring and line the tart shell in front of them. There were four or five judges standing there with clipboards, and I was terrified. But I managed to focus and do my thing: I rolled out the dough and lined the ring, making sure that I left no space at the bottom of the ring and that the dough was an even thickness all the way around. I was then going to put the lined ring on a sheet pan to make a tart. But before I could put it on the sheet pan the judges ripped the ring from my hands and rolled it, like a wheel, down the length of the 8-foot table. If the ring had not been properly lined, the dough would have collapsed inward. Nobody had warned me about this test; but my dough held. I passed my CAP with one of the highest grades in Alsace.

PÂTE SABLÉE

INGREDIENTS	WEIGHT	MEASURE (APPROXIMATE) OR OUNCE WEIGHT
Butter (French style, 82% fat)	175 grams	6 ounces
Sea salt	3 grams	Scant ½ teaspoon
All-purpose flour	290 grams	2 cups plus 3 tablespoons
Almond flour, skinless	35 grams	Rounded ⅓ cup
Confectioners' sugar	110 grams	1 cup
Vanilla extract	3 grams	½ teaspoon
Egg yolks	80 grams	4 to 5 yolks

BEFORE YOU BEGIN

→ Get out the following equipment and allow all of the ingredients to come to room temperature:

Digital scale, set to metric weights
1 sifter
3 small mixing bowls
KitchenAid or stand mixer fitted with the paddle attachment
1 bowl scraper
Plastic wrap

NOTE: The butter should be soft. Sift the flour, the almond flour, and the confectioners' sugar into separate bowls.

→ Read this recipe through twice from start to finish.

Sablée is a different type of dough that is richer in butter and egg yolks than *pâte sucrée* (Sweet Dough, PAGE 138), thus more crumbly (*sable* means sand). This recipe contains almond flour, which gives the dough a rich nutty flavor. Because *pâte sucrée* makes a sturdier crust, you would choose to use it if you wanted to make, say, a strawberry tart that would keep for 2 days. It would stay firm despite the juice from the strawberries. But if you want a flakier, richer-tasting crust and you plan on eating the tart on the same day, *sablée* would be the dough to make.

METHOD

DAY 1

1 Place the butter, sea salt, and sifted all-purpose flour in the bowl of your mixer. Mix on low speed with the paddle until the mixture is crumbly. Do not mix longer or you will allow the gluten in the flour to develop, which will result in rubbery dough. Add the almond flour and the sifted confectioners' sugar and mix on low speed until the ingredients are just mixed together. Add the vanilla and egg yolk and mix on medium just until all the ingredients come together.

2 Scrape the dough out of the bowl and press it into a ½-inch-thick rectangular block. Wrap airtight in plastic wrap and refrigerate overnight.

DAY 2

1 Roll out and line tart pans following the directions following Sweet Dough on PAGE 138. For best results refrigerate overnight before pre-baking.

2 To pre-bake, preheat the oven to 325°F/160°C. The low oven temperature will allow all of the water to evaporate, resulting in a very flaky crust. Use pie weights for the first 15 minutes of baking (see Note, PAGE 140). Bake with the pie weights for 15 minutes, then remove them and continue to bake for 5 to 15 minutes, until the dough is dry and light golden brown on the edges and an even light brown in the center. Remove from the heat and cool on a rack.

IT'S DONE WHEN IT'S DONE

Whether using this for a tart shell or a cookie, the finished product should be golden brown on the edges and an even light brown color in the center. This means that you have baked it long enough. If either a cookie or tart shell is completely white in the center it means that it is not baked enough and it will not be flaky.

STORAGE

The unbaked dough can be double wrapped airtight in plastic and stored in the refrigerator for 3 days or in the freezer for up to 1 month. Once baked, crusts and cookies can be kept in airtight containers in a dry place or in the freezer, but never in the refrigerator, or they will get soggy.

SABLÉE COOKIES

To make cookies with this dough, roll it out to ⅛ to ¼ inch thick and cut out with cookie cutters. Bake them at 325°F/160°C for 10 to 15 minutes, until golden brown on the edges. If you want to make *sablée* dough free of nuts, replace the almond flour with all-purpose flour.

VARIATION

HAZELNUT SABLÉE: Substitute hazelnut flour for the almond flour.

Since *sablée* dough is more delicate than sweet dough, I use all-purpose flour in it. All-purpose flour contains slightly more gluten than cake flour, and will hold the dough together and prevent it from crumbling apart. The almond flour contributes a rich nutty flavor to the dough. Egg yolk also helps bind the dough and contributes great flavor, texture, and color to the final product. The lecithin in the yolk is what makes it a great binder. I use confectioners' sugar in this recipe because it melts and mixes much faster with the other ingredients than regular sugar.

The butter contributes rich flavor and is the main reason why the dough is so flaky.

There is twice as much salt in this dough as in the *pâte sucrée*. The salt contributes to the delicate texture.

Methods for Making Pie Dough: Creaming vs. Sanding

There are two main ways to mix sweet doughs, the creaming method and the sanding method. The creaming method is done by mixing the butter with the sugar first, then adding eggs or egg yolks, and finally the flour. When we cream the butter and sugar we introduce some air bubbles into the dough and the water in the butter and eggs activates the gluten in the flour. The result is a sweet dough that is somewhat flaky because of the air bubbles introduced when mixing, but stable at the same time. We use the creaming method with the Sweet Dough on PAGE 138.

The second method is called sanding; it's the method we use for *sablée* dough. We first mix the butter with the flour, allowing the fat in the butter to wrap itself around the gluten in the flour. This prevents the gluten from developing, which would cause the dough to be rubbery. This method is typically used for short doughs. The higher fat content in *sablée* dough also makes the dough flaky and slightly more fragile compared to a sweet dough mixed using the creaming method.

The method you choose depends on the type of dough you wish to achieve, and that depends on what you intend to use it for. You can use a creaming technique with a *sablée* recipe and vice versa. For example, if the *sablée* recipe you want to use calls for a sanding technique but you want a more stable dough—say you want to keep the tart you are making for a few days—you can always change the mixing method to a creaming method. Or you can use the sanding method for a sweet dough if you want your dough to be more flaky and fragile.

Even when using the creaming method, avoid incorporating too much air into the dough or you will end up with a very airy and porous dough that will get soggy as soon as it is in contact with the humidity of a cream or the refrigerator. Air bubbles also like to puff open during the baking process, which will make the baked dough separate very slightly, so it won't be as stable and resistant to becoming soggy.

PÂTE BRISÉE / SAVORY PIE DOUGH

YIELD | ENOUGH FOR TWO 9-INCH TART RINGS OR PANS, 684 TO 700 GRAMS

2- OR 3-DAY RECIPE

INGREDIENTS	WEIGHT	MEASURE (APPROXIMATE) OR OUNCE WEIGHT
Sea salt	7 grams	1 teaspoon
Water	92 grams	6 tablespoons
Butter (French style, 82% fat)	222 grams	8 ounces
All-purpose flour	370 grams	3 cups minus 2 tablespoons

This is a wonderful flaky pie dough that can be used for sweet or savory applications. In French it is also known as *pâte à foncer*, which means "dough used to line tart shells." It is one of the very first recipes that I made during my apprenticeship. I learned it from my master pastry chef Jean Clauss, who himself learned it during his apprenticeship. Good recipes stand up from one generation to the next not only because they taste great and receive positive feedback from customers over the years, but also because they are well proportioned and offer consistent results. This is how recipes become classics, and classics are the essence of French pastry.

METHOD

DAY 1

In a small bowl or measuring cup mix the sea salt with the water using a rubber spatula until the salt has dissolved. Place the soft butter and the flour in the bowl of your mixer. Mix with the paddle at the slowest speed until the mixture is well combined; do not over-mix or you will activate the gluten in the flour. Add the water and mix only until the dough comes together; again, do not over-mix. Scrape the mixture out onto a sheet of plastic wrap and flatten it into a square so that it will not take up too much room in the refrigerator. Cover tightly and refrigerate overnight.

DAY 2

Follow the directions in the Sweet Dough recipe (PAGE 138) for rolling out, lining the tart pans or rings, and pre-baking. For savory tarts that require a thoroughly pre-baked pâte brisée you will be instructed to pre-bake the dough for a longer time.

BEFORE YOU BEGIN

→ Get out the following equipment and allow all of the ingredients to come to room temperature:

Digital scale, set to metric weights
1 sifter, if necessary
1 small bowl or measuring cup
1 rubber spatula
KitchenAid or stand mixer fitted with the paddle attachment
1 bowl scraper
Plastic wrap

→ The butter should be soft. Sift the flour if lumpy.

→ Read this recipe through twice from start to finish.

UNDERSTANDING INGREDIENTS

This recipe uses the sanding method of mixing the butter with the flour. The fat in the butter wraps itself around the gluten in the flour and this slows down its action. Otherwise the dough will be rubbery and shrink in the oven. We use all-purpose flour here because it has just the right amount of gluten. Cake flour does not contain enough gluten and would result in a crust that falls apart in the oven. Bread flour contains too much gluten and would result in a dough that is more akin to a rubber band than a pie crust.

IT'S DONE WHEN IT'S DONE

The unbaked dough will be completely homogenized and will feel slightly tacky. When pre-baked, it should be golden brown on the edges and light golden brown and evenly colored in the center.

STORAGE

This dough can be stored in the refrigerator for 3 days, and frozen for up to 1 month. The fact that it is shaped in a flat square instead of in a ball will allow it to defrost fairly quickly. Remove from the freezer and let sit on the countertop for 1 hour, or transfer from the freezer to the refrigerator and let sit overnight.

JACQUY'S TAKEAWAYS

→ I recommend that you make this dough by hand a few times so that your hands develop a memory of how the dough should feel. Mix the butter and flour in a mixing bowl with your fingers, then add the water and salt.

→ I always like to have enough *pâte brisée* for a fruit tart on hand in my freezer. You never know when you will find perfect fruit at your farmers market and will be inspired to make a delicious seasonal tart.

APPLE NOUGAT TART

YIELD | ONE 9-INCH TART

2-DAY RECIPE

INGREDIENTS	WEIGHT	MEASURE (APPROXIMATE) OR OUNCE WEIGHT
Sweet Dough (PAGE 138) or Pâte Brisée (PAGE 147)	One 9-inch crust (½ recipe, about 350 grams)	One 9-inch crust (½ recipe, about 12³⁄₁₀ ounces)
Braeburn apples, peeled and cored	370 grams (peeled and cored weight)	3 apples
Lemon juice, freshly squeezed	6 grams	1¼ teaspoons
Butter (French style, 82% fat)	27 grams	2 tablespoons
Turbinado sugar	40 grams	¼ cup less 1 teaspoon
Vanilla extract	8 grams	1¾ teaspoons
NOUGAT TOPPING		
Egg whites	56 grams	¼ cup (about 1½ whites)
Granulated sugar	56 grams	¼ cup plus ½ teaspoon
Sliced almonds	56 grams	Scant ½ cup
Ceylon cinnamon	Pinch	Pinch

This is much like the apple tart that I learned to make during my apprenticeship. It's filled with lightly caramelized apples topped with a simple nougat mixture of egg whites, sugar, and thinly sliced almonds. We pastry chefs like to have at least three different textures in a pastry. This one has the crust, the apples, and the crisp nougat topping; all these textures make it very exciting to eat.

We like to cook the apples before we fill the tart. That's how we control for variation in cooking times and textures. Apples vary from variety to variety and from season to season; some are crisper than others, some are juicier, some better for eating than for cooking. Some fall apart, some are fibrous, some floury. Depending on the variety and the season, they will react differently to heat. If it's winter in Chicago and you are making this apple tart, you can be sure that the apples you buy in the supermarket have been in cold storage for several months and will take longer to soften than the apples you can buy if you live in California. Another reason why we cook the apples first is that by doing so the apples lose some of their moisture in the pan rather than in the crust, which would make the crust soggy. By sautéing them in butter with some sugar until they have softened you've established a degree of control—another thing we pastry chefs love.

BEFORE YOU BEGIN

→ Get out the following equipment and allow all of the ingredients to come to room temperature:

Equipment for the dough of your choice
Digital scale, set to metric weights
2 medium mixing bowls
1 sheet pan lined with parchment paper or a silpat
1 large skillet
1 high-heat rubber spatula
1 fork

→ Read this recipe through twice from start to finish.

UNDERSTANDING INGREDIENTS

Over the years I've found that Braeburn apples can take a lot of abuse and will retain moisture the best without falling apart. Pink Ladies also have some of these qualities, but Braeburns stand up to cooking best of all. The fresh taste of an apple does not always transfer when it is cooked, but a plain apple such as a Braeburn carries other flavors really well.

Turbinado sugar (also known as "sugar in the raw") is the perfect medium between brown sugar and granulated sugar. It has the property of granulated sugar but enough molasses flavor to make it interesting. Molasses has such a strong flavor and aroma that it can overwhelm the other flavors in a dessert, but the balance is just right in turbinado sugar.

JACQUY'S TAKEAWAYS

→ Do not sauté the apples too long or they will be dry; you want them to still be juicy in the center. If you want juicier apples you can always cut them in larger pieces or sauté them for a shorter time.

→ The nougat topping can be replaced with Streusel (PAGE 9). You will need about 120 grams (1 cup).

→ Serving this apple tart warm and topped with a scoop of vanilla ice cream takes it to the level of pastry heaven.

METHOD

DAY 1

Mix up the dough. Refrigerate overnight, then roll out and line your tart pan or ring. Let rest in the refrigerator for several hours or preferably overnight.

DAY 2

1   Pre-bake your tart shell according to the directions on PAGE 138 and let cool.

2   Preheat the oven to 350°F/180°C. Cut the apples in ½-inch dice and toss with the lemon juice in a medium bowl. Line a sheet pan with parchment paper or a silpat.

3   Heat a large skillet over high heat and add the butter. Wait until it becomes light brown and add the diced apples, turbinado sugar, and vanilla. Sauté until golden brown, about 5 to 7 minutes. *You will succeed in this only if you let the pan get hot enough to sear the apples, so that they can hold their juice.* Allow the apples to brown on one side before you flip them. Scrape them out onto the lined sheet pan and allow to cool completely. The apples should be brown and soft on the outside but still slightly firm in the center.

4   Spread the cooled apples evenly over the pre-baked tart shell.

5   Make the nougat/almond topping. Beat the egg whites lightly in a bowl with a fork, just until loosened up. Stir in the sugar, almonds, and cinnamon. Spread the topping evenly over the apples.

6   Place the tart in the preheated oven and bake 25 to 30 minutes or until the crust and topping are golden brown. Remove from the oven and cool on a rack.

IT'S DONE WHEN IT'S DONE

The tart shell should be a medium dark brown color and the nougat topping should be golden brown and glossy.

STORAGE

This tart has a shelf life of 2 days at room temperature and can be refrigerated for 1 day but after that will get soggy. I prefer to eat it the day it's baked. It can also be double-wrapped and frozen. My thawing instructions are often the same: I like to let the product thaw out at room temperature and then I flash it at 400°F/200°C for 1 minute to regain the crisp texture.

WILD BLUEBERRY TART

INGREDIENTS	WEIGHT	MEASURE (APPROXIMATE) OR OUNCE WEIGHT
Sweet Dough (PAGE 138), Pâte Sablée (PAGE 144), or Pâte Brisée (PAGE 147)	One 9-inch crust (½ recipe, about 350 grams)	One 9-inch crust (½ recipe, about 12³⁄₁₀ ounces)
1 egg, beaten with 1 tablespoon water, for egg wash	65 grams	2³⁄₁₀ ounces
Frozen wild blueberries	280 grams	10 ounces or 2¼ cups
Granulated sugar	51.5 grams	¼ cup
Lemon juice, freshly squeezed	6 grams	1¼ teaspoons
Water	6 grams	1¼ teaspoons
Cornstarch	2.5 grams	1 teaspoon
Vanilla bean	½ bean	½ bean
Egg yolks	36 grams	2 yolks plus 1 teaspoon
Whole milk (3.5% fat)	56 grams	¼ cup
Heavy cream (35% fat)	56 grams	¼ cup
Streusel (PAGE 9), fully baked	17 grams	2 tablespoons plus 1 teaspoon

Every summer my mother would take me to see my crazy uncle Antoine in Turckheim, a village in the beautiful Colmar region of Alsace. My mother, Oncle Antoine, my godmother, Thérèse, and I would spend hours each day gathering blueberries in the hills above the village. Oncle Antoine carried special metal combs set in wooden frames that he used to comb the blueberries from the bushes. The blueberries would lodge between the wires of the combs and the leaves would stay behind.

We would set out in the late morning, each of us carrying two large buckets. We'd pick berries for a while, then sit down in the grass and stop for a lunch of sandwiches and cold beer. After lunch we'd continue with our gathering. Going down from the hills at the end of the day was always a challenge because our buckets would be filled with anywhere from 5 to 8 kilos—10 to 15 pounds—of berries.

Antoine used most of his berries for schnapps, which really didn't taste much like blueberries at all. But my mom and I brought our blueberries home to make delicious tarts. This tart is a simple mixture of wild blue-

BEFORE YOU BEGIN

→ Get out the following equipment and allow all of the ingredients to come to room temperature:

Equipment for the dough of your choice
Digital scale, set to metric weights
1 pastry brush
1 medium saucepan
1 high-heat rubber spatula
1 medium mixing bowl
1 paring knife
1 stainless steel hand whisk
1 sheet pan

→ Read this recipe through twice from start to finish.

Wild blueberries are much closer to the blueberries we use in France and should always be used for blueberry tarts. They are blue and juicy in the center, whereas farmed blueberries are white inside and not as juicy.

We make a slurry with cornstarch because we don't know how much juice will emerge from the fruit as the tart bakes. Juice always raises a red flag for pastry chefs because it can make the tart crust soggy. The amount will vary with the season and the fruit. Since we are all about control, we use the slurry because it binds the juice and prevents it from ruining our tart or pie. Otherwise, the tart won't set properly and the juice may ooze through the dough or bubble upward as the tart bakes.

The egg wash is brushed on the tart shell and will prevent it from becoming soggy (nothing yuckier than a soggy tart shell!) and extend the shelf life by 1 day. The proteins in the egg congeal when exposed to the heat of the oven and create a barrier that protects the shell from the liquids in the filling. The streusel absorbs liquid as well, adding additional protection.

berries, which are blue through and through, unlike cultivated blueberries, and custard, baked until just set.

METHOD

DAY 1

Mix up the dough. Refrigerate overnight, then roll out and line your tart pan or ring. Let rest in the refrigerator for several hours or preferably overnight.

DAY 2

1   Pre-bake your tart shell following the directions on PAGE 138 and allow to cool.

2   Preheat the oven to 325°F/160°C with the rack positioned in the middle. Brush the fully baked tart shell with egg wash and bake for 5 minutes. The surface should be shiny. Allow to cool.

3   In a medium saucepan, combine the blueberries and 1 teaspoon of the sugar and bring to a boil. Turn the heat to medium low and boil for 2 minutes.

4   Meanwhile, whisk together the lemon juice, water, and cornstarch in a medium bowl. Gradually stir the mixture into the berries and simmer 1 minute, until thickened. If the blueberries are very juicy and the juice remains watery, dissolve another ½ teaspoon cornstarch in a tablespoon of the juice and stir in. Continue to simmer until thickened. Remove from the heat.

5   Using a paring knife, split the vanilla bean lengthwise in two and scrape the seeds out into a medium bowl. Add the egg yolk and remaining sugar and beat together with a whisk. Add the milk and cream and beat together until the sugar is dissolved. Stir in the blueberries.

6   Sprinkle the streusel in an even layer over the bottom of the tart shell. Spread the blueberries on top. Place on a sheet pan. Bake 30 to 40 minutes, until just set. Remove from the oven and place on a wire rack to cool completely.

7   Sprinkle with granulated sugar or dust with confectioners' sugar before serving.

IT'S DONE WHEN IT'S DONE

The filling will be set around the edges but just set in the middle. If you shake the pan gently the middle will jiggle a little bit under the surface until it cools, when it will firm up.

STORAGE

The baked tart will keep for 2 days outside the refrigerator and 3 days in the refrigerator. It is best eaten at room temperature. It can also be double-wrapped and frozen. Thaw overnight in the refrigerator, or at room temperature in a few hours. Once thawed, reheat briefly for 1 minute in a 400°F/200°C oven to re-crisp the crust and evaporate any liquid on the surface.

JACQUY'S TAKEAWAYS

→ It is important to pre-bake the streusel. Using raw streusel will not work because the steam from the blueberries will prevent it from baking and crisping.

→ You could also top the blueberry tart with additional pre-baked streusel before baking it. This would add another texture to the tart.

→ **$50 TRICK:** Place the scraped split vanilla bean in an open container in a dry place. Once dry, place it in a jar of granulated sugar to create vanilla-scented sugar, or grind in a spice mill or food processor and use as vanilla powder.

How Long Can I Keep Baked Goods in the Freezer?

My students always ask me how long we can freeze a product, and my answer is 50 million years. They look at me with puzzled expressions. Then I explain that in Antarctica they find frozen mammoths that are at least that old. A product that is placed in the freezer will stay frozen as long as the freezer is functioning. The true question is how long I can keep my blueberry tart frozen before it picks up the smell of the freezer or the smells of other items in my freezer such as fish, meat, seafood, and so on. And that answer depends on what you have sitting next to your tart in the freezer. As a general rule and in a perfect world, I do not keep things frozen for more than 1 month.

PLUM TART / TARTE AUX QUETSCHES

(See page 134 for photo)

INGREDIENTS	WEIGHT	MEASURE (APPROXIMATE) OR OUNCE WEIGHT
Pâte Brisée (PAGE 147)	One 9-inch crust (½ recipe, about 350 grams)	One 9-inch crust (½ recipe, about 12³⁄₁₀ ounces)
Ripe Italian or red plums	800 to 900 grams	1¾ to 2 pounds
Streusel, made with hazelnuts (PAGE 9), fully baked	120 grams	1 cup
Granulated sugar	50 grams	¼ cup
Ground cinnamon	1 gram	½ teaspoon

Quetsches are dark purple plums that are grown mainly in the northeast of France. They are about 1½ inches long and oblong in shape. The closest plums you will find in the United States are sugar plums, French plums, d'Agen plums, or Italian plums, which you can find from August to October. Their nice acidic flesh contrasts well with sweet flavors. In Alsace *quetsches* are the king of plums, along with small yellow plums called *mirabelles*. We make many different types of pastries and desserts out of them, from clafoutis and jam to sorbets, tarts, and even eau de vie. When they were in season my dad would announce it to our customers, and that would be the tart they would buy at the bakery. We would make twenty large tarts at a time, and they would fly off the shelves.

METHOD

DAY 1

Mix up the dough. Refrigerate overnight, then roll out and line your tart pan or ring. Let rest in the refrigerator for several hours or preferably overnight.

DAY 2

1 Preheat the oven to 325°F/160°C. Following the directions on PAGE 140, line the dough with pie weights and pre-bake for 20 minutes. Remove the pie weights. Return to the oven if necessary and bake another 5 to 10 minutes. The bottom should be lightly browned.

2 Turn up the oven to 375°F/190°C.

3 Wash the plums and dry them with a paper towel. Leave them to air dry for 30 minutes.

4 Sprinkle the baked streusel on the bottom of the par-baked tart shell.

5 Cut the Italian plums in half lengthwise and remove the pits. Then, using a paring knife, make a lengthwise incision about ¾ inch long in the middle of the end of each half (SEE ILLUSTRATION). Beginning at the rim, arrange the plum halves in the pastry shell all the way around and then making your way toward the center, skin side down but standing up slightly with the incised end sticking up. It is very important to pack the tart very tightly with as many plums as possible. They should be squeezed together with the incised tips upright. If you fail to do that there will be empty spots in between the plums after they soften up when they bake.

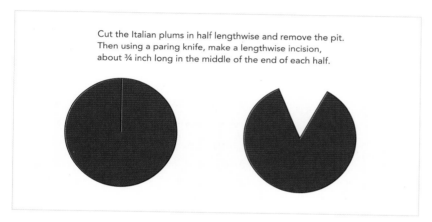

Cut the Italian plums in half lengthwise and remove the pit. Then using a paring knife, make a lengthwise incision, about ¾ inch long in the middle of the end of each half.

6 Mix the cinnamon with the granulated sugar in a bowl and sprinkle half of the mixture on the plums. Bake at 375°F/190°C for 45 to 50 minutes, until the tips of the plums are beginning to color and the crust is baked crisp. Remove from the oven and cool on a wire rack. Once cool, sprinkle on the remaining cinnamon sugar. The tart is ready to eat and is best at room temperature.

IT'S DONE WHEN IT'S DONE

When they are baked, the plums should be tender but not mushy or soupy.

STORAGE

You can leave the tart out at room temperature for 1 to 2 days. You can also refrigerate it and keep it for 3 to 4 days, but then the crust will get very soggy. The longer you wait to eat it, the more the juices will make their way into the crust. I don't advise you to freeze this tart.

UNDERSTANDING INGREDIENTS

The amount of water that oozes out of fruit when you work with it in pastry depends on the molecular structure and cell walls of the fruit. Strawberries, for example, will release a lot of water compared to apples. These are all things that you need to take into consideration before experimenting with different fruits and pastry. Plums release a fair amount of water, especially if they are not completely ripe. For this reason I recommend that you use ripe fruit. As in jam, good ripe fruit makes good pies.

When you make a fruit tart with stone fruits like plums you must take care to fill the tart shell with as much fruit as you can squeeze in. As the tart bakes the fruit loses a lot of volume as much of its liquid evaporates. The way we cut the plums also affects the outcome of the tart. We make a small incision in the top end of each half to allow water to escape. If you just cut the plums in half and don't make the incision they retain too much water, which will make the tart soggy.

Since the juices will be released during the baking process, you need something to absorb them. I usually use baked nut crumble or Streusel (PAGE 9). The crumble has to be fully baked; using raw crumble would be fatal, as the juice would soak through and prevent it and the crust from baking. If you want to make this a nut-free dessert you could use crushed cookies or even crumbled sponge cake that you dry out in a 300°F/150°C oven for 15 minutes.

I like to use Pâte Brisée (PAGE 147) for this baked fruit tart because of its nice flaky texture. It does not have to be fully baked first, because the tart does not involve any type of custard that would penetrate a partially baked crust, and the streusel will protect it from the juice from the plums.

CHOCOLATE TART/TARTE AU CHOCOLAT WITH NOUGATINE TOPPING

YIELD | ONE 9-INCH TART

2-DAY RECIPE

INGREDIENTS	WEIGHT	MEASURE (APPROXIMATE) OR OUNCE WEIGHT
Pâte Sablée (PAGE 144)	One 9-inch crust (½ recipe, about 350 grams)	One 9-inch crust (½ recipe, about 12³⁄₁₀ ounces)
Chocolate Nougatine Crisp (PAGE 59)	½ recipe	½ recipe
Dark chocolate couverture (65%), chopped or coins	160 grams	5³⁄₅ ounces
Whole eggs	50 grams	1 extra-large egg
Whole milk (3.5% fat)	25 grams	2 tablespoons
Heavy cream (35% fat)	150 grams	⅔ cup
Whole milk (3.5% fat)	50 grams	¼ cup

No pastry book should be without a chocolate tart recipe, and this one has always been a family favorite in my house. The recipe is fairly easy even though it involves three different elements—a *sablée* crust, a chocolate nougatine topping, and a chocolate custard filling. It's the combination of those three textures—the flaky crust, the creamy filling, and the crispy/crunchy topping—that makes this chocolate tart truly special and delicious.

Let's not fool ourselves: there's nothing healthy or light about chocolate tart. It's a celebration of the undeniable power of chocolate, with its rich and complex flavor profile. The ingredients here are simple, but when you taste the tart you'll understand yet again that making good pastry is not about using exotic, difficult-to-find ingredients. It's about using fresh, top-quality ingredients and applying the right technique to them. The texture of the chocolate custard is outstanding. Follow the directions below and it's sure to come out smooth and creamy.

You will need to make your *pâte sablée* at least a day ahead, and I recommend that you also make the chocolate nougatine crisp ahead. You also must allow at least 2 hours for your tart to set before eating.

METHOD

DAY 1

1 Mix up the dough. Refrigerate overnight, then roll it out and line your tart pan or ring. Let it rest in the refrigerator for several hours or preferably overnight.

BEFORE YOU BEGIN

→ Get out the following equipment and allow all of the ingredients to come to room temperature:

Equipment for Pâte Sablée (PAGE 144)
Equipment for Chocolate Nougatine Crisp (PAGE 59)
Digital scale, set to metric weights
1 large chef's knife
1 medium microwave-safe bowl
1 rubber spatula
1 digital thermometer
1 strainer
1 small mixing bowl
1 medium saucepan
1 stainless steel hand whisk

→ Read this recipe through twice from start to finish.

The three elements of this custard—eggs, dairy, and chocolate—have one common ingredient: fat. When working with all three in a recipe the goal is to have those fats fuse together and mix well with the water that's present in the ingredients. Follow the recipe carefully, especially in regard to the temperature of the melted chocolate and the custard (which is important for pasteurizing the egg) and the way you combine the two.

The chocolate nougatine crisp is a perfect flourish for this chocolate tart. The sliced almonds in the crisp allow it to be so thin that you will be able to cut right through it when you serve the tart. If you used pecans for your nougatine your crisp would be about ¼ inch thick, making the tart impossible to cut. Another reason why we use almonds here is that their flavor won't overpower the taste of the chocolate.

2 Make the chocolate nougatine crisp, and weigh out half of it for this recipe. Store the crisp in an airtight container as directed.

DAY 2

1 Pre-bake your 9-inch *pâte sablée* following the directions on PAGE 144 and set aside. Preheat the oven to 325°F/160°C.

2 If not using chocolate coins, chop your chocolate into approximately ¼-inch pieces. Place the chopped chocolate or chocolate coins in a microwave-safe bowl and microwave at 50 percent power for 1 minute. Stir with a rubber spatula for 20 seconds and microwave for another 30 seconds at 50 percent power. Microwave again at 50 percent power for 30 seconds if necessary to melt the chocolate, and stir again. Insert a thermometer and stir until the chocolate reaches 113°F/45°C. If you are not comfortable with a microwave you can melt the chocolate by placing the bowl over a double boiler and heating to 113°F/45°C. Place a strainer over the bowl with the melted chocolate and set aside but keep warm.

3 In a small mixing bowl, beat together the egg and the 25 grams of milk.

4 Combine the cream and the 50 grams of milk in a medium saucepan and place over medium heat. Bring to a boil, then remove from the heat. Making sure that it is not boiling, whisk half into the egg mixture to temper the egg. Then whisk the tempered egg back into the milk mixture, scraping all of it out of the bowl with a rubber spatula. (See my Understanding Ingredients in the Vanilla Custard Sauce recipe, PAGE 35.)

5 Return the saucepan to low heat and insert a thermometer. Whisk constantly, making sure to whisk along the bottom and sides of the saucepan, until the mixture reaches 158°F/70°C. This should not take more than 2 minutes. As soon as it reaches 158°F/70°C remove from the heat and strain the hot custard over the melted chocolate. If the mixture looks broken or separated, pour it immediately into a tall container and blend with an immersion blender for 10 seconds; using a regular blender works as well.

6 Using a rubber spatula, carefully stir the chocolate and hot custard mixture from the center of the bowl out to the sides until the mixture is completely homogenized. It is important to stir and not to whip so that you don't incorporate unnecessary bubbles into the custard.

7 When the mixture is homogenized, pour into the pre-baked *sablée* shell and place in the preheated oven. Bake for 8 to 9 minutes, until you see the sides become thicker and slightly more set than the middle. The middle will look liquid when you remove the tart from the oven, but during the cooling process it will thicken due to the solids and fat from the dairy and chocolate.

8 Remove from the oven and set aside to cool for 30 minutes.

9 Cover the entire surface of the tart with pieces of nougatine crisp and place in a cool room for 2 hours. Serve at room temperature. If you do not have a cool place to put the baked tart, allow it to cool for 30 minutes, then refrigerate for 1 hour before placing the nougatine on top. Remove from the refrigerator, cover with the nougatine and serve; do not refrigerate again.

IT'S DONE WHEN IT'S DONE

The custard should not be too loose, but set and creamy. There should be no cracks. The nougatine crisp should be crunchy and the *sablée* shell flaky and golden brown.

STORAGE

The shelf life for this tart is 2 days, but the best way to enjoy it is to make it and eat it the same day so that the tart is never refrigerated; this will ensure a rich and creamy custard. Refrigerating it will set the fat crystals very hard and the custard will lose some of its creamy texture. If you must refrigerate this tart, do not top with the nougatine crisp, as it would get soggy in the refrigerator. Whenever you plan on serving it, let it come to room temperature for 2 hours without the nougatine crisp and then place it in a 400°F/200°C oven for 30 seconds only. This will slightly soften the upper layer of the custard so that you can stick the nougatine crisp on top.

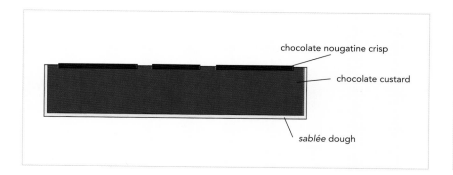

chocolate nougatine crisp

chocolate custard

sablée dough

LEMON CREAM TART
WITH MERINGUE TEARDROPS

YIELD | ONE 9-INCH TART

2-DAY RECIPE

INGREDIENTS	WEIGHT	MEASURE (APPROXIMATE) OR OUNCE WEIGHT
Pâte Sablée (PAGE 144)	One 9-inch crust (½ recipe, about 350 grams)	One 9-inch crust (½ recipe, about 12³/₁₀ ounces)
LEMON CREAM		
Butter (French style, 82% fat), softened and cut into small pieces	192 grams	6⁷/₁₀ ounces
Lemon zest	½ lemon	½ lemon
Granulated sugar	200 grams	1 cup
Lemon juice, freshly squeezed	140 grams	5 fluid ounces
Whole eggs	175 grams	3 eggs plus 1 yolk
Sea salt	0.5 gram	Pinch
TART		
Seven 3-inch Meringue Teardrops (PAGE 65), dusted with sugar crystals and/or roasted chopped nuts before baking	7 pieces	7 pieces
One 2½-inch round Meringue (PAGE 65), dusted with sugar crystals and/or chopped nuts before baking	1 piece	1 piece
Candied Peel (PAGE 87), for garnish	As desired	As desired

Whatever continent I've worked on and whatever the job, lemon tarts have always been one of the most requested desserts. Creamy, smooth, tangy lemon curd topped with sweet, crunchy meringue inside a flaky tart shell is the perfect combination of sweet and acidic, creamy and crunchy.

Lemon tarts always make me think of the lemon trees that I had in my backyard in Menlo Park near San Francisco, which was the first place in the United States I lived.

I loved the weather in California, but initially it was a huge culture shock for a young Alsatian from a small, old-fashioned French village where everyone was disciplined. I was expecting something like the America I saw in *Starsky & Hutch*, one of my favorite television shows when I was a kid—something more midwestern, with everyone driving big, fast cars. It didn't take me very long to see that California was dif-

BEFORE YOU BEGIN

→ Get out the following equipment and allow all of the ingredients to come to room temperature:

Equipment for Pâte Sablée (PAGE 144)
Digital scale, set to metric weights
1 vegetable brush
1 microplane
1 lemon press
1 small bowl
1 medium mixing bowl
1 stainless steel hand whisk
1 medium saucepan
1 digital thermometer
1 strainer
1 rubber spatula
1 immersion blender

NOTE: Make sure the butter is soft.

→ Read this recipe through twice from start to finish.

UNDERSTANDING INGREDIENTS

There are a few critical issues in this recipe.

- First, the butter must be soft and at room temperature; this takes time. It's best to scale the butter the day before and let it sit at room temperature overnight in a bowl. You can also speed up the process by cutting the butter into small pieces and letting it sit at room temperature. Adding cold butter to the lemon curd mixture will make it seize up (see the Troubleshooting section below).
- I prefer to use a microplane to make lemon zest, as it just grates the skin of the lemon where the natural lemon oil is and not the bitter white pulp.
- Eggs coagulate with heat, but that coagulation can also be activated when the eggs come in contact with an acid. Because of this, lemon juice, which is highly acidic, cannot just be added to the eggs. In order to prevent coagulation, we add some sugar to the lemon juice and use it as a buffer. Sugar added straight to eggs can also coagulate them, which is why we add a little milk to the egg yolks when we make pastry cream or vanilla sauce.
- It's important to bring the lemon curd to the proper temperature to make sure that the coagulation has been properly executed. Then it is crucial to let the mixture cool to 140°F/60°C before adding the butter. Use a hand blender and follow the recipe carefully when adding the butter. A soft butter added to a cream cooled to 140°F/60°F will blend perfectly and make a very smooth and shiny mixture because the fat crystals are blended into the mixture at the perfect temperature. Then the cream will set properly.

ferent, more like a country unto itself; that the 1960s had spawned a population that was liberated, carefree, and happy. A week after I arrived I went to my first concert, which was quite an experience; of course it was the Grateful Dead, an unknown band at the time in France. The next day I realized that I was likely the only person in the audience who actually remembered the concert afterward. It took me a while to get used to the California pace, but I still miss that backyard, where lemons and oranges were a constant reminder of the West Coast way of life.

METHOD

DAY 1

1 Mix up the dough. Refrigerate overnight, then roll it out and line your tart pan or ring. Let it rest in the refrigerator for several hours or preferably overnight.

2 Make your meringue following the instructions on PAGE 65; pipe 3-inch teardrops and one 2½-inch-round dome, sprinkle them with crystallized sugar or chopped roasted nuts, and bake as directed. Set aside. (You can also make these on Day 2.)

DAY 2

1 Pre-bake your tart shell following the directions on PAGE 138 for a fully baked shell and cool thoroughly.

2 Before making the cream, make sure that the butter is soft. To make the lemon cream, wash the lemons thoroughly and brush with a small brush to remove all the waxes that are covering them. Zest a half a lemon using the microplane. Squeeze the lemon juice with the press. Divide the sugar into 2 equal portions of 100 grams each. In a small bowl combine 1 portion of the sugar with the lemon juice and sea salt and stir with a whisk until dissolved.

3 In another medium bowl, whisk the eggs with the remaining sugar for 30 seconds. Whisk in the lemon juice mixture and add the zest.

4 Create a water bath by bringing 1 inch of water to a simmer in a medium saucepan. Rest the bowl with the egg and lemon mixture on the saucepan, making sure that the bottom is not touching the simmering water (otherwise the eggs will scramble). Place a digital thermometer in the bowl and whisk the mixture over the water bath until it thickens and reaches 176° to 179.6°F/80° to 82°C. The speed of the whisking is not important, but it is crucial to whisk all the time and everywhere. Ignoring a side of the bowl will result in scrambled eggs. Immediately remove from the heat and strain into a bowl, using a rubber spatula to push the mixture through a fine mesh strainer.

5 Allow to cool to 140°F/60°C; this should not take more than 5 minutes. Then add half of the soft butter and blend with the immersion blender. Add the second half of the butter and blend. When all of the butter has been added blend for another 30 seconds to a minute, until smooth and homogenized. You can also use a blender for this step.

6 Pour the lemon cream into the baked and cooled crust. Refrigerate for at least 2 hours before serving; the cream will set and you will be able to get clean slices when you cut the tart.

7 Shortly before serving decorate the top with the meringues, arranging the round meringue in the middle and the teardrops around it with the skinny tails facing the center like petals of a flower (SEE ILLUSTRATION). Garnish with thin strips of candied citrus peels.

MERINGUE PLACEMENT

IT'S DONE WHEN IT'S DONE

The finished lemon cream should be bright yellow and thick like mayonnaise, but once refrigerated it should be set and stiff enough to cut cleanly. Keep the tart refrigerated, but take it out of the refrigerator 1 hour before serving so that the cream is nice and creamy and not too cold. Do not decorate with the meringues until you are ready to serve because they will become soggy in the refrigerator.

TROUBLESHOOTING

THE LEMON CREAM DID NOT SET UP: The mixture was too warm when you added the butter, causing the butter to melt. This will destroy its original crystal form and prevent it from setting properly. To fix this, melt the entire mixture completely in a double boiler. Then set the bowl in a bowl of ice and whisk until you see the mixture come together. Blend with an immersion blender for 30 to 60 seconds to make it smooth.

THE LEMON CREAM LOOKS LIKE A BUTTER CREAM: The butter was too cold when you added it, or the lemon mixture was too cold. To fix, warm up the mixture very slightly in the microwave for 5 to 10 seconds only at full power. Blend with the immersion blender; you should see it becoming smoother. Repeat the heating and blending once more if needed.

STORAGE

The tart will keep for 24 hours in the refrigerator. After that the tart and especially the meringues get soggy.

> ### JACQUY'S TAKEAWAYS
>
> → You can substitute other types of citrus juice or acidic fruit juices like passionfruit for lemon juice and make different types of citrus or exotic fruit creams using this method. You can even make a blend of more than one flavor.
>
> → The lemon zest can be increased or omitted. It contributes a distinctive lemon oil flavor that some people really like and others don't.
>
> → Never use aluminum pans or bowls when working with acidic fruit. The acid will react with the metal and make the cream unsafe to eat.

ALSATIAN SOUR CREAM AND BERRY TART / TARTE AU FROMAGE BLANC ET AUX FRUITS ROUGES

INGREDIENTS	WEIGHT	MEASURE (APPROXIMATE) OR OUNCE WEIGHT
Pâte Brisée (PAGE 147)	1 recipe	1 recipe
BERRY FILLING		
Cornstarch	6 grams	1¾ teaspoons
Water	6 grams	2 teaspoons
Raspberries	124 grams	4½ ounces
Blackberries, cut in half	55 grams	2 ounces
Strawberries, cut in ½-inch chunks	35 grams	1¼ ounces
Granulated Sugar	65 grams	⅓ cup plus 2 teaspoons
SOUR CREAM FILLING		
Cornstarch	3 grams	1 teaspoon
Cake flour	2 grams	1 teaspoon
Granulated sugar	20 grams	1 tablespoon plus 2 teaspoons
Whole milk (3.5% fat)	4 grams	1 teaspoon
Vanilla extract or paste	4 grams	1 teaspoon
Egg yolks	20 grams	1 yolk plus 1 teaspoon
Heavy cream (35% fat)	8 grams	2 teaspoons
Sour cream	100 grams	⅓ cup
Egg whites	40 grams	About 1⅓ eggs
Granulated sugar	40 grams	3½ tablespoons

BEFORE YOU BEGIN

→ Get out the following equipment and allow all of the ingredients to come to room temperature:

Equipment for Pâte Brisée (PAGE 147)
Digital scale, set to metric weights
12 small tart rings, individual tart pans, or ramekins
1 small mixing bowl
1 medium saucepan
1 rubber spatula
3 medium mixing bowls
1 sheet pan lined with parchment paper
1 medium stainless steel hand whisk
1 medium chef's knife
KitchenAid or stand mixer fitted with the whisk attachment
1 bowl scraper
1 pastry bag fitted with a ½-inch round tip, optional
1 offset spatula

→ Read this recipe through twice from start to finish.

Every Alsatian *pâtisserie* serves *tarte au fromage blanc,* a cross between a baked cheesecake and a tart. It consists of a *pâte brisée* tart shell filled with a light baked cheesecake mixture. Some chefs place raisins on the bottom of the tart. I prefer to use a berry puree, which, along with the meringue that I fold into the filling, gives the tarts a lighter quality than the traditional version.

French *fromage blanc* is an inherently low-fat soft cheese with a nice sour flavor. In Alsace, the making of *fromage blanc* goes back centuries. It is also very popular in the north of France and in Belgium. In the old days the cow's milk was left in a warm spot until its lactose degraded and the natural lactic acid curdled the milk. The milk would then be poured into a clay strainer so that all the water would drain off. The firm cheese that remained in the strainer would then be mixed until smooth and creamy.

So far I have not been lucky enough to find good and smooth *fromage blanc* in the United States, so I adapted the recipe using sour cream. I also added a berry filling that goes very well with the sour cream flavor. Although *tarte au fromage blanc* is always served at room temperature in Alsace, I think that this adaptation is best served fresh from the oven like a soufflé. I recommend that you make individual tarts instead of one large one because the warm berry filling will ooze out and make it impossible to serve nice slices.

METHOD

DAY 1

Make the *pâte brisée* and refrigerate overnight. Roll it out and line 12 individual tart rings or tart pans. Let it rest for several hours or overnight in the refrigerator.

DAY 2

1 Dock the tart shells and pre-bake following the instructions on PAGE 138. They should be fully baked and golden brown, which could take up to 30 minutes in a regular oven.
2 Make the fruit puree. In a small mixing bowl, make a slurry by mixing together the cornstarch and water. Place the fruit and the sugar in a medium saucepan. Bring to a simmer

This cheesecake soufflé mixture is thickened with three different thickening agents: cornstarch, cake flour, and egg yolks. Using only one of them would not work, as cornstarch would make the mix too starchy, the cake flour would make it too rubbery due to the gluten, and if you used more egg yolks their flavor might dominate. Using a combination of the three is the best of all worlds. The meringue made by beating egg whites and sugar together to stiff peaks lightens the filling and turns it into a soufflé.

JACQUY'S TAKEAWAYS

→ It's best to whip the egg whites and sugar just before baking.

→ The berries can be interchanged with other berries or fruit such as peaches, cut into ½-inch dice.

and cook over medium heat until the fruit starts to soften, about 3 to 4 minutes. Add the slurry and cook until the mixture has a marmalade-like consistency, another 1 to 3 minutes. It is crucial to cook this mixture enough or it will be too watery and will make the tart shell soggy. Also, not cooking it enough after adding the slurry will leave an unpleasant starchy texture. Transfer to a medium bowl or container, cover, and refrigerate. You can refrigerate the fruit for up to 3 days or freeze for up to 1 month.

3 Preheat the oven to 375°F/190°C. Unmold the pre-baked tart shells and place them on a sheet pan lined with parchment paper.

4 Make the sour cream filling. In a mixing bowl mix together the cornstarch, cake flour, and the 20 grams of granulated sugar with a whisk. In another mixing bowl, whisk together the milk, vanilla extract or paste, egg yolk, and heavy cream. Add the dry ingredients to the milk mixture and whisk together. Whisk in the sour cream and set aside.

5 Place the egg whites in the bowl of your stand mixer fitted with the whisk attachment and whip on high speed for 10 seconds. Add half of the 40 grams of sugar and whip on high speed for 2 minutes. Scrape down the sides of the bowl, add the rest of the granulated sugar, and whip on high speed for another 2 minutes. You should have a meringue with firm peaks (see meringue pictures on PAGES 70-71).

6 Gently fold the meringue into the sour cream mixture until you see no separate traces of meringue. Spread 1 tablespoon of berry mixture on the bottom of each pre-baked tart shell. Spoon or pipe the sour cream mixture into the tart shells. Fill them up to the rim, then use an offset spatula to carefully level them off. Dust with confectioners' sugar.

7 Place the sheet pan in the preheated oven and bake for 15 minutes or until puffed and light brown. Serve immediately; the soufflés will collapse quickly.

IT'S DONE WHEN IT'S DONE

The fruit mixture should be cooked but not completely mushy. It should have the consistency of marmalade, and not be watery at all. The sour cream mixture should be puffed and light brown.

STORAGE

The cooked fruit and the sour cream base can be made a day in advance and refrigerated. Bring to room temperature before making the meringue and finishing the tarts. The tarts could be left to cool and consumed at room temperature, but they will be slightly heavier.

RASPBERRY AND HAZELNUT TART / TARTE AUX FRAMBOISES ET NOISETTES

YIELD | ONE 9-INCH TART

2-DAY RECIPE

INGREDIENTS	WEIGHT	MEASURE (APPROXIMATE) OR OUNCE WEIGHT
Pâte Sablée (PAGE 144), made with hazelnut flour	One 9-inch crust (½ recipe, about 350 grams)	One 9-inch crust (½ recipe, about 12 ³⁄₁₀ ounces)
Raspberry Jam (PAGE 80)	150 grams	½ cup
Whole hazelnuts, toasted and skinned (PAGE 55)	30 grams	¼ cup
Hazelnut flour	70 grams	¾ cup
Confectioners' sugar	70 grams	¾ cup
Cornstarch	2 grams	¾ teaspoon
Cake flour	2 grams	1 teaspoon
Butter (French style, 82% fat)	70 grams	2½ ounces or 5 tablespoons
Sea salt	0.6 grams	Pinch
Vanilla extract or paste	2 grams	½ teaspoon
Whole eggs	50 grams	1 egg
Dark rum, optional	12 grams	1 tablespoon
Fresh raspberries	250 grams	9 ounces or about 2 cups
Powdered sugar, for dusting	As needed	As needed

This is another deceptively easy recipe with delicious results: a *sablée* crust made with hazelnut flour instead of almond flour, filled with hazelnut cream and fresh raspberries. To me, raspberries are the most flavorful of all berries and hazelnuts are the most flavorful of all nuts. Together they make a wonderful combination.

You will need one 9-inch tart ring or pan lined with *unbaked* hazelnut *sablée* dough (PAGE 144) and 150 grams of Raspberry Jam (PAGE 80).

METHOD

DAY 1

1 Make the *pâte sablée* using hazelnut flour instead of almond flour. Refrigerate overnight, then roll it out and line your tart pan or ring. Let it rest in the refrigerator for several hours or preferably overnight.

2 Begin making the raspberry jam.

BEFORE YOU BEGIN

→ Get out the following equipment:

Equipment for Pâte Sablée (PAGE 144)
Digital scale, set to metric weights
1 sheet pan lined with a silpat or parchment paper
1 pastry bag
1 rolling pin
1 medium mixing bowl
1 sifter
KitchenAid or stand mixer fitted with the paddle attachment
1 bowl scraper
1 pastry bag fitted with a ½-inch round piping tip
1 fork or dough docker
1 small offset spatula
1 paring knife
1 powdered sugar shaker or sieve

NOTE: Allow all of the ingredients except the *sablée* dough to come to room temperature. Keep the 9-inch *pâte sablée* in the refrigerator until ready to use.

→ Read this recipe through twice from start to finish.

Hazelnuts have good moisture absorption power, but not as great as almonds. Even so, when baked this filling stays moist for 2 days. You can make the cream using another type of nut flour such as almond or pistachio, or you can tone down the hazelnut flavor by using half almond flour and half hazelnut. Nut flours are sometimes called nut powders; they're the same ingredient.

DAY 2

1 Finish making the raspberry jam and allow to cool. Scale the ingredients you need for the rest of the recipe.

2 Preheat the oven to 325°F/160°C. Line a sheet pan with parchment paper or a silpat. Place the whole hazelnuts on the sheet pan and place in the oven for 15 minutes. Remove from the oven, cool for 15 minutes, and place them in a pastry bag. Hold the bag shut and gently roll over the nuts with a rolling pin, just to crush them into halves. Set aside.

3 Sift together the hazelnut flour, confectioners' sugar, cornstarch, and cake flour in a medium bowl.

4 Place the soft butter, sea salt, and vanilla in the bowl of your mixer fitted with the paddle and mix at medium speed for 1 minute. Turn off the machine, scrape down the sides of the bowl, and add the nut flour mixture to the machine. Mix at medium speed for 1 minute. Gradually add the egg and mix at medium speed until it is incorporated, which should take no more than 2 minutes. Add the rum and mix until incorporated. Scrape down the sides of the bowl and transfer the mixture to a pastry bag fitted with a ½-inch round tip if desired.

5 Remove the tart ring or pan lined with the hazelnut *sablée* dough from the refrigerator. With a fork or dough docker, poke holes in the dough every inch. Pipe or spoon the cream over the bottom of the crust in an even layer, then use an offset spatula to smooth.

6 Bake the tart for 40 minutes, until the cream and the crust are golden brown and the tip of a paring knife comes out clean when inserted. Remove from the oven, let cool on a wire rack for 30 minutes, then remove the tart from the ring.

7 With a small offset spatula, spread the raspberry jam over the surface in an even layer. If the jam is too stiff to spread easily, warm it slightly first.

8 Place the fresh raspberries on the jam, distribute the roasted hazelnuts among the raspberries if serving right away, and dust with confectioners' sugar. If not serving right away, wait until serving before you arrange the hazelnuts and dust with confectioners' sugar.

IT'S DONE WHEN IT'S DONE

The finished baked *sablée* and hazelnut cream should have a nice golden brown color. When you place the tip of a paring knife in the center, it should come out clean. If the hazelnut cream looks broken it is most probably

→ When mixing up the cream it's important to be careful not to incorporate too much air, which you will do if you beat for too long or at high speed. This will fill the mixture with air bubbles that will burst and make the cream rise during the baking process, only to deflate and collapse afterward. Additionally, if the baked hazelnut cream is porous, it will allow humidity to make the finished crust soggy.

→ **$50 TRICK:** If your hazelnut cream or any other butter mixture breaks during the mixing, just warm up the bottom of the bowl slightly so that the fat can come to room temperature and incorporate with the rest of the ingredients. Simply take the mixing bowl out of the mixer, put an inch of hot tap water in a large mixing bowl or your sink, place the bowl in the water for 20 to 30 seconds, and then resume the mixing. You will be amazed to see how it comes together and how much better it looks.

because either the butter or the eggs were not brought to room temperature before mixing. When butter is emulsified and cold it will break, because the butter crystals will clump together and separate from the water in the mixture.

STORAGE

The hazelnut cream can be used in the tart right away or transferred to a plastic container and refrigerated for up to 3 days. You can also divide it into 100-gram batches and freeze for up to 1 month.

You can enjoy this tart right away or refrigerate it for 1 day. I recommend that you sprinkle on the roasted hazelnuts just before serving the tart so that they are nice and crunchy.

VARIATION

You can buy an additional 50 grams of raspberries and press them into the raw hazelnut cream before baking the tart. The raspberries will release their juices into the cream during the baking process, but they do not contain enough juice to make the cream fall apart and get soggy. When you bake a tart that contains fruit that falls apart and releases water it is important to use a filling that does not contain too much water (such as this cream) so that it can absorb that moisture. But certain fruits, such as strawberries, release too much water. Even with the hazelnut cream they will create unpleasant wet spots when baked.

LINZER TART MY WAY / TARTE DE LINZ MA FAÇON

YIELD | ONE 9-INCH TART

2-DAY RECIPE

INGREDIENTS	WEIGHT	MEASURE (APPROXIMATE) OR OUNCE WEIGHT
Raspberry Jam (PAGE 80)	300 grams	1 cup
Hazelnuts	25 grams	Scant ¼ cup
Hazelnut flour	55 grams	⅔ cup
Butter (French style, 82% fat), for the pan	As needed	As needed
Butter (French style, 82% fat)	88 grams	3 ounces
Confectioners' sugar	28 grams	¼ cup
Sea salt	0.8 grams	¼ teaspoon
Vanilla bean	½ bean	½ bean
Confectioners' sugar	55 grams	½ cup
Ground Ceylon cinnamon	2 grams	1 teaspoon
Ground clove, optional	0.6 grams	1 clove
All-purpose flour	100 grams	¾ cup
Whole eggs	110 grams	2 extra-large eggs less 2 teaspoons

In Alsace I grew up with *tarte de Linz*. Most Alsatian pastry chefs make it in one way, shape, or form. It is usually made with a type of sweet or *sablée* crust that contains hazelnut flour and spices. The crust is then filled with raspberry jam and baked. It is one of those recipes that became famous internationally, just like chocolate mousse, crème brûlée, tiramisu, and Black Forest cake. During my travels I saw Linzer tarts on all four continents that I worked on. The originality of this version is that the dough is much softer than regular sweet dough and no rolling is required. It is piped into the tart pan and the lattice is piped over the jam.

⊹ ORGANIZING YOUR TIME ⊱

This recipe calls for the homemade Raspberry Jam on PAGE 80. Do not substitute commercial jam, as it will be too watery and using it will result in a soggy crust. What you gain in convenience you will lose in flavor and texture. Remember that to make the jam you must begin a day ahead so that the jam and the first half of the sugar, once brought to a boil, can sit

BEFORE YOU BEGIN

→ Get out the following equipment and allow all of the ingredients to come to room temperature:

Digital scale, set to metric weights
Food processor fitted with steel blade
1 pastry bag
1 rolling pin
1 sheet pan lined with parchment paper
1 pastry brush
One 9-inch tart ring or pan
KitchenAid or stand mixer fitted with the paddle attachment
1 bowl scraper
1 sifter
2 pastry bags, each fitted with a ¼-inch round piping tip
1 rubber spatula
1 small offset spatula
1 confectioners' sugar shaker or sieve

→ Read this recipe through twice from start to finish.

overnight in the refrigerator. The jam must also have time to cool before you use it in the tart, and the tart will bake for close to an hour, then requires at least 30 minutes of cooling time.

METHOD

DAY 1

Begin making a recipe of the raspberry jam. But first make sure to crush the raspberries in a food processor for 3 full seconds—see "Understanding Ingredients." Then cook the jam as instructed.

DAY 2

1 Finish making the jam and allow it to cool.

2 Place the hazelnuts inside a pastry bag and gently roll over them with a rolling pin to just crush them into halves. You may have to do this in batches. Be careful not to pulverize the nuts.

3 Preheat the oven to 325°F/160°C. Line a sheet pan with parchment paper. Spread the hazelnut flour on one side and the halved hazelnuts on the other. Place in the oven and roast for 10 minutes, until light brown and toasty. Remove from the oven and allow to cool, then transfer to separate containers. Using a brush and soft butter, lightly grease a 9-inch tart pan or ring. If you can see the butter on the ring, you've used too much.

4 Place the butter and the first 25 grams of confectioners' sugar, the sea salt, and the scraped vanilla bean in the bowl of a stand mixer fitted with the paddle attachment and cream for 3 full minutes at medium speed. Scrape down the sides of the bowl and the paddle.

5 Meanwhile, sift together the hazelnut flour, the remaining 50 grams of confectioners' sugar, the ground cinnamon and the clove, and the all-purpose flour.

6 Reduce the speed of the mixer to low. Add half the eggs to the butter mixture, then half of the dry ingredients. Beat until incorporated and repeat with the rest of the eggs and dry ingredients. This method will prevent lumps from forming.

7 Stop mixing and scrape down the sides of the bowl and the beater. Transfer half of the mixture into a pastry bag fitted with a ¼-inch piping tip. Hold the bag vertically over the tart pan and with the tip facing down start piping a tight spiral beginning from the center all the way to the rim. If there are spaces between the coils or the batter looks uneven, smooth with a small offset spatula. Then pipe a single ring along the perimeter of the pan. Use a rubber spatula and spread the ring upward on the edge of the pan so that it sticks to it and eventually makes an outside crust.

According to the history books, Linzer tart, also commonly called Linzertorte, is the creation of an Austrian pastry chef named Jindrak, who created the tart in his native city of Linz in 1653. The Austrians are famous for fighting for the rights to call a pastry theirs and original, as they did in a seven-year court case over the label "The Original Sacher Torte," so I'll go along with the history books. I'm less interested in the history and more interested in how a pastry tastes, in any case. This should always be the main concern of the pastry chef: flavor should always come before looks, colors, and shapes, and it should never be hindered by them.

UNDERSTANDING INGREDIENTS

Hazelnut flour contributes a wonderful nutty flavor and crunchy texture to the dough. One of my tricks is to pre-toast the hazelnut flour slightly so that it dries out and has a stronger flavor; during the baking process it will bake more and release its full aroma. You can do that with other nut flours as long as you don't need them to absorb the moisture in a recipe.

By now you know that I love the combination of raspberries and hazelnuts. Two spices also define Linzer tart: cinnamon and cloves. Cinnamon is a wonderful spice when used judiciously so that the flavor remains subtle. Ceylon cinnamon is my favorite because of its floral undertones. Because of my personal history with cloves (PAGE 178) I have made them optional in this recipe—but the spices bring a new and wonderful dimension to my favorite flavor combination.

It's worth stopping and reflecting on the notion of adding new flavors to an existing combination. As soon as you add a new flavor to a pastry, everything changes. You might have to adjust the quantities of all the existing ingredients or alter the method to make sure

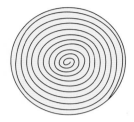

1 Hold the piping bag vertically over the tart pan and with the tip facing down start piping a tight spiral beginning from the center all the way to the rim.

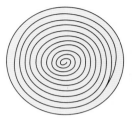

2 Pipe a single ring along the perimeter of the pan.

8 Place the jam in the second pastry bag and pipe it into the middle of the tart, leaving a ½-inch margin around the outside border. Spread it evenly with a small offset spatula.

9 Place the remaining Linzer mix in the pastry bag you used for the bottom crust and pipe a crisscross lattice design of the mix on top of the tart, from one edge of the pan to the other. Pipe 1 last ring or teardrops along the edge of the ring and arrange the hazelnuts on top. There should be enough halved hazelnuts to form a ring all the way around the edge of the tart.

10 Bake for 45 to 55 minutes. Remove from the oven and let cool for 30 minutes. Before serving dust lightly with confectioners' sugar. The tart is best eaten at room temperature when freshly baked.

3 Place the jam in the second pastry bag and pipe it into the middle of the tart, leaving a ½-inch margin around the outside border.

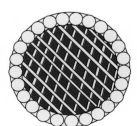

4 Place the remaining Linzer mix in the pastry bag you used for the bottom crust and pipe a crisscross lattice design of linzer mix on top of the tart, from one edge of the pan to the other. Pipe one last ring or a teardrop border along the edge of the ring.

IT'S DONE WHEN IT'S DONE

The dough and the crushed hazelnuts should be golden brown. The raspberry jam should be red with a very light tint of brown, and it should not have bubbled out of control (though it will bubble somewhat) during baking.

STORAGE

This tart lasts forever, meaning you can have it sitting on the counter for a week (though it usually never lasts that long since we love it so much). If you refrigerate it, it will become soggy. You can also double-wrap it and freeze it for 1 month.

JACQUY'S TAKEAWAYS

→ This recipe is definitely a faster and easier way to make Linzer tart than the traditional way. The dough results in a finished product that is somewhere between a crust and a cake. Taking a sweet dough and increasing the butter or decreasing the flour to obtain a dough that you can pipe is a very interesting concept that you could also apply to other tarts.

---

that all of the ingredients—hazelnuts, raspberries, and spices, in this case—are represented at their best, and that one doesn't overpower another. This is one of the most difficult aspects of pastry making, and of cooking in general—achieving a balance of flavors—and one that is very important to think about. I taste far too many pastries that are overpowered by one ingredient, such as ginger or cinnamon. The result is that it's impossible for me to detect and appreciate the other ingredients.

Regarding the jam, it's important to understand that once the tart is filled with the jam it is baked in the oven. A jam that is too loose or still too full of water will bubble out of control in the oven due to the water evaporation. To stabilize this jam there is an important extra step in the jam recipe on PAGE 80. Before you begin the jam, you grind the raspberries in a food processor for 3 full seconds so that the seeds are crushed open. This way they will release their natural pectin. You then cook the jam as instructed; it will set slightly firmer.

CLOVES AND MY TEETH

CLOVES LEAVE A BAD TASTE in my mouth partly because I associate the spice with painful dental work. In the family bakery I grew up in my mom sold candies from a giant 18 × 16–foot wall display. On the way to school I would walk through the store past that huge display and would be allowed one candy. Now let's be real—what kid will only take one candy when he sees more than what an entire day of trick-or-treating would yield? So I ate *a lot* of candies when I was young, and I was lazy when it came to brushing my teeth. I began to get cavities, and they hurt. My grandmother would have me sit on a chair, open my mouth, and point at the cavity; then she would shove a clove into it. The good news is that cloves contain a chemical called eugenol that has been known for centuries to act as an antiseptic and anesthetic; the bad news is that you have cloves on your breath for the entire day.

I would then have to go to the dentist, whom I called the butcher. He did not have any patience for young brats who thought that candies were a food group, nor did he believe in novocaine. The pain was horrible, and to this day the sound of the dentist's drill brings chills down my spine.

As far as cloves in a Linzer tart are concerned, I don't want the Austrians to come after me, so I've added one to this recipe as an optional ingredient.

RHUBARB TART
WITH HAZELNUT CRUMBLE

YIELD | ONE 9-INCH TART

2-DAY RECIPE

INGREDIENTS	WEIGHT	MEASURE (APPROXIMATE)
Pâte Brisée (PAGE 147)	One 9-inch crust (½ recipe, about 350 grams)	One 9-inch crust (½ recipe, about 12³/₁₀ ounces)
Rhubarb, peeled if necessary and cut in ½-inch chunks	250 grams	2 cups
Vanilla bean	1 bean	1 bean
Water	295 grams	1¼ cups
Granulated sugar	295 grams	1½ cups less 1 tablespoon
Cornstarch	1.5 grams	½ teaspoon
Cake flour	1 gram	½ teaspoon
Granulated sugar	30 grams	2½ tablespoons
Whole milk (3.5% fat)	100 grams	7 tablespoons
Crème fraîche	75 grams	⅓ cup
Egg yolks	30 grams	1½ to 2 yolks
Vanilla extract	5 grams	1 teaspoon
Streusel, made with hazelnuts (PAGE 9), fully baked	120 grams	1 cup
Confectioners' sugar, for dusting	As needed	As needed

Rhubarb tart is one of the most traditional tarts in Alsace, as rhubarb grows all over our beautiful region. When I was a young boy, my mom would always make me peel off the outer skin to get rid of the stringy parts and get it ready for tart making. Rhubarb is great for desserts because it is very acidic and contrasts beautifully with sweet flavors.

METHOD

DAY 1

1 Mix up the dough. Refrigerate overnight, then roll it out and line your tart pan or ring. Let it rest in the refrigerator for several hours or preferably overnight.

2 Wash the rhubarb and cut off the bottoms of the stems. Peel if they seem stringy. Cut into ½-inch chunks. Split the vanilla bean in half and scrape out the seeds with the tip of a paring knife. Place the water and the 295 grams of

BEFORE YOU BEGIN

→ Get out the following equipment and allow all of the ingredients to come to room temperature:

Equipment for Pâte Brisée (PAGE 147)
Digital scale, set to metric weights
1 large chef's knife
1 small paring knife
1 medium saucepan
1 strainer
1 medium mixing bowl
1 medium stainless steel hand whisk

→ Read this recipe through twice from start to finish.

UNDERSTANDING INGREDIENTS

Rhubarb is a perennial plant with origins in Asia; it is actually classified as a vegetable in the buckwheat family, along with garden sorrel. The leaves contain a type of acid that makes them poisonous, so be sure to use only the stalks. Different types of rhubarb are available from May to August.

Before you use the rhubarb, cut away the bottoms of the stalks and peel only if it is stringy. (Freshly harvested young rhubarb usually does not need to be peeled.) Wash it thoroughly, as it can be slightly muddy. Weigh it after you have cut it up. Rhubarb does not refrigerate well because it becomes soggy after a while, but because of its texture, it freezes very well. When it's in season, cut it into ½-inch chunks, weigh them out into 250-gram parcels, and package them in airtight plastic bags to be frozen so that they are ready for your tarts.

granulated sugar in a saucepan, add the vanilla bean and seeds, and bring to a boil over medium heat. When the syrup comes to a boil add the rhubarb and poach on medium heat for 5 minutes or until the rhubarb softens slightly but stays intact. Do not overcook or it will turn to mush. Set a strainer over a bowl and carefully transfer the rhubarb to it. Refrigerate and let drip overnight.

DAY 2

1 Bake the tart shell following the directions on PAGE 147 and allow to cool.

2 Preheat the oven to 350°F/180°C. Make a flan mixture by mixing the cornstarch, flour, and granulated sugar together in a mixing bowl. Whisk in the milk, crème fraîche, egg yolk, and vanilla.

3 Arrange the poached rhubarb evenly over the bottom of the pre-baked tart shell. Fill the tart with the flan mixture four-fifths of the way, leaving a rim of crust still exposed. Bake for 20 minutes and pull out of the oven.

4 Sprinkle on a generous layer of baked hazelnut streusel and return to the oven. Bake for another 20 to 30 minutes, until the tart is set and the crumble is brown and crisp. Remove it from the oven, allow to cool for 30 minutes, and dust the top with confectioners' sugar.

IT'S DONE WHEN IT'S DONE

After the first 20 minutes of baking the flan should have set; if it hasn't, add another 5 minutes. The finished tart should be golden brown and the flan should be set.

STORAGE

This tart is best eaten the day it's made. It can be refrigerated and consumed the next day, but it will be slightly soggier.

→ Any fruit that can be poached without falling apart would be a good candidate for this recipe. I chose this method for the rhubarb to make sure that it is fully cooked once it goes in the tart shell. It is a great way to soften stringy or woody rhubarb.

→ **$50 TRICK:** The syrup left over from poaching the rhubarb can be used in different ways, two of which are my favorites. In the first, I freeze it in a shallow pan and stir it with a fork every 30 minutes until it makes an icy, refreshing granita (we call it *granité* in French). In the second, I make a jelly out of it by weighing the syrup and adding 3 percent gelatin bloomed in 15 grams (1 tablespoon) of water. You can use the jelly in a layered dessert, in a glass with fresh strawberries, French Meringues (PAGE 65), and perhaps some crumbled hazelnuts. If you don't want to make either of the above, spoon the poaching syrup over homemade vanilla ice cream (PAGE 271).

→ During the last 2 minutes of the poaching, you could always add 10 percent sliced strawberries to the rhubarb. Strawberries are very sweet and pair well with the acidic rhubarb.

This is one of my favorite photos, taken by my friend Paul Strabbing during our marathon photo shoot. These are rhubarb skins that we dried in a dehydrator in case we wanted to use them as a decoration.

FRENCH MACARON
(SEE PAGE 221 FOR RECIPE)

· CHAPTER 4 ·

COOKIES

I have a weakness for cookies. We are all guilty of sneaking into the cookie jar at one time or another during our childhood, and some of us, like me, are still secretly reaching into the metal tin as adults. What makes us act so irrationally? We don't sneak into the refrigerator for a piece of steak or a plate of pasta. I don't see any member of my family getting as worked up about any other type of food. Is it their small size that makes these irresistible pastries seem like only very small temptations to us?

My brothers and sisters and I grew up making cookies at my family's bakery. My dad made coconut *rochers* (PAGE 215), which we call coconut macaroons in the United States, by the ton all year round. And one of our after-school tasks was putting 25 pounds of *spritz* cookie dough (PAGE 194) through a commercial cookie press and placing the cookies on sheet pans while my dad was taking his afternoon nap.

Alsace has a huge tradition of festive Christmas cookies. They are called *bredele de Noël*—little Christmas breads—and we know that the tradition goes back at least to the fourteenth century, although Alsatians will tell you that they have been making these cookies since the beginning of time. They include such family favorites as rich, buttery Christmas Sablés (PAGE 187) and Cinnamon Stars, or *Zimtsterne* (PAGE 197). Hundreds of years ago the dough for cookies like these was pressed into carved wooden molds, some of which you can still see in museums in the region. The cookies were sold in the Strasbourg Sablés Market, which began in the sixteenth century and still takes place every year during the month of December. With over 300 vendors around the famous Strasbourg Cathedral, today this is one of the ten most visited Christmas markets in the world. You will find many of the cookies in this chapter there, as well as other Alsatian Christmas specialties like stollen, if you ever have the good fortune to visit Strasbourg at this time of year.

Some of the recipes in this chapter are French classics: Almond Tuiles (PAGE 217) are deceptively easy to make and so good that you will have a hard time keeping them in the jar. Palmiers, also known as Elephant Ears (PAGE 227), showcase the wonders of flaky puff pastry combined with caramelized sugar. Other recipes, like Fours de Lin (PAGE 205), are cookies that I learned to make during my apprenticeship. These irresistible chocolate-dipped sandwich cookies unite the flavor of a butter cookie, hazelnut paste, and dark chocolate. It would have been a crime not to include Macarons (PAGE 221) in this chapter, as they are now an obsession for gourmets around the world. They can be technically challenging at first, but I hope that with the help of my recipe you will "crack the code" and be able to make and enjoy them.

Cookie making always brings me back to the 1970s and working in my father's bakery during the busy holiday season. It was not as fun then as it is now to be helping my entire family make huge amounts of cookies every weekend for the month before Christmas, especially since we were forced to listen to the French music that my father loved—Edith Piaf, Charles Trenet, Maurice Chevalier. It seemed like the ultimate torture for us kids to be working instead of enjoying ourselves and listening to the Beatles. Of course, now I continue the ritual of getting the family together to make cookies while listening to traditional music every Christmas. We don't make as many as we had to make for my dad, but we make enough so that all the parties involved can go home with multiple jars that they can then pass on to family, neighbors, and friends. There is something about showing up at a neighbor's house with a tin of homemade cookies; it may seem old-fashioned, but to me it is possibly the best present a person can get.

CHRISTMAS SABLÉS / SABLÉS DE NOËL

INGREDIENTS	WEIGHT	MEASURE (APPROXIMATE) OR OUNCE WEIGHT
All-purpose flour	300 grams	2⅓ cups
Almond flour, skinless	100 grams	1 cup
Ground cinnamon	2 grams	1 teaspoon
Butter (French style, 82% fat)	200 grams	7 ounces
Vanilla extract or paste	10 grams	2 teaspoons
Granulated sugar	150 grams	¾ cup plus 2 teaspoons
Sea salt	3 grams	⅜ teaspoon
Whole eggs	40 grams	1 extra-large egg less 4 teaspoons
Egg Wash (PAGE 7)	1 recipe	1 recipe

Sablés de Noël, one of the traditional cookies we call *bredele de Noël*, are usually shaped like Christmas trees, stars, or snowmen, which are all symbolic of the December holidays. These simple, luscious cookies, made from a rich buttery dough flavored with vanilla, ground cinnamon, and almonds, can be addictive.

I can remember a time when the *bredele* were tied with ribbons to the Christmas tree as a decoration, together with actual small candles that were held to the branch with a small clip base. On Christmas Eve we would light the candles, taking great care not to set the house on fire! Though the candle tradition has died out, my mom still makes *bredele de Noël* every year during the month of December. She was one of nine children from a family of very modest means. When she and her brothers and sisters were children *bredele de Noël*, a mandarin orange, and a piece of chocolate were what they got as Christmas presents. To her this was a piece of heaven. I hope that when you try these cookies, you will feel the same way.

METHOD

1 Sift the flour and the almond flour and combine them in a bowl. Add the cinnamon.

2 Place the butter, vanilla, sugar, and sea salt in the bowl of your mixer and mix with the paddle for 2 minutes on medium speed. Add the egg and mix

BEFORE YOU BEGIN

→ Get out the following equipment and allow all of the ingredients to come to room temperature:

Digital scale, set to metric weights
1 sifter
1 medium mixing bowl
KitchenAid or stand mixer fitted with the paddle attachment
1 rubber spatula
1 bowl scraper
Plastic wrap
1 sheet pan lined with parchment paper
1 rolling pin
Assorted cookie cutters
1 pastry brush

NOTE: The butter should be soft.

→ Read this recipe through twice from start to finish.

UNDERSTANDING INGREDIENTS

We use all-purpose flour for these cookies because it gives the dough more
structure than cake flour. If you use
bread flour, which contains more gluten,
your dough will be rubbery. If you want
a more delicate, crumbly cookie you
can substitute cake flour for half of the
all-purpose flour. The almond flour contributes a rich nutty flavor to the dough.
The butter gives it rich flavor and is the
main reason why the dough is so flaky.

for another 2 minutes. Scrape the bottom of the mixing bowl with a rubber
spatula to make sure that all the ingredients are mixed together.

3 Add the dry ingredients and mix until they just come together. Stop the
machine and scrape the bottom and sides of the bowl and the paddle, then
beat again just until the dough is amalgamated. Do not over-beat or you
will activate the gluten in the flour and the dough will be rubbery. Scrape
the dough out of the mixer onto a sheet of plastic wrap. Divide into 2 equal
pieces and press each piece gently until it is about ½ to ¾ inch thick. Wrap
airtight and refrigerate for at least 2 hours and preferably overnight to allow
the flour to absorb the water in the dough. This will make the dough much
more stable and easier to roll out.

4 When you are ready to roll out the dough and shape and bake the cookies, preheat the oven to 325°F/160°C with the rack positioned in the middle.
Line the sheet pans with parchment paper. Lightly dust your work surface or
a silpat with flour. It may be easiest to cut each piece of dough in half and
roll out 1 small piece at a time. Take the piece you are going to roll out from
the refrigerator and let sit at room temperature for 5 minutes. Then roll out
to ³⁄₁₆ of an inch. Cut into shapes with the cookie cutters of your choice and
place on the sheet pans. Do not cut on the silpat.

5 Brush the tops of the cookies lightly with egg wash, taking care not to
allow it to drip down the sides of the cookies. Let sit for 10 minutes and apply
a second thin layer of egg wash.

6 Bake for 15 to 20 minutes, reversing the pan front to back halfway through,
until they are golden brown throughout. The low oven temperature will allow
all of the water to evaporate, resulting in a very flaky cookie.

IT'S DONE WHEN IT'S DONE

The finished product should be golden brown throughout. This means that
you have baked it long enough.

STORAGE

The cookies will keep for 1 month in a tin or an airtight container.

ANISE COOKIES /
PETITS FOURS À L'ANIS / ANIS BREDELE

YIELD | 60 COOKIES

INGREDIENTS	WEIGHT	MEASURE (APPROXIMATE)
Cake flour	150 grams	1⅓ cups
Spanish anise seeds	4 grams	2 teaspoons
Whole eggs	90 grams	2 eggs less about 4 teaspoons
Granulated sugar	150 grams	¾ cup
Sea salt	1.5 grams	Scant ¼ teaspoon

These round, dry cookies have a white shell on top and a golden brown foot on the bottom. Their delicious anise flavor is subtle at first but becomes more distinctive as they mature. Though the shell of this cookie looks like a *macaron* shell, anise cookies are never sandwiched together like *macarons* and they are dry all the way through. They are great to eat with coffee or tea. When I was a kid I liked to dip mine in coffee, even though my mom grimaced when she saw me do it and insisted that dipping cookies was not done. But I still like to dip my anise cookies today.

Anise was one of the first spices to be used in Alsace. Green anise (not to be confused with star anise, a different plant altogether) originated in Asia and adapted well to the European climate. It has been used medicinally as a muscle relaxant since antiquity. Some say that it has aphrodisiac properties, but after years of eating anise cookies I am still waiting for those effects to kick in.

Records of anise cookies go back as far as the 1600s. Called *anisbredele* or *anisbrot*, they were made during Advent and were one of the most popular end-of-the-year holiday cookies. Two types of anise cookies that utilize different techniques eventually emerged. One type is the piped cookies that we are making in this recipe, where the batter is piped onto parchment paper–covered sheet pans and left to dry before they are baked. The other type of cookie is made from a stiffer dough that is rolled out and pressed, like gingerbread cookies, into wooden molds called *springerle.*

BEFORE YOU BEGIN

→ Get out the following equipment and allow all of the ingredients to come to room temperature:

Digital scale, set to metric weights
1 sifter
KitchenAid or stand mixer fitted with the whisk attachment
1 rubber spatula
1 bowl scraper
1 pastry bag fitted with a ⅜-inch round tip
2 sheet pans lined with silpats

→ Read this recipe through twice from start to finish.

The moisture in the whole eggs is what makes these cookies puff when they bake. The mixture is similar to a sponge mixture and it is handled like a *macaron*, in the sense that you pipe small rounds of the batter onto a silpat-lined sheet pan and then let them dry out for 45 minutes or longer, until a skin forms on top. When the cookies bake the water in the eggs escapes upward, making the cookies rise slightly.

For this recipe I use green (Spanish) anise seeds, a spice that originally came from Asia but is now common in many parts of the world. Anise seeds have a strong but not overpowering flavor (star anise is much stronger). In pastry, we use them in gingerbread recipes and confectionery. Green anise is also used in the famous French aperitif called pastis. My grandmother would sprinkle anise seeds around the house during the summer to keep bugs away. This recipe requires seeds; do not substitute ground anise or star anise, as the flavor of those ingredients is too strong.

JACQUY'S TAKEAWAYS

→ This is a sponge mixture, and like all sponge mixtures you cannot refrigerate or freeze the raw dough or it will collapse.

METHOD

1 Sift the flour and add the anise to it.

2 Place the eggs, sugar, and sea salt in the mixer and whip on high speed for 3 minutes. Lower the speed to medium and whip for another 3 minutes.

3 Remove the mixing bowl from the stand, add the flour and anise to the egg mixture, and gently fold in, making sure that with each fold you scrape the bottom of the bowl with your spatula and tilt the bowl so that the dry ingredients don't settle on the bottom. Fold only until the flour is completely incorporated—no longer, or the mixture will start to collapse.

4 With the bowl scraper, scrape the mixture into the pastry bag fitted with the ⅜-inch round tip and pipe 1 ¼-inch rounds onto the sheet pans lined with silpats. Leave 1 inch of space between each cookie and stagger the rows. When you first pipe the rounds you will see a small tip, but it should disappear on its own and the cookie should look like a round, smooth disk. Sprinkle the cookies evenly with granulated sugar. Let the cookies dry at room temperature for 45 minutes or longer, up to 24 hours in humid weather, until a skin has formed on the surface. You should be able to touch the surface without leaving a mark and without the batter sticking to your finger. The temperature and humidity in your room will be a factor in the time it takes for the cookies to form a skin.

5 Meanwhile, preheat the oven to 350°F/180°C and arrange the rack in the middle.

6 When the cookies have formed a skin, bake 1 sheet pan at a time, opening the oven door quickly so that you do not lose too much heat. Close the door and let the cookies bake at 350°F/180°C for 10 minutes, until they start to rise, then turn the heat down to 300°F/150°C and bake them for another 8 minutes. Remove from the oven and cool.

IT'S DONE WHEN IT'S DONE

The tops of the cookies should be rounded, and they should have a foot created by the rising. The foot should be golden brown, but the top of the cookie should be off-white.

STORAGE

This is a dry cookie that can be kept in an airtight tin for 1 month. They cannot be refrigerated or frozen.

If you are ever in Alsace, don't miss La Maison Lips in Gertwiller, a bakery owned by Michel Habsiger that has specialized in gingerbread for over 200 years. The bakery houses a fascinating gingerbread museum where you can see a beautiful collection of *springerle*, or wooden cookie molds, as well as antique earthenware molds.

SPRITZ COOKIES / SPRITZ BREDELE

INGREDIENTS	WEIGHT	MEASURE (APPROXIMATE) OR OUNCE WEIGHT
Egg yolks, cooked using instructions below	80 grams	6 to 7 yolks
Sea salt	Pinch	Pinch
All-purpose flour	275 grams	2⅕ scant cups
Baking powder	1.5 grams	½ teaspoon
Butter (French style, 82% fat), softened	175 grams	6 ounces
Sea salt	1 gram	⅛ teaspoon
Granulated sugar	150 grams	¾ cup
Vanilla extract	5 grams	1 teaspoon
Almond flour, skinless	40 grams	Rounded ⅓ cup
Finely chopped hazelnuts	75 grams	½ cup

BEFORE YOU BEGIN

→ Get out the following equipment and allow all of the ingredients to come to room temperature:

Digital scale, set to metric weights

1 medium saucepan

Ice cubes

1 sieve or sifter

1 small bowl or cup

Plastic wrap

KitchenAid or stand mixer fitted with the paddle attachment

1 rubber spatula

1 cookie press with ½-inch star attachment

3 sheet pans lined with parchment paper

→ Read this recipe through twice from start to finish.

This pressed cookie is another iconic Alsatian Christmas cookie. The dough is a type of *sablée* dough but has the particularity of using cooked egg yolks. A fresh uncooked egg yolk consists of 50 percent water, which binds all the ingredients in the dough together and makes it firmer due to the gluten activation. If you cook the egg yolks you eliminate some of the water in the mixture. This makes the raw dough more difficult to roll out and the baked cookie more crumbly because there is less gluten activation. The good news is that you do not have to roll out this dough; instead you put it straight into a cookie press. If you do not have a cookie press, you can shape the dough into a log and cut round cookies. They won't look like traditional *spritz* but they will taste great.

My siblings and I know a lot about making *spritz* cookies. From the time we were tall enough to reach the top of a worktable we were allocated the task of making them. My dad would make 25 pounds of dough the day before, and our job was to press out the *spritz* cookies after we came back from school, while he was napping. We would place the dough in a manual meat grinder fitted with a star-shaped attachment, a system that resembles toy clay extruders. The meat grinder was carefully attached to the wooden worktable. One of us would fill the opening of the machine with dough and turn the hand crank while another would catch the cookies as they came out and press and place them in rows on large sheet

We use cooked egg yolks in this recipe in order to produce a more crumbly cookie. The almond flour contributes a nice flavor and the chopped hazelnuts add great texture.

pans. It was a very efficient way to make the cookies, but at the time it seemed more like forced labor than fun. Twenty-five pounds of dough felt like 2,000. We would bicker about who should be doing what, and eventually we would switch jobs because our arms would hurt from the heavy cranking. Every once in a while someone would clip the end of a finger on the spiral inside the meat grinder. That taught us to be careful.

When my dad woke up at around five p.m. he would bake the cookies and we were always allowed to eat some. They were a labor of love, and they tasted fantastic. Every time I eat a *spritz* cookie the image of us children extruding pounds and pounds of these cookies pops into my head. It always makes me smile. I encourage you to cultivate the tradition of making cookies with your children; as long as you don't force them to press 25 pounds of dough, they will thank you later in life for doing so.

METHOD

1 Place 7 whole eggs in a medium saucepan and fill the pan with cold water, making sure that there is at least ¾ inch of water above the eggs. Add a pinch of sea salt and bring to a boil over medium-high heat. When the water reaches a boil reduce the heat to medium and cook for 10 minutes. Place the saucepan in the sink and pour out most of the hot water. Run cold water into the saucepan for 30 seconds and turn it off. Add ice cubes to the pan and set aside. Let the eggs cool completely; it should take 20 minutes. Peel the eggs under a small stream of water. Cut in half and separate the yolks and whites. Weigh out 80 grams of egg yolks and put them through a sieve or sifter. Set aside in a small bowl or cup, covered with plastic wrap.

2 Preheat the oven to 325°F/160°C with the rack positioned in the middle.

3 Sift the all-purpose flour with the baking powder.

4 Place the soft butter with the sea salt and granulated sugar in the bowl of your mixer. Mix with the paddle for 1 minute on medium speed. Scrape down the sides of the bowl and the paddle. Add the cooked egg yolk, vanilla, and almond flour and mix for another minute on medium speed. Scrape down the bowl and beater. Add the flour and baking powder mixture as well as the finely chopped hazelnuts. Mix only until the dough comes together.

5 Scrape the dough into a cookie press fitted with a ½-inch star attachment and press out long strips, then make S shapes or U shapes and place on sheet pans lined with parchment paper. Leave ½ inch of space between the cookies and stagger the rows.

6 Bake 1 sheet pan at a time for 15 to 18 minutes, rotating the tray front to back halfway through, until golden. Remove from the heat and allow to cool completely before handling.

IT'S DONE WHEN IT'S DONE

The cookies should be golden brown and crunchy once they are cool.

STORAGE

Keep in an airtight container such as a metal tin. They will keep for 2 to 3 weeks.

CINNAMON STARS / ETOILES À LA CANELLE / ZIMTSTERNE

YIELD | 45 TO 55 COOKIES (DEPENDING ON THE SIZE)

INGREDIENTS	WEIGHT	MEASURE (APPROXIMATE) OR OUNCE WEIGHT
COOKIE DOUGH		
Almond flour, skinless	250 grams	2½ cups
Granulated sugar	250 grams	Scant 1¼ cups
Ground cinnamon	10 grams	1 tablespoon plus 2 teaspoons
Egg whites	50 grams	About 1½ whites
Lemon juice, freshly squeezed	20 grams	1 tablespoon plus 2 teaspoons
ROYAL ICING		
Confectioners' sugar	250 grams	2 cups
Lemon juice, freshly squeezed	5 grams	1 teaspoon
Egg whites	25 grams	About ¾ white
Water or kirschwasser	As needed	As needed
Additional almond flour	As needed	As needed

Zimtsterne, or cinnamon stars—moist, chewy, spiced, star-shaped, almond-meal cookies glazed with royal icing—date back to the fourteenth century and are among the most iconic of the many Alsatian Christmas cookies. The cookie is somewhat labor intensive to make, as it involves rolling out dough, brushing it with royal icing, and cutting many stars, then remixing the scraps with more almond flour and rolling, icing, and cutting again, and so on until all of the dough is used up. But the cookies are worth the time, and today I find them enjoyable to make, especially since the number I make now is small compared to the number I had to make during the days of my apprenticeship.

The Christmas-cookie season always involved a fair amount of friction among the apprentices when I was learning my craft. Our boss would dispatch the schedule for his holiday production to his two main pastry chefs, who would then allocate each individual task to the apprentices. Fierce negotiations would take place in our dorm at night after work. We could argue only so much, though, since any reports of insubordinate behavior from the chefs to the boss would open the gates of hell for the entire holiday season.

When I told this story to my colleague at the French Pastry School, Chef Pierre Zimmermann, he said that he never had this problem at his

BEFORE YOU BEGIN

→ Get out the following equipment and allow all of the ingredients to come to room temperature:

Digital scale, set to metric weights
1 sifter
KitchenAid or stand mixer fitted with the paddle attachment
1 bowl scraper
1 silpat
Two ⅜- to ½-inch-high bars
Parchment paper
1 rolling pin
1 offset spatula
1 small bowl
One 2-inch-wide star cookie cutter
2 sheet pans lined with silpats or greased parchment paper

→ Read this recipe through twice from start to finish.

family bakery. His father, Albert, would always make the cinnamon stars alone on his day off during the holiday baking season. Apparently he would look at it as a way to relax and meditate. Indeed, pastry making, which requires so much patience and attention, can be a meditative activity.

METHOD

1 Sift the almond flour. Place the almond flour, granulated sugar, and cinnamon in a mixer and mix with a paddle for 30 seconds on low speed. Add the egg whites and lemon juice and mix on medium speed until the dough comes together. Scrape out onto a silpat and place on your work surface.

2 Place a ⅜- to ½-inch bar on each side of the dough to facilitate even rolling. Top the dough with a sheet of parchment paper and roll out the dough until it is ⅜ to ½ inch thick. Let it sit while you prepare the royal icing.

3 Prepare the royal icing. Sift the confectioner sugar into the bowl of your mixer. Attach the paddle and mix at low speed while you add the lemon juice and then the egg whites. Turn the speed up to medium and mix on medium speed for 3 minutes or until the icing looks like toothpaste. If it is too thick add a very small amount of egg whites (be careful, as a little goes a long way). If the mixture is too soft, add some sifted confectioners' sugar.

4 Using your offset spatula, spread a thin, even layer of the royal icing, about ⅟₁₆ inch thick, over the top of the dough.

5 Fill a small bowl with water or kirschwasser (traditional in Alsace, the kirschwasser gives the cookies a wonderful flavor). Dip your cookie cutter into the water or kirschwasser and cut out the cookies. Dip your cutter each time you cut a cookie to prevent the dough from sticking. You still may have to ease it out of the cookie cutter when you transfer it to the sheet pan. Place each cookie on a sheet pan lined with a silpat or a sheet of greased parchment paper, taking care to leave ½ inch of space in between each of them. Make sure to position the cookie cutter close to the previous cut so that you don't have much waste.

6 Once all the cookies are cut, weigh the excess dough and place in the mixing bowl. Add 10 percent of almond flour to it and mix for 30 seconds, until the dough comes together. It should have the same consistency as the original dough; if it seems too soft, add a little more almond flour. Roll the dough again. Beat the icing again and spread a thin layer over the dough using an offset spatula. Cut out more stars and repeat the process, weighing the excess dough each time and mixing with 10 percent almond flour or as needed, until you have no more dough. If the royal icing hardens add a little more egg

UNDERSTANDING INGREDIENTS

This is a very moist cookie, and, as always, when moisture is called for in a pastry, almonds are your nut and almond flour your flour. This cookie also owes its moist texture to the fact that it is not fully baked in the center. We achieve this by transferring the shaped cookie dough directly from the refrigerator or even the freezer to the oven. The heat of the oven will do what it usually does—bake things from the outside in—and the cookie will be baked on the outside while the center is just about coagulated but not fully baked. The cookie will not spoil over time because of the acidity of the cinnamon and lemon juice. The royal icing provides a nice look, but it is also a great protection for the cookie, allowing it to remain moist for weeks.

For the cinnamon I prefer Ceylon cinnamon.

white; it should always have the consistency of toothpaste. Place the cookies in the freezer for 2 hours.

7 Preheat the oven to 350°F/180°C. Bake 1 sheet pan at a time for 10 minutes, until the royal icing begins to color slightly. Remove from the heat and allow to cool before removing from the sheet pan.

IT'S DONE WHEN IT'S DONE

The royal icing should be a little off-white, and the baked cookies should not stick to the paper or silpat once they are cool.

STORAGE

Keep the cookies in an airtight container; they will stay moist for 2 to 3 weeks.

LEMON MIRRORS / MIROIRS CITRON

INGREDIENTS	WEIGHT	MEASURE (APPROXIMATE) OR OUNCE WEIGHT
ICING		
Confectioners' sugar	50 grams	½ cup
Lemon juice, freshly squeezed	6 to 12 grams	1¼ to 2½ teaspoons
Water	6 grams	1 teaspoon
ALMOND CREAM FILLING		
Candied Lemon Peel (PAGE 87)	20 grams	1 tablespoon
Almond Cream (PAGE 43)	100 grams	6 tablespoons
MERINGUE COOKIE BASE		
Confectioners' sugar	50 grams	½ cup
Almond flour, with skin	50 grams	½ cup
Egg whites	100 grams	3 whites plus 1 tablespoon
Sea salt	0.5 gram	Pinch
Cream of tartar	0.5 gram	Pinch
Granulated sugar	10 grams	2 teaspoons
TOPPING		
Sliced almonds, with skin	50 to 100 grams	Scant ½ to 1 cup
Apricot jelly	100 grams	Scant ¼ cup

These delicate, nutty cookies are called mirrors because the final glaze makes them shiny and almost reflective, like a mirror. The cookies consist of piped rings of nutty meringue filled with almond cream that are baked and glazed first with apricot jam, then with sugar icing.

The recipe requires Almond Cream (PAGE 43) and Candied Lemon Peels (PAGE 87). You can, however, make these cookies if you don't have lemon peel on hand: simply use twice as much lemon juice in the icing and no water.

METHOD

1 Make the sugar icing by mixing together the sifted 50 grams of confectioners' sugar with 6 grams of lemon juice and 6 grams of water. If you are not using candied lemon peel, use 12 grams of lemon juice and omit the water.

2 Chop the candied lemon peel, if using, until it becomes a paste and

The almond flour gives the meringues their nutty flavor. When the meringue is baked, it turns slightly crispy and protects the almond cream filling from becoming dry. I like to use almonds with skin for this cookie just because it adds character to the recipe, but skinned almonds work as well. The apricot jelly and sugar icing both give the cookie its mirror-like sheen and prevent the cookie from drying out.

combine with the almond cream in a medium mixing bowl. Scrape the lemon almond cream into a disposable pastry bag fitted with a ¼-inch tip and set it aside.

3 Preheat the oven to 325°F/160°C.

4 Sift together the confectioners' sugar and almond flour onto a sheet of parchment paper.

5 Place the egg whites, sea salt, and cream of tartar in the bowl of your standing mixer and whisk together for 10 seconds on medium. Add the sugar and whip on high for 1 to 2 minutes, until you have a meringue with soft peaks (SEE PAGE 69). Gently and carefully fold in the sifted confectioners' sugar and almond flour with a rubber spatula until the mixture is homogenous. *Make sure that you do not over-mix. Over-mixing the meringue mixture will make it soupy and the baked cookies will be gummy.*

6 Using a bowl scraper, carefully transfer the mixture to a pastry bag fitted with a ⅜-inch round tip. Do this gently so that you don't deflate the mixture. Pipe 1½-inch rings onto the sheet pan lined with parchment paper, leaving ½ inch of space between each cookie and making sure to stagger the rows. Sprinkle the edge of each ring with sliced almonds.

7 Pipe the almond cream into the center of each ring.

8 Place in the preheated oven and bake for 15 minutes, until golden brown.

9 While the cookies are baking, warm the apricot jelly in a small saucepan just until it becomes liquid. Have it ready for brushing the cookies, along with the sugar icing.

10 As soon as you pull them out of the oven, brush each cookie with the apricot jelly while hot, then right away with the sugar icing. Keep the apricot jelly warm over the lowest heat possible so that it won't seize up. If this happens, just warm it up a little more and it will become liquid again. Allow the cookies to cool completely before removing from the parchment paper.

IT'S DONE WHEN IT'S DONE

The cookies should be golden brown. The double glazing should create a mirror-like appearance and the surface of the cookie should not be sticky anymore. Once cool, they should release easily from the parchment paper.

STORAGE

The cookies keep for 1 week in an airtight container at room temperature. They should not be refrigerated or frozen once they are baked or they will become soggy.

DURING MY APPRENTICESHIP, Tuesday was cookie production day. It was always a difficult day for us, as Jean Clauss made a huge selection of petits fours—in this book I'm only giving you a snippet of the repertoire we made on a regular basis—so we had to come in very early after our day off, Monday, when many pastry shops in France are closed. We were never at the top of our game on Tuesday morning, and that made Jean Clauss crankier than usual, since he had to rally us to not only make the bakery recipes for Tuesday morning but also begin cookie production for the entire week.

Because Jean Clauss was so old-fashioned and set in his ways (like every true Alsatian), he didn't use much parchment paper in his pastry shop, and silpats didn't exist back then. We would pipe *miroirs* directly onto black steel sheet pans. Part of my job as a first-year apprentice was cleaning those sheet pans—about 100 of them—every day. First I would have to scrape them off to remove all of the flour and grease that had been baked on. Then I would wipe them with a rag. The black sheet pans got their patina from the grease burned into the metal, and the smell of that grease is forever embedded in my brain. To this day, I am bothered by pans that smell like rancid grease.

To make the *miroir* cookies I would first brush the sheet pans with melted butter and then dust them with a thin layer of flour. Then I would pipe rings of nutty meringue—another great way for me to sharpen my piping skills—and spoon a blob of almond cream filling in the middle. These are two very different techniques that I would have a chance to practice every Tuesday. Practice piping these cookies for a while, and soon you will be so comfortable that you may come up with your own design.

INGREDIENTS	WEIGHT	MEASURE (APPROXIMATE) OR OUNCE WEIGHT
Hazelnut Praline Paste (PAGE 57)	200 grams	⅔ cup
Cake flour	125 grams	1 cup plus 4 teaspoons
Butter	150 grams	5¼ ounces
Sea salt	1 gram	⅛ teaspoon
Granulated sugar	80 grams	Heaped ⅓ cup
Almond flour, skinless	60 grams	½ cup plus 1 tablespoon
Egg whites	30 grams	1 extra-large white less 1 to 2 teaspoons
Vanilla extract	5 grams	1 teaspoon
Tempered dark chocolate (PAGE 208)	200 grams	7 ounces

This is one of many cookies that I learned to make during my apprenticeship, a delicious piped butter cookie sandwiched together with hazelnut praline paste and dipped in chocolate. The butter cookie, hazelnut, and chocolate combination is one of the most appealing and popular flavor combinations in pastry.

Making these cookies is a great way for you to practice your piping. Follow my piping directions on PAGES 15–20, and after a few batches you should become very comfortable with making teardrops.

METHOD

1 Make the praline paste ahead of time and set aside in a disposable pastry bag fitted with a ¼-inch round tip.

2 Sift the flour into a bowl and set aside.

3 Place the soft butter with the sea salt and sugar in the bowl of your standing mixer and mix with the paddle for 1 minute on medium speed. Add the almond flour, egg whites, and vanilla extract and mix just until incorporated.

4 Add the sifted flour and mix for 30 seconds only on low speed, just until incorporated. Do not over-mix or you will activate the gluten in the flour and your cookies will not be delicate.

5 Using a bowl scraper, scrape the mixture into a pastry bag fitted with a ⅜-inch star tip. Pipe 1½-inch-long flat teardrop cookies onto the parchment paper–lined sheet pans, leaving ½ inch space in between them and stagger-

BEFORE YOU BEGIN

→ Get out the following equipment and allow all of the ingredients to come to room temperature:

Digital scale, set to metric weights
1 pastry bag fitted with a ¼-inch round tip
1 sifter
1 medium mixing bowl
KitchenAid or stand mixer fitted with the paddle attachment
1 bowl scraper
1 pastry bag fitted with a ⅜-inch star tip
2 sheet pans lined with parchment paper

→ Read this recipe through twice from start to finish.

I like to use cake flour for this recipe because with its low gluten content it results in a very delicate cookie. But if you find that the cookies flatten out during baking, then try using half cake and half all-purpose flour. There's a lot of butter in these cookies, which gives them a rich flavor and makes the batter creamy and easy to pipe.

The butter cookies will be "glued" together with hazelnut praline paste, but it is actually the cookie that keeps the paste moist and creamy. The dark chocolate keeps the two firmly stuck together and contributes wonderful flavor.

JACQUY'S TAKEAWAYS

→ You could substitute another type of nut flour such as hazelnut for the almond flour, and use a different nut for the praline paste. You can also interchange the type of chocolate. Lastly, you can vary the fillings, using jam or ganache instead of the praline paste.

---

ing the rows. Hold the pastry bag with the tip at a 45-degree angle, close to the sheet pan (about ¼ inch away). Continue to press on the bag and swing the tip toward you while you progressively stop pressing, so that the teardrop ends in a tail.

6 Let the cookies rest at room temperature for 1 hour. Meanwhile, 30 minutes before baking preheat the oven to 375°F/190°C.

7 Bake the cookies for 15 minutes, until golden brown. Remove from the heat and cool completely.

8 Once cool, flip half of the cookies over and pipe on a small amount of praline paste. Top with another cookie and press down lightly to sandwich together.

9 Temper the chocolate following the instructions beginning on PAGE 208. Dip the tail of each cookie into the tempered chocolate following the instructions on PAGE 211 and place the cookies on parchment paper. Let the chocolate harden and then keep the cookies in an airtight container.

IT'S DONE WHEN IT'S DONE

The baked cookies will have flattened out very slightly and should be golden brown when baked; they should be very buttery.

STORAGE

Store the cookies in an airtight container. They will keep for at least 2 weeks. Do not refrigerate. They can be frozen for up to 1 month, but they will lose some of their crunch.

BEFORE YOU BEGIN

✦ Get out the following equipment:

Digital scale, set to metric weights
1 medium microwave-safe bowl
1 large rubber spatula
1 paring knife
Twelve 1 × 1–inch parchment paper
   squares
1 digital thermometer
1 hand towel

✦ Read this recipe through twice from start to finish.

NOTE: It is very difficult for any fat to crystallize when it is in a warm environment. To temper chocolate you need to work in a cool room that is no hotter than 75°F.

When you temper chocolate, you make it stable so that it will remain in its solid state after it cools. To get it to this state, the chocolate is very slowly heated and cooled in such a way that it hardens and stabilizes, or "sets." Chemically you are causing the fat molecules in the chocolate—the cocoa butter—to crystallize in such a way that the crystals are uniform and small. This is necessary for the chocolate to set properly.

When you temper chocolate you should only use couverture, which is chocolate that contains at least 31 percent cocoa butter, the element in chocolate that makes it melt in your mouth. Do not use coating chocolate, which uses artificial fats that imitate cocoa butter but have the taste and properties of paraffin. They do not crystallize in the same way as cocoa butter, and proper crystallization is the key to tempering chocolate.

You can temper dark, milk, or white chocolate as long as it's couverture. Dark chocolate couverture consists of cocoa paste (the natural cocoa solids in the cocoa bean), granulated sugar, and cocoa butter (the natural fat in the cocoa bean). Milk chocolate is the same, but milk powder is added to those ingredients, making this a pleasant chocolate to eat. White chocolate contains cocoa butter, granulated sugar, and milk powder but no cocoa solids.

No matter which chocolate couverture you want to use, it is important to know that the water content of all of these chocolates is zero. This explains their long shelf life. Without the presence of water, bacteria cannot easily grow. That's why chocolate never needs to be kept in a refrigerator or freezer; it should always be kept at room temperature, protected with plastic wrap.

When you need to melt chocolate couverture so that you can use it as a decoration or coating, as we do in Fours de Lin (PAGE 205), the chocolate must be melted in a controlled way so that some of the cocoa butter remains in crystal form and all of the crystals are small and of a uniform size once the chocolate hardens. If you have more crystallized cocoa butter molecules present in the melted chocolate than melted ones the chocolate will set properly. If too much of the cocoa butter in the chocolate is melted it will not set, or at least not for several hours.

The cocoa butter in the chocolate couverture that you purchase has already been put through the tempering process; the crystals have been reduced to a small and uniform size, which makes them stable and will ensure that the chocolate will set properly. Tempering chocolate will ensure that they don't lose this structure after the chocolate has been heated and cooled.

METHOD

Here are two ways to temper chocolate; both methods work well. The first is called the direct method, and the second is called the seeding method. No matter which process you use, it's best to use a microwave at 50 percent power rather than a water bath or double boiler to heat the chocolate. It would be disastrous if a drop of water got into the chocolate. Since chocolate does not contain any water at all, if any liquid gets in, the solids absorb it in a second and the chocolate will clump. Trying to stir in the clump actually speeds up the clumping process. You will not be able to use the chocolate for tempering and will have to begin again.

It's also best not to try to temper all of the chocolate you have at once. That way if your chocolate couverture gets too hot, you can add solid pieces of chocolate couverture to it (the seeding method described in the second method below) to even out the crystallization. Always have 33 percent of the weight of the chocolate you are heating set aside.

One thing to keep in mind is that the more chocolate you use, the slower the cooling process, because the more you use, the more it retains its heat. If you are working with a small amount of chocolate it will cool more quickly and you will have to heat it more often and thus risk overheating it. If you only need a small amount of tempered chocolate for your recipe, it's better to temper more than you need and store the leftovers.

DIRECT METHOD

The direct method is simple; it assumes that the chocolate couverture you are using is made with the right type of small, uniform crystals for tempering. The method does not require a thermometer, just close attention. It involves melting the chocolate couverture slowly so that you always have more crystallized cocoa butter crystals than melted ones in the mixture.

1 Let's say you have a 450-gram (1-pound) bar of chocolate couverture or 450 grams of chocolate couverture coins. If working with a bar, chop it finely and evenly into ¼-inch pieces. Place 300 grams of the finely chopped chocolate couverture or chocolate couverture coins in a microwave-safe bowl and microwave for 1 minute at 50 percent power. It's crucial to always use 50 percent power, as 100 percent power is too hot and will burn the chocolate. Remove from the microwave, stir with a rubber spatula, and microwave for another full minute. Stir again. When you stir make sure that the bottom of the spatula is submerged in the chocolate and constantly touching the bottom of the mixing bowl. Make sure that your mixing bowl is small enough to allow this. It's very important that you stir and not fold, as when you fold you introduce air into the chocolate and create air bubbles.

2 Now microwave the chocolate for 30 seconds at 50 percent power and stir for a full minute. You should now see that the chocolate is starting to melt, which is good news. The trick is not to overheat it at this point. Dip the end of a paring knife or the corner of one of the 1 × 1–inch squares of parchment paper into the melted portion of the chocolate and put it on the counter for 2 full minutes. The chocolate should set. If it does not, refer to the Troubleshooting section at the end of the recipe.

3 Now you will heat the chocolate in shorter and shorter blasts (always at 50 percent power), stirring it after each time and testing the chocolate with the paring knife or parchment paper, until it is just about smooth. The smaller amount of chocolate you are tempering, the quicker this process will be. By observing the proportion of lumps remaining in the chocolate you will determine how many more times you should microwave it, but each time should be shorter than the time before. The more you melt it, the smoother it gets and the fewer lumps of hard chocolate you will see. Seeing a couple of unmelted chocolate coins or pieces in the chocolate should be encouraging, as it indicates that the chocolate has not overheated. But only the paring knife/parchment paper test will prove that. The closer you get to having a smooth chocolate, the more careful you have to be with your microwaving; some microwaves are more powerful than others. If you are not sure about the length of time to use, always be conservative.

4 Once almost all the chocolate is melted, stir for 1 full minute and make a final test with the paring knife. If the chocolate sets within 2 minutes you are ready to go.

SEEDING METHOD

The seeding method is also simple. It involves controlling the crystallization of the melting chocolate by introducing unmelted chocolate into the mix. The amount you add to the mix is 33 percent of the weight of the first amount you melted. For example, if you begin with 300 grams of finely chopped chocolate couverture or chocolate couverture coins you will need to also weigh out 99 grams of finely chopped chocolate couverture or chocolate couverture coins. This method requires a thermometer.

1 Place 300 grams of finely chopped dark chocolate couverture or chocolate couverture coins in a medium-sized microwave-safe bowl. Microwave for

1 minute at 50 percent power. Remove from the microwave, stir with a rubber spatula, and microwave for another full minute at 50 percent power. Stir again for 20 seconds. When you stir, make sure that the bottom of the spatula is submerged in the chocolate and constantly touching the bottom of the mixing bowl. Make sure that your mixing bowl is small enough to allow this. It's very important that you stir and not fold, as when you fold you introduce air into the chocolate and create air bubbles. Continue this process until you see the chocolate melt; once this happens, reduce the microwave time to 30 seconds at 50 percent power.

2   Take the temperature of your melted chocolate. Melt dark chocolate in 30-second increments at 50 percent power until it reaches 113°F/45°C. Melt milk and white chocolates to 104°F/40°C.

3   Place the bowl of melted chocolate on your counter and add 99 grams of finely chopped chocolate couverture or chocolate couverture coins. Stir for 3 full minutes, taking care to keep your spatula submerged in the chocolate the entire time. The long stirring is required to equalize the temperature of the melted chocolate and the hard chocolate. Dip the end of a paring knife or the corner of a 1 × 1–inch square of parchment paper into the chocolate and set on the counter for 2 full minutes. The chocolate should be hard. If it is not, refer to the Troubleshooting section at the end of the recipe.

4   At this point your chocolate is probably lumpy. In order to make it nice and fluid, you need to melt most of the lumps. The trick is to do this very carefully without melting too much cocoa butter. I recommend microwaving the chocolate in 10- to 15-second increments at 50 percent power and stirring for 1 full minute after each blast to make sure that the temperature has a chance to even out. Test the chocolate with the paring knife or parchment paper after each microwave zap and stir to make sure that the chocolate still sets. The more the lumps melt, the closer you get to having a perfectly fluid chocolate, but also the closer you get to having more melted cocoa butter crystals than solid ones. If you are not sure about the length of time to use, always be conservative and use less. I like to see 1 or 2 small lumps at the end of the process. You can now use the chocolate and dip the cookies.

DIPPING THE COOKIES

Place the bowl on a folded towel and dip your cookies. The towel will create a buffer between the bowl and the table and prevent the chocolate from seizing up too quickly. If the chocolate does begin to feel thick, do not stir it, because you will emulsify the fat and create air bubbles that cannot be removed. Instead, warm it again for a short time at 50 percent power in the microwave and then stir. The amount of time you warm the chocolate for will depend on the amount you have, but always be conservative. You can also heat the chocolate a little bit and seed it with some more coins or pieces to keep it stable.

IT'S DONE WHEN IT'S DONE

When chocolate is well tempered it is very fluid, as you have melted a lot of the cocoa butter, but it can still have a few solid pieces in it. It will also have a nice rich brown color. When you look at the light reflecting in the chocolate you should see a smooth, even, and shiny surface. Streaks indicate the trace of cocoa butter that is on the verge of crystallizing, which means the chocolate is getting too cold.

Once the chocolate is set it should have a nice crunch to it. We call this a snap. It should also have a nice rich brown color.

STORAGE

Once you are done working with the tempered chocolate, while it is still liquid pour it onto a sheet pan lined with parchment paper and spread it out thinly. Allow it to harden, and once it is cold, break it up and store in an airtight container or wrap it in plastic. You can then reuse it and it will be easier to chop it up rather than melting it in a big block. If it hardens in the bowl, simply heat the bowl in a warm oven or over a bain-marie for 30 seconds (being very careful not to let any water get into the chocolate) or until the chocolate releases from the bowl. Heat it enough to spread on the parchment paper as directed. Chocolate products should always be stored in a cool room, never in a refrigerator or a freezer. Should you have a wine cooler at home this is the absolute perfect place to store chocolate products, at around 60°F/15.5°C and 60 percent humidity.

TROUBLESHOOTING

Your chocolate can be too cold or get too hot. Both are simple problems to fix.

MY CHOCOLATE IS GETTING THICK: Eventually the melted chocolate that you are using to dip your cookies in will cool and thicken because the cocoa butter crystals get cold and seize. This is normal. You just need to warm up the chocolate slightly in the microwave for 15 seconds at 50 percent power; stir for a full minute, then do the paring knife/parchment paper test before you use it. If the test sets up, you can continue using the chocolate.

JACQUY'S TAKEAWAYS

→ The more chocolate you use in tempering, the slower the cooling process, because the more you use, the more it retains heat.
→ Properly tempered chocolate always sets in about 2 minutes.
→ Never dip fresh sliced fruit into chocolate as the juices will drip into it and make the chocolate lumpy.

MY CHOCOLATE IS NOT SETTING UP: If your chocolate is not setting up after 2 minutes it means that you have overheated it. In order to fix this, all you need to do is to crystallize some of the melted cocoa butter and cool the chocolate by adding chocolate couverture coins to it and start the process from the beginning. The amount to add is 33 percent of the weight of the chocolate.

THE CHOCOLATE SETS UP AFTER A WHILE BUT IT IS NOT SHINY: This means that it was slightly too hot. You need to cool the chocolate by adding coins (33 percent of the weight of the chocolate).

THE CHOCOLATE ON MY COOKIES WAS SHINY BUT AFTER A FEW DAYS IT LOOKS CLOUDY: Two things can cause this. The first is called "fat bloom," and it happens when finished chocolate products are exposed to a hot environment such as the closet light bulb or a heated room. The cocoa butter present in the chocolate melts on the surface and when it eventually crystallizes the crystals will be larger than usual, creating a cloudy look. The second reason is what we call "sugar bloom." This happens when there is condensation on the chocolate, resulting, for example, from having been kept in the refrigerator. In the old days air conditioning didn't exist in many homes and people kept their chocolate in the refrigerator so that it wouldn't melt. Nowadays we do not have this problem, and chocolate should always be kept at room temperature. If, for instance, you keep your chocolate candies in a refrigerator and then bring them out to room temperature to serve to your guests, you will observe a thin layer of condensation created by the change of temperature. The condensation water will melt the sugar present on the surface of the chocolate, and once the water has evaporated a cloudy finish caused by the crystals of sugar will appear.

WATER GOT INTO MY CHOCOLATE: A water bath can be used to melt chocolate, but you have to be very careful about contaminating it with the water. If a drop of water falls into the chocolate, stop stirring at once. Cut a small piece of paper towel and dip it into the area where the water is. Let the water be absorbed by the towel. Repeat the operation until all the water is gone, then continue using the chocolate as normal. If too much water gets into the chocolate and you decide to stir, the only remedy is to make a chocolate sauce with it by whisking in an equal weight of boiling cream.

COCONUT MACARON /
ROCHER À LA NOIX DE COCO

YIELD | 3 DOZEN COOKIES

2-DAY RECIPE

INGREDIENTS	WEIGHT	MEASURE (APPROXIMATE) OR OUNCE WEIGHT
Egg whites	100 grams	About 3 whites
Granulated sugar	160 grams	¾ cup
Unsweetened fine coconut flakes	100 grams	1⅓ cups
Apricot compote or applesauce	10 grams	2 teaspoons
Sea salt	1.5 grams	Scant ¼ teaspoon

My father used to make these coconut "rocks" (*rocher* means "rock" in French) nonstop year round and sell them by the kilo (a little over 2 pounds). They are a favorite in Alsace, where cookies in general are a big deal. I don't know how they became so popular; Alsace is about as far away from the land of coconuts as you can get.

The cookie always makes me think of my father's impressive strength. He would put about 5 kilos—11 pounds—of coconut—50 times more than we are making here—with all the sugar and egg whites into one big pot, set it on the gas stove, and stir the mixture with a huge spatula for what seemed like hours. He was used to stirring big quantities of dough and batter and had the muscles for it. When he trained as a baker in the early 1940s, before there was any mechanization to speak of, they would mix huge quantities of dough by hand in a big vat called a *pétrin* (*pétrir* means "to knead"). It's an amazing exercise for your fingers, arms, and forearms, and my father's were incredibly strong. He had to stir the *rocher* batter quickly or the heat would fry the egg whites (we use a double boiler for that reason), and he had to stir for a long time, about a half hour, in order to bring such a big batch to the right temperature. When I watched him do this I would always be stunned by his power. Punk that I was, one day I asked if I could try, but of course I got tired right away.

The dough for these sweet cookies is cooked on the stove until the egg whites coagulate. Then we let it rest until the moisture in the mixture is absorbed by the coconut flakes and by the pectin in the small amount of apricot or apple compote in the recipe. The baking in the oven is just to give the cookies a nice crust and color.

BEFORE YOU BEGIN

→ Get out the following equipment and allow all of the ingredients to come to room temperature:

Digital scale, set to metric weights
1 medium saucepan
1 stainless steel bowl that is larger than the saucepan
1 medium stainless steel hand whisk
1 digital thermometer
1 bowl scraper
Plastic wrap
2 sheet pans lined with parchment paper or silpats
1 small (1½-inch) ice cream scoop

→ Read this recipe through twice from start to finish.

UNDERSTANDING INGREDIENTS

I like to use fine coconut flakes for this recipe; the finer the coconut, the more it will absorb and retain moisture. If you can only find coconut in large flakes, blend them in a food processor with the sugar until you obtain a fine flake, about 1⁄16 inch wide.

This is a very sweet cookie; the salt in the recipe offsets some of the sweetness. The applesauce or apricot compote contains a good amount of pectin, which will absorb and retain the moisture in the mixture, keeping these cookies very moist.

JACQUY'S TAKEAWAYS

→ Another way to make these cookies is to pipe them onto a sheet pan with a 3⁄4-inch star tip. A smaller tip will not work, as the coconut likes to clump up. I also like to pipe them into 11⁄2 × 11⁄2–inch pyramid-shaped silicone Flexipan molds, then bake them straight in the molds. To unmold them, let them cool for 1 full hour. They will come out easily when they are completely cool.

→ You can use them frozen as part of a tropical ice cream sundae—for example combined with mango ice cream, roasted pineapple chunks, and a litchi coulis. Because they're so sweet they go well with tart tropical fruits. They also taste great dipped in tempered chocolate (PAGE 208).

Ideally, you should cook the batter on one day and let it rest overnight before making the cookies.

METHOD

DAY 1

1 Create a double boiler by pouring 3⁄4 inch of water into the saucepan and placing it on the stove over medium heat.

2 Place all the ingredients in the mixing bowl and mix them together with a whisk. Reduce the heat under the saucepan to low and place the bowl on top. It should not be touching the water. Stir continuously with a whisk—not like a maniac, but being sure to reach all areas of the bowl so that the egg whites don't coagulate throughout the mix into small white pieces. Stir until the mixture thickens and reaches 167°F/75°C. Remove from the heat, take the bowl off the pot, and wipe the bottom dry. Scrape down the sides of bowl.

3 Place a piece of plastic wrap directly over the mixture, taking care to lay the plastic right on the surface of the batter so that it is not exposed to air. Cover the bowl as well and refrigerate for at least 2 hours or preferably overnight.

DAY 2

Preheat the oven to 375°F/190°C and arrange the rack in the middle. Line the sheet pans with parchment paper or silpats and, using the 11⁄2-inch ice cream scoop, scoop the coconut mixture onto the sheet pan, leaving 1 inch between each cookie and staggering the rows. Each scoop should be leveled so that all the cookies are the same size and bake the same way. Bake the cookies for 15 to 20 minutes, 1 sheet pan at a time, until golden brown.

IT'S DONE WHEN IT'S DONE

The cookies should be a beautiful shiny and golden brown color. I like mine a little on the darker side to offset the sweetness.

STORAGE

The unbaked mixture can be refrigerated for 2 to 3 days, but you might see liquid separating in the bottom of the bowl. This is the sugar that has turned to syrup—you can just mix it back together. We do not usually freeze the mixture. You can keep the cookies for weeks in an airtight container or you can freeze them. Even frozen, they do not get hard (my wife loves to eat them that way).

TUILES AUX AMANDES

INGREDIENTS	WEIGHT	MEASURE (APPROXIMATE)
Egg whites	100 grams	About 3 whites
Sea salt	Pinch	Pinch
Granulated sugar	120 grams	½ cup plus 4 teaspoons
Cake flour	40 grams	⅓ cup
Melted butter	40 grams	1⅖ ounces
Sliced almonds	100 grams	About ¾ cup plus 2 tablespoons

Tuiles are deceptively simple and easy to make, and they are so wonderful. What makes them so special is their crisp texture. The word means "roof shingle" in French, and in French pastry we use the term in general to describe a very thin crispy cookie that can be flat, rounded, or even shaped like a bowl. When I was a boy *tuiles* were always sold from huge glass jars in French pastry shops. They would break if they were handled too roughly because they're so fragile.

The batter is very easy to mix. You just whip some egg whites with a fork to loosen them up, then add sugar, a little flour, and sometimes melted butter. Then it's ready to go. No air is whipped in, and that's one of the reasons the cookie is so crispy. The way we get the shape is by spreading a small amount of batter thinly on a silpat, sprinkling nuts on top, baking in a low oven, and, while the thin-baked cookie is still warm, draping it over a rolling pin. When I learned to make *tuiles* the recipes had the nuts mixed into the batter, but I find this inefficient, as the nuts get in the way when you are trying to spread the batter on the silpat.

It's crucial that *tuiles* bake very slowly so that all of the water in the batter has time to evaporate before the cookies get too brown. Then they'll stay crispy for weeks in a cookie tin. When properly baked, whatever nuts you put in them—almonds, in this recipe—get nice and dark, and very crunchy.

METHOD

1 Preheat the oven to 325°F/160°C.

2 Place the egg whites and the sea salt in a medium mixing bowl and whip with a fork for 30 seconds. Exchange the fork for a whisk.

BEFORE YOU BEGIN

→ Get out the following equipment and allow all of the ingredients to come to room temperature:

Digital scale, set to metric weights
1 medium mixing bowl
1 fork
1 medium stainless steel hand whisk
1 small rubber spatula
1 small spoon
4 sheet pans lined with silpats
1 small offset spatula
1 wire rack
1 rolling pin

→ Read this recipe through twice from start to finish.

3 Mix the granulated sugar with the cake flour and whisk into the egg whites. Now switch to a rubber spatula and stir in the warm melted butter.

4 Using the small spoon (a measuring teaspoon is perfect), spoon a 1¼-inch round of batter onto your silpat-lined sheet pans. Spread the mixture with the small offset spatula to obtain a flat, thin cookie that is 3 inches wide. The action of spreading is back and forth, wax on, wax off, like window wipers, with the spatula slightly angled. The *tuiles* do not have to be perfectly round; the shape can be irregular and there can be some empty spaces within the cookie. The important thing is to be sure that you leave ¾ inch of space between each *tuile* and that you stagger the rows; you will only get 5 to 6 pieces onto each sheet pan. Sprinkle sliced almonds onto each *tuile*.

5 Place the first sheet pan in the oven. Set up a wire rack on your work surface, with a rolling pin and offset spatula next to it. You will use the rolling pin to shape the *tuiles*, so place a heavy object against it to make sure that it is secured from rolling left or right. Bake the *tuiles* for 10 to 15 minutes, until the edges are golden brown. Remove from the oven and set the sheet pan on the wire rack. Allow to cool for exactly 1 minute, then slide an offset spatula under each *tuile* and place it on the rolling pin; press on it to make sure that it has a nice curved shape. The *tuiles* resting on the rolling pin will cool and hold their shape in a matter of 60 seconds. If you do not have time to shape them all and the *tuiles* on the sheet pan get hard, just put them back in the oven for 2 to 3 minutes and they will soften again.

6 Continue until you have used up all of the batter. Once the cookies have cooled, store them in an airtight container.

IT'S DONE WHEN IT'S DONE

The *tuiles* and the sliced almonds should be golden brown. This will ensure that they're sufficiently baked and that they will be crispy when they cool. It is important that the *tuiles* be fully baked. If your *tuiles* brown very quickly on the edges but not in the center, your oven is too hot; turn it down 25 degrees. *Tuiles* that are too light in the middle will not be crispy.

STORAGE

Place *tuiles* in an airtight container to keep them dry and crispy. They will keep for 2 to 3 weeks.

UNDERSTANDING INGREDIENTS

The reason we whip the egg whites just slightly when we begin mixing the batter is to break down the albumen. This will prevent the mixture from coagulating in a big block and will result in a crispier *tuile*. Flour is necessary to bind the moist mixture together, and I prefer cake flour to all-purpose flour because of its low gluten content; there is less risk of the cookies having a rubbery texture. As always, melted butter contributes a nice rich flavor.

JACQUY'S TAKEAWAYS

→ You can vary the flavorings and garnishes, using different kinds of nuts, candied peel, or spices like ground cinnamon, which you would mix in with the flour.

→ We like eating *tuiles* as cookies, but we also use them in other recipes. They can be made large enough to serve as a bowl for desserts, or a topping for a tart or a frozen mousse (see the Frozen Coffee and Chocolate Mousse on **PAGE 289**). Sometimes the batter is even spread raw on a brioche and then baked to form a crisp coating. To shape them like a bowl, drape them over a cup or a ramekin, rather than the rolling pin, while warm.

FRENCH MACARONS

YIELD | 56 *MACARONS* (112 SHELLS)

3-DAY RECIPE—5 DAYS UNTIL READY TO EAT

INGREDIENTS	WEIGHT	MEASURE (APPROXIMATE) OR OUNCE WEIGHT
Almond flour, skinless	250 grams	2½ cups
Confectioners' sugar	250 grams	2 cups
Aged egg whites (see below)	95 grams	4 fresh eggs (you will lose some weight with evaporation)
Sugar	250 grams	Scant 1¼ cups
Water	63 grams	¼ cup
Corn syrup	50 grams	2 tablespoons
Liquid food coloring	15 grams	1 tablespoon
Aged egg whites (see below)	95 grams	About 4 fresh eggs (you will lose some weight with evaporation)
Filling of your choice, such as Ganache (PAGE 72), Lemon Cream (PAGE 163), or Raspberry Jam (PAGE 80)	250 grams	8⅘ ounces

Macarons have been around for decades, but they have been enjoying a revival over the last 10 years because of their colorful and attractive look, as well as their moist and creamy textures. They're made by combining almond flour with an Italian meringue. The mixture is then piped in round flat spheres onto a sheet pan and left to dry until a skin forms on the spheres. After they are baked, two of the round shells are put together like a tiny sandwich with a stable filling like ganache, a butter cream, or jam. The cookies should be moist in the center with a thin, semi-hard shell.

⊰ ORGANIZING YOUR TIME ⊱

The trick to making successful *macarons* is to allow your egg whites to age for at least 24 hours and your almond flour to dry out. When you make this recipe, organize your time so that you give the flour 48 hours to dry before you mix up the batter. Once made, the *macarons* require a minimum of 48 hours in the refrigerator before they are moist enough to consume.

BEFORE YOU BEGIN

→ Get out the following equipment:

Digital scale, set to metric weights
1 sifter
2 to 6 sheet pans lined with parchment paper
2 medium mixing bowls
Plastic wrap
1 food processor
1 large mixing bowl
1 hard plastic or wood spatula
KitchenAid or stand mixer fitted with the whisk attachment
1 small saucepan
1 large rubber spatula
1 pastry brush
1 digital thermometer
1 bowl scraper
1 pastry bag fitted with a ⅜-inch round tip
1 spoon or a small pastry bag fitted with a ¼-inch round tip

→ Read this recipe through twice from start to finish.

NOTE: Follow Day 1 Step 1 48 hours before beginning to mix the batter.

UNDERSTANDING INGREDIENTS

Macarons require a great deal of sugar in order to form a brittle, shiny shell on the surface. You cannot reduce the amount or the recipe will fail.

Almonds are the nuts of choice because their flour absorbs moisture like no other nut flour. You cannot obtain a real French *macaron* with any other variety of nut flour. The dryer the almond flour, the more it will be able to absorb and retain moisture from the other elements in the batter. That is why we let it air dry for a few days before making the *macarons*. Seek out almond flour made from skinned almonds—the skin has no absorption value—and the finer the almond flour, the more it can absorb water. If your almond flour is coarse, blend it in a food processor with the confectioners' sugar for 10 seconds.

The egg whites are the last main component and an important one, as the albumen is what is holding all the air bubbles together in the meringue. Egg whites contain mainly water, some of which we want to evaporate before we make the *macarons*. Aged egg whites are egg whites that have been left uncovered in your refrigerator for a minimum of 24 hours. This allows some of the water to evaporate, resulting in more concentrated, stronger egg whites that can hold more air. Leaving them out on the counter overnight in a dry cool room will speed up the process. Sometimes to bypass the egg white drying process bakers add pure egg white powder—3 percent of the total weight of egg whites in the recipe. You can find egg white powder in many supermarkets and health food stores.

For all you germaphobes I have good news: Bacteria cannot grow in egg whites easily, mostly due to lack of

METHOD

DAY 1 (AND 2)

Forty-eight hours prior to making the recipe, sift the almond flour and confectioners' sugar together onto 2 sheet pans lined with parchment paper. Leave the mixture uncovered to dry for a minimum of 48 hours and up to several days. Also, separate 8 eggs and place half the whites in one bowl and half the whites in another. Cover each bowl with plastic wrap, then poke several holes in the plastic wrap in order to allow the water in the egg whites to evaporate, or cover with cheesecloth. Allow the egg whites to age and dry at room temperature overnight or in the refrigerator for 48 hours. Weigh out 95 grams of aged egg whites from each batch and keep separate.

DAY 3

1 When you are ready to mix the batter, place the almond flour and confectioners' sugar in a food processor fitted with the steel blade and run it for 10 seconds. Transfer to a large mixing bowl and stir together with a wooden or stiff plastic spatula. Place the first 95 grams of egg whites in the bowl next to it and set aside.

2 Make an Italian meringue. Wash the bowl of your stand mixer thoroughly with hot water and soap, and dry with a clean kitchen towel. Begin whipping the second 95 grams of egg whites on the lowest speed. Double-check the temperature of the egg whites by feeling the bottom of the bowl. If it is at all cold, fill a sink with 1 inch of hot water. Stop the machine, unlock the bowl, and place it in the hot water for 1 full minute while mixing by hand with the whip attachment or a whisk. Remove the bowl from the water and wipe dry. Feel the temperature with your hand; it should feel neither cold nor hot. Return the bowl to the mixer and resume whipping on low speed.

3 Meanwhile, place the water in the small saucepan and pour the sugar into the center of the pan. With a rubber spatula, stir very slowly to mix the sugar and water together, being careful not to wipe or splash the mixture onto the sides of the saucepan. If you do, wipe it back down with a wet pastry brush. Otherwise, sugar crystals will adhere to the sides and once you begin to heat the pan and the sides get hot, the sugar crystals will fall back into the syrup and cause the entire mixture to crystallize, rendering it unusable. Use a lot of water on the brush when you wash down the sides of the pan. You don't have to worry about adding excess water to the recipe, since once the syrup reaches 244°F/118°C it will have the same consistency no matter how much water was added. The excess water will just make the cooking process take longer. Add the corn syrup and the food coloring.

4 Begin heating the mixture over medium heat. Once the syrup comes to a boil, do not stir or it will crystallize. Insert your digital thermometer and cook the syrup to 244°F/118°C. Keep an eye on your egg whites while you are heating the syrup. When the syrup is at 230°F/110°C your egg whites should be semi-foamy. If they are not, increase the speed slightly. At 239°F/115°C the syrup is just about ready to be poured into the egg white. Check the bottom of the mixing bowl, and, if necessary, tilt the machine so that the egg whites at the bottom of the bowl are also beaten until foamy.

5 Turn the mixer to its highest speed. When the syrup reaches 244°F/118°C remove it from the heat immediately and very gradually stream it into the egg whites, taking great care to pour the syrup right between the whisk and the sides of the bowl. This is crucial, because if the hot syrup engages with the whisk before it hits the egg whites, all of it will splatter onto the sides of the bowl instead of going into the egg whites (and it could splatter on your hands and burn you). Once this happens you cannot undo it; you will have to scale a new recipe and begin again. If you pour the hot syrup between the whisk and the sides of the bowl as instructed, most of it will go into the egg whites and the recipe will work. No matter how careful you are, though, there will always be a small amount of syrup that splashes onto the bowl, so that you will have a thin candy-like layer of sugar around the inside of the bowl above the meringue.

6 Once all of the syrup has been added, whip on high speed for 1½ minutes while you combine the almond and confectioners' sugar mixture with the first 95 grams of egg whites that you set aside. Add the egg whites to the mixture and stir together with a wooden or hard plastic spatula. The mixture will be stiff.

7 Reduce the speed of the mixer with the meringue to medium speed and whip for another 3 minutes. Turn the mixer off and scrape out the meringue into the almond mixture. Using a large rubber spatula fold until the mixture is homogenized and one color; it will be somewhat compact.

8 At this point you need to "*macaronner*," which means to over-mix the mixture. If you don't do this, when you pipe small rounds onto your silpat-lined sheet pan, the tail left by the pastry bag will never disappear. In order to prevent this, continue folding the mixture for 20 seconds, then lift the rubber spatula up into the air and let some mixture drip onto the surface of the *macaron* mixture. Wait for 15 seconds to see if the drip disappears slowly into the mixture. If it does, then it is ready; if not, mix for another 10 seconds and repeat the process.

nutrients. In the bakeries I worked in in France egg whites for meringue were left out at room temperature for days in buckets that were placed on a shelf. The bucket with the oldest whites would be on the left and the freshest on the right. Whenever we separated eggs we would have to always make sure to add the fresh egg whites to a new bucket on the right side and push the older ones to the left.

You can find natural food coloring at www.amazon.com.

Here is more proof that egg whites fight against bacteria. I use the inner skin of a freshly cracked egg as a natural Band-Aid when I have a slight cut or a small burn. I make sure that the wound is covered with fresh albumen, then I cover it with a regular Band-Aid. I usually change the egg Band-Aid on a daily basis; it works wonders.

If you are using parchment paper on your sheet pan and you find that when you pipe the parchment paper comes up off the sheet each time you lift the pastry bag, glue down the corners of the parchment paper with a small dab of batter.

9 Scrape the mixture into the pastry bag fitted with a ⅜-inch round tip. Holding the bag vertically over the sheet pan with the tip pointing straight down, pipe 1½-inch rounds onto the silpats or parchment paper; make sure that they are not larger than this and take care to leave a 1-inch space between each round and to stagger the rows. Let the *macarons* sit at room temperature for 45 minutes or until they form a skin. The time will vary depending on the humidity in your kitchen. Meanwhile, preheat the oven to 300°F/150°C and arrange the rack in the middle.

10 Bake 1 sheet at a time in the middle of the 300°F/150°C oven for 15 minutes. Remove from the oven and allow to cool completely. They will release from the silpat or parchment paper once cooled.

11 Turn half of the rounds over and spoon or pipe on a small amount of the filling of your choice—about 5 grams. Top with another round. There should be enough filling for it to spread out and be just visible between the two halves. Place in the refrigerator, uncovered, for 48 hours. Check to see if the *macarons* are moist enough in the center. If they are not, you will have to leave them for 1 more day. When they are moist in the center, *macarons* are ready to be consumed.

IT'S DONE WHEN IT'S DONE

When the shells are baked they will be hard to the touch, but they should not brown in the oven. The bottoms might be ever so slightly darker than the rest, but the only color you should see is the color that you added.

STORAGE

Once they have softened in the refrigerator the *macarons* can be frozen for up to 1 month.

TROUBLESHOOTING

THE *MACARON* BATTER IS VERY STIFF: This is probably due to the fact that your syrup got too hot and the meringue mixture is on its way to becoming taffy. If the syrup goes above 244°F/118°C, add ¼ cup water to it and the temperature will drop. Then wait for the syrup to reach 244°F/118°C and immediately take it off the heat.

THE *MACARONS* CRACKED IN THE OVEN: Either you did not allow them to dry out enough before baking or, like many of my students, you piped the *macaron* too wide, larger than 1½ inches. The excess batter in a larger *macaron* holds more water, and as the *macaron* heats up in the oven the excess water evaporates, making the shell crack. The amount of time you need to leave the *macarons* to dry before baking depends on the humidity in your kitchen. On a hot and humid summer day the drying process might take longer.

THE *MACARONS* RAN OUT TO ONE SIDE: If your *macarons* run to one side you might want to rotate the sheet pan after 6 minutes of baking. Make sure that your sheet pans are level, and that you allow the *macarons* enough time to dry out sufficiently before baking.

JACQUY'S TAKEAWAYS

→ *Macaron* shells are always made with almond flour. The only variation is the color, which is determined by the filling you are using—green for pistachio, red for raspberry, yellow for lemon cream, and so on. The *macaron* shell itself is usually not flavored, as adding a flavoring ingredient would completely change its texture and it would bake differently in the oven.

→ As for fillings, they must be stable. Butter creams, ganaches, curds, and jams are all good candidates. I recommend flavors that are not too sweet, to offset the sweetness of the *macaron* shells. Coffee, chocolate, caramel, and lemon are some of my favorites.

ELEPHANT EARS / PALMIERS

YIELD | 24 COOKIES

2-DAY RECIPE

INGREDIENTS	WEIGHT	MEASURE (APPROXIMATE) OR OUNCE WEIGHT
Puff Pastry (PAGE 28), 4 turns only	½ recipe	½ recipe
Granulated sugar	150 grams, or as needed	¾ cup, or as needed

I don't know anyone who doesn't like a well-made *palmier*. An extremely simple pastry, this cookie consists of layers of puff pastry held together with sugar. The puff pastry is folded into a log and cut in slices that are baked slowly after an initial blast in a moderately hot oven. The sugar caramelizes as the cookies bake while the pastry puffs, dries out, and becomes flaky. The flakiness of the pastry is set against the caramel, and the nutty flavor of the butter—when you bake puff pastry all the way through the browned butter takes on a hazelnut flavor—is irresistible.

Like everything in pastry, *palmiers* take a little practice; the better you get at making puff pastry, the better your *palmiers* will be. The puff pastry layers need to be nice and straight, the slices must be all the same thickness, and you need to give them time to dry out in the refrigerator for a while before you bake them so that they have the right shape once baked, and don't open up.

These were some of the first pastries I made when I was a kid, beginning at age seven or eight. When my dad had made puff pastry and had scraps left over I was allowed to make creations with the bits he didn't recycle into his next batch. When I got home from school while my father was sleeping, between one and four p.m., if I saw that there was leftover dough I'd ask my mom if I could make creations with it. She was happy to let me, as it gave me something to do. I'd sprinkle sugar over the dough and shape it in different ways, then I'd bake my creations in the brick oven that was still hot from my father's baking. If the dough got too warm while I was handling it, I'd chill it in the refrigerator, then once it was cold again I'd go back to it. This was how I learned to handle puff pastry.

Most doughs do not have much of a chance to be used a second time, but puff pastry is definitely an exception. Scraps can be used for *palmiers,* cocktail snacks, and Mille-feuilles (PAGE 116). Adding sugar to the dough to make *palmiers* completely changes its identity.

BEFORE YOU BEGIN

→ Get out the following equipment and allow all of the ingredients to come to room temperature:

Digital scale, set to metric weights
Equipment for Puff Pastry (PAGE 28)
4 small mixing bowls
1 large chef's knife
2 to 3 sheet pans lined with parchment paper
1 medium offset spatula

→ Read this recipe through twice from start to finish.

UNDERSTANDING INGREDIENTS

Palmiers are made with puff pastry. Puff pastry is not sweet at all, so when we make *palmiers,* we replace the dusting flour with granulated sugar in the last 2 book folds. A generous amount of sugar is needed to turn this into a sweet pastry. Abundant sugar is also required to obtain a nice caramel finish during the baking process. The glossy finish also has a wonderful taste, and the combination of that caramel flavor and the rich, flaky puff pastry is hard to resist. As for all puff pastry, you must bake it initially in a very hot oven in order for the water in the layers to turn into steam and force the layers to separate. But because of all the sugar the temperature for *palmiers* will be a little lower than in the basic puff pastry recipe—375°F/190°C as opposed to 400°F/200°C. If the temperature is too high the sugar will burn before the puff pastry is cooked through.

JACQUY'S TAKEAWAYS

→ Puff pastry usually puffs upward, but in this case it will puff sideways, since the layers are lying on their side. This is why you need to leave enough space between each *palmier.*

→ The amount of sugar you use for sprinkling the dough will look like an insanely large amount, but you will see when you try one that the *palmiers* are not too sweet.

DAY 1

Make half a batch of puff pastry dough following the recipe on PAGE 28. Apply 4 bookfolds and refrigerate overnight.

DAY 2

If you have made a full batch of puff pastry (this recipe only requires a half batch), divide it in 2 and freeze half of it. Make sure to label the batch that you freeze and note that it only has 4 folds. Divide the sugar into 4 equal portions and place each portion in a separate bowl.

1 Bowl 1: Put the dusting flour away and place one of the bowls of granulated sugar next to your silpat or your rolling surface. Place a very generous amount of sugar on the silpat or rolling surface, place the dough on it, and spread a generous amount of sugar on top of the dough. Start rolling out the puff to make the next fold, following the directions on PAGE 28. Sprinkle more sugar underneath and on top of the dough as needed, in the same way you would dust with flour. When it is time to fold the dough, sprinkle an even and generous amount of sugar over the middle third of the dough and fold one end of the dough over it. Sprinkle the folded half evenly with sugar and bring the other side over it for the fifth turn. Sprinkle evenly with sugar. Wrap in plastic and let the dough rest in the refrigerator for 30 minutes.

2 Bowl 2: Place the next bowl of granulated sugar next to the dough and repeat the rolling and folding for the last bookfold, sprinkling the dough with sugar as in the previous step. Wrap and refrigerate for 30 minutes.

3 Bowl 3: Place the third bowl of granulated sugar next to your silpat or rolling area. Roll out the puff pastry to a 13 × 26–inch rectangle, dusting it underneath and on top with the sugar. Ultimately you want to have a 12 × 24–inch rectangle, but since the dough will shrink you should roll it a little bigger at first. With a ruler measure half of the rectangle and make a small indent at the 12-inch (or midpoint) mark with the back of a paring knife or your ruler. Fold in one end of the dough so that the edge is at the middle of the rectangle, right at the midpoint (SEE ILLUSTRATION). Repeat with the other end. Fold the folded pastry in half at the middle into a log, with one side on top of the other. If you look at it from the end it should look like a heart (SEE ILLUSTRATION). Place the log on a sheet pan lined with parchment paper and freeze for 30 minutes.

4 Place the log on a cutting board and, using a large chef's knife, cut twenty-four ½-inch-thick slices. Place 1 slice, cut side down, on a parchment paper–lined sheet pan. Place another *palmier* on the sheet pan 2 inches away from the first one but facing the other way (SEE ILLUSTRATION). Repeat with all the *palmiers,* using 2 or 3 sheet pans. Now pull apart the 2 sides of each

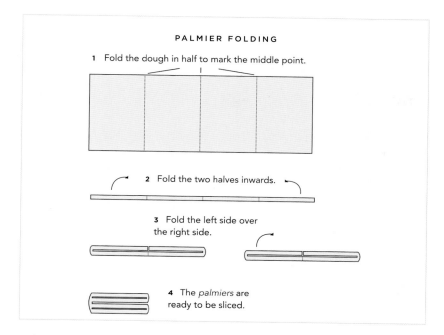

PALMIER FOLDING

1 Fold the dough in half to mark the middle point.

2 Fold the two halves inwards.

3 Fold the left side over the right side.

4 The *palmiers* are ready to be sliced.

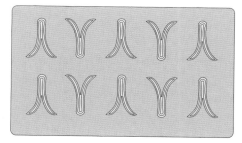

palmier slightly while gently pressing with your index fingers in the middle, so that each one looks like a stick figure (SEE ILLUSTRATION).

5 Place the sheet pans with the shaped *palmiers* in the refrigerator for 2 hours to dry out. Otherwise the cookies will open up when they bake.

6 Bowl 4: Preheat the oven to 375°F/190°C. Sprinkle the sugar from the fourth bowl over the palmiers. Bake 1 sheet pan at a time for 20 minutes, until the *palmiers* have expanded to their final size. Remove the sheet pan from the oven and turn the heat down to 325°F/160°C. Using your offset spatula, flip the *palmiers* over and place them back in the oven for another 15 to 20 minutes, until they are baked fully and the sugar is caramelized. Remove from the oven and allow the cookies to cool completely before eating. Repeat with the other sheet pan(s). If the sugar is caramelizing too quickly, turn the oven down to 300°F/150°C.

IT'S DONE WHEN IT'S DONE

The puff pastry is fully baked when it is light brown all the way through and the caramelized sugar has a glossy rich amber color.

STORAGE

The best way to store *palmiers* is to keep them in an airtight box. You can freeze them, but if you do you will need to re-crisp them in a 325°F/160°C oven for 5 to 10 minutes before serving

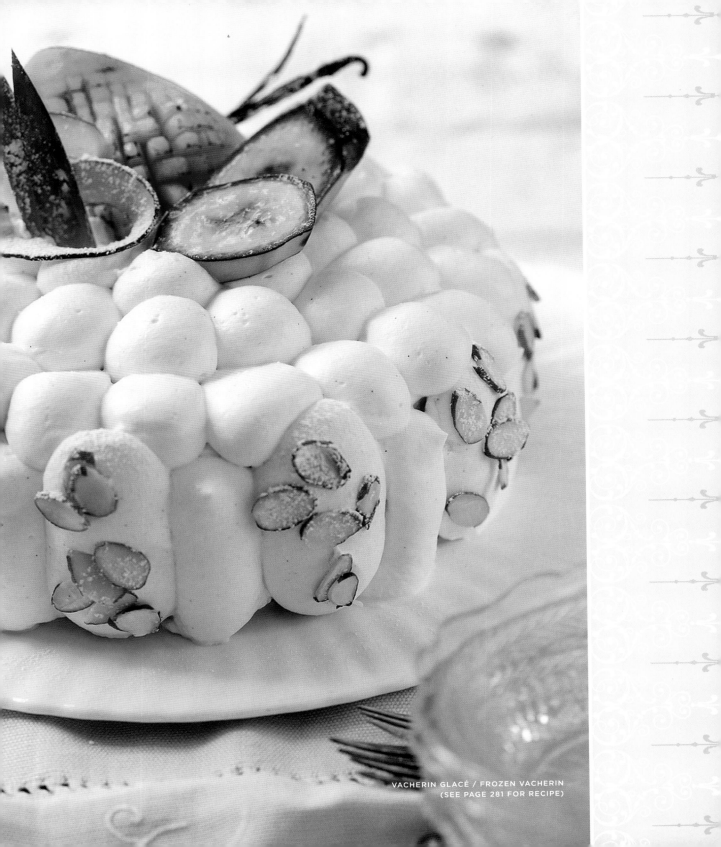

VACHERIN GLACÉ / FROZEN VACHERIN
(SEE PAGE 281 FOR RECIPE)

· CHAPTER 5 ·

CAKE AND ICE CREAM

*I*n French this chapter would be described as *"l'incontournable"*—
essential reading. When you learn to make pastry you learn to
make cake, be it a buttery pound cake, a light and elegant mousse
cake, or a refreshing ice cream cake. Cake is usually the first type of
pastry a French child makes at home.

If you're new to making cakes you can get your feet wet with the
simple but interesting Deerback (PAGE 233), a rich pound cake that also
includes a layer of ganache. Then you can move on to more serious
projects. Like so many products in French pastry, cakes are "built"
from fundamental recipes. First master the Sponge Cake, or Génoise
(PAGE 237), the Jelly Roll Sponge (PAGE 241), and the Flourless Chocolate
Sponge (PAGE 246), and then you will be able to make more complex
classics like Chocolate and Hazelnut Yule Log (PAGE 249) and Black
Forest Cake (PAGE 259).

When you are making a cake, think of yourself as an architect or
a builder and you will succeed. Imagine your cake as a structure with
sponge cake as the foundation, different floors filled with mousse, and
walls made of frosting. If you don't think like a builder you can have
mixed results, cakes that I call "organic" looking. Let's say you make a
cake that has a surfeit of mousse but not enough sponge layers: that
cake will collapse in no time because the foundation is weak. But once
you have the mind-set of a cake builder you'll be able to master projects

like my modern version of Black Forest cake, an old time classic that never loses its appeal.

Some beloved French cakes like Gâteau St. Honoré (PAGE 253) are built from pastry basics that are not cakes or mousses. The St. Honoré is built from puff pastry and *pâte à choux* cemented together with hot caramel. Technically it is a step further into cake construction, and it is so worth the effort. Today pastry chefs are even building cakes in glasses (PAGE 267); these have great visual appeal and they're fun and delicious to eat.

Since ice cream and cake go together and sometimes cakes are made with ice cream, I decided to combine the two in the same chapter. Making an ice cream cake involves the same architectural approach as making a mousse cake, but it has the added challenge of handling the ice cream. Again, we begin with the fundamentals. Vanilla ice cream is the key to all other ice creams; take the time to master it, understand what it means to give it the time to set properly in the freezer. Then go on to try the more intricate Vacherin Glacé (PAGE 281), an ice cream cake with a meringue foundation, whipped cream "walls," and, in this version, "floors" filled with fruity ice cream and sorbet that contrast perfectly with the sweet meringue base.

Frozen desserts don't stop at ice cream and sorbet. You'll also find frozen mousse desserts in this chapter, such as a traditional Kougelhof Glacé (PAGE 275) frozen in a Bundt-shaped mold that will introduce you to frozen honey mousse, and for your next dinner party a frozen coffee mousse with a rich chocolate layer on the bottom, frozen in individual ramekins and topped with a crisp coffee-pecan *tuile* and a spiced whipped cream quenelle (PAGE 289).

When I see a delicious and beautiful whole cake presented on a platter I always have the urge to put it on a pedestal and worship it. Your guests may feel the same way after you've worked your way through these recipes and appear victorious in your living room, presenting them with the most gorgeous cake they've ever seen.

CHOCOLATE, ALMOND, AND GANACHE
POUND CAKE / DEERBACK

INGREDIENTS	WEIGHT	MEASURE (APPROXIMATE) OR OUNCE WEIGHT
Soft butter, for the pan	30 grams	1 ounce or 2 tablespoons
Sliced almonds, with skin	75 grams	¾ cup
Cocoa powder	16 grams	3 tablespoons
Confectioners' sugar, sifted	60 grams	Scant ½ cup
Almond flour, skinless, sifted	80 grams	Rounded ¾ cup
Cake flour	20 grams	2 tablespoons
Cornstarch	18 grams	2 tablespoons
Butter (French style, 82% fat)	52 grams	1⅘ ounces
Almond flour, skinless, sifted	75 grams	¾ cup
Confectioners' sugar, sifted	30 grams	¼ cup
Egg yolks	50 grams	3 yolks
Clover honey	20 grams	2 teaspoons
Whole eggs	50 grams	1 egg
Vanilla extract	5 grams	1 teaspoon
Lemon zest	½ lemon	½ lemon
Orange zest	¼ orange	¼ orange
Egg whites	160 grams	⅔ cup or about 4½ whites
Granulated sugar	80 grams	⅓ cup
Ganache (PAGE 72)	75 grams (make ½ recipe and store what you don't use)	2³⁄₁₀ ounces

This is a modified version of a moist chocolate and almond pound cake that I used to make during my apprenticeship in Strasbourg. I had actually forgotten about it until I began working on this book. Writing this book has revived so many old memories and brought recipes out of drawers where they had been stored for more than twenty years. The cake has a rich chocolate and almond outer layer, contains a center made of a moist almond cake infused with orange and lemon zest, and is filled with a generous amount of ganache that puts it in the category of "devilishly good."

BEFORE YOU BEGIN

→ Get out the following equipment and allow all of the ingredients to come to room temperature:

Digital scale, set to metric weights
Equipment for Ganache (PAGE 72)
1 pastry brush
1 loaf pan
1 sifter
Parchment paper
1 small saucepan
1 wide spatula
KitchenAid or stand mixer fitted with the paddle and whisk attachments
1 large mixing bowl
1 small mixing bowl
1 rubber spatula
1 small offset spatula
1 sheet pan
1 paring knife
1 wire rack
1 hand towel
Plastic wrap
1 serrated knife

→ Read this recipe through twice from start to finish.

METHOD

1 Using a pastry brush, grease your loaf pan very generously with soft butter and pour the sliced almonds into it. Tilt the pan in all directions so that the almonds coat the sides thoroughly and evenly, forming a natural outside lining of your cake. Once the sides are coated, turn the pan over and allow the excess almonds to fall out. Set the excess aside for another purpose and place the pan in the refrigerator for 15 minutes.

2 Preheat the oven to 350°F/180°C with the rack positioned in the center. Sift the cocoa powder, 60 grams of confectioners' sugar, and 80 grams of sifted almond flour together onto a sheet of parchment paper and set aside. Sift the cake flour together with the cornstarch onto another piece of parchment paper or into a small bowl and set aside.

3 Place the butter in a small saucepan and set over low heat. Allow the butter to melt, then stir slowly with the spatula until it turns light brown, about 5 to 7 minutes. Remove from the heat and strain into a small bowl so that it does not continue to brown. Set it aside to cool for 5 minutes.

4 Meanwhile, place the 75 grams sifted almond flour, the 30 grams sifted confectioners' sugar, the egg yolks, honey, whole egg, and vanilla in the bowl of your stand mixer fitted with the paddle. Mix on medium speed for 5 minutes, until the mixture is pale and light. Add the lukewarm browned butter and mix on medium speed for 30 seconds. Take the bowl out of the mixer and scrape out the mixture into a large bowl. Using a wide spatula, gently fold in the lemon and orange zests and the cake flour and cornstarch mixture. Wash the mixer bowl thoroughly with hot, soapy water, rinse, dry, and return to the stand. Change to the whisk attachment. Immediately move on to the next step so that the flour does not sit too long in the egg mixture.

5 Place the egg whites in the bowl of your mixer fitted with the whisk. Whip on medium speed for 10 seconds. Add the granulated sugar and whip for 1½ to 2 full minutes on high speed, until semi-stiff but not dry. Remove the mixing bowl from the machine, place a small bowl on your scale, and weigh out 120 grams of the meringue. Fold this into the egg yolk mixture. Do not over-fold or you will deflate the batter and your cake will be tough. Return the mixing bowl to the machine and continue to whip the remaining meringue on the lowest speed just to maintain it.

6 Stop the mixer, take out the bowl and, using a rubber spatula, gently fold in the cocoa powder mixture. Scrape into the almond-lined bread pan and, using a small offset spatula, gently spread it evenly all over the sides and bottom of the pan to create a chocolate meringue shell.

UNDERSTANDING INGREDIENTS

When it comes to nutty pound cakes I lean toward almond flour as my nut flour of choice because almonds do the best job at retaining moisture. Other nuts contain more fat, and the more fat there is, the less moisture can be absorbed, since fat and water do not mix.

Folding whipped egg whites into a pound cake always lightens the texture, and the air bubbles are also great at trapping moisture. Usually I add salt or cream of tartar to my meringues, but for this recipe I did not because I didn't want the acidity to clash with the acidity of the chocolate.

I recommend using cake flour because of its low gluten content, and cornstarch so that the cake will not get tight and rubbery. A mix of lemon and orange zest will bring both acidity and a great flavor profile. I make a brown butter for this recipe because it has a wonderful nutty flavor, which you can only achieve if you melt the butter slowly. If you place the butter over high heat it will burn, and burned butter has an unpleasant flavor and aroma.

The reason that I instruct you to make more ganache than you will need for the cake is that making a very small amount of ganache can be tricky, as the ganache can break easily because it cools down much more quickly. You can freeze what you don't use; it's always nice to have some ganache on hand in the freezer.

Fill the chocolate shell with the cake batter and smooth the top with the small offset spatula. The pan will be about ⅔ or ¾ full. Place the mold on a sheet pan and bake for 25 minutes at 350°F/180°C. Reduce the heat to 325°F/160°C and bake for another 20 minutes, until firm. Insert the tip of a paring knife into the center of the cake; it should come out clean. If it does not, bake for another 5 to 10 minutes. Remove from the oven and immediately reverse the cake onto a wire rack, unmold, and gently wrap the cake in a towel. Allow the cake to cool to room temperature; this will take 1 hour.

8 In the meantime, make a half recipe of Ganache (PAGE 72), cover with plastic wrap, and allow it to cool in the refrigerator for 30 minutes. Weigh out 75 grams and store the remaining ganache, wrapped airtight, in the refrigerator or freezer (it's great for making hot chocolate! Just add a tablespoon to a cup of hot milk, blend, and voilà!).

9 Place the cake on a cutting board with the bottom facing up. Using a long serrated knife, create a V cut by slicing from the edge of the cake to the middle on an inward 45-degree angle. Repeat on the other side of the cake so that you can now remove the triangular slice. Using a small offset spatula, spread the surface of the V cut with the 75 grams of ganache. Return the triangular slice to the cake, setting it right on top of the ganache filling and pressing down gently but firmly so that it sticks to the ganache. Place the cake back in its original mold and refrigerate for 30 minutes. This will allow the ganache to set and keep the whole cake together. Let it come to room temperature for 30 minutes and unmold. The cake is now ready to be served.

IT'S DONE WHEN IT'S DONE

Both the chocolate cake and yellow cake should be moist; the ganache should be nice and creamy.

STORAGE

This cake keeps in a cool place for 2 to 3 days wrapped in plastic wrap.

JACQUY'S TAKEAWAYS

→ The reason you have to unmold the cake right away is that if you let it sit in the pan the steam will have nowhere to go and will hit the side of the metal pan and turn into water, resulting in a wet cake.

→ The V cut is challenging to do at first. You can always choose to fill the cake like a layer cake, cutting it into 2, 3, or 4 slices. If you make a layer cake you will use more of the ganache, which will make a more chocolaty cake.

→ Deerback would also be delicious made with hazelnut flour or pecan flour, but if you choose to use one of these flours combine it half and half with almond flour so that you will not lose moisture. Chocolate, hazelnut, or pecan with orange are great flavor combinations.

SPONGE CAKE (CAKE PAN VERSION) / GÉNOISE

INGREDIENTS	WEIGHT	MEASURE (APPROXIMATE) OR OUNCE WEIGHT
Butter (French style, 82% fat), clarified according to instructions below	125 grams for 100 grams clarified	$4^2/_5$ ounces for $3^1/_2$ ounces clarified
Softened butter, for the pan	30 grams	1 ounce
Cake flour	120 grams	1 cup
Cornstarch	14 grams	1½ tablespoons
Whole eggs	200 grams	About 4 eggs
Granulated sugar	100 grams	½ cup
Vanilla extract	10 grams	2 teaspoons
Clover honey	20 grams	1 tablespoon

Nothing compares to a freshly baked moist, buttery sponge with a crumb as light as a feather. I don't even mind when the cake is a little overbaked and has a rich brown crust. Génoise is a pillar recipe in pastry; you will find it in a wide range of desserts. It is obviously the main element of many traditional cakes, but it can also end up in plated desserts, ice cream cakes, individual mini pastries, and desserts in a glass (*verrines*).

You can flavor génoise with a few different components. My favorite is vanilla, the traditional choice that is used by most chefs. I also like citrus zest, which brings a great zing to the cake. Cocoa powder will transform the génoise into a delicious chocolate cake. Some chefs add hazelnut paste or flour for a rich, nutty flavor profile.

METHOD

1 Make the clarified butter. Place 125 grams of butter in a small saucepan over low heat and heat it slowly until it comes to a boil. The boiling butter will be noisy at first because of the water droplets hitting the bottom of the pan. After about 2 to 3 minutes the noise will stop because all of the water in the butter will have evaporated. You will now see that some of the protein solids have risen to the top, and you should skim them off with a fine-mesh skimmer or a large spoon. The other proteins or solids will stick to the bottom of the pan. Let the butter cook for another 3 minutes, being careful not to let it brown, and turn off the heat. Set it aside for 30 minutes, then strain through a fine-mesh or cheesecloth-lined strainer into a bowl. The butter should now be

BEFORE YOU BEGIN

→ Get out the following equipment and allow all of the ingredients to come to room temperature:

Digital scale—set to metric weights
1 small saucepan
1 digital thermometer
1 mesh skimmer or large spoon
1 fine-mesh strainer or regular strainer lined with cheesecloth
1 small bowl
1 pastry brush
One 9-inch cake pan
Parchment paper
Scissors
1 sifter
KitchenAid or stand mixer fitted with the whisk attachment
1 stainless steel hand whisk
1 large mixing bowl
1 large rubber spatula or balloon whisk
1 sheet pan
1 paring knife

→ Read this recipe through twice from start to finish.

UNDERSTANDING INGREDIENTS

To make a sponge recipe for a cake pan I prefer to use a method where the whole eggs and sugar are whipped and heated together to 149°F/65°C so that the eggs can coagulate while the aeration is happening. This will make a much more stable sponge mixture than the cold-method process that I use in the jelly roll sponge recipe for the Yule log on PAGE 249, as the coagulated egg will encase the air bubbles more firmly.

Sugar acts as a buffer and prevents the eggs from scrambling.

Honey is a very sweet inverted sugar. Its structure helps emulsify the fat in the egg yolk and makes it bind with the water in the recipe.

I prefer to use cake flour because of its weak gluten content; nobody likes a rubbery cake. I have seen sponge cake recipes that actually use bread flour, but only when the sponge contains an unusually high amount of butter, which makes the cake super rich but also super fragile, requiring more gluten to hold it together. Also, in this recipe I use some cornstarch. Cornstarch improves the suppleness of the sponge because it does not contain gluten.

When it comes to making a moist sponge, fat is required. Oil would do the trick very nicely, but who wants to eat an oil-soaked sponge? Oil will never taste like butter. The next best thing is clarified butter, which is butter that is cooked slowly until all the water has evaporated and the proteins have separated from the fat. The mixture is strained and will act just like oil—but still taste like butter.

clear of all solids. Scale 100 grams of the clarified butter and set it aside in a small bowl to cool to 105°F/41°C. If there is any left over, keep in the refrigerator; it is great for pan-frying. Wash your thermometer probe and dry it.

2 Preheat the oven to 350°F/180°C with the rack positioned in the middle. Brush a 9-inch cake pan with softened butter. Place the cake pan on top of a piece of parchment paper and mark it with a pencil; cut on the inside of the line to obtain an 8¾-inch round piece of parchment paper and place it in the bottom of the pan. Cut a long strip of parchment paper the same height as your cake pan and line the sides of the pan with it.

NOTE: Never use oil or pan spray to grease a baking pan, as they leave a greasy aftertaste.

3 Sift the flour with the cornstarch onto a sheet of parchment paper.

4 Place 1 inch of water in a small saucepan. Combine the whole eggs, granulated sugar, vanilla, and honey in the bowl of a stand mixer. Place the bowl on top of the saucepan; the bottom should not be touching the water. Turn the heat on low under the double boiler, or bain-marie. Using a hand whisk, whip the egg mixture continuously over the bain-marie until it reaches 149°F/65°C, making sure to rotate the bowl and whisk everywhere to prevent the eggs from scrambling. Immediately remove from the heat and place the bowl on the mixing stand.

5 Fit the mixer with the whisk attachment, turn to the highest speed, and beat for 3 minutes. The mixture should now be fluffy, light, and pale in color. Turn the speed down to medium and beat for another 3 minutes.

6 Check the temperature of the clarified butter. It should have cooled to 105°F/41°C. Turn down the speed to low and slowly drizzle the butter into the egg mixture.

7 Stop the mixer and, using a rubber spatula, carefully transfer the egg mixture to a large mixing bowl. Add half of the flour and cornstarch mixture and, using a wide spatula, gently fold in. Make sure that each time you fold you reach down all the way to the bottom of the bowl with your spatula, as this is where the flour likes to settle. Add the remaining flour and continue to fold until you see no more traces of flour. Some recipes call for the use of a whisk to fold in the flour. I am not opposed to that as long as you realize that, compared to a rubber spatula, a whisk is much more efficient because of its multiple metal wires, so you will have to fold less than you fold with a spatula. If you over-fold you will make the sponge collapse.

8 Using a rubber spatula to scrape out every last bit, pour all of the mixture into the cake pan, distributing it evenly.

9 Place the cake pan on a sheet pan in the preheated oven and bake for 30 to 35 minutes, until light golden brown and a paring knife comes out clean when inserted in the middle. Unmold onto a wire rack, cover with a towel, and allow to cool.

IT'S DONE WHEN IT'S DONE

The cake should be golden brown and very moist in the center. Check the doneness by inserting a paring knife into the middle of the cake. If the cake is done it should come out clean. Otherwise, bake for another 5 minutes.

STORAGE

You can keep this baked cake refrigerated, wrapped tightly in plastic wrap, for 2 to 3 days or frozen for 1 month.

VARIATION

To make this a chocolate cake, replace the cornstarch with cocoa powder.

JACQUY'S TAKEAWAYS

→ You can grease the cake pan with the butter and flour mixture on **PAGE 8** instead of lining the mold with parchment paper.

→ You can use a silicone pan instead of a metal cake pan, in which case you would not have to butter the mold or line it with parchment paper. You can also use metal pans that come in different shapes. In Alsace we make a lamb-shaped cake called *lamele* or *lamala* at Easter using an earthenware mold. If using a shaped mold, use the butter and flour mixture on **PAGE 8** to grease it.

ONE EARLY DECEMBER MORNING three months into the first year of my apprenticeship with Jean Clauss, my boss asked me to make génoise for the Yule logs that it was time to begin producing for the holiday season. Our recipe for a full batch of génoise called for 40 eggs and 1200 grams of sugar, which we'd whip until hot on the stove as we do in this much smaller recipe. Jean Clauss knew that I was new at pastry and probably didn't have the muscles in my forearms to whip 40 eggs, so he had me do a half batch. But I didn't have the forearms for 20 eggs, either; I was a soccer player and my legs were a lot stronger than my arms. Jean Clauss explained to me how it was done and I began to whip. After a few minutes my hands began to cramp and I began to freak out because I knew I needed to stop—but Jean Clauss was staring at me. The more I whipped and agonized the more he would stare, in disbelief that a strong young man like me wasn't up to the task. After 3 or 4 minutes of whipping I looked at him, turned off the stove, put down the whisk, and told him I couldn't do it. He became furious and began one of his rants, calling me a wimp and worse, telling me that I would never make it in the business.

But it was just that my muscles for this task hadn't developed yet. The muscles needed for pastry making are not obvious ones; they're in our forearms and wrists. I always tell my students that they should never give up. There is some discomfort at first, but with the right mind-set you can block it out enough to continue to do the work for as long as it takes to develop the necessary muscles. By the following December I had the forearms, and I was in charge of making all of the sponges for all of the Christmas Yule logs that year. One day I made 40 full batches of génoise—40 eggs in each batch—in a row, nonstop like a machine, without breaking a sweat. I was very proud that I'd stuck with it and that now I could do the task.

JELLY ROLL SPONGE / GÉNOISE ROULADE

YIELD | ONE 12 × 17-INCH CAKE (1 SHEET PAN)

INGREDIENTS	WEIGHT	MEASURE (APPROXIMATE) OR OUNCE WEIGHT
Melted butter, for the pan	As needed	As needed
Whole eggs	190 grams	3 eggs plus about 1½ tablespoons beaten egg
Granulated sugar	90 grams	⅓ cup plus 2 tablespoons
Vanilla extract	5 grams	1 teaspoon
Clover honey	5 grams	¾ teaspoon
All-purpose flour	45 grams	⅓ cup
Cornstarch	45 grams	⅓ cup

This recipe makes a thin, moist rectangular sponge cake that you can use for a Yule log, a jelly roll, or even a layered cake. Because of the method and ingredients in my recipe, this génoise is a very pliable cake and is easy to roll. Unlike in the previous recipe—the génoise is baked in a cake pan—you don't heat the eggs and sugar before whipping them together until they're cool. Flat cakes baked on sheet pans have to be moist enough to roll without breaking; using this cold process, in which the room-temperature eggs and sugar are whipped without being heated first, prevents any loss of moisture, something that can happen if the warming method is used.

METHOD

1 Line a sheet pan with parchment paper. Brush the parchment paper with a thin layer of melted butter. Never use oil or pan spray, as they leave a greasy aftertaste. Preheat the oven to 400°F/200°C with the rack positioned in the middle.

2 Combine the whole eggs, granulated sugar, vanilla, and honey in the bowl of a stand mixer fitted with the paddle attachment. Mix for 30 seconds at low speed to combine the ingredients.

3 Turn the mixer to the highest speed and beat for 5 minutes. The mixture should now be fluffy, light, and pale in color. Turn the speed down to medium and beat for another 3 minutes.

4 Meanwhile, sift the flour with the cornstarch onto a sheet of parchment paper.

BEFORE YOU BEGIN

→ Get out the following equipment and allow all of the ingredients to come to room temperature:

Digital scale, set to metric weights
1 sheet pan lined with parchment paper
1 pastry brush
KitchenAid or stand mixer fitted with the whisk attachment
1 sifter
Parchment paper
1 large rubber spatula
1 large mixing bowl
1 offset or flat metal spatula

→ Read this recipe through twice from start to finish.

Honey is a very sweet sugar. Its structure helps emulsify the fat in the egg yolk. It also breaks down droplets of fat into smaller ones, making the mixture feel lighter.

Usually sponges are made with flour only. In this recipe I use half flour and half cornstarch. Cornstarch improves the flexibility of the sponge because it does not contain gluten.

JACQUY'S TAKEAWAYS

→ The best thing to do after baking the cake is to leave it on the parchment paper until you need it. This sponge, like all sponges, can be frozen at the baked stage, but the batter can never be frozen at the raw stage. Double-wrap airtight in plastic before freezing. If you are freezing more than one, stack them between sheets of parchment paper, then double-wrap airtight in plastic.

→ **$50 TRICK:** If your sponge bakes too long and turns out dry and hard like a cracker, keep it in the sheet pan and place it uncovered in the refrigerator overnight. The moisture in the refrigerator will make it soft and usable again.

5 Using a rubber spatula, carefully transfer the egg mixture to the large mixing bowl. Pour half of the flour and cornstarch into the egg mixture and gently fold in with a large rubber spatula. Make sure that each time you fold you reach down all the way to the bottom of the bowl with your spatula, as this is where the flour likes to settle. Add the remaining flour and cornstarch and continue to fold until you see no more traces of dry ingredients.

6 Using the rubber spatula to scrape out every last bit, pour all of the mixture into the sheet pan, distributing it equally between the middle of the pan and all the corners. Using an offset or a flat metal spatula (offset is easier) held at a slight angle, spread the mixture evenly over the pan with a back-and-forth, wax-on, wax-off motion. Use your rubber spatula to scrape the batter that adheres to the offset spatula back into the pan. It is important to do this efficiently and fairly quickly in order to not deflate the batter. The finished mixture should be about ½ inch thick, with visible air bubbles.

7 Place the sheet pan in the preheated oven and bake for 7 to 8 minutes, until light golden brown. Cool on a rack.

IT'S DONE WHEN IT'S DONE

The cake should be light golden brown but still moist in the center. It may be a little browner in the center than on the edges. The edges should not be crisp. The oven temperature might seem very high for this thin cake, but it is precisely because the sponge is so thin that a hot oven is required to bake the cake quickly without drying it out. Baking it in a lower oven would be fatal, as the cake would require too much time in the oven, and it would completely dry out.

VARIATION

Some bakers add melted butter to their génoise to produce a richer cake. The proportion of butter added is 20 percent of the weight of the eggs. (So for this recipe you would use 38 grams of butter.) I prefer to use clarified butter (SEE PAGE 237), but for a small amount like this you can also use melted butter that isn't clarified. Melt the butter at 50 percent power in a microwave or over low heat on the stove. Once you have finished folding your flour into the egg mixture, add a small amount of batter to the melted or clarified butter, then gently fold this into the génoise batter.

ALMOND BISCUIT ROULADE

YIELD | ONE 12 × 17-INCH CAKE
(1 SHEET PAN)

INGREDIENTS	WEIGHT	MEASURE (APPROXIMATE) OR OUNCE WEIGHT
Melted butter, for the pan	As needed	As needed
Almond flour, skinless	95 grams	1 cup plus 1 tablespoon
Confectioners' sugar	95 grams	1 cup
Cake flour	23 grams	¼ cup
Granulated sugar	30 grams	2 tablespoons plus 1 teaspoon
Whole eggs	60 grams	1 extra-large egg
Whole eggs	60 grams	1 extra-large egg
Egg whites	85 grams	⅓ cup
Granulated sugar	70 grams	5 tablespoons
Sea salt	0.5 grams	Pinch
Butter (French style, 82% fat)	17 grams	1 tablespoon

Like the jelly roll sponge in the previous recipe, this thin, rectangular almond sponge cake can be used for a jelly roll or a layered cake. A sponge cake is called a biscuit when a meringue is used in the recipe. Otherwise the sponge is called a génoise. The reason we use the egg whites whipped into a soft meringue in this type of cake is that the meringue gives the cake a soft texture that will allow you to manipulate it without its falling apart.

METHOD

1 Line a sheet pan with parchment paper. Brush the parchment paper with a thin layer of melted butter. Never use oil or pan spray, as they leave a greasy aftertaste. Preheat the oven to 400°F/200°C with the rack positioned in the middle.

2 Sift the almond flour, confectioners' sugar, and cake flour and combine with the 30 grams of granulated sugar in the bowl of a stand mixer fitted with the paddle attachment. Mix for 30 seconds at low speed.

3 Stop the machine and add the first 60 grams of whole eggs to the bowl. Slowly turn the speed up to medium and mix for 4 minutes. Stop the mixer, lower the bowl, and scrape the bottom of the bowl with a rubber spatula, making sure to stir any dry residue into the rest of the mixture. Add the

BEFORE YOU BEGIN

→ Get out the following equipment and allow all of the ingredients to come to room temperature:

Digital scale, set to metric weights
1 sheet pan lined with parchment paper
1 pastry brush
1 sifter
KitchenAid or stand mixer fitted with
    the paddle and whisk attachments
1 large rubber spatula
1 medium mixing bowl
1 small microwave-safe bowl
1 large mixing bowl
1 offset or flat metal spatula

→ Read this recipe through twice from start to finish.

UNDERSTANDING INGREDIENTS

Most of the flour in this cake is almond flour. Compared to other nuts, almonds have a relatively low fat content; therefore they can absorb and retain water well, resulting in a very moist sponge that is easy to manipulate. This is why we use the almond flour here and why you see it as an ingredient in many other cakes. You can also make the cake using other nut flours such as hazelnut flour or a mixture of half almond flour and half pistachio, pecan, walnut, or macadamia nut flour. You wouldn't want to use all pistachio or macadamia nut flour because their high fat content would result in a greasy biscuit. Using all pecan or walnut flour would produce a cake that is too bitter.

Confectioners' sugar is granulated sugar that has been ground to a very fine powder. It melts and incorporates into the batter more quickly than granulated sugar. You could use granulated sugar, but you'd have to mix the batter longer in order for it to melt and be incorporated.

second 60 grams of whole eggs and mix for 4 more minutes on medium speed. The mixture should now be fluffy, light, and pale in color.

4 Using a rubber spatula, transfer the mixture to a medium mixing bowl. Wash the bowl of your mixer very well with soap and hot water. Rinse, dry thoroughly, and return to the stand.

5 Combine the egg whites, the 70 grams of sugar, and the sea salt in the bowl of your electric mixer. Using the whisk attachment, whip for 3 minutes on medium speed to obtain a soft meringue (SEE PAGE 69). The meringue should be shiny and creamy looking. When you pull out the whisk and hold it up, the meringue should make a bird's beak, curving down rather than up (SEE PAGE 70). If this is not what you are seeing, mix the meringue for an additional minute. Be careful not to over-whip, however. If you over-whip a meringue the egg whites will incorporate too much air, more than they can hold, and the meringue will break. If this happens you can make another one, or let it sit for 30 minutes on the counter so that the air bubbles deflate, then mix it at high speed for 30 seconds only. The meringue should be creamy and somewhat soft, like the rest of the cake mixture. If it is too stiff you'll have to mix too much to incorporate it, and you'll deflate the sponge.

6 Place the butter in a small microwave-safe bowl, cover with a sheet of paper towel, and melt in a microwave at 50 percent power for 1 minute.

7 In a large mixing bowl, fold together half of the egg and almond flour mixture, half of the meringue, and the melted butter with a large rubber spatula. When folding it is important that with each fold you bring the spatula all the way underneath the mixture to the bottom of the bowl, then fold the mixture up and over itself.

8 Gently fold together the remaining egg and almond flour mix and meringue. Take care to use a light touch, which will keep the mixture light and fluffy. Using a rubber spatula to scrape out every last bit, pour all of the mixture into the sheet pan, distributing it equally between the middle of the pan and the corners. Using an offset or a flat metal spatula (offset is easier) held at a slight angle, spread the mixture evenly over the pan with a back-and-forth, wax-on, wax-off motion. Use your rubber spatula to scrape the batter that adheres to the offset spatula back into the pan. It is important to do this efficiently and fairly quickly in order to not deflate the batter. The finished mixture should be about ¼ inch thick, with visible air bubbles.

9 Place the sheet pan in the preheated oven and bake for 8 to 10 minutes, until uniformly light golden brown. Cool on a rack.

IT'S DONE WHEN IT'S DONE

The cake should be light golden brown but still moist in the center. The oven temperature might seem very high for this thin cake, but it is precisely because the sponge is so thin that a hot oven is required to bake the cake quickly without drying it out. Baking it in a lower oven would be fatal, as the cake would require too much time in the oven, and that would completely dry it out.

STORAGE

The best thing to do after baking the cake is to leave it on the parchment paper until you need it. This sponge, like all sponges, can be frozen at the baked stage but never at the raw stage. The most efficient way to freeze a few of them would be to stack them between sheets of parchment paper, then double-wrap them airtight in plastic.

JACQUY'S TAKEAWAYS

→ **$50 TRICK:** If your sponge bakes too long and turns out dry and hard like a cracker, place it on the sheet pan, uncovered, in the refrigerator overnight. The moisture in the refrigerator will make it soft and usable again.

FLOURLESS CHOCOLATE SPONGE

INGREDIENTS	WEIGHT	MEASURE (APPROXIMATE) OR OUNCE WEIGHT
Egg yolks	120 grams	About 8 yolks
Granulated sugar	70 grams	6 tablespoons
Dark chocolate couverture (64%)	70 grams	2⅓ ounces
Unsweetened dark chocolate	11 grams	⅖ ounce
Egg whites	150 grams	4½ to 5 whites
Sea salt	Pinch	Pinch
Granulated sugar	70 grams	6 tablespoons

BEFORE YOU BEGIN

→ Get out the following equipment and allow all of the ingredients to come to room temperature:

Digital scale, set to metric weights
2 sheet pans, 1 lined with parchment paper
KitchenAid or stand mixer fitted with the whisk attachment
1 large rubber spatula
1 large mixing bowl
1 small microwave-safe mixing bowl or bowl that will fit over a double boiler
1 wide spatula or large stainless steel hand whisk
1 offset spatula
1 paring knife
Parchment paper

→ Read this recipe through twice from start to finish.

It would be difficult to find anyone who does not like flourless chocolate sponge. It is so smooth that there is a fine and delicious line between a sponge and a ganache. The fact that it does not contain flour makes it melt in your mouth at the first bite. In pastry we can use the flourless chocolate sponge as a component in a traditional chocolate cake, but I have seen it also end up in an ice cream cake, because it never completely hardens, even when it is frozen. The cake is also perfect as an element in a chocolate tart or a *verrine*, a dessert served in a glass (SEE PAGE 267). Enjoy this simple but excellent cake and be adventurous with it.

METHOD

1 Preheat the oven to 350°F/180°C. Line a sheet pan with parchment paper.
2 Place the egg yolks and 70 grams of granulated sugar in the bowl of your mixer fitted with a whisk. Whip for 3 minutes on high speed. Stop the machine and scrape down the sides of the bowl with a rubber spatula. Whip for another 3 minutes on medium until the mixture is thick and pale in color. Stop the machine and lift the whisk from the batter. The mixture should be at the ribbon stage, falling from the whisk in thick bands. Transfer to a large bowl with a rubber spatula and set aside. Wash the bowl of your mixer thoroughly with hot water and detergent and dry.
3 Place the dark chocolate couverture and unsweetened chocolate in a small mixing bowl over a double boiler on low heat and melt the chocolate; be careful not to burn it. You can also put it in a microwave-safe bowl and melt it with three 30-second zaps at 50 percent power. Stir gently with a rubber spatula until thoroughly melted.

4 Place the egg whites and sea salt in the clean, dry bowl of your electric mixer fitted with a whisk and whip for 10 seconds on medium speed. Add 70 grams of granulated sugar and whip on high to a stiff but not dry meringue, about 1½ minutes. Reduce the speed to low to maintain the meringue while you fold the chocolate into the egg yolk mixture.

5 Gently fold the melted chocolate into the egg yolk mixture with a large rubber spatula. Make sure to scrape the bottom of the bowl with each fold, as the chocolate will settle on the bottom.

6 Stop the mixer and, using a wide spatula or a balloon whisk, gently fold the meringue into the yolk mixture. Pour the mixture into different areas of the sheet pan and gently spread it evenly with an offset spatula. Try to spread the sponge quickly and efficiently so that you don't deflate it.

7 Bake for 12 minutes, until the tip of a paring knife inserted into the center of the cake comes out clean. Remove from the oven and let cool.

8 To remove the cake from the pan and the parchment paper, first run a paring knife between the edges of the cake and the sides of the sheet pan to separate them from the pan. Place a sheet of parchment paper on top of the chocolate sponge and set a sheet pan on top of the parchment paper so that the 2 sheet pans are stacked with the baked chocolate sponge and second sheet of parchment paper in between. Hold the 2 sheet pans together and flip them over. Remove the sheet pan that is now on top and very gently peel off the parchment paper. If it sticks, tear it off in strips.

IT'S DONE WHEN IT'S DONE

The surface should have a skin but the center should be moist, though not liquid (it shouldn't stick to a knife or skewer).

STORAGE

You can keep this sponge refrigerated for 2 days or frozen for up to 1 month. Like other sponges, the batter cannot be frozen.

JACQUY'S TAKEAWAYS

→ This is a great sponge to have on hand, as everyone likes a good flour-less cake; it would even make a good candidate to use in a Yule log (PAGE 249).

A flourless sponge is never baked in a tall pan because without flour it wouldn't hold its shape. Flour contains not only gluten that binds all the ingredients together, but also solids that allow sponge cakes to become firm. When you make this type of sponge you need to use ingredients that contain enough solids to mimic the properties of the flour so that the cake will hold together. Egg whites do not contain a lot of solids, since they consist of 85 to 90 percent water; some solids come from the egg yolks, but they come mostly from the sugar and the chocolate, which contain no water. Sugar and chocolate can seem to liquefy when they are heated and melt, but once they cool they harden again and make mixtures set up.

I like to combine 64 percent dark chocolate couverture with a small amount of unsweetened chocolate, which contributes a nice dark chocolate kick. I have little patience for chocolate desserts, candies, or cakes that are too sweet and have no punch; they should knock you off your chair. If you can't find unsweetened chocolate you can always combine the weight of the two types and use 85 grams of a darker chocolate couverture, such as a 70 percent.

Do not attempt to make flourless cake with milk chocolate or white chocolate, as your sponge will be overly sweet. Technically speaking, since there is no flour in this recipe, one of the only main solids is sugar. If you use milk or white chocolate for this recipe instead of staying with dark chocolate, the milk powder lactose present in these chocolates will clash with the rest of the ingredients and especially with the sugar, making the cake extremely sweet. I have never had a good milk chocolate or white chocolate flourless cake.

CHOCOLATE AND HAZELNUT YULE LOG / BÛCHE DE NOËL

INGREDIENTS	WEIGHT	MEASURE (APPROXIMATE) OR OUNCE WEIGHT
Hazelnut Praline Paste (PAGE 57)	1 recipe (use only half the caramelized nuts for the paste and the other half for sprinkling)	1 recipe (use half the caramelized nuts for the paste and half for sprinkling)
Jelly Roll Sponge (PAGE 241; do not include butter)	1 recipe	1 recipe
GANACHE AND CHOCOLATE MOUSSE FILLING		
Heavy cream (35% fat)	250 grams	1 cup plus 1 teaspoon
Dark chocolate couverture (64%)	450 grams	1 pound
Vanilla bean	1 bean	1 bean
Heavy cream (35% fat)	415 grams	1¾ cup plus 1 teaspoon
Butter (French style, 82% fat)	50 grams	1¾ ounce
Clover honey	30 grams	1½ tablespoons
GARNISH		
Cocoa powder	As desired	As desired
Crushed caramelized hazelnuts	As desired	As desired
Confectioners' sugar	As desired	As desired
Vanilla Custard Sauce (PAGE 35), optional	As desired	As desired

BEFORE YOU BEGIN

→ Get out the following equipment and allow all of the ingredients to come to room temperature:

Digital scale, set to metric weights
Equipment for Caramelized Hazelnuts (PAGE 51) and Hazelnut Praline Paste (PAGE 57)
Equipment for Jelly Roll Sponge (PAGE 241)
Equipment for Ganache (PAGE 72)
Equipment for Vanilla Custard Sauce (PAGE 35), optional
1 sheet pan lined with parchment paper
1 small offset spatula
KitchenAid or stand mixer fitted with the whisk attachment
1 large bowl
Plastic wrap
1 sheet pan lined with plastic wrap
1 medium or large rubber spatula
1 stainless steel hand whisk
1 digital thermometer
1 pastry bag
1 rolling pin
1 microwave-safe bowl, if necessary
1 serrated knife
1 set of round cookie cutters, different sizes, or jar caps

→ Read this recipe through twice from start to finish.

NOTE: Clear a space in the refrigerator large enough for a sheet pan.

Bûche de Noël is the traditional French Christmas cake. It represents the giant log (*bûche*) that families customarily lit in their fireplaces on Christmas Eve, a log so big that it was meant to burn until the first of January. Families used the ashes from their Yule logs for medicinal purposes and as a fertilizer for their crops. Yule logs thus symbolized hope for a good harvest.

At my family's bakery, my parents would make hundreds of *bûches de Noël* for the holidays. The entire family—aunts and uncles and cousins—would come over to help make them. The logs were usually filled with vanilla, coffee, or chocolate butter cream and frosted with ganache.

Parchment paper not being readily available at the time, bakers cut

their flour sacks down to sheet-pan size and used them as liners. Sometimes my dad ran out of flour sacks so he'd use newspaper; I'd know
because I could often see the lead print from the papers on the sponges.
That's pretty terrifying now to think about, but then no one would ever
notice and apparently no harm was done.

This recipe involves three different procedures, but your hard work
will be rewarded by the final result. You can get ahead by making the
caramelized hazelnuts up to 2 weeks before you make the cake. The combination of the moist sponge, a thin layer of hazelnut praline paste topped
with crunchy caramelized hazelnuts, the chocolate mousse filling, and the
thick chocolate ganache icing studded with more caramelized hazelnuts
makes a killer combination. Sinfully rich, it's a perfect end-of-the-year
celebration cake that your guests will never forget.

METHOD

1 Make a recipe of caramelized hazelnuts using the ingredient amounts for
the hazelnut praline paste recipe on **PAGE 57** and following the method you
prefer on **PAGE 51**. Use half the caramelized nuts for the hazelnut praline paste
and set aside the other half in an airtight container.

2 Make the jelly roll sponge following the instructions on **PAGE 241** (do not
include the optional butter). Once it has cooled completely, place another
sheet pan upside down on your work surface, line it with parchment paper,
and flip the sheet pan with the génoise over onto the parchment paper.
Carefully remove the paper from the underside of the génoise.

3 Using a small offset spatula, carefully spread the nut paste in a very thin
layer over the génoise, leaving a ½-inch border all the way around.

MAKING THE GANACHE AND THE MOUSSE FILLING

1 First whip the 250 grams of heavy cream until semi-stiff (**SEE PAGE 114**). Be
careful not to over-beat. If the cream is whipped until stiff you will not be able
to fold it evenly into the ganache to achieve a smooth mousse. Transfer to a
bowl, cover with plastic wrap, and refrigerate.

2 Line a sheet pan with plastic wrap. Make the ganache recipe with the
remaining ingredients listed, following the method for making ganache on
PAGE 72. Once the ganache is made, scale 700 grams of it (about 2¾ cups)
and scrape onto the plastic-lined sheet pan with a spatula. Cover airtight with
another sheet of plastic wrap and place in the refrigerator for 15 minutes.

3 Fold the whipped cream into the remaining ganache, first with a whisk for
20 seconds, then with a rubber spatula. It is important that the ganache not

be too cold. I recommend a temperature of 104°F/40°C. Do not over-fold, just mix until the ganache and whipped cream are amalgamated, with no more visible traces of ganache or whipped cream. This is your chocolate mousse filling.

ROLLING AND FINISHING THE CAKE

1 Carefully pour all of the chocolate mousse onto the nut paste–covered génoise and, leaving a ½-inch border all the way around, spread evenly over the cake with an offset spatula, taking care not to deflate it.

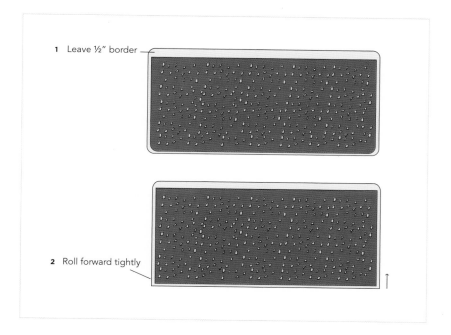

1 Leave ½" border

2 Roll forward tightly

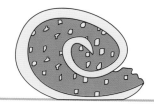

1 Improper loose rolling:
The Yule log won't hold its shape.

2 Place half the caramelized hazelnuts in a pastry bag and tap lightly with a rolling pin to crush them coarsely. You want to keep some big chunks. Sprinkle the crushed nuts evenly over the chocolate mousse.

3 Roll up the cake. Begin by lifting the corners of the parchment paper that the génoise is sitting on to help you roll it. Roll it tightly and gradually, rolling over once, then tightening gently and peeling back the parchment paper, then rolling over again and so on, so that the log is round and not flat (SEE ILLUSTRATION). Don't worry if the cake cracks a little as you roll it or if the outer skin comes off; you will be covering it with plenty of ganache. Place the rolled cake in the refrigerator for 20 minutes.

4 Remove the ganache from the refrigerator and make sure that it is not too cold. It should be spreadable; if it is too stiff, transfer it to a microwave-safe

2 Proper tight rolling:
The Yule log will hold its shape.

bowl and microwave for 15 seconds at 50 percent power, then stir with a rubber spatula. Repeat if necessary.

5   Take the Yule log out of the refrigerator, and check to see if the outer skin of the sponge comes off (it may have come off and stuck to the parchment paper when you rolled it). If it does, peel it off. Spread a thin layer of ganache onto the log with an offset spatula. We call this first thin layer a crumb coat. Then spread all but a small amount of the remaining ganache in a generous layer over the entire log. Run an offset spatula horizontally along the log to make a striped pattern on the surface resembling wood bark. With a serrated knife, cut off each end of the log at an angle and glue the end pieces on top of the log to create the look of knots on the log. Spread a small amount of ganache over and around the 2 knots as well as over both ends of the log. Dust the log with cocoa powder and, using different sizes of round cookie cutters or jar caps, create the look of rings on cut wood by making small indentations on the top of each knot. Dust with cocoa powder if desired. Lightly crush the remaining caramelized nuts and sprinkle over the Yule log. Dust with confectioners' sugar. Place in the refrigerator for 1 hour so that it will firm up. Once the Yule log is firm you can transfer it to a serving platter. Keep refrigerated until 2 hours before you wish to serve.

STORAGE

The Yule log will last 48 hours in a refrigerator but you can also freeze it for up to a month. To do this, freeze uncovered for 2 hours, then wrap it airtight to store in your freezer. Unwrap and defrost in the refrigerator. It should take about 6 hours to defrost.

JACQUY'S TAKEAWAYS

→ Remember to remove the cake from the refrigerator 2 hours before serving so that the ganache and mousse are creamy.

→ The log is delicious served with Vanilla Sauce (**PAGE 35**).

GÂTEAU ST. HONORÉ

YIELD | ONE 9-INCH CAKE

2- OR 3-DAY RECIPE | YOU WILL NEED TO
MAKE PUFF PASTRY AT LEAST 1 DAY BEFORE
YOU MAKE THIS CAKE. IDEALLY, MAKE IT
2 DAYS AHEAD SO THAT WHEN YOU ROLL
IT OUT YOU CAN LET IT REST FOR A FULL
DAY BEFORE CUTTING THE CAKE ROUND.

INGREDIENTS	WEIGHT	MEASURE (APPROXIMATE) OR OUNCE WEIGHT
Puff Pastry (PAGE 28)	150 grams	5³⁄₁₀ ounces
Pâte à Choux (PAGE 11)	½ recipe	½ recipe
Egg Wash (PAGE 7)	1 recipe	1 recipe
CRÈME LÉGÈRE		
Pastry Cream (PAGE 39)	1 recipe	1 recipe
Cold heavy cream (35% fat)	75 grams	⅓ cup less 1 tablespoon
CRÈME CHANTILLY		
Cold heavy cream (35% fat)	200 grams	1 cup less 1 tablespoon
Vanilla extract	3 grams	¾ teaspoon
Granulated sugar	30 grams	2 tablespoons
CARAMEL		
Granulated sugar	150 grams	⅔ cup plus ½ teaspoon
Water	50 grams	¼ cup
Corn syrup	50 grams	2 tablespoons
Fresh raspberries	1 pint	1 pint

This is by far one of my favorite desserts in the entire French pastry repertoire. It involves four of my very favorite pastry components—*pâte à choux*, pastry cream, caramel, and puff pastry—in one magical combination. A puff pastry base is topped with a round of *pâte à choux* and baked, then topped with *pâte à choux* puffs. The cake and the puffs are filled with a silky pastry cream mixed with whipped cream and glazed with caramel, and finally piped with a layer of sweetened whipped cream called *crème chantilly*. A layer of raspberries is hidden inside the pastry cream and another layer decorates the cake. It does not get much better than that! You can make one big gâteau St. Honoré or several individual pastries.

Although the 9-inch cake only requires half a batch of *choux* pastry, I recommend that you make the entire recipe, and with the extra dough pipe different shapes that you can freeze for later. It's always nice to have some cream puff, éclair, and *salambo* shells on hand in the freezer!

It's important to give yourself plenty of time to make this cake so that the puff pastry will have enough time to rest. Once you have completed

BEFORE YOU BEGIN

→ Get out the following equipment and allow all of the ingredients to come to room temperature:

Equipment for Puff Pastry (PAGE 28)
Equipment for Pâte à Choux (PAGE 11)
Equipment for Pastry Cream (PAGE 39)
Equipment for Caramel (PAGE 47)
One 9-inch ring, tart pan insert, or plate
Scissors
2 sheet pans lined with parchment paper
1 pastry bag fitted with a ½-inch round tip
1 pastry brush
1 fork
1 KitchenAid or standing mixer fitted with the whisk attachment, stainless steel hand whisk, or handheld electric mixer
1 small bowl
1 rubber spatula
2 medium mixing bowls
1 paring knife
1 pastry bag fitted with a ¼-inch round tip
Aluminum foil
Latex gloves
1 small offset spatula
1 pastry bag fitted with the St. Honoré tip (see below) or a ½-inch star tip

→ Read this recipe through twice from start to finish.

NOTE: A St. Honoré piping tip has a special deep V that creates the peaked tips used to decorate a classic gâteau St. Honoré. You can find these tips online at **http://www.backmann24.com/**.

all of the turns and rolled out the pastry to a thin sheet, ideally you will be able to refrigerate it for a full day before cutting the round cake base. If you don't let it rest sufficiently the round will shrink the moment you've cut it because of the gluten in the flour, and the base will be oval. I have watched my students try to rush through the process and after all that work they end up with an oval cake.

METHOD

DAY 1

Make a recipe of puff pastry following the recipe on PAGE 28, or if you have some puff pastry and/or puff pastry scraps on hand in the freezer, allow them to thaw. You will need approximately 150 grams.

DAY 2 (OR DAY 2 AND DAY 3)

1 Complete the puff pastry turns and roll out to a thickness of ⅛ inch. Place on a sheet pan and, using a dough docker or a fork, dock the pastry every ½ inch. Let rest in the refrigerator for several hours or overnight.

2 Place the rested puff pastry on a cutting board and place a 9-inch ring, tart pan insert, or plate on top near the edge (so that you don't waste any dough). Cut out a 9-inch circle, turn the disk over, and place it on a parchment paper–lined sheet pan, leaving enough room for 13 cream puffs on one side. Refrigerate while you prepare the *pâte à choux*.

3 Preheat the oven to 400°F/200°C. Prepare a recipe of *pâte à choux* following the recipe on PAGE 11. Place the mixture in a pastry bag fitted with a ½-inch round tip.

4 Make a recipe of egg wash. Remove the sheet pan with the puff pastry from the refrigerator and glaze the circumference of the disk with a small amount of egg wash. Hold the pastry bag vertically 1 inch above the disk and slowly and carefully pipe a ring of *pâte à choux* onto the egg-washed edge of the puff pastry disk (SEE ILLUSTRATION). Then, holding the bag 1 inch above the disk, pipe a loose spiral of *pâte à choux*, starting in the center and working your way out (SEE ILLUSTRATION). The piping should not be too tight, and you should leave 1 inch of space between the concentric circles so that some of the base is exposed. There should still be enough *choux* pastry in the bag to pipe thirteen 1-inch circles.

UNDERSTANDING INGREDIENTS

Puff pastry is the dough of choice for this cake, but pie dough is also a good candidate if you happen to have some in the freezer. Parts of the dough will be covered with piped *choux* pastry, which will slow down its baking time, so it is very important to roll the dough out thin enough—⅛ inch—so that it has a chance to bake thoroughly. Once it is baked it will be covered with *crème légère*, a mix of pastry cream and whipped cream, and if the dough below it isn't thoroughly baked it can become soggy very quickly. This is also true for the *choux* pastry puffs; they must be baked until dry or they will become soggy once filled. It's important too that when you make the pastry cream you cook it fully so that it is not too moist; otherwise it will become soupy when you fold in the whipped cream. Before making the caramel, review the method on PAGE 47 so that you will be comfortable making it.

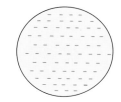

1 Dock the puff pastry.

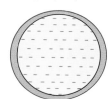

2 Pipe a ring of *pâte à choux* around the puff pastry.

3 Pipe a loose spiral of *pâte à choux* starting in the center and working your way out.

1 Glue the puffs at the 12 o'clock mark, the 6 o'clock, 3 o'clock, and 9 o'clock marks.

2 Glue two puffs between each mark so that you have 12 puffs on the edge of the base.

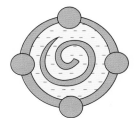 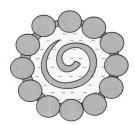

A Little Bit of History

It is interesting to know that St. Michel is the patron saint of grocers, mariners, paratroopers, policemen—and pastry chefs. Every year pastry chefs in France celebrate him from September 21 to 29 by making different kinds of cakes in his honor. St. Honoré is the patron of millers and bakers. No special celebration takes place for him, but the St. Honoré cake was invented in his honor by Maison Chiboust at the Palais Royal, so he is celebrated all year round. It is comforting to know that not one but two saints are watching over you while you are making this recipe; this should definitely increase your confidence in successfully making the cake.

5 Now pipe thirteen 1-inch puffs onto the parchment paper next to the disk. Glaze all of the piped *pâte à choux*, both the circles on the base and the puffs, with a small amount of egg wash. Using a fork, lightly score them to ensure that the *choux* pastry rises evenly.

6 Place the sheet pan in the preheated oven and bake for 10 to 15 minutes, until the puffs rise. Reduce the heat to 325°F/160°C and bake for another 25 minutes, until the round puffs are golden brown. After 35 to 40 minutes of baking quickly remove the sheet pan from the oven and close the oven door. Remove the baked puffs and immediately place the sheet pan with the base back in the oven. You do not want to interrupt the baking of the base for too long. Bake for another 15 minutes, until golden brown, and let cool completely.

7 While the cake bakes in the oven you will have time to make the pastry cream, following the directions on **PAGE 39**. While it is cooling in the freezer and then the refrigerator, whip the 75 grams of cold heavy cream to semi-stiff peaks about as stiff as shaving cream (**SEE PAGE 114**). Transfer to a small bowl with a rubber spatula and refrigerate.

8 Once the pastry cream is cold, place in a medium bowl and mix with a hand whisk, a KitchenAid or stand mixer, or an electric handheld mixer until it is loose, shiny, and free of lumps. Using a rubber spatula, gently fold in one-third of the 75 grams of whipped cream. Fold in the remaining two-thirds until the mixture is just homogenized, and place in the refrigerator. This enriched pastry cream is called *crème légère*.

9 Using a paring knife or a very pointy piping tip, poke a ¼-inch-wide hole on the bottom of each puff. Prepare a pastry bag fitted with a ¼-inch round tip and fill it halfway with *crème légère*. Insert the tip into the puff hole and fill the puffs. If cream emerges from the hole, scrape it onto the edge of your mixing bowl.

10 Make the *crème chantilly*. In a medium bowl whip the 200 grams of cold heavy cream with the vanilla and the sugar to semi-stiff peaks and refrigerate.

11 Make the caramel. Combine the water, corn syrup, and sugar in a small pan. Place a bowl of cold water large enough to accommodate the bottom of the pan on the stove nearby. Follow the caramel-making directions on **PAGE 47** and cook on medium heat until the caramel reaches 325°F/160°C. Dip the bottom of the pan into the bowl of cold water for 10 seconds to stop the cooking and keep your caramel at the right color and flavor. Keep warm so that the caramel stays loose. You can keep the pan on a wire rack, over a pad of paper towels or a heating pad to keep it warm, or gently reheat if it begins to stiffen as you dip the cream puffs.

12 Line a sheet pan with parchment paper or a silpat. Fold a small piece of aluminum foil over the edge of your caramel pot. Wearing latex gloves, hold a puff by the bottom and dip the rounded top about one-third of the way into the caramel. Scrape the edge on the foil-covered side of the pan and place the puff on the sheet pan. Repeat with the other puffs.

13 Once all of the puffs are glazed, reheat the caramel if necessary so that it is soft and suitable for dipping. Place the round puff pastry base in front of you. Hold a cream puff by the top, dip the bottom part into the soft caramel, and glue it onto the ring at the 12 o'clock mark. Repeat with 3 more puffs and glue at the 6 o'clock, 3 o'clock, and 9 o'clock marks. Glue the remaining puffs, placing 2 puffs between each mark so that you have 12 puffs on the edge of the base.

14 Fill the pastry bag with the remaining *crème légère* and pipe half of it into the center of the cake in a ½-inch layer. Press half the fresh raspberries into the cream and cover with another ½ inch of *crème légère*. Smooth it flat with a small offset spatula.

15 Fit a pastry bag with a St. Honoré tip (**SEE PAGE XXVI**) or a ¾-inch star tip and fill with the *crème chantilly*. Pipe the *chantilly* on top of the *crème légère*. Place the last puff in the middle of the cake and decorate with the remaining fresh raspberries.

IT'S DONE WHEN IT'S DONE

The baked *pâte à choux* and puff pastry cake should be golden brown and firm.

STORAGE

Because this cake is made with pastry cream and caramel it is best eaten the same day; it will get soggy overnight in the refrigerator.

JACQUY'S TAKEAWAYS

→ The pastry cream for the *crème légère* could be flavored with coffee, caramel, chocolate, or praline paste.

→ You can create another look with the cream puffs by dipping them into the caramel and placing them dipped side down on a silpat so that the caramel side ends up flat.

→ To make individual St. Honorés, cut 3- to 4-inch puff pastry disks and pipe *pâte à choux* rings around the circumference but not in the middle. Glue 3 small puffs onto each ring.

BLACK FOREST CAKE

2-DAY RECIPE

INGREDIENTS	WEIGHT	MEASURE (APPROXIMATE) OR OUNCE WEIGHT
CHOCOLATE SPONGE		
Butter and flour mixture for greasing pans (PAGE 8) if using a regular cake pan	1 recipe	1 recipe
Cake flour	75 grams	⅔ cup
Cocoa powder	20 grams	2½ tablespoons
Egg yolks	75 grams	4 to 5 yolks, depending on the size of the eggs
Granulated sugar	45 grams	3 tablespoons
Egg whites	110 grams	3 whites plus 2 tablespoons
Granulated sugar	60 grams	¼ cup
Sea salt	Pinch	Pinch
CHERRIES IN SYRUP		
Dark cherries, pitted	285 grams	10 ounces
Granulated sugar	100 grams	½ cup
Organic cherry juice	165 grams	⅔ cup
Kirschwasser	5 grams	1 teaspoon
Vanilla Custard Sauce (PAGE 35)	½ recipe	½ recipe
Chocolate Mousse (PAGE 78)	1 recipe	1 recipe
CHERRY SOAKING JELLY		
Gelatin	1.5 grams	½ teaspoon
Organic cherry juice	5 grams	1 teaspoon
Cherry juice (from cherries in syrup)	100 grams	⅓ cup plus 1 tablespoon
Kirschwasser	10 grams	2 teaspoons
BAVARIAN CREAM		
Heavy cream (35% fat)	105 grams	½ cup
Gelatin	2.5 grams	1 teaspoon
Water	12.5 grams	1 scant tablespoon
Kirschwasser	10 grams	2 teaspoons
Vanilla Custard Sauce (PAGE 35)	150 grams	5³⁄₁₀ ounces or about ⅞ cup
Dark chocolate couverture (64%) block, for decoration	One 50-gram block	One 1⅖-ounce block
Cherries, whipped cream, and confectioners' sugar, for decoration	As desired	As desired

BEFORE YOU BEGIN

→ Get out the following equipment and allow all of the ingredients to come to room temperature:

Digital scale, set to metric weights
One 6¾- or 7-inch Flexipan cake mold or one 7-inch metal cake pan
1 sifter
KitchenAid or stand mixer fitted with the whisk attachment
1 large mixing bowl
1 rubber spatula
1 sheet pan
1 paring knife
1 wire rack
Plastic wrap
1 small saucepan
1 small stainless steel hand whisk
1 strainer
Two ¾-inch-high bars
1 serrated knife
1 small bowl
1 double boiler
1 pastry brush
1 medium mixing bowl
One 3-inch cookie cutter or vegetable peeler
1 medium offset spatula
1 digital thermometer
1 strip of 2-inch-high acetate (if using Method 2 to decorate)
Cutting board lined with parchment paper (if using Method 2)

→ Read this recipe through twice from start to finish.

There are many variations of this popular cake. In the last four decades I have seen it go from an old-fashioned layer cake to a domed cake where all of the components are hidden beneath the chocolate sponge, to an individual pastry to a plated dessert. But no matter what form it takes, it will always combine cherries, chocolate, whipped cream, and a kirsch-flavored vanilla cream or mousse of some kind.

What lies beneath the success of the Black Forest cake is the complex and subtle relationship between all of the flavors. Sweet and slightly acidic cherries with sweet chocolate is a match made in heaven, but sour cherries and very bitter chocolate would not work at all. As always the flavors have to complement each other and not fight. That is the key to creating successful pastries.

With its German origins, it should come as no surprise that this is the cake of choice in the eastern part of France where I grew up. But you can find it in other regions as well. Its universal appeal and expatriate chefs like me who travel with their recipe books have given Black Forest cake an international reputation.

·⊱ ORGANIZING YOUR TIME ⊰·

Black Forest cake takes longer to make than many cakes, but the reward is worth it. It has several components and you must begin work on this recipe at least 1 day ahead to have all of them ready. It's definitely not the cake to decide to make on the morning of your spouse's birthday for his or her party that night. Here is the way you need to organize your time:

DAY 1
Make the chocolate sponge
Make the cherries in syrup
Make the vanilla custard sauce
Start the chocolate mousse

DAY 2
Prepare the cherry soaking syrup and soak the cake
Make the Bavarian cream
Assemble the cake
Make the chocolate shavings
Finish the chocolate mousse
Decorate the cake

METHOD

DAY 1

MAKING THE CHOCOLATE SPONGE

1 Preheat the oven to 350°F/180°C. If you are not using a Flexipan, grease a regular 7-inch cake pan with the butter and flour mixture. Sift together the flour and the cocoa powder.

2 Place the egg yolks and the first 45 grams of sugar in the bowl of your mixer, attach the whisk, and whip on high speed for 3 minutes. Reduce the speed to medium and mix for another 3 minutes. The mixture should be pale and frothy. Transfer it to a large mixing bowl with a rubber spatula. Thoroughly wash the electric mixing bowl and whisk attachment with hot soapy water to make sure that no traces of egg yolks are left on the bowl or beater, as they would prevent the egg whites from setting up. Dry and place back on the stand.

3 Place the egg whites with the next 60 grams of sugar and the pinch of sea salt in the clean and dried mixing bowl and whip the mixture on high speed until it becomes a soft-peaks meringue (PAGE 69), about 1 minute.

4 Using a large rubber spatula, gently fold the flour mixture into the egg yolk mixture along with a third of the egg white mixture, making sure that you reach all the way down to the bottom of the mixing bowl with every fold. Gently fold in the rest of the meringue. The folding is complete when the mixture has one uniform color.

5 Place your round Flexipan or 7-inch buttered and floured cake pan on a sheet pan. Carefully pour the sponge mixture into the pan. Place in the oven and bake for 30 to 35 minutes. Check the doneness by inserting a paring knife into the center of the cake; it should come out clean. Bake another 5 minutes if it does not.

6 Unmold the cake and let it cool on a wire rack for 1 hour, then wrap it in plastic wrap and keep at room temperature.

The reason we always remove cakes from the cake pan or Flexipan right away is that the steam from the baked cake would hit the sides of the mold or pan and create wet spots in the cake.

MAKING THE CHERRIES IN SYRUP

Place the pitted cherries, sugar, and cherry juice in a small saucepan and stir to dissolve the sugar. Bring to a simmer over medium heat and simmer for 5 minutes. Turn off the heat and stir in the kirschwasser. Immediately cover with plastic wrap and let cool for 1 hour. Refrigerate overnight.

MAKING THE VANILLA CUSTARD SAUCE

Make the vanilla sauce following the recipe on PAGE 35. Measure out 150 grams for the Bavarian cream. You will use the rest as a sauce for the cake. Cover and refrigerate overnight.

UNDERSTANDING INGREDIENTS

The cake component of Black Forest cake is a chocolate sponge that is specifically designed to be soaked with syrup or, in this instance, cherry juice. For this reason the cake does not contain butter, and I've increased the proportion of flour so that the sponge is on the dry side. These two factors will help the sponge absorb and retain the cherry juice. The juice has a little bit of gelatin added to it so that the soaked cake doesn't fall apart. When you brush the sponge make sure to use up all of the juice or the cake will be dry.

I usually use cake flour for my sponges as it is low in gluten; no one likes a rubbery cake. For chocolate sponges, I shy away from using natural cocoa powder, which has a very acidic flavor that might overpower the subtle but distinctive flavor profile of this cake. I prefer to use Dutch-process cocoa powder; this type of processing neutralizes the acidity in the cocoa. Dutch-process cocoa powder has a strong chocolate flavor and a dark brown color, as opposed to natural cocoa powder, which is lighter.

A Bavarian cream is made with crème anglaise that is cooled down and mixed with whipped cream, resulting in a mousse that is slightly liquid. To help it hold its shape, we fold in a small amount

MAKING THE CHOCOLATE MOUSSE

Make the chocolate mousse following the recipe on PAGE 78. Refrigerate the ganache overnight as instructed and whip the mousse on Day 2 (see below).

DAY 2

1 Drain the cooked cherries through a strainer set over a bowl. Set out a 7-inch Flexipan mold or a 7-inch cake pan lined with plastic wrap.

2 Place the chocolate sponge cake on a cutting board and place a ¾-inch bar on each side. Using a serrated knife positioned parallel to your cutting board, with the side of the blade resting on the bars to ensure an even slice, slice a layer off the top of the cake. The key to getting an even layer is to keep the blade flat against the bar and to saw back and forth gently; don't try to force the knife into the cake. Wrap the top layer of the sponge tightly in plastic wrap and place in the freezer for another use. Place the bottom sponge slice in the lined cake pan.

MAKING THE CHERRY SOAKING SYRUP

In a small bowl, combine the gelatin and 5 grams of cherry juice and stir together. Let sit for 2 minutes, at which point the gelatin should have softened, or "bloomed." It will not look dry anymore and will have absorbed most of the water. Set over a double boiler until the mixture melts, and remove from the heat. Whisk in 100 grams of cherry cooking syrup (about ⅓ cup plus 1 tablespoon) and the kirshwasser. Using a pastry brush, soak the sponge generously with the syrup. Wait 5 minutes for the sponge to absorb the syrup and then brush it one more time. Continue to brush until all of the syrup has been used up. Distribute the cherries evenly on top of the sponge.

MAKING THE BAVARIAN CREAM

1 Whip the heavy cream until it is semi-stiff and place in the refrigerator. Mix the 2.5 grams of gelatin with the 12.5 grams of water in a medium mixing bowl and let soften for 2 minutes. Place it over a double boiler until it melts. Remove from the heat. Whisk in the kirschwasser and the 50 grams of the vanilla sauce you set aside for the Bavarian cream. If the mixture thickens right away it is slightly too cold; place it on the double boiler for a minute and whisk until it is loose again. Remove from the heat and add the remaining vanilla sauce. Using a rubber spatula, fold in the whipped cream.

2 Pour the Bavarian cream over the cherries and place the cake pan in the freezer for 1 hour so that the cake can firm up.

FINISHING THE CHOCOLATE MOUSSE

1 While the cake is in the freezer, make the chocolate shavings and finish the chocolate mousse. Take a block of chocolate and scrape off a large plate full of shavings using a round 3-inch cookie cutter, a vegetable peeler, or a special tool for shaving chocolate (SEE PAGE XXVI).

2 To finish the chocolate mousse, place the ganache for the mousse in the bowl of your mixer and fit with the whisk attachment. Whip for 1 minute on high speed. Scrape down the sides of the bowl and whip on high speed for another minute, until the ganache is transformed into a mousse. Do not over-whip or the mousse will be grainy. Remove the whisk and place the bowl in the refrigerator until you are ready to finish the cake.

FINISHING THE BLACK FOREST CAKE

There are two different ways to finish the cake.

METHOD 1: Unmold the cake and place it on a cutting board. Using a medium offset spatula, frost the top and sides with the chocolate mousse. Using a tablespoon, arrange the shaved chocolate in a ring around the bottom of the cake. Clean and dry the offset spatula and use it to pick up shavings from the ring and press them onto the sides of the cake. Sprinkle a generous amount on the top (but handle them as little as possible because they will melt from the heat of your hands). Using a wide spatula, transfer the cake carefully to a platter and let it defrost in the refrigerator for 2 hours, or in a cool room for 1 hour. Dust confectioners' sugar on the top or decorate with whipped cream rosettes and cherries, and serve with additional vanilla sauce on the side.

METHOD 2: This method is a little more labor intensive, as it requires tempered dark chocolate. Prepare an acetate strip that is 2 inches tall (it should be ¼ inch taller than the cake) and 1 inch longer than the circumference of your cake pan (to find food-grade acetate, see the supplier list on PAGE XXVI). Temper 100 grams of dark chocolate couverture following the directions on PAGE 208.

Line a cutting board with parchment paper. Remove the cake from the freezer and unmold onto the parchment paper. Place the acetate strip flat on the counter and spread a thin layer of tempered chocolate on it using an offset spatula. Immediately wrap the cake: hold the strip with an end in each hand and wrap the cake left to right, with the chocolate-coated side of the acetate facing the cake. The end will overlap slightly, which is normal. Let the cake sit for 5 minutes to allow the chocolate to set and then remove the strip of acetate from right to left. Fill the top generously with chocolate shavings

of gelatin into the mousse. Bavarian creams are very creamy and smooth in texture. They can be used as a component in layered cakes or as a stand-alone mousse served with berries and perhaps a crumble.

For the cherries in syrup I use fresh dark cherries when they are in season. Otherwise I use frozen dark cherries; these also work very well. Canned cherries and morello cherries do not work well for this, as they don't have enough flavor and morello cherries are too sour. Cherries are best eaten fresh, and I usually do not use them to flavor mousses, as they do not have a lot of flavor compared to other stone fruit. A good way to bring out their flavor is to cook them in syrup made with organic cherry juice and sugar. This also preserves their color; once cherries are cut open, they react with the oxygen in the air and turn brown unless you cook them with sugar or preserve them by pickling them with an acid such as vinegar.

The kirshwasser is usually a must in a Black Forest cake, as it brings out the flavor of the cherries very nicely. The amount here is quite small, and you can reduce it by one-third if you want even less of an alcohol flavor and more of a cherry flavor.

and refrigerate. Let the cake defrost in the refrigerator for 2 hours or in a cool room for 1 to 2 hours or up to 48 hours before serving. Dust with confectioners' sugar and a few cherries and serve with vanilla sauce on the side.

OPTION 1

Using a medium offset spatula frost the top and sides with the chocolate mousse. Press chocolate shavings onto the sides of the cake: sprinkle a generous amount of chocolate shavings on the top.

OPTION 2

Spread a thin layer of tempered chocolate on a strip of acetate using an offset spatula. Immediately wrap the cake: hold the strip with an end in each hand and wrap the cake left to the right, with the chocolate-coated side of the acetate facing the cake.

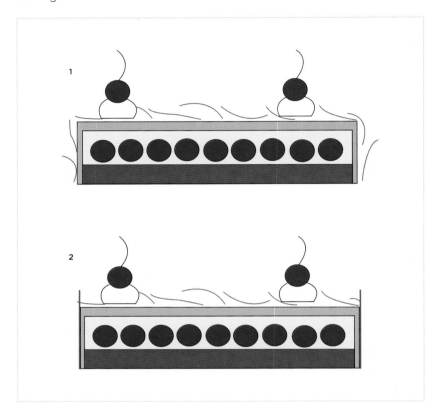

IT'S DONE WHEN IT'S DONE

The mousse should be soft but not icy; the sponge should be moist but not wet. You should taste the intricate flavor interaction between the cherries, the chocolate, the vanilla, and the kirschwasser. Remember that you can increase or reduce the liquor to taste (but don't increase by more than 5 percent or the flavor of the cake will be overpowered), or even omit it if it is unpleasant for you or if your children do not like it.

STORAGE

You can keep this finished cake in the freezer for up to 1 month and it keeps for 2 to 3 full days in the refrigerator.

BLACK FOREST CAKE ALWAYS MAKES ME THINK of a young chef named Keegan Gerhard, who worked for me when I was the pastry chef at the Sheraton Hotel in Chicago and now has two restaurants of his own. This story is about how Keegan got his start in pastry.

The Chicago Sheraton is a big hotel with the largest ballroom in the Midwest. Keegan applied for the assistant pastry chef position. He was an experienced savory chef, and despite his lack of experience in pastry he had all the other qualities a chef must have—self-motivation, commitment to quality, and a great attitude. I always tell my students that I can teach them all the pastry techniques in the world but I cannot teach them to have a great attitude. That has to come from them. Great attitude can help people lift mountains, and for Keegan it helped him get his break in pastry. He had just been hired, and on his second day of work he was touring the hotel with eight other newly hired employees as part of their orientation. I pulled him out of the tour and asked him, "Keegan, you are part German, right? Have you ever made a Schwarzwalder Kirschtorte?"—the German name for Black Forest cake.

He answered, "Yes, Chef, when I was a kid I made one once with my Oma [grandmother]."

"Great!" I said. "We need 368 nine-inch Black Forest cakes for the day after tomorrow."

His jaw dropped, but he said, "Yes, Chef."

That is all I wanted to hear. I knew then and there that he was the right person for the job. The wrong person would have come up with all sorts of excuses, not realizing that I was testing him. We already had the Black Forest cake production laid out, but we integrated Keegan into it; it was his boot camp. His first cakes looked very rustic, but by the end they looked stellar; repetition and practice is everything in our business.

The large events that we were catering forced my team and me to be very organized. I trained them to time themselves and see how long it actually took to plate up 4,000 slices of Black Forest cake with sauce and decoration, so that we would be ready when the desserts had to be served. After a trial run, we concluded that it took 4 seconds to plate one slice; this, multiplied by 4,000, was 16,000 seconds—about 4 hours and 45 minutes. For such large banquets we also had to count, measure, and multiply everything that ended up on the plate by 4,000 to make sure that we did not run out of anything. After working together for a while my team had this type of detail down to a science. They knew how many strawberries, raspberries, or blueberries are in a pint or how many cherries are in a #10 can. These details were lifesavers for us.

Although you may never need to make 4,000 servings of Black Forest cake, the ability to do it begins with knowing how to make one good one.

CHOCOLATE MOUSSE CAKE IN A GLASS / GÂTEAU MOUSSE AU CHOCOLAT EN VERRINE

YIELD | 8 SERVINGS

2-DAY RECIPE

INGREDIENTS	WEIGHT	MEASURE (APPROXIMATE) OR OUNCE WEIGHT
CHOCOLATE MOUSSE		
Heavy cream (35% fat)	390 grams	1¾ cups
Corn syrup	33 grams	1 tablespoon plus 1 teaspoon
Clover honey	33 grams	1 tablespoon plus 1 teaspoon
Dark chocolate couverture (64%)	158 grams	5½ ounces
VERRINE		
Chocolate Mousse (PAGE 78)	1 recipe	1 recipe
Caramelized Hazelnuts (PAGE 51), whole or crushed (to taste)	80 grams	½ cup
Flourless Chocolate Sponge (PAGE 246)	1 recipe	1 recipe
Chocolate Nougatine Crisp (PAGE 59)	40 grams	2⅘ ounces
Hazelnut Praline Paste (PAGE 57)	100 grams	½ cup
Chocolate Shavings, for decoration (PAGE 378)	20 grams (shave from a 50-gram block)	⁷⁄₁₀ ounce (shave from a 1.76-ounce block)
OPTIONAL DECORATION		
Hazelnut Caramel Curls (PAGE 376)	8 curls	8 curls

Dessert in a glass is quite a concept. I included this recipe, called a *verrine* in French, because I want you to see how easy it is to come up with a quick and impressive dessert with components that you can have on hand. French pastry shops have been making *verrines* for a decade now. Made with multiple components—as a general rule I like to have three main flavors and at least three to five different textures—layered in tall see-through plastic glasses, *verrines* showcase very nicely. They're convenient, because the customers can take them home and serve them as they are.

Once you have mastered many of the techniques in this book you will not mind doubling certain recipes in order to create a small stock of items like frozen Sponge Cake (PAGE 237), Streusel (PAGE 9), or Caramelized Almonds and Hazelnuts (PAGE 51). This is how a professional pastry

BEFORE YOU BEGIN

→ Get out the following equipment and allow all of the ingredients to come to room temperature:

Digital scale, set to metric weights
Equipment for Chocolate Mousse
  (PAGE 78)
Equipment for Caramelized Hazelnuts
  (PAGE 51)
Equipment for Flourless Chocolate
  Sponge (PAGE 246)
Equipment for Chocolate Nougatine
  Crisp (PAGE 59)
Equipment for Hazelnut Praline Paste
  (PAGE 57)
Equipment for Caramel (PAGE 47), if
  using the optional hazelnut garnish
8 tall glasses
Round cookie cutters or paring knife
1 pastry bag fitted with a ½-inch
  round tip
1 vegetable peeler

→ Read this recipe through twice from start to finish.

Entertaining in the French Style

You will see that once you embrace the fun of cooking or baking you will want to invite family and friends over more often. For the French, entertaining is one of our ultimate joys. We place a lot of importance in general on our quality of life, and fine dining, both in homes and in restaurants, is a vital part of our heritage. It is so important to us that France successfully lobbied UNESCO to include "The French Gastronomic Meal" on the organization's "Intangible Culture Heritage of Humanity" list.

In this age of distractions caused by the technology that is running our lives it is crucial for everyone, French or not, to keep the art of entertaining alive. Otherwise someday we might end up losing our social traditions and be forced to have virtual dinners on our computers. I can assure you that they will not taste anything like this luscious dessert in a glass.

chef thinks—if you make a component for one cake, why not make it for more than one and freeze the extra for future desserts? Now you've got some Flourless Chocolate Sponge (PAGE 246) in the freezer, some Caramelized Hazelnuts (PAGE 51) in a jar, and some Chocolate Nougatine Crisp (PAGE 59) in another jar. With some of the caramelized hazelnuts you can make Hazelnut Praline Paste (PAGE 57)—or maybe you already have that in the refrigerator. Thinking a day ahead, all you have to make is the chocolate mousse. The amount of mousse required for 8 *verrines* is a bit more than the basic recipe on PAGE 78 yields, so I've listed the ingredient quantities. The mousse is easy but requires an overnight rest in the refrigerator before you whip it. With these elements you can build a beautiful, dramatic dessert in a glass for your next dinner party.

METHOD

DAY 1

Scale the ingredients for the chocolate mousse using the quantities listed, which makes 50 percent more than the basic recipe on PAGE 78. Follow the instructions for making chocolate mousse on PAGE 78. Refrigerate the mixture overnight.

DAY 2

1 Whip your chocolate mousse, following the recipe on PAGE 78. Take care not to over-beat or your mousse will be grainy.

2 Prepare 8 glasses of your choice. I like to use tall ones so that guests can see all the beautiful layering. My suggestion for quantities and order of each layer is meant to be used as a guideline; it doesn't have to be set in stone. The thickness of the layers will depend on the shape of your glasses. The weights will give you a sense of how to organize your ingredients. If you want to be able to visualize how much of each element I'm suggesting for each layer, before you begin to assemble the *verrines* weigh out the amount of each ingredient called for onto a small piece of parchment paper, or pipe into a glass.

3 With the actual glass that you are using for the dessert, cut 16 round pieces of sponge; for tapered glasses find the right cutter so that the sponge slides nicely into the glass. Break some of the nougatine crisp into ¾-inch pieces. Transfer the hazelnut praline paste to a pastry bag fitted with a ½-inch tip. Do the same with the chocolate mousse in a second bag. If you only have one ½-inch tip, use a spoon for the hazelnut praline paste.

4 Pipe a layer of chocolate mousse (about 25 grams) onto the bottom of the glass. Sprinkle with a small number (about 5 grams) of caramelized hazelnuts; you can leave them whole or crush them. Place a round of flourless chocolate sponge on top. Pipe a layer of chocolate mousse—about 25 grams—on top of the cake. Top with a thin layer of nougatine crisp (about 5 grams). Pipe or spoon a thin layer—about 12 grams—of hazelnut praline paste over the nougatine crisp. Sprinkle about 5 grams of caramelized hazelnuts on top of the praline paste. Repeat the layering with the rest of the cake and chocolate mousse. Save some chocolate nougatine crisp for garnishing just before serving. The *verrines* will only have 1 layer of hazelnut praline paste. If you have extra you can create another layer. Place glasses in the refrigerator.

5 Shave off 8 large chocolate curls from a block of chocolate, following the recipe on PAGE 378. Make the hazelnut caramel curls following the recipe on PAGE 376, and prepare 8 large pieces of chocolate nougatine crisp. Keep the garnishes in airtight containers.

6 Before serving the desserts decorate each glass with a shard of nougatine crisp, a chocolate curl, and a hazelnut caramel curl.

STORAGE

You can make these 3 hours ahead but I prefer to make them just 1 hour before serving in order to keep all the textures intact. You can also make this an interactive dessert where you assemble the *verrines* in front of your guests.

JACQUY'S TAKEAWAYS

→ The hazelnut caramel curl decorations are optional but they add a whimsical effect to the dessert.

→ The components of this dessert and their quantities are all suggestions. I encourage you to be creative.

VANILLA ICE CREAM / CRÈME GLACÉE À LA VANILLE

YIELD | 1 QUART

2-DAY RECIPE (3 DAYS IF YOU INFUSE YOUR MILK WITH VANILLA FOR A DAY)

INGREDIENTS	WEIGHT	MEASURE (APPROXIMATE) OR OUNCE WEIGHT
Whole milk (3.5% fat)	520 grams	2⅓ cups
Heavy cream (35% fat)	250 grams	1 cup plus 1½ tablespoons
Egg yolks	80 grams	About 4½ yolks
Sugar, divided into 2 equal parts	175 grams	1 cup less 2 tablespoons
Vanilla bean	1.5 beans	1½ beans

Americans are the world's biggest consumers of ice cream per capita, and I definitely contribute to this statistic. I cannot refrain from eating ice cream or sorbet once it is placed in front of me.

The history of ice cream making is fascinating. It is almost as old as snow itself, as this is how the idea for ice cream got its start. Flavors were mixed with snow or run over blocks of ice. Later it was discovered that salt absorbs heat, and if you plunge a container of liquid into a salty brine the temperature will go down. Ice cream was produced that way for many years until the invention of refrigeration, which made the ice cream maker's life so much easier. With today's efficient ice cream machines it's hard to imagine how difficult it must have been a hundred years ago to make a smooth, cold ice cream, but chefs managed to do it.

This recipe is a great place to start if you're new to making ice cream. Follow the instructions for the basic Vanilla Custard Sauce on PAGE 35 but use the ingredient proportions below and you will end up with a delicious, creamy vanilla *glace*. The custard base, without the vanilla, will be your master recipe for all ice creams that are infused with flavors such as coffee, tea, spices, flowers, dried fruits, and dry flavors like vanilla.

No matter what flavor of ice cream you make, it's important to make the base a day before you freeze it and to let it chill overnight. This method will provide you with the maximum flavor and a very cold base that will freeze efficiently in your home ice cream machine.

METHOD

DAY 1 (DAY 2 IF YOU HAVE INFUSED THE MILK WITH VANILLA)

1 Make a vanilla sauce using the ingredients listed above and following the method in the recipe on PAGE 35. Chill the sauce overnight.

BEFORE YOU BEGIN

→ Get out the following equipment and allow all of the ingredients to come to room temperature:

Digital scale set to metric weights
Equipment for Vanilla Custard Sauce
  (PAGE 35)
1 small saucepan or bowl
1 paring knife
One 1-quart container
1 immersion blender
1 electric ice cream maker

The day before you make your vanilla ice cream base, scale the milk and place all but 50 grams (about ¼ cup) in a saucepan or bowl. On a cutting board, cut the vanilla bean in half lengthwise, scrape the seeds into the milk with the tip of your knife, and add the pod. Cover and refrigerate overnight. (Note: If you forget to do this step the day before, bring the milk with the vanilla to 158°F/70°C, remove from the heat, cover tightly, and allow to infuse for 15 to 30 minutes.)

→ Read this recipe through twice from start to finish.

UNDERSTANDING INGREDIENTS

When making ice cream it's important to calculate an accurate proportion of fats, solids, water, and sugar in order to get a creamy, smooth result. Too many solids can make the ice cream grainy; too much fat will also produce a grainy finished product full of fat crystals. Too much sugar will prevent the ice cream from freezing, but not enough sugar and too much water will make it icy.

This recipe contains slightly more sugar than the custard sauce on PAGE 35. We want more sugar because of the way it changes the molecular composition of the water crystals present when the two are heated and transformed into a syrup. This results in a creamier ice cream with fewer ice crystals.

DAY 2

2 Place a 1-quart container in the freezer. Remove the vanilla sauce from the refrigerator and blend it for 1 minute with an immersion blender. Freeze in an ice cream maker following the manufacturer's instructions. Transfer to the chilled container and place in the freezer for at least 3 hours to pack.

3 Check the ice cream before you want to serve it; if it is very hard, transfer to the refrigerator for 15 to 30 minutes before serving so that it softens and becomes creamy again.

STORAGE

You can keep ice cream in the freezer in a well-sealed container for 1 month.

Making Fruit Ice Creams

When it comes to making an ice cream with fruit, I do not recommend using fresh fruits, as they contain a considerable amount of water. Fresh strawberries, for example, contain around 85 percent water; lemon juice is 91 percent water. The resulting ice cream will be too icy due to the water introduced by the fruit. Bananas can be the exception to this rule, as they are not a juicy fruit. But they do have to be ripe, both because of the flavor and because when ripe they contain less water. I recommend two ways to make fruit ice creams.

1   The first way is to use freeze-dried fruit, using 4 percent of freeze-dried fruit by weight.

Peaches and strawberries work very well, but you can be adventurous and try raspberries, mangoes, or bananas. I don't recommend pears or apples, as they do not release enough flavor. In this recipe you would use 41 grams, which is 4 percent of 1025 grams, the total weight of the ingredients in the vanilla base. Most supermarkets sell a wide range of dehydrated or freeze-dried fruit, and they are surprisingly tasty. If you have a dehydrator you could make your own by slicing fresh fruit in very thin slices (1/16 inch) and putting them in the dehydrator for a few hours until they are completely dry. Make the custard base, and as soon as you take it off the heat stir in the freeze-dried fruit. Cool the mixture as directed and refrigerate overnight. The next day, use your immersion blender to liquefy the base with the fruit. Strain it if you don't like the small pieces of fiber from the fruit, and spin as directed in your ice cream maker.

2 **The second way to make fruit ice cream is to add semi-candied fruit at the end of the churning process.**

To make semi-candied fruit, cut up 200 grams of fruit into ½-inch cubes and place in a bowl. Make a simple syrup using 500 grams water (about 2 cups) and 675 grams sugar (about 3⅓ cups). Pour the hot syrup over the fruit and refrigerate overnight. The following day, drain and fold the fruit into your ice cream at the end of churning.

An alternative way to candy fruit is to use a cold process. This process takes 6 days, but the advantage is that the fruit is never overheated and maintains its tangy flavor profile. Cut the fruit into ½-inch pieces and mix with 20 percent sugar by weight (in this case use 200 grams (7 ounces) of fruit and mix with 40 grams of sugar). Stir once, cover the bowl with plastic, and refrigerate overnight. For the next 5 days stir it once a day and return to the refrigerator. After 6 days, the fruit should be completely cured. When you are ready to fold the fruit into the churned ice cream, place a strainer over a bowl and drain it. Use the fruit only in the ice cream and use the juice as a sauce.

KOUGELHOF ICE CREAM CAKE /
KOUGELHOF GLACÉ

YIELD | 1 BUNDT-SHAPED ICE CREAM CAKE, SERVING 10 TO 12 PEOPLE

2- TO 3-DAY RECIPE

INGREDIENTS	WEIGHT	MEASURE (APPROXIMATE) OR OUNCE WEIGHT
Pâte Sablée (PAGE 144)	½ recipe, about 350 grams	½ recipe, about 12³/₁₀ ounces
CARAMEL ICE CREAM		
Egg yolks	80 grams	4½ yolks
Whole milk (3.5% fat)	520 grams	2 cups plus 2⅓ tablespoons
Heavy cream (35% fat)	250 grams	1 cup plus 1 tablespoon
Vanilla bean	1.5 beans	1½ beans
Water	60 grams	¼ cup plus 1 teaspoon
Sugar	185 grams	⅞ cup
Corn syrup	60 grams	3 tablespoons
Sea salt	0.5 grams	Pinch
FROZEN MOUSSE		
Cold heavy cream (35% fat)	325 grams	1½ cups less 1 teaspoon
Caramelized Almonds (PAGE 51)	100 grams	⅔ cup
Dried apricots, optional	50 grams	¼ cup
Aged egg whites (PAGE 222)	85 grams	About 3 whites or ⅓ cup plus 1 teaspoon
Water	15 grams	1 tablespoon
Granulated sugar	45 grams	3 tablespoons
Corn syrup	25 grams	2¾ teaspoons
Clover honey	70 grams	¼ cup less 1 teaspoon
FINISHED CAKE		
Cocoa powder, for dusting	As needed	As needed
Fresh or frozen apricots, optional	100 grams	3½ ounces
Granulated sugar, optional	15 grams	1 tablespoon
Whipped cream, optional	As desired	As desired

BEFORE YOU BEGIN

→ Get out the following equipment and allow all of the ingredients to come to room temperature:

Digital scale, set to metric weights
Equipment for Caramelized Almonds (PAGE 51)
Equipment for Pâte Sablée (PAGE 144)
Plastic wrap
1 medium mixing bowl
1 small saucepan or microwave-safe bowl or cup
1 paring knife
1 large mixing bowl
Ice cubes
1 large stainless steel saucepan
1 high-heat rubber spatula
1 pastry brush
1 large mixing bowl filled with ice water
1 digital thermometer
1 small white plate
1 ladle
1 stainless steel hand whisk
1 strainer
1 ramekin
One 9-inch silicone or metal Bundt mold
1 immersion blender
1 ice cream maker
KitchenAid or stand mixer fitted with the whisk attachment
1 chef's knife
1 small offset spatula
1 rolling pin
1 blender

→ Read this recipe through twice from start to finish.

This is a somewhat elaborate ice cream cake molded in a metal Bundt pan or, more efficient and much easier to unmold, a kougelhof-shaped silicone mold. The first kougelhof *glacé* was created by the late Maurice Ferber, a famous pastry chef in Niedermorschwihr, Alsace. Maurice mentored many young people who aspired to join our wonderful profession, the

UNDERSTANDING INGREDIENTS

Making caramel ice cream is like making regular vanilla ice cream (PAGE 271), but you transform the sugar in the vanilla sauce base into caramel first. That's the twist, and the trick is to make sure that you do not let your caramel get too dark, or you will end up with bitter ice cream. Unfortunately, when you let your caramel cook too dark, the burned flavor can't be masked; if this happens, the best remedy is to throw out the caramel and start over. If it's been a while since you've made caramel I recommend that you read my caramel-making instructions on PAGE 47. When you make caramel, the sugar is inverted; because of this it will not set up as much when it is frozen, and will bring a very smooth texture to the ice cream. A hint of sea salt will bring out the caramel flavor and temper the sweetness.

Frozen mousse made with an Italian meringue always has a light and airy texture, ensuring a soft result. Added to that, the honey, which brings a great flavor profile, is naturally an inverted sugar that does not set up hard even when frozen. Given these two factors, we need to introduce an element that will give the frozen mousse some structure so that it will be somewhat firm. That's where the whipped cream comes in. The caramelized nuts add a great crunch; never use raw nuts, as they get soggy very quickly. Dried apricots (as opposed to fresh) are used in this recipe because they are candied and will not harden even when frozen. If you want a simpler mousse, you can omit them. The best way to make the fruit coulis that will be used as a sauce is to blend pitted, peeled ripe fruit in season with 10 to 15 percent of sugar by weight. You never want to cook it, as that would kill its acidity.

most famous one being his own daughter, Christine Ferber, who is world renowned mostly for her delicious jams but is an accomplished pastry chef as well.

I have seen many versions of this frozen cake. Mine consists of a layer of salted caramel ice cream and a layer of frozen honey mousse filled with caramelized nuts and dried apricots. The cake sits on a flaky *sablée* base. I like to serve this wonderful refreshing cake with a tangy apricot sauce.

You need to be organized when you make kougelhof *glacé*, beginning with making a *sablée* dough and ice cream mix at least 2 days and preferably 3 days before you plan on serving it. That way, once you have finished assembling the cake on the second day, it will have 24 hours in the freezer and will set nice and hard in the mold. It will then be easy to unmold (especially if you make it in a silicone mold), and you will have time to return it to the freezer if necessary, and then to let it sit in the refrigerator for 15 to 30 minutes before serving so that it will be at the optimal temperature for a creamy texture.

METHOD

DAY 1

1 Make a recipe of caramelized almonds (PAGE 51) as well as a recipe of *sablée* dough (PAGE 144). Divide the dough in half, wrap each half airtight, and place one half in the refrigerator, the other half in the freezer to use for another purpose.

2 Make the caramel ice cream. Place the egg yolks in a medium bowl. Place the milk and cream in a saucepan or a microwave-safe bowl or cup; split the vanilla beans in half lengthwise and scrape the seeds out with the tip or the blunt edge of a paring knife. Add the bean and seeds to the milk and cream and set aside. Fill a large bowl halfway with ice and set aside. You will use this again in Step 7, below.

3 To make the caramel, place the water in a large stainless steel saucepan. Pour the sugar into the center of the pan. With a high-heat rubber spatula, stir very slowly to mix the sugar and water together, being careful not to wipe or splash the mixture onto the sides of the saucepan. Add the corn syrup and slowly stir together. Examine the saucepan closely, and if you see sugar on the sides, wash it back into the mixture with a clean, wet pastry brush. You will not stir the mixture again until the end of cooking.

4 Place the large mixing bowl filled with ice water on the stove. Place the saucepan on medium heat and bring to a boil without stirring. The sugar will dissolve, and the mixture is now a syrup. Insert a digital thermometer and continue to cook until the mixture reaches 300°F/150°C; start warming up the milk and cream.

5 When the syrup reaches 325°F/160°C it will be golden brown. Turn off the heat and dip the bottom of the pan into the bowl of cold water for 10 seconds to stop the cooking. Using the rubber spatula, place a drop of caramel on a small white plate; it will cool in about 15 seconds. Taste it and see if the caramel is bitter enough; the plate will also allow you to see the color of the caramel; the darker it is, the more bitter it will be. Cook it a little more if you prefer a slightly more bitter flavor, but be careful not to let it get too dark. Once the right flavor is obtained, turn off the heat and carefully add a ladle of hot cream and milk to the caramel; the caramel will bubble up and create a lot of steam for 5 seconds. After 5 seconds slowly stir the mixture with a high-heat rubber spatula for 10 seconds. Repeat with another ladle of milk and cream; after the third ladle, switch to a hand whisk. Once all the milk and cream is incorporated, add the sea salt. Remove the vanilla beans from the liquid, set on paper towels to dry, and, once dry, store.

6 Whisk 3 ladles of the hot caramel mixture into the egg yolks. Slowly whisk the tempered egg yolks into the hot caramel mixture in the saucepan. Wash out the bowl, dry, and place near your saucepan with a strainer on top. Place the saucepan back on low heat. Using a rubber spatula, stir constantly and everywhere until you feel the mixture starting to thicken; stirring in a figure 8 helps to assure that your spatula touches the entire bottom of the pan. To test whether or not your sauce is thick enough, lift your spatula from the saucepan with some sauce on it and run your finger down the middle. It should leave a canal. Place a thermometer in the saucepan and continue to stir constantly until the temperature reaches between 165°F/75°C and 185°F/85°C.

7 Immediately strain the mixture into the clean dry mixing bowl and set this bowl in the large bowl filled halfway with ice. Placing a ramekin under the mixing bowl will keep it steady once the ice begins to melt. Stir for a few minutes, then just once in a while, until the mixture has cooled. It is important that the egg mixture cools down in 20 minutes or less so that salmonella bacteria do not have a chance to reproduce and it is safe to use. (If you do not have ice on hand, place the bowl in your freezer and stir once in a while.) Once cool, transfer to a container, cover tightly, and refrigerate for at least 2 hours or preferably overnight.

DAY 2

1 Place the silicone mold or metal Bundt mold in a large mixing bowl and place it the freezer. Remove the caramel mixture from the refrigerator and blend it for 1 minute with an immersion blender. Freeze in an ice cream maker following the manufacturer's instructions. Scrape the caramel ice cream into the mold, and using a rubber spatula, spread it on all sides of the mold, leaving the middle empty; freeze for 1 hour. Spread the ice cream again if it has settled on the bottom of the mold, so that it coats the sides of the mold. This can happen if your home ice cream maker does not freeze the mixture hard.

2 Make the frozen mousse. First whip the heavy cream to soft peaks, transfer to a mixing bowl, and refrigerate. Roughly chop the caramelized nuts and cut the dried apricots into ¼-inch dice. Set aside.

3 Begin whipping the egg whites in the mixer on the lowest speed using the whisk attachment. Double-check the temperature of the egg whites by feeling the bottom of the bowl. If it is at all cold, fill a sink with 1 inch of hot water. Stop the machine, unlock the bowl, and place it in the hot water for 1 full minute while mixing by hand with the KitchenAid whip or a whisk. Remove the bowl from the water and wipe dry. Feel the temperature with your hand; it should feel neither cold nor hot. Return the bowl to the mixer and resume whipping on low speed.

4 Meanwhile, place the water in the small saucepan and pour the sugar into the center of the pan. With a rubber spatula, stir very slowly to mix the sugar and water together, being careful not to wipe or splash the mixture onto the sides of the saucepan. Add the corn syrup and honey. Examine the saucepan closely; if you see sugar on the sides, wash it back down with a clean, wet pastry brush. Place the saucepan over medium heat. Once the syrup comes to a boil do not stir. Insert a digital thermometer, and cook the syrup to 244°F/118°C.

5 Keep an eye on your egg whites while you are heating the syrup. When the syrup is at 230°F/110°C your egg whites should be semi-foamy. If they are not, increase the speed slightly. At 239°F/115°C the syrup is just about ready to be poured into the egg whites. Check the bottom of the mixing bowl; if necessary, tilt the machine so that the egg whites at the bottom of the bowl are also beaten until foamy.

6 Turn on the mixer at its highest speed. When the syrup reaches 244°F/118°C remove from the heat and very gradually stream it into the egg whites, taking great care to pour the syrup right between the whisk and the sides of the bowl. This is crucial, because if the hot syrup engages with the whisk before it hits the egg whites, all of it will splatter onto the sides of the bowl instead of going into the egg whites (and it could splatter onto your hands and burn you). Once all of the syrup has been added, whip on high speed for 2 minutes, then reduce to medium speed and whip for another

6 minutes. The meringue should have cooled to room temperature; take the bowl out of the mixture and, using a rubber spatula, gently fold in the whipped cream, the chopped caramelized nuts, and the diced dried apricot.

7 Take the cake mold out of the freezer and fill it with the honey mousse. Smooth the top with a small offset spatula and freeze overnight.

DAY 3

1 Preheat the oven to 325°F/160°C. Roll out the *sablée* dough to a ⅛-inch thickness and cut a disk that is ½ inch shorter than the diameter of your mold. Cut a hole out of the center if the mold has a hole in the center. Bake for 20 minutes, or until golden brown. Remove from the heat and allow to cool. Take the cake out of the freezer and gently press the *sablée* disk onto the bottom of the frozen mousse. Unmold the cake onto a platter. If you have used a metal mold you will need to dip the mold ¾ of the way into a bowl of hot water for about 30 seconds. Remove from the water, dry the mold with a kitchen towel, then reverse onto the platter. Once unmolded, immediately return to the freezer for 30 minutes to reset the ice cream.

2 Thirty minutes before you wish to serve the cake, remove from the freezer, dust with cocoa powder, and place in the refrigerator.

3 If serving with the apricot coulis, wash, peel, and pit the ripe apricots, place them in a blender with the 15 grams of sugar, and blend until smooth. Cut the cake into slices and serve with the apricot coulis and, if you wish, a dollop of whipped cream.

IT'S DONE WHEN IT'S DONE

The cake should be covered with a very thin layer of cocoa powder; the ice cream and frozen mousse should be easy to slice even at the frozen stage. The *sablée* should be baked all the way through and should be easy to slice through.

STORAGE

This cake can be kept in the freezer for up to 1 month.

JACQUY'S TAKEAWAYS

→ You can use different honeys, but beware of chestnut honey, which is very bitter and will clash with the caramel flavor.

→ Other types of caramelized nuts such as hazelnuts, or just simply roasted nuts, can be used instead of the caramelized almonds.

→ Apricots contribute a great fruity and tangy element to the cake's flavor profile, but you can omit them or use other dried fruits if you prefer.

→ It's best to use a silicone mold for this; it will simplify the unmolding process, which can be tricky. If you do use metal, make sure that it is not aluminum, as aluminum would give the ice cream a metallic taste. Ceramic molds do not work for this application.

→ When making an ice cream cake I advise you to get some dry ice from your local ice cream shop. It can come in very handy if you need to cool your ice cream cake quickly, or transport it. But always wear gloves when handling dry ice and be careful, as it can burn your hands.

THE BIGGEST TIP IN MY LIFE:
AN ICE CREAM CAKE STORY

DURING MY APPRENTICESHIP WE SOMETIMES had to make deliveries for our boss. Every time we were called upon for this job it was like escaping prison for a half an hour or hour. We'd always get yelled at when we got back for taking so long, but the little bit of freedom was worth it. We used a cargo tricycle called a *triporteur*, which was sort of like an old-fashioned ice cream vendor's tricycle. There was a wooden box in the front, with two wheels in the front and one in the back. They were a lot of fun to ride because you couldn't tip over.

One day I was told to deliver an ice cream cake to a customer. It was a beautiful spring day in Strasbourg and I rode along on the *triporteur* whistling and having the time of my life, the ice cream cake in the box kept cold by a frozen liquid element. I was going fast, but not so fast that I didn't spot a beautiful girl walking along on my right. I looked at the girl and she looked at me . . . and the next thing I knew I was lying on the pavement. I'd crashed into the car in front of me and gone flying over the handlebars, and now the angry driver of the car was yelling at me and asking me where I worked. In tears, I begged him not to mention the accident to Jean Clauss and told him how much trouble I would get into. Luckily the man's car wasn't damaged, so he just huffed and drove away.

I parked the *triporteur* and inspected the cake. It was smashed. I continued on to the home of the woman who had ordered the cake. An older woman in her fifties, she was happy to see me and the cake from Jean Clauss. But I was in tears, and when she asked me what was wrong I told her about the accident; of course I left out the real cause of the accident.

"Are you okay?" she asked. Though I was badly bruised, I said, "I'm okay—but I think your cake is damaged." We had a look, and then she said, "Yes, this is going to be a problem." I told her that I could not go back and tell Jean Clauss about this. I was afraid he'd kill me. I would have run away or just gone home to Marlenheim rather than face my boss. It would be the last day of my apprenticeship. I begged her to not say anything and to let me try to fix the cake. Kind woman that she was, she agreed. With two spatulas in the kitchen, she let me fix it as best I could, and we put it in the freezer. She even offered to give me a tip, but I said, "No, you have already given me the biggest tip of my life. Thank you so much."

VACHERIN GLACÉ / FROZEN VACHERIN

(See page 230 for photo)

YIELD | ONE TALL 7-INCH CAKE, SERVING 12 PEOPLE

2- TO 3-DAY RECIPE

INGREDIENTS	WEIGHT	MEASURE (APPROXIMATE)
MERINGUE		
French Meringue (PAGE 65)	1 recipe	1 recipe
Sliced almonds	25 grams	¼ cup
BANANA ICE CREAM		
Whole milk (3.5% fat)	520 grams	2⅓ cups
Heavy cream (35% fat)	250 grams	1 cup plus 1½ tablespoons
Granulated sugar	100 grams	½ cup
Vanilla bean	1 bean	1 bean
Egg yolks	80 grams	About 4½ yolks
Granulated sugar	100 grams	½ cup
Ripe banana, peeled	260 grams peeled	2 medium bananas
Lemon juice, freshly squeezed	20 grams (½ lemon)	1½ tablespoons (½ lemon)
Ground nutmeg	Pinch	Pinch
PINEAPPLE SORBET		
Fresh pineapple, peeled and cored	645 grams peeled and cored	1 small pineapple
Corn syrup	45 grams	2 tablespoons
Granulated sugar	55 grams	¼ cup
Clover honey	15 grams	2¾ teaspoons
MANGO COULIS		
Fresh ripe mango, peeled and diced	280 grams peeled and diced	About 1⅓ cups peeled and diced or 1½ medium mangoes
Clover honey	15 grams	2¾ teaspoons
FROSTING AND DECORATION		
Heavy whipping cream	450 grams	2 cups
Confectioners' sugar	75 grams	¾ cup
Vanilla extract	5 grams	1 teaspoon
Fruit, for decoration	As desired	As desired
Confectioners' sugar, for dusting	As needed	As needed

BEFORE YOU BEGIN

→ Get out the following equipment and allow all of the ingredients to come to room temperature:

Digital scale, set to metric weights
Equipment for French Meringue
  (PAGE 65)
1 sheet pan
Pencil
Parchment paper
1 pastry bag fitted with a ¾-inch
  round tip
1 flat spatula
1 large mixing bowl
Ice cubes
1 ramekin or shallow cup
1 medium saucepan (do not use
  aluminum)
1 paring knife
1 medium mixing bowl
1 medium stainless steel hand whisk
1 small plate
1 medium strainer
1 large rubber spatula
1 digital thermometer
1 immersion blender
1 blender
1 ice cream maker
One 8- or 9-inch springform pan or
  ring, optional
1 small offset spatula
1 large chef's knife

→ Read this recipe through twice from start to finish.

UNDERSTANDING INGREDIENTS

It's important to understand that an ice cream cake requires a base that will cut well even when frozen. I once broke a tooth on an ice cream cake in which the chef had used biscotti as a base; biscotti are hard to begin with and serving them frozen is just asking for trouble. Frozen meringue cuts easily and will offer no resistance to your teeth; instead, it melts in your mouth.

In a *vacherin*, the ice cream and/or sorbet are surrounded by baked meringue and whipped cream. This is because these two components have an incredible insulating power. Hard meringue is made of sugar and egg white; the egg white's albumen traps and encloses thousands of air bubbles, and once baked its texture is comparable to Styrofoam. Whipped cream is also a product where air bubbles are walled in, but this time it's the fat in the cream that traps them. These two elements provide a great shield and will keep the frozen component very cold. After I tested this cake I transferred it from the freezer to an insulated box and brought it home. From there it stayed in the box at room temperature for 3 hours; when it was time to eat it, the center was still frozen.

When making an ice cream cake it is important to use components that will all have a similar texture when the cake

Whenever I eat a slice of *vacherin* or make this recipe I am transported to a summer day in 1975 when our family went to L'Auberge de l'Ill, a famous Michelin three-star restaurant in the Alsatian village of Illhaeusern. There I had the best vacherin I had ever tasted. It consisted of a layer of Tahitian vanilla ice cream and a layer of raspberry sorbet set between two meringue disks and topped with whipped cream: so simple, so well made, and so good! I was fourteen at the time and had already begun to toy with the idea of becoming a pastry chef. Eating the *vacherin* on that day sealed the deal: I knew for sure that this was what I wanted to do.

I have made many *vacherins* in the years since. In this version, I've opted to go with tropical flavors. The filling consists of a delicious creamy banana ice cream, a smooth mango coulis, and a tangy pineapple sorbet that I created for the *Meilleur Ouvrier de France* competition. Classic French meringue disks are the top and bottom for the ice cream cake, the frosting is vanilla-infused whipped cream, and more meringue shells decorate the sides. The result is very fruity and refreshing; the acidity of the fruit ices contrasts nicely with the sweet meringue.

The recipe requires at least 2 days, as the meringue shells need to bake and the ice cream mixture needs to chill and mature. Given that many home ice cream makers do not freeze ice cream stiff enough to shape right away, you will need to give yourself plenty of time on the second day, or you can make the cake over 3 days, icing the cake on Day 3. I recommend this if you are planning on serving this as a dessert for a dinner party.

METHOD

DAY 1

You can make the meringues before or after you make the ice cream bases.

MAKING THE MERINGUES

1 Preheat the oven to 325°F/160°C. Place the sliced almonds on a sheet pan and toast for 15 minutes, until golden brown. Remove from the heat and allow to cool. Reduce the oven to 250°F/120°C.

2 Using a pencil, draw two 7-inch circles on parchment paper. Flip the paper over and place on a sheet pan. On another piece of parchment paper use a pencil to draw twelve 2-inch-long by ¾-inch-wide lines, flip the paper over, and place on a sheet pan.

3 Make a recipe of meringue following the instructions on **PAGE 65**. Transfer the meringue to the pastry bag fitted with a ¾-inch round piping tip. Hold the bag vertically 1 inch above the center of one of the circles and pipe a tight spiral from the inside out. Repeat with the second circle. With the rest of the meringue pipe twelve 2-inch-long by ¾-inch-wide meringue sticks. Sprinkle some toasted sliced almonds onto the sticks, and dust all of the meringues with confectioners' sugar. Place in the oven and bake 1 hour. Remove with a flat spatula and let cool. Set aside at room temperature.

MAKING THE BANANA ICE CREAM BASE

1 Fill a large bowl with ice and set a ramekin in the middle that you can balance a medium bowl on.

2 Set aside 50 grams of the milk (about ¼ cup) and place the rest of the milk, all of the cream, and the first 100 grams of sugar in a medium saucepan. On a cutting board, cut the vanilla bean in half lengthwise, scrape the seeds into the saucepan with the tip of your knife, and add the pod to the saucepan. Place over medium heat and stir for 10 seconds to make sure that the sugar does not stick to the bottom of the pan.

3 Meanwhile, combine the egg yolks and the remaining 100 grams of sugar in a medium mixing bowl and whisk immediately for 30 seconds. The sugar will create a buffer around the egg yolk proteins, which helps prevent the coagulation from taking place too quickly. Add the 50 grams of milk you set aside to the egg yolk mixture.

4 When the milk comes to a boil in the saucepan, turn off the heat. Remove the split vanilla pods, scrape all of the seeds adhering to them into the milk mixture, and place the pods aside on a plate (allow to dry and store in a jar or in a jar of sugar). Whisking constantly, pour about 2 cups of the hot milk into the egg yolk mixture. Whisk the egg yolk mixture back into the hot milk in the saucepan. Quickly rinse and dry your medium bowl and place it in the bowl of ice with a strainer set on top.

NOTE: If you set the bowl on a piece of shelf paper or on a coiled towel it won't slide around when you whisk in the milk.

5 Place the saucepan back on low heat. Using a rubber spatula, stir constantly and everywhere until you feel the mixture starting to thicken. Stirring in a figure 8 helps to assure that your spatula touches the entire bottom of the pan. To test whether or not your sauce is thick enough, lift your spatula from the saucepan with some sauce on it and run your finger down the middle. It should leave a canal. Place a thermometer in the saucepan and continue to stir constantly until the temperature reaches between 165°F/75°C and 180°F/82°C.

is served. No layer should be too hard and be difficult to cut, or so soft that it melts, causing the cake to collapse. The corn syrup in the pineapple sorbet and the honey used in both the pineapple sorbet and the mango coulis are inverted sugars that do not harden too much in the freezer, allowing those layers of the *vacherin* to have a nice soft consistency like the banana ice cream layer, and preventing the mango coulis from becoming hard and icy.

When you make banana ice cream it is important to use perfectly ripe bananas; they should be deep yellow with some brown flecks. Never use over-ripe bananas, as they have a foul smell. If you need to ripen bananas you can leave them at room temperature and wait for them to get the right look, or to speed up the process you can place them in a brown bag with an apple or a tomato. When a fruit ripens it releases ethylene, which creates enzymes that cause starches and acids to break down into sugar. These enzymes also break down the cell walls and soften the fruit. Apples and tomatoes speed up the ripening process because they produce a lot of ethylene.

L'Auberge de l'Ill

More than 150 years ago the Haeberlin family opened a modest restaurant that would become L'Auberge de l'Ill in the small Alsatian village of Illhaeusern, on the banks of the Ill River. Despite two world wars, when the region of Alsace was occupied by the German army, the family managed to pass on their knowledge of fine cooking from one generation to the next and persevere in their pursuit of excellence. Their reward for this was the coveted three-star Michelin rating, which they obtained in 1967. This is the highest rating that a restaurant can obtain; it encompasses all aspects of serving the perfect meal to a customer, from impeccable service to divine cooking to a soothing ambiance.

L'Auberge de l'Ill is housed in a large ancient Alsatian mansion. On fine days and warm summer evenings guests can enjoy an aperitif on the terrace that looks out over the lawn, where giant willow trees cascade over the river. The

6 Immediately strain the mixture into the clean dry mixing bowl set in the ice. The ramekin under the bowl will keep it steady once the ice begins to melt. Stir for a few minutes, then just once in a while, until the mixture has cooled. It is important that the egg mixture cools down in 20 minutes or less so that salmonella bacteria do not have a chance to reproduce and it is safe to use. If you do not have ice on hand, place the bowl in your freezer and stir once in a while. In the meantime, using an immersion blender, blend the ripe banana with the lemon juice and the nutmeg to a puree. Once the ice cream is cool, add the pureed banana to it, blend the entire mix, and transfer it to a container. Cover tightly and refrigerate overnight.

MAKING THE PINEAPPLE SORBET BASE

Place all the ingredients for the pineapple sorbet in a blender and blend until completely smooth. Transfer to a container and refrigerate overnight.

DAY 2

BUILDING THE CAKE

1 On the second day, place the 2 disks of meringue on a plate in the freezer.

2 Blend the banana ice cream for 1 minute using an immersion blender and freeze in an ice cream maker. Place in the freezer for 1 to 2 hours or until it is stiff enough to shape a cake layer but not packed hard.

3 Place a frozen meringue disk on a plate, flat side down. If you wish, place the plate in a larger springform mold to facilitate turning the cake while you build it up. Using a rubber spatula and working quickly, transfer 1 quart of the banana ice cream (freeze the rest to enjoy on its own) to the disk and first smooth it out with a small offset spatula, then build the sides up so that you create an indent in the center. This is where the mango coulis will go. Freeze for 15 to 30 minutes or until set.

4 In the meantime, puree the fresh mangoes in a blender. Weigh out 80 grams (about ¼ cup) and mix with the honey. Transfer the remaining puree to a container and refrigerate.

5 Blend the pineapple sorbet mix again and freeze in your ice cream maker. Place in the freezer for 1 hour or until it is stiff enough to shape a cake layer but not packed hard.

6 Remove the plate with the *vacherin* in progress from the freezer. Pour the mango puree and honey mixture into the indent and smooth so that the layer is flat. Freeze for at least 30 minutes.

7 Spread the pineapple sorbet over the banana and mango layer in an even layer. Smooth flat with an offset spatula and top with the second meringue disk, the flat side up. Freeze for 1 hour or overnight.

8 In the meantime, whip the heavy cream until stiff enough to pipe, but be careful not to over-whip it or it will be grainy. Add the confectioners' sugar and the vanilla and mix for an additional 5 seconds.

9 If the cake is in a springform pan, remove it from the pan. Transfer two-thirds of the whipped cream to the cake and, using a flat metal spatula, frost it so that the top and sides are covered in an even layer. Glue the meringue sticks to the side of the cake. First glue 4 of them at even intervals like the 12, 3, 6, and 9 on a clock, then glue 2 between each, leaving even spaces between each meringue. Transfer the rest of the whipped cream to a bag fitted with a ½-inch round tip and pipe cream between each meringue stick or decorate the spaces between with slivered almonds. Pipe round bulbs or teardrops on the top on the vacherin. Freeze for at least 1 hour so that all elements are stable and cold.

10 Before serving, transfer the vacherin to the refrigerator for 1 hour. Decorate the top with the fruit of your choice. Dust with confectioners' sugar and serve with the chilled mango coulis. To serve, dip a large chef's knife in warm water, wipe it dry with a towel, and slice. Repeat between each slice.

IT'S DONE WHEN IT'S DONE

When you eat the cake, the ice cream should be soft but it should not melt and drip.

STORAGE

This cake can be kept for 1 month in the freezer, covered with plastic wrap.

decor inside the old mansion is a mix of traditional Alsatian style combined with Asian-inspired minimalist modern touches.

The Haeberlin family has maintained its high standards over the decades since I had my epiphany there. In France, even families with modest means will go to a three-star Michelin restaurant for special occasions. For my family, it would be to celebrate a big birthday, such as my grandmother's seventieth, or a major wedding anniversary.

When I went there more than three decades later with my own family, the meal we enjoyed was as wonderful and memorable as the one I reveled in as a fourteen-year-old boy. That day we were the guests of Pierre Zimmermann, master baker and twice world baking champion, and his family. Pierre joined the faculty at the French Pastry School a couple of years after that and he now heads up our baking program.

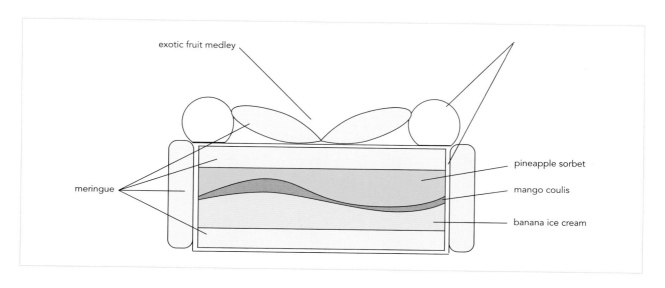

$\mathcal{S}\,O\,R\,B\,E\,T\,S$

Sorbet is made with water, sugar, and fruit. Most contain no dairy (milk or heavy cream). The more water in a sorbet, the greater the possibility of an icy finished product; the more solids, the greater the possibility of a grainy and dry sorbet. I have seen various systems in pastry books for calibrating the sugar/water/fruit ratios in sorbet recipes, such as placing an egg on the sorbet mixture once it is prepared and seeing if the egg floats—if it does, the mixture is ready. I think that if we put a man on the moon we can do a little better at figuring out sorbets than that archaic system. Other recipes call for the use of a universal syrup recipe for sorbets, which can give you a decent finished product but is not always precise.

One needs to know that all fruit contains mainly water. The solids consist of fiber or cellulose and sugars (fructose or glucose, for the most part). The range of water/solid ratio is very broad from one fruit to another, going from 9 percent solids and 91 percent water for lemons to 17 percent solids and 83 percent water for strawberries to 25 percent solids and 75 percent water for bananas. So if you are making a lemon sorbet, you will have a low amount of solids and a high amount of water and will have to balance this by increasing the sugar and decreasing the water in your syrup. On the other hand, if you want to make a banana sorbet, you will have to decrease the amount of sugar and increase the amount of water in your syrup.

When it comes to flavor, I have seen recipes for sorbets where the water, sugar, and fruit are brought to a boil, cooled down, and then spun in the ice cream maker. I would never ask you to cook the fruit;

you would lose the tanginess that makes it so delicious and obtain more of a compote taste. You might as well make a tart if you're going to cook the fruit.

Although many sorbets include water, you could just add sugar to the fruit without making a syrup first, as we do in the pineapple sorbet in this recipe. Then the sorbet will be even fruitier. A touch of honey will prevent the water in the fruit from crystalizing because of its very high degree of sweetness. Like honey, corn syrup is an inverted sugar and has an anti-crystallizing effect on the water crystals.

Every fruit has a different amount of fructose, so there is no hard-and-fast rule about sweetening amounts. I always replace some granulated sugar with corn syrup, and sometimes add a little honey, because these inverted sugars help prevent ice crystals from forming. As a general rule I use a maximum of 5 percent by weight of corn syrup and 15 to 20 percent by weight of granulated sugar. The amount you use depends also on your taste for sweetness.

Most fruit contains enough acid to prevent it from going bad or turning brown in the freezer (have you ever seen a lemon sorbet go bad?), though some fruit like pears can turn brown faster than others. I recommend adding a little bit of fresh lemon juice for these sorbet mixtures. Only a very few fruits such as cherries will still turn brown even with the lemon juice treatment. If you add more lemon juice you won't be able to taste the flavor of the cherries. The solution for these stubborn fruits is a very low heat pasteurization, which involves cooking the fruit with 10 percent of its weight in sugar for 30 minutes at 149°F/65°C, then cooling the mixture down over an ice bath.

FROZEN COFFEE AND CHOCOLATE MOUSSE / MOUSSE GLACÉE AU CAFÉ ET AU CHOCOLAT

INGREDIENTS	WEIGHT	MEASURE (APPROXIMATE) OR OUNCE WEIGHT
COFFEE MOUSSE		
Coffee beans	39 grams	½ cup
Coriander seed	1 seed	1 seed
Whole milk (3.5% fat)	264 grams	1⅛ cups
Dark chocolate couverture (64%)	40 grams	1⅖ ounces or about ¼ cup coins
Cold heavy cream (35% fat)	176 grams	¾ cup
Granulated sugar	126 grams	½ cup plus 2 tablespoons
Egg yolks	55 grams	About 3 yolks
Dark rum	6 grams	1½ teaspoons
Clover honey	22 grams	1 tablespoon plus ¼ teaspoon
Vanilla extract	6 grams	1⅛ teaspoons
COFFEE TUILE		
Brewed espresso	85 grams	⅓ cup plus 1 teaspoon
Heavy cream (35% fat)	35 grams	2 tablespoons
Sea salt	0.5 gram	Pinch
Granulated sugar	70 grams	5 tablespoons
Corn syrup	35 grams	2 tablespoons
Butter (French style, 82% fat)	18 grams	⅗ ounce or 1 rounded tablespoon
Chopped pecans	50 grams	⅓ cup plus 1 tablespoon
SPICED WHIPPED CREAM		
Cold heavy cream (35% fat)	250 grams	1 cup plus 1 tablespoon
Ground cinnamon	1 gram	½ teaspoon
Ground nutmeg	0.3 gram	¼ teaspoon
Ginger powder	0.3 gram	⅛ teaspoon
Cardamom powder	Pinch	Pinch
Confectioners' sugar	30 grams	⅓ cup (¼ cup tightly packed)
DECORATION		
Candied Lemon Zest (PAGE 87), optional	As desired	As desired
Chocolate Curls (PAGE 378), optional	As desired	As desired

BEFORE YOU BEGIN

→ Get out the following equipment and allow all of the ingredients to come to room temperature:

Digital scale, set to metric weights
KitchenAid or stand mixer fitted with the whisk attachment or a handheld electric mixer
1 pastry bag
1 rolling pin
1 medium saucepan
Plastic wrap
1 chef's knife
2 small mixing bowls
2 medium mixing bowls
1 strainer lined with cheesecloth
1 stainless steel hand whisk
1 high-heat rubber spatula
1 digital thermometer
1 immersion blender
8 ramekins (4 inches round and ¾ inches high) (also sold as crème brûlée dishes)
1 offset metal spatula
2 or more sheet pans lined with a silpats; make sure the pans are perfectly flat
1 round measuring teaspoon or a 1-inch ice cream scoop
1 soup spoon

→ Read this recipe through twice from start to finish.

UNDERSTANDING INGREDIENTS

The technique for this frozen mousse shows a completely different way of using a vanilla sauce. First, the milk is infused with coffee beans and coriander seed. The more water there is in a liquid, the stronger the infusion, since it is the water in the liquid that absorbs the flavors. So milk will absorb more coffee flavor than heavy cream, because it contains more water.

When it comes to flavoring egg-based creams I like to use crushed coffee beans instead of ground or instant coffee, as the beans deliver a rounder flavor profile that marries very well with the egg. For a coffee infusion, the finer the coffee is crushed, the stronger the infusion. In this recipe we only crush the beans slightly so that the flavor is not too strong and so that the vanilla sauce has a good texture and doesn't have to be put through a very fine strainer to get rid of powdery coffee residue. You should choose coffee beans that are light brown in color, as darker ones signify that the coffee has been over-roasted and will be very bitter. This will clash in a bad way with the bitterness of the chocolate. Also, since there is a lot of coffee in this dessert, you might want to use decaffeinated beans or reduce the amount by 10 percent.

Many different textures and flavors come together in this pleasing dessert. The frozen mousse, served in a ramekin, combines the wonderful aroma of coffee with the complexity of coriander and chocolate. It is topped with a spiced whipped cream and a delicious crispy coffee and pecan *tuile*. The recipe is a fairly simple one, and you could do the entire dessert in a day, though it's possible and may be more practical for you to make it over the course of 2 or 3 days. The mousse can be frozen for up to a month and the *tuiles* will keep for a week.

METHOD

MAKING THE FROZEN MOUSSE

1 Chill a mixing bowl or the bowl of your stand mixer for 15 minutes.

2 Place the coffee beans and coriander seed in a disposable pastry bag, hold the end shut, and crush the beans slightly with a rolling pin. Be careful not to crush to a powder.

3 Place the whole milk in a medium saucepan and add the crushed beans and the coriander seed. Bring to a boil over low heat. Immediately turn off the heat and cover with plastic wrap. Infuse for 15 minutes.

4 Meanwhile, if working with a block of chocolate and not coins, chop the chocolate finely with a chef's knife on a cutting board and transfer to a small mixing bowl (there is no need to chop coins). Set aside.

5 Place the 176 grams of cold cream in the cold bowl you refrigerated, fit the stand mixer with the whisk attachment or use a handheld electric mixer, and beat at medium speed until the cream reaches soft peaks (PAGE 114). Watch the cream carefully and stop beating before the cream is stiff. If it becomes too stiff it will not fold into the coffee mousse properly. Transfer to a small mixing bowl and refrigerate.

6 Place a strainer lined with cheesecloth over a medium bowl and strain in the milk infusion. Weigh the strained liquid; you should have 187 grams. If necessary add a little more milk. Discard the cheesecloth and coffee beans.

7 Divide the sugar into two equal (63-gram) portions. In a medium mixing bowl, mix the egg yolks with ¼ cup of the infused milk, the first 63 grams of granulated sugar, the dark rum, honey, and vanilla. Return the remaining coffee-infused milk to the saucepan, add the remaining 63 grams of sugar, and stir with a spatula. Heat to a simmer, stirring, then turn off the heat. When it is no longer at a simmer, whisk the hot coffee infusion into the egg yolk mixture. Pour the mixture back into the pan and place over low heat. Stirring constantly with a rubber spatula or a whisk, heat the mixture to 179.6°F/82°C.

It is important to stir everywhere with the rubber spatula or whisk in order to prevent the mixture from curdling. If the mixture should get too hot and curdle, blend it immediately with an immersion blender and strain. When the mixture reaches 179.6°F/82°C remove it from the heat and stir for another 30 seconds.

8 Place the chocolate bowl on the scale with a strainer set over the bowl. (Make sure to reset the scale at 0.) Strain in 120 grams of the hot coffee crème anglaise. Stir gently with a rubber spatula or a whisk until the chocolate is melted and the mixture is homogenized.

9 Immediately strain the rest of the coffee crème anglaise into the bowl of your stand mixer and whisk on medium-high speed for 8 minutes or until the mixture is foamy and reaches the ribbon stage. *Do not let the mixture cool before you perform this step.* When a hot coagulated egg yolk mixture is whipped to cool, it "shrinks" and has the ability to trap air only at this point of the process. You cannot cool an egg yolk mixture and whip air into it afterward.

10 Meanwhile, using an immersion blender, blend the chocolate mixture for 30 seconds, until smooth. Set out your 8 ramekins and pour a thin layer of the chocolate mixture—it won't be more than ⅛ inch—into each one. Tilt the ramekins if necessary so that the chocolate layer covers the bottom. Place in the refrigerator for 20 minutes.

11 Take the mixing bowl out of the stand, transfer to a wider bowl if desired, and gently fold in the soft-peak whipped cream using a large rubber spatula. Remove the ramekins from the refrigerator and spoon in the mousse. Scrape the top flat with an offset spatula and freeze for 2 hours or longer uncovered. If not serving on the same day, cover the ramekins with plastic wrap once they have been in the freezer for a couple hours.

MAKING THE *TUILES*

1 Combine the liquid espresso, heavy cream, sea salt, granulated sugar, corn syrup, and butter in a medium saucepan and heat to 230°F/110°C over medium heat. The mixture should thicken and become somewhat gooey. Make sure to heat it all the way to 230°F/110°C, otherwise the batter will run too much when you make the cookies. Take the pan off the heat and transfer the mixture to a small bowl. Cool for 30 minutes. The mixture will thicken as it cools.

2 Meanwhile, preheat the oven to 325°F/160°C, place the rack in the center, and line your sheet pans with silpats. Using a chef's knife, chop the pecans into ⅛-inch pieces. Stir into the cooled espresso mixture.

Once infused, the vanilla sauce is cooked to 179.6°F/82°C and then cooled down by being whipped until cold, thick, and foamy. When a hot coagulated egg yolk mixture is whipped to cool, it "shrinks" and has the ability to trap air. At this point it's a mousse-like base. Whipped cream is then folded into it and the mixture is frozen.

The trick when preparing a frozen mousse is to make it in such a way that it will never harden completely in the freezer and will maintain its creamy texture even when frozen. To ensure this we use honey in the mixture, because honey is a very sweet inverted sugar and, like the dark rum we also include here, it does not harden completely when it freezes. These ingredients will help the frozen mousse remain creamy.

The coffee *tuile* brings together caramel, pecans, and coffee, three flavors that combine very nicely. Delicate like nougatine crisp and sweet and nutty like praline, the wonderful crunchy texture of the *tuile* works very nicely with the smooth whipped cream and frozen mousse. The spicy flavors and creaminess of the whipped cream complete the picture.

3 Using a round measuring teaspoon or a very small ice cream scoop, scoop out 4 spoonfuls of batter onto a sheet pan lined with a silpat, making sure to leave at least 2 inches of space between each one, as they will spread a lot. Make sure that your sheet pans are perfectly flat, otherwise the batter will run in all directions when you bake these. Repeat with a second sheet pan. Bake 1 sheet pan at a time for 12 to 14 minutes, until the *tuiles* are dark brown in color and the nuts look roasted. Remove from the oven and let them cool for 15 minutes. Do not be impatient, as the *tuiles* are very fragile and will break if you try to peel them off too soon. Gently turn the silpat over and slowly peel them off. Work very carefully as you peel off the silpats so that the *tuiles* remain intact. Continue until all of the batter is used up. Place the *tuiles* in an airtight container. They will keep for a week, and you will have more than you need for this one dessert.

FINISHING THE DESSERT

1 Whip the 250 grams of cold heavy cream until it forms very soft peaks. Add the confectioners' sugar and spices and whip until it reaches semi-stiff peaks. Take care not to over-beat or the cream will be grainy. It should be stiff enough for you to shape into a quenelle that will hold its shape, but not so stiff that it looks grainy. The texture should be nice and smooth.

2 Transfer the ramekins from the freezer to the refrigerator 10 to 15 minutes before serving.

3 To serve, place a small amount of hot water in a tall container and place a soup spoon in it. Place a *tuile* on top of each ramekin. Using the hot wet spoon make a spiced whipped cream quenelle by dipping the hot spoon into the cream and slowly twisting it and turning it over in the cream to get a nice smooth oval of cream in the spoon. Slide the whipped cream quenelle out of the spoon onto the *tuile*. Dust with a little confectioners' sugar and if desired set another *tuile* over or leaning on the side of the quenelle. Decorate the desserts with a chocolate curl and candied lemon zests if desired.

IT'S DONE WHEN IT'S DONE

The chocolate layer should be soft, the frozen mousse should be frozen but creamy, and the *tuiles* should be thin and crispy.

STORAGE

The ramekins can be made up to a month in advance and kept frozen. The *tuiles* can be kept in an airtight container for up to 1 week.

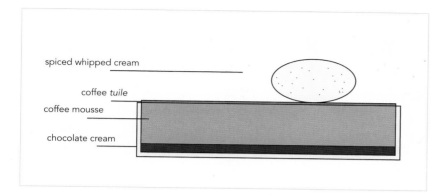

spiced whipped cream

coffee *tuile*

coffee mousse

chocolate cream

TARTE FLAMBÉE
(SEE PAGE 364 FOR RECIPE)

· CHAPTER 6 ·

SWEET AND SAVORY ALSATIAN SPECIALTIES

O f all the chapters in this book, this one is the closest to my heart. Each recipe brings back a wonderful memory from my childhood, from the delicious breakfast pastries like Chinois (PAGE 315), our version of cinnamon rolls, to the iconic Bundt-shaped Kougelhof (PAGE 297), a raisin-filled, almond-studded brioche that every Alsatian family buys on Saturdays for Sunday-morning breakfast. There are many brioche-based breakfast pastries in the Alsatian repertoire. We bake them in cake pans and top them with streusel, fill them with pastry cream, and coat them with an almond glaze for the popular Bee Sting Brioche (PAGE 311); and we make a wonderful Alsatian version of French toast, Brioche Bostock (PAGE 319), in which slices of stale brioche are dipped into an almond syrup, then topped with a thin layer of almond cream and sliced almonds, and crisped up in a hot oven until golden brown.

There are other Alsatian recipes here and there in this book, such as many of the cookies in Chapter 4 and some of the tarts in Chapter 3. Gastronomic traditions run deep here, and all of these dishes come with a little bit of history. The land is abundant and we take pride in the many fresh foods we produce—dairy and meat, fruits and vegetables, famous wines. Our savory dishes are rustic country fare that can accurately be described as comfort food. You'll understand what

I mean when you try Warm Alsatian Meat Pie (PAGE 367), the succulent puff pastry pie filled with Riesling-marinated pork and veal strips, the Onion Tart (PAGE 357), slow-cooked and then topped with bacon lardons, Beer Quiche (PAGE 361), the vegetable quiche enhanced with beer, or Tarte Flambée (PAGE 364), one of the culinary symbols of Alsace, a paper-thin flatbread covered with sour cream, onions, and bacon lardons that is baked in a very hot wood-burning oven. It is so good that I installed a special *tarte flambée* oven from Alsace at my home in Chicago so that I can enjoy this delicacy the way I remember it.

In our region, as in most of France, bread is present at all meals. Our breads are hearty. You will discover the wonderful Seeded Bread (PAGE 346), full of texture and a great candidate for your sandwiches, and the delicious and beautiful Beer Bread (PAGE 341), which has an extremely moist crumb and a delightful crust. While on the subject of beer, as a true Alsatian I could not deny you a recipe for Pretzels (PAGE 351), the snack that is most often served with beer. With their soft texture in the center and crunchy, salty crust, they are addictive.

There is a seasonality to many of the recipes in this chapter. When cherries are in season we make a simple yet very tasty type of bread pudding with fresh black cherries called Bettelman aux Cerises (PAGE 339); it is to die for. During the Christmas holiday season we make spice bread, lots of cookies, and a rich panettone-type brioche called Stollen (PAGE 303); and at Mardi Gras we make scrumptious Beignets (PAGE 323) filled with fresh raspberry jam, and small orange-flavored Carnival Fritters (PAGE 331). The entire region looks forward to Mardi Gras and its special pastries, even though it foreshadows Lent, when we must give up some of our favorite pleasures. I hope that you will immerse yourself in my region with me. A trip to Alsace can't help but follow.

KOUGELHOF

YIELD | 2 MEDIUM (6-INCH) OR 1 LARGE (9-INCH) KOUGELHOF

BASE TEMPERATURE | 60°C

INGREDIENTS	WEIGHT	MEASURE (APPROXIMATE) OR OUNCE WEIGHT
POOLISH		
Whole milk (3.5% fat)	50 grams	3 tablespoons plus 2 teaspoons
Dry yeast	12 grams	1 tablespoon plus ¼ teaspoon
All-purpose flour	50 grams	⅓ cup
DOUGH		
Golden raisins	120 grams	⅔ cup
Kirschwasser	10 grams	1 tablespoon
Granulated sugar	80 grams	½ cup less 1½ tablespoons
Bread flour	450 grams	3½ cups plus 1 rounded tablespoon
Whole eggs	125 grams	About 2½ extra-large eggs
Whole milk (3.5% fat)	125 grams	½ cup plus 2 teaspoons
Sea salt	10 grams	1¼ teaspoons
Butter (French style, 82% fat)	150 grams	5³⁄₁₀ ounces
Whole almonds	40 grams	28 almonds
Water	50 grams	Scant ¼ cup
Butter (French style, 82%), softened, for greasing molds	As needed	As needed
Confectioners' sugar, for dusting	As needed	As needed

Kougelhof is the signature bread of Alsace, the region's celebration bread par excellence. Rare is the Alsatian family that does not buy or make a kougelhof on a Saturday, which means that bakers are extremely busy every weekend. A brioche-type bread filled with kirsch-soaked golden raisins, studded with almonds, and dusted with confectioners' sugar, kougelhof is not as rich as Parisian brioche; there's less butter in it. Over centuries of on-and-off occupation by the Germans, Alsatians learned to be frugal.

What distinguishes kougelhof from other brioches is its shape—it has a hole in the center—and the fact that it's baked in a glazed ceramic mold. These molds have been used in Alsace since the Middle Ages.

BEFORE YOU BEGIN

→ Get out the following equipment and allow all of the ingredients to come to room temperature (except for the milk):

Digital scale, set to metric weights
KitchenAid or stand mixer fitted with the hook attachment
1 rubber spatula
1 small bowl
1 dough scraper
Plastic wrap or a damp hand towel
1 pastry brush
One 9-inch or two 6-inch ceramic or silicone kougelhof molds
1 sheet pan

→ Read this recipe through twice from start to finish.

METHOD

1 Make the *poolish* with a base temperature of 60°C. (See **PAGE 23** for an explanation of base temperature.) Let's say that your room and flour are both 20°C (68°F): add room temperature + flour temperature (20°C + 20°C) = 40°C. Subtract the sum from the base temperature of 60°C: 60°- 40°= 20°. This means that your milk should be heated to 20°C (68°F). Adjust the 50 grams of milk to the right temperature. Place it in the bowl of your stand mixer and add the yeast. Stir together. Sprinkle the all-purpose flour over the top. Let sit for 10 to 15 minutes, until cracks form on the surface of the flour. This signifies that the yeast is fermenting. This liquid fermentation is called a *poolish*, and acts a little like a starter to jump-start the action of the yeast.

2 Place the raisins in a small bowl and add the kirsch. Toss together and set aside. If not using kirsch, toss the raisins with a tablespoon of water.

3 Adjust the rest of the milk to the right temperature. Add the sugar, bread flour, eggs, the rest of the milk, and lastly the sea salt to the bowl of your mixer. Attach the hook to the mixer and mix on slow speed for 1 minute. Stop the mixer and, using a rubber spatula, scrape the bottom of the bowl to make sure that all the ingredients on the bottom of the mixer get mixed with the rest of the dough. If for some reason the dough looks very stiff, add a tablespoon of milk; if the dough is too soft, add a little bit of all-purpose flour.

4 Turn up the speed to medium and mix for 5 minutes on medium speed. Stop the mixer and, using a dough scraper, scrape the sides of the bowl as well as any dough that has worked its way up the hook. This will help the dough to come together faster. Repeat this twice—5 minutes on medium speed, stop and scrape the sides of the bowl and the dough hook, then another 5 minutes. The dough should now be shiny, elastic, and wrapped around the hook. The gluten has now been activated. Only when the dough has reached this stage can it absorb the next addition, which is the soft butter.

5 Make sure that the butter is at room temperature and soft; you might want to let it sit outside the night before making the dough, or you can microwave it for 5 to 10 seconds but do not melt. Add half of the soft butter and mix on medium speed for about 3 to 5 minutes, until the butter is incorporated. Add the rest of the soft butter and mix for about 3 to 5 more minutes on medium speed, until the butter is completely incorporated. The dough should again be smooth and elastic.

6 Drain the raisins if there is any liquid in the bowl, and add them to the dough. Knead in by hand if easier, or mix on a slow speed to incorporate. Mix the raisins or knead for 1 minute only to avoid crushing them, until they are evenly incorporated. Remove the dough hook, sprinkle a very small amount

UNDERSTANDING INGREDIENTS

The reason why I choose to use two different flours is that bread flour in the United States has a very strong gluten content that can make the dough rubbery and the bread chewy. All-purpose flour contains less gluten and will prevent this from happening.

Soaking the raisins in kirsch is not necessary, but it adds the distinctly Alsatian flavor. If you don't use kirsch, substitute with water to moisten the raisins before adding them to the dough. This moisture will then transfer to the dough and keep the kougelhof fresh.

Salt controls the action of the yeast by slowing down the speed of the fermentation: too much salt would prevent the dough from rising; not enough would allow the dough to ferment out of control. Never sprinkle the salt straight onto the yeast, as this will kill the yeast.

Kougelhof contains less butter than brioche, but it will still be very moist, especially during the first 48 hours after baking; after that it tastes great toasted. As with all brioche doughs, it is very important that the butter be soft before you try to work it into the dough. You can leave it out the night before or microwave it for 5 to 10 seconds (be sure not to melt it, though).

Kougelhof Molds

Each time you make kougelhof the ceramic mold absorbs the scent of your baking bread, and this contributes to the flavor of your next batch. The bread bakes slowly in the ceramic, allowing a golden crust to form. That's why it's important to use pottery and not something like a metal Bundt pan, which would bake the bread too quickly. Although we schlepp the molds back from Alsace for the French Pastry School, you can find ceramic kougelhof molds or monkey bread molds online through retailers. If you want to order them directly from Alsace, there is a site called **www.alsace-depot.com** that will ship. You can also bake them in a kougelhof silicone mold sold through **www.demarleathome.com**, which is a great and very practical option, though of course you won't have the patina that a ceramic mold develops.

Yeast breads are not normally baked in ceramic molds, but in Alsace we have been baking our kougelhof this way since the Middle Ages. In addition to the classic *couronne* with the hole in the middle, the old ceramic molds come in many different shapes, each one symbolizing a specific holiday. There are fleurs-de-lis for rich kings, stars for the Christmas holidays, lambs for Easter, couples for marriages, and more. I have been collecting antique Alsatian molds for years, beginning with the black ceramic kougelhof mold that I salvaged from my father's bakery on the day that it was sold.

of flour on the surface of the dough, and cover the bowl with a damp towel or with plastic wrap. Set in a warm spot (not hotter than 80.6°F/27°C or the butter will melt out of the dough) and let rise until double in volume, 1 to 1½ hours. You can create a makeshift proofer if your oven does not have a pilot light by placing a small pan filled halfway with freshly boiled water on the oven floor and the bowl inside the oven. Make sure the temperature does not exceed 80.6°F/27°C.

7 While the dough is rising, soak the almonds in the water in a small bowl.

8 Using softened butter and a pastry brush, grease your kougelhof molds. Should you use a silicone mold, you will not need to grease it. Drain the almonds and place on the bottom of the kougelhof molds, between each crease, with the pointy ends facing the center (otherwise they will burn during baking).

9 When the dough has doubled in volume (but not height), place it on a lightly dusted work surface. If making 2 breads, cut the dough in half using the flat edge of a scraper. Cup the dough with your hands on either side and shape it into a ball by making clockwise circular motions. At all times the sides of your hands should be touching the table. Make a hole in the center with your thumb. Place the dough in the mold and press it down so that it makes contact with the almonds. Repeat with the second piece of dough and the second mold. If you do not have 2 molds and want to make 2 breads, place the other half of the dough in a bowl, cover with plastic, and refrigerate. When you are ready to bake it, allow it to come to room temperature and reshape as above.

10 Cover the mold with plastic wrap or a towel. Let the dough rise at room temperature until it doubles in size, about 1½ hours. Do not allow the dough to get too warm (the temperature should not exceed 80.6°F/27°C).

11 Preheat the oven to 350°F/180°C and adjust the rack to one lower than the middle level. Place the kougelhofs on a sheet pan, leaving at least 2 inches of space between them.

12 Bake for 1 hour for a 9-inch kougelhof, 50 minutes for 6-inch kougelhofs. If the top begins to get too dark before the end of baking, cover loosely with a piece of aluminum foil. Remove from the oven using oven mitts and flip over onto a wire rack. Remove the breads from the molds and allow the kougelhofs to cool for 30 minutes to 1 hour. Dust lightly with confectioners' sugar and serve.

NOTE: *Never wash* ceramic molds; just wipe them clean while still warm with a paper towel. They will take on the wonderful aroma of baked kougelhof in time.

IT'S DONE WHEN IT'S DONE

When baked, the almonds on the top surface should be crunchy; the top of the kougelhofs should be golden brown while the bottom should be darker.

STORAGE

The baked kougelhof is good for 2 days at room temperature wrapped in a towel or a cloth bread bag; it can be frozen for 1 month. As a general rule, if you need to wrap a baked bread with plastic wrap, always ensure that it has cooled completely to room temperature. This can easily take 1 hour for a loaf of bread. Otherwise the leftover steam will be trapped in the plastic and the crust will become completely wet. In France, we usually don't wrap bread in plastic wrap; every family has a cloth bread bag.

JACQUY'S TAKEAWAYS

→ The rule of thumb for yeast doughs is that you fill your pan halfway full with dough. This will leave enough room for it to rise.

→ Never, ever refrigerate bread. Refrigerating bread causes it to become soggy. Bread molds faster in the refrigerator than it does when kept at room temperature because there is usually more moisture inside a refrigerator then outside of it. The bread will also pick up smells from your refrigerator.

→ You can now get silicone molds for kougelhof from the company Demarle. They're a great alternative to the ceramic molds, especially if you want to make small kougelof as they also come in a sheet of individual pieces. I recommend using 75 grams of dough per individual mold.

www.demarleathome.com

YIELD | 1 STOLLEN LOAF, SERVING 10 TO 12 PEOPLE

BASE TEMPERATURE | 60°C

INGREDIENTS	WEIGHT	MEASURE (APPROXIMATE) OR OUNCE WEIGHT
FRUIT		
Candied Orange or Lemon Peel (PAGE 87)	40 grams	1½ tablespoons
Golden raisins	40 grams	Scant ⅓ cup
Dark rum	15 grams	1½ tablespoons
POOLISH		
Whole milk (3.5% fat)	50 grams	¼ cup less 1 teaspoon
Dry yeast	8 grams	2 teaspoons
All-purpose flour	50 grams	⅓ cup
DOUGH		
Whole milk (3.5% fat)	90 grams	⅓ cup plus 1 tablespoon
Granulated sugar	30 grams	2 tablespoons
Bread flour	220 grams	1⅔ cups
Whole eggs	50 grams	1 large egg
Almond flour, unskinned	12 grams	3 tablespoons
Cardamom powder	0.8 grams	Scant ½ teaspoon
Sea salt	3 grams	½ teaspoon
Butter (French style, 82% fat)	115 grams	4 ounces
Chopped almonds	75 grams	½ cup whole almonds
GLAZE		
Butter (French style, 82% fat)	30 grams	1 ounce
Confectioners' sugar	30 grams	¼ cup

BEFORE YOU BEGIN

→ Get out the following equipment and allow all of the ingredients except for the milk and the eggs to come to room temperature:

Digital scale, set to metric weights
1 chef's knife
1 medium jar
1 digital thermometer
KitchenAid or stand mixer fitted with the dough hook
1 rubber spatula
1 bowl scraper
1 medium mixing bowl, if needed
Plastic wrap or hand towel
1 sheet pan lined with parchment paper
1 pastry brush
1 small saucepan
1 sifter

→ Read this recipe through twice from start to finish.

Stollen, a celebration bread that has been a Christmas tradition since the fifteenth century, is an eastern European type of brioche that is similar to Italian panettone. The rich oblong bread is loaded with butter, nuts, raisins, and candied citrus peels, and lasts for weeks due to the rum in the recipe, which acts as a curing agent, and to the melted butter and confectioners' sugar coating that is applied when the bread comes out of the oven, creating a seal that keeps the bread moist. The bread is also called Christstollen, and its shape is supposed to represent the baby Jesus wrapped in a blanket.

You can make this bread in a single day; the dough does not require a 2-day process like many other brioche doughs.

UNDERSTANDING INGREDIENTS

Authentic stollen was developed to be
kept for weeks or months, but personally I prefer this recipe, which is more
like a rich brioche and can be kept for
a week. As in many of my yeast raised
dough recipes, I choose to use two
different flours; bread flour has a very
high gluten content that can make the
dough rubbery and the bread chewy,
and using some all-purpose flour, which
contains less gluten, will prevent this
from happening. The addition of alcohol,
in this case rum, acts on the dough as a
preserving agent and extends the shelf
life of the stollen for days.

Salt controls the action of the yeast
by slowing down the speed of the fermentation: too much salt would prevent the dough from rising; not enough
would allow the dough to ferment out
of control. The large amount of butter
will make this a very rich bread and
will contribute to its long shelf life.
The cardamom adds complexity to
the flavor profile.

METHOD

1 Cut the candied citrus peel into a medium dice and mix it together with
the raisins and the rum so that the mixture can marinate. This step can be
done days or weeks ahead and the mixture kept at room temperature in a jar.

2 Make the *poolish* using a base temperature of 60°C. Take the temperature
of the flour and the room (convert to Celsius) and add them together. Adjust
your milk temperature (Celsius) so that the sum of the three ingredients is 60.
For instance, if your room temperature is 70°F, converted to Celsius you will
get 21°C, and your flour is 72°F (22°C), add 21°C + 22°C to get 43°C. 60
minus 43 = 17°C (62.6°F), the temperature you need to bring your milk to.

3 Place the 50 grams of milk in the bowl of your stand mixer and add the
yeast. Stir together and sprinkle the all-purpose flour over the top. Let sit
undisturbed for 10 to 15 minutes, or until cracks are visible on the surface
of the flour, which indicates that the yeast is fermenting.

4 Once the yeast has been activated it is time to mix and knead the dough.
Adjust the temperature of the 90 grams of milk to the same temperature as
the 50 grams. Before beginning the mixing process place an extra ¼ cup of
milk next to the mixer, just in case the dough is too dry. Add the sugar, bread
flour, eggs, almond flour, 90 grams of milk, cardamom powder, and finally the
sea salt to the *poolish*. Mix on medium speed with the dough hook for 30 seconds to 1 minute and observe the dough. If it looks very dry and lumpy add
a very small amount of extra milk to it. This can happen if you are in a dry environment where the flour is very dry; then it might need more hydration than
usual. The dough should start coming together after a full minute of mixing
on medium speed. Watch carefully and add liquid if necessary. Unattended
stollen dough that is very dry in the early stages of the mixing will have lumps
that will be impossible to get rid of later on. Mix the dough for 5 minutes on
medium speed and stop the machine. Using a rubber spatula or a dough
scraper, scrape the dough that is stuck to the bottom and sides of the bowl.
If the dough seems very wet and loose, add a tiny amount of all-purpose flour
to it. Mix again for 5 minutes, stop and scrape the bowl and dough hook, and
repeat once more. Depending on the amount of dough, after about 15 minutes of mixing the dough you should hear a slapping sound and the dough
should be very elastic and completely wrapped around the hook. It should
now look shiny and you should be able to stretch out a small piece of it like
a piece of cloth; this technique is called windowpane (SEE PHOTO ON PAGE 24).

5 Add half of the soft butter to the dough and mix on low to incorporate it,
about 2 minutes. At the beginning it will look like the butter will not incorporate, but eventually it will. After 2 minutes, stop the machine and scrape the

butter together with the dough with a rubber spatula, then mix for another 2 minutes. Eventually it will all be absorbed. Add the remaining soft butter and repeat this mixing procedure at medium speed for a total of 4 to 5 minutes. The dough should once again be elastic and shiny and the butter should now be completely incorporated. Add the nuts, raisins, and citrus peels to the dough and mix for 1 to 2 minutes on low until everything is incorporated.

6 Place the dough in a medium bowl (or, if not using the mixer again, allow the dough to rise in the mixing bowl), dust the surface with a small amount of all-purpose flour, and cover the bowl with plastic wrap or a towel. Place it in a warm spot to rise for 1 hour or until the dough doubles in volume. You can create a makeshift proofer if your oven is not a gas oven with a pilot light by placing a small pan filled halfway with freshly boiled water on the oven floor. Make sure the temperature does not exceed 80.6°F/27°C or the butter will melt out of the dough.

7 Line a sheet pan with parchment paper. Dust your work surface lightly with flour and turn out the dough. Press out the first gases created by the action of the yeast. Lightly dust your hands with flour, take the dough in your hands, and fold it over itself to shape into a ball. Cup the dough with your hands on each side and start pressing on it while turning it in clockwise circles on the counter. At first you need to press hard so that the dough sticks to the work surface a little, then ease up on the pressing and tighten your cupped hands around the dough; the sides of your hands should always be touching the counter. When the shaping is done you should have a perfectly round sphere of dough. If the dough sticks to the table too much, stop shaping and dust the work surface again with a very small amount of flour, keeping in mind that over-flouring the dough will make it dry and impossible to shape. Dust the top of the dough sphere and roll or press it into a 9-inch disk. Flip it over on the countertop and, using a pastry brush, brush the top surface with a little bit of water. Fold in half with one side overlapping the other like a calzone pizza.

8 Place the shaped stollen dough on the sheet pan and set it, uncovered, back in the makeshift oven proofer with the hot water next to it and the door closed, or in the warm spot where it rose the first time. Let proof for 45 minutes; if it is rising in the oven, take it out of the oven. Preheat the oven to 375°F/190°C with the rack adjusted to the center, and remove any racks that may be above it, as they could block the rise in the oven. Place the stollen in the oven and bake 35 to 40 minutes, until golden brown. While it bakes, melt 30 grams of butter in a small saucepan, and prepare a brush and a sifter with 30 grams of confectioners' sugar.

9 When the stollen comes out of the oven immediately brush it with all the melted butter that you have. Dust with the confectioners' sugar and let it cool completely. The confectioners' sugar and melted butter will create a natural crust. Eat when cooled, or store for up to 1 week.

IT'S DONE WHEN IT'S DONE

The baked stollen should have a dark brown color. To check doneness, insert a knife for 1 full second. Remove the knife; if there is no residue on the blade, the bread is done.

STORAGE

This stollen has a 7-day shelf life at room temperature on a platter or wrapped in a towel or a cloth bag. Do not seal it in a plastic bag, as it will not be able to breathe and will spoil faster. Stollen can be wrapped airtight and kept frozen for up to 1 month.

JACQUY'S TAKEAWAYS

→ The type of nuts, raisins, and candied fruit can be interchanged. Rum or kirschwasser are usually the alcohols of choice.

BRIOCHE STREUSEL / STREUSSEL BRIOCHE

YIELD | ONE 9-INCH CAKE

2-DAY RECIPE

INGREDIENTS	WEIGHT	MEASURE (APPROXIMATE) OR OUNCE WEIGHT
Brioche dough (PAGE 21)	½ recipe	½ recipe
Streusel (PAGE 9, kirsch optional)	125 grams	4²⁄₅ ounces
Melted butter, for the pan	As needed	As needed
Egg Wash (PAGE 7)	1 recipe	1 recipe
Confectioners' sugar, for dusting	As needed	As needed

Brioche streusel, another bread I grew up with, is a coffee cake made with brioche dough sprinkled with streusel. In Alsace it is called *streussel brioche* and in the United States we call the topping "crumble," but no matter what you call this wonderful pastry or how you spell the name, what people remember about it is the way it tastes. It allies two of my favorite textures, the smooth, delicate crumb of brioche and the crunch and butter of streusel topping. I like mine dusted with a little bit of confectioners' sugar. It is heavenly when served slightly warm with morning café au lait and some homemade jam.

As in the recipe for Bee Sting Brioche on PAGE 311, you will only use half the brioche dough for this, but I recommend that you make an entire batch and freeze what you don't use. The same applies to the streusel. Bake what you don't use for the coffee cake and keep in the freezer. Then you'll have it on hand to sprinkle it on ice cream. Yum!

METHOD

DAY 1

1 Make a recipe of brioche dough following the instructions on PAGE 21 and refrigerate overnight as instructed.

2 Make the streusel following the instructions on PAGE 9 and allow to cool. Weigh out 125 grams and place the rest in a labeled, dated container in the freezer.

DAY 2

1 If using a metal cake pan, grease it with melted butter. If you use a 9-inch round silicone Flexipan mold you will not need to grease it. Remove the

BEFORE YOU BEGIN

→ Get out the following equipment and allow all of the ingredients to come to room temperature:

Digital scale, set to metric weights
Equipment for Brioche (PAGE 21)
Equipment for Streusel (PAGE 9)
One 9-inch round cake pan, preferably silicone
1 chef's knife
Plastic wrap
1 rolling pin
1 pastry brush
1 digital thermometer
1 wire rack

→ Read this recipe through twice from start to finish.

brioche dough from the refrigerator, weigh it, and divide into 2 equal pieces. Wrap 1 piece in plastic and freeze for another purpose (or make a regular brioche following the recipe on PAGE 21).

2 Dust your work surface lightly with flour and make sure you have a lot of space in front of you for shaping the dough. Lightly dust your hands with flour and place your hands over the dough with the sides of your hands resting on the table so that they are cupping the dough. Cup the dough and press on it at the same time while sliding it around on the table in clockwise circles. At first you need to press hard so that the dough sticks to the table a little, and then you ease the pressing while tightening the cupping. When the shaping is done you should have a perfectly round sphere of dough. Take your rolling pin and start rolling it out to a 9-inch circle. Roll for 5 seconds, then turn the dough a quarter turn and roll again for 5 seconds. Do not forget to dust with a little bit of flour if the dough is sticky. Repeat until the dough is rolled out to a 9-inch circle.

3 Place the dough in your prepared pan and press it out so that it reaches the sides of the pan. Brush the top with egg wash and sprinkle on the streusel in an even layer, making sure not to put too much in the middle or the brioche will collapse when it bakes.

4 Place the bread in a warm place—but no hotter than 80.6°F/27°C—to rise for 1 to 1½ hours. You can create an ideal environment for rising in your oven if it doesn't have a pilot light by filling a medium saucepan halfway with boiling water and placing it in the cold oven. Set the dough in the oven along with the pan of steaming water. The hot water will provide heat and humidity. This system works very well, as it will also keep the dough away from drafts.

5 To check if the dough has risen enough, poke the surface with your finger and see how it bounces back; if the dough still seems very tight and bounces back rapidly the brioche will probably need another 20 to 30 minutes of rising. If after you poke it the dough barely bounces back and you can see a slight mark left by your finger, then the brioche has risen enough. If using the oven as a proofer, remove dough from the oven. Preheat your oven to 350°F/180°C.

6 Bake the brioche for 40 to 45 minutes, until golden brown and the streusel is crunchy. Remove from the oven, unmold right away, and place on a wire rack so that it can cool completely. This will take 1 full hour. Once cool sprinkle with confectioners' sugar and serve.

→ This is a classic Alsatian cake that is very simple but so good. The streusel can be flavored in different ways; see the suggestions in the streusel recipe.

→ You can also make individual brioche streusel rolls. Use 40 grams of brioche and 15 grams of crumble for each roll. They should proof for about 75 minutes and bake for 15 to 20 minutes at 350°F/180°C.

→ I have made countless versions of this brioche. You can build it upside down, placing the streusel on the bottom of a silicone mold and the raw brioche on top. It rises nicely, and when you unmold it the top will be a nice flat crust.

→ Brioche streusel is usually served for breakfast, but in another version I transform it into a tart. I use half the amount of brioche and roll it out to line a tart ring. Before I roll out the brioche I sauté some sliced or diced apples in butter with some vanilla extract and sugar, let them cool, and place them on the raw brioche. The whole thing is then topped with streusel; when baked together, these three textures combine magically.

IT'S DONE WHEN IT'S DONE

The sides of the brioche should be golden brown and the streusel should be very crunchy.

STORAGE

You can keep this bread for 2 days at room temperature or you can freeze it for 1 month.

BEE STING BRIOCHE / BRIOCHE NID D'ABEILLE

YIELD | ONE 9-INCH CAKE

2-DAY RECIPE

INGREDIENTS	WEIGHT	MEASURE (APPROXIMATE) OR OUNCE WEIGHT
Brioche dough (PAGE 21)	½ batch (make the entire recipe and freeze half the dough)	½ batch (make the entire recipe and freeze half the dough)
PASTRY CREAM		
Whole milk (3.5% fat)	175 grams	Scant ¾ cup
Heavy cream (35% fat)	18 grams	4 teaspoons
Butter (French style, 82% fat)	30 grams	1 ounce
Granulated sugar	18 grams	18 grams
Vanilla bean, split and scraped	1 bean	1 bean
Cornstarch	11 grams	1 tablespoon plus 1 teaspoon
All-purpose flour	6 grams	2 teaspoons
Granulated sugar	18 grams	2 tablespoons plus scant 2 teaspoons
Egg yolks	36 grams	2 yolks
Heavy cream (35% fat), for whipping	42 grams	3 tablespoons plus 1 teaspoon
Melted butter, for the pan	As needed	As needed
TOPPING		
Granulated sugar	25 grams	1 tablespoon plus 2 teaspoons
Clover honey	25 grams	1 tablespoon
Butter (French style, 82% fat)	25 grams	⁹⁄₁₀ ounce
Sliced almonds	25 grams	Scant ¼ cup

BEFORE YOU BEGIN

→ Get out the following equipment and allow all of the ingredients to come to room temperature:

Digital scale, set to metric weights
Equipment for Brioche (PAGE 21)
Equipment for Pastry Cream (PAGE 39)
KitchenAid or stand mixer fitted with the whisk attachment
1 large mixing bowl
Plastic wrap
One 9-inch round cake pan, preferably silicone
1 chef's knife
1 rolling pin
1 small saucepan
1 high-heat rubber spatula or wooden spatula
1 digital thermometer
1 small offset spatula
1 wire rack
1 serrated knife
1 pastry bag fitted with a ½-inch star piping tip

→ Read this recipe through twice from start to finish.

The bee sting cake is a wonderful cross between a breakfast and a dessert. It is very traditional in Alsace and can be found in every *boulangerie/pâtisserie*. It's made with brioche dough that is spread with a sticky bun–like mixture of sugar, butter, honey, and almonds, then baked and filled with a rich mixture of pastry cream and whipped cream called *crème diplomate*.

The cake is called *nid d'abeille* (honeycomb) in France, as it resembles a bee's nest covered with swarming bees. In Alsace we call it *binenstich*, which means "bee sting." Oddly, it is quite similar to another French pastry called *tarte Tropezienne*, which was apparently invented for Brigitte

UNDERSTANDING INGREDIENTS

The ingredients in this pastry are simple, but once you are comfortable with the recipe you can try some variations. You could use "sugar in the raw" (also called turbinado sugar) instead of granulated sugar or you could use a mix of half brown sugar and half granulated. You can substitute other types of honey for the clover honey, which has a lovely neutral flavor; just don't use chestnut honey, as its flavor is too strong. You can also play around with different nuts, but make sure to chop them small so that they bake fully.

The topping mixture is cooked to 222°F/105°C before it is spread on the raw brioche dough. Just melting the mixture and omitting to precook it would result in a liquid mixture that runs down the sides of the brioche as the brioche rises. The mixture would also be too soft and chewy, and stick to your teeth. In pastry nothing should stay stuck to your teeth.

Bardot in the 1950s by a Polish pastry chef. The only difference is that the tart has a layer of butter cream in addition to the pastry cream and is covered with a layer of coarse sugar crystals.

This recipe is a 2-day process: you will make brioche dough the first day and let it proof overnight in the refrigerator. You will only use half the dough for the cake, but that leaves you another half for the Brioche Streusel on PAGE 307, or just for your freezer. You can never have too much brioche on hand!

METHOD

DAY 1

1 Make a recipe of brioche dough following the instructions on PAGE 21 and refrigerate overnight as instructed.

2 Make the pastry cream. Line a sheet pan with plastic wrap. In a medium stainless steel saucepan combine all but ¼ cup of the milk, the 18 grams of cream, 30 grams of butter, 18 grams of the sugar, and the vanilla bean seeds and pod. Stir with a whisk and place over medium heat.

3 Meanwhile, in a medium bowl whisk the cornstarch and the flour together with the remaining 16 grams of sugar. Add the ¼ cup of milk that you set aside and whisk in the egg yolks.

4 When the milk mixture comes to a boil, turn off the heat and remove the vanilla bean (set it on a sheet of paper towel to dry). Whisk half of the hot milk mixture into the egg yolk mixture. Strain the egg yolk mixture back into the saucepan with the remaining milk.

5 Turn the heat back to medium and whisk, making sure to whisk everywhere—bottom and sides and bottom edges of the pan—so that the mixture does not scorch. As soon as you feel that the mixture is becoming slightly thick on the bottom of the pan, remove it from the heat and whisk until the mixture is thick and thoroughly uniform. This will allow a slow and even coagulation of the eggs and result in a nice, creamy pastry cream. Return to the heat and bring back to a boil, whisking constantly. Cook, whisking, for 1 minute to cook out the starch flavor.

6 Immediately remove from the heat and transfer to the plastic-lined sheet pan. Spread in an even layer and place another sheet of plastic wrap directly on top of the cream, so that the pastry cream is not in contact with the air. This will prevent the pastry cream from developing a dry skin. Place the sheet pan in the freezer to cool the cream rapidly and stop the growth of bacteria. This should only take 15 minutes. Remove from the freezer and refrigerate.

7 Meanwhile, whip the 42 grams of cream to medium-stiff peaks (PAGE 114). Once the pastry cream is cool, place in a large bowl and fold in the whipped cream. Cover the bowl and refrigerate overnight.

DAY 2

1 If using a metal cake pan, grease it with melted butter. If you use a 9-inch round silicone Flexipan pan, you will not need to grease it. Remove the brioche dough from the refrigerator, weigh it, and divide into 2 equal pieces. Wrap one half in plastic and freeze for another purpose (or make a regular brioche following the recipe on PAGE 21).

2 Dust your work surface lightly with flour and make sure you have a lot of space in front of you for shaping the dough. Lightly dust your hands with flour and place your hands over the dough with the sides of your hands resting on the table so that they are cupping the dough. Cup the dough and press on it at the same time while sliding it around on the table in clockwise circles. At first you need to press hard so that the dough sticks to the table a little, and then you ease the pressing while tightening the cupping. When the shaping is done you should have a perfectly round sphere of dough. Take your rolling pin and start rolling it out to a 9-inch circle. Roll for 5 seconds, then turn the dough a quarter turn and roll again for 5 seconds. Do not forget to dust with a little bit of flour if the dough is sticky. Repeat until the dough is rolled out to a 9-inch circle.

3 Place the dough in your prepared pan and press it out so that it reaches the sides of the pan.

4 Make the bee sting topping. Place the sugar, honey, and butter in a small saucepan over medium heat and heat to 222°F/105°C. This should take around 5 minutes. Remove from the heat, let sit for 1 minute, and stir in the almonds. Stir for 10 seconds.

5 Immediately pour the mixture evenly onto the brioche and spread it flat and evenly with a small offset spatula.

6 Place the bread in a warm place—but no hotter than 80.6°F/27°C—to rise for 1 to 1½ hours. You can create an ideal environment for rising in your oven if it doesn't have a pilot light. Fill a medium saucepan halfway with boiling water and place in the cold oven. Set the dough in the oven along with the pan of steaming water. The hot water will provide heat and humidity. This system works very well, as it will also keep the dough away from drafts. To check if the dough has risen enough, poke the surface with your finger and see how it bounces back; if the dough still seems very tight and bounces back

→ The reason why you cut the top of the cake before setting it back on the filling is that otherwise the top pieces might slide off and the cream might ooze out when you cut the cake. If you do want to preserve the look of the whole uncut cake I recommend an electric knife as the best tool for cutting it. A sharp serrated knife is the second-best tool.

→ This brioche can be shaped into individual pieces. If you choose to do this, use silicone muffin molds and place 10 grams of bee sting mixture into each cup first. Bake for 10 minutes at 350°F/180°C and then let cool completely. Shape 40 grams of brioche into a ball, press it flat, and then place it on top of the bee sting mixture; repeat for all the dough. Proof for 1 hour and 15 minutes and bake at 350°F/180°C for 15 to 20 minutes, until golden brown. Let cool completely in the mold for 45 minutes. Take them out of the mold and inject some *crème diplomate* into the roll with a pastry bag fitted with a ¼-inch round tip.

→ I make many versions of this cake. I vary the type of nuts and also the flavoring of the pastry cream. Who could resist a bee sting made of brioche, hazelnut topping, and chocolate hazelnut pastry cream? *Pas moi.*

rapidly the brioche will probably need another 20 to 30 minutes of rising. If after you poke it the dough barely bounces back and you can see a slight mark left by your finger, then the brioche has risen enough.

7 If your dough has risen in the oven, remove it from the oven. Preheat your oven to 350°F/180°C. Bake the brioche for 35 to 40 minutes, until golden brown. Remove from the oven, unmold right away, and place on a wire rack so that it can cool completely. This will take 1 full hour.

8 Place the brioche on a cutting board and slice it in half horizontally. Remove the top and set it aside. Place the pastry cream in a pastry bag fitted with a ½-inch star tip and pipe teardrop shapes all around the edge of the bottom half of the brioche. Once the entire border is piped, pipe a second row of teardrops, staggering the drops between the drops in the first row. Continue piping circles of teardrops until the entire bottom half of brioche is covered (see photo on PAGE 13). Using a serrated knife cut the top part into 12 equal slices and place them on the piped cream, reassembling the top in its original shape.

Serve at once or refrigerate. If you do refrigerate this cake, let it come to room temperature for 1 hour before you serve it.

IT'S DONE WHEN IT'S DONE

The sides of the brioche should be golden brown and the bee sting mixture should also be golden brown and crunchy. The pastry cream should be shiny.

STORAGE

You can keep bee sting brioche for 2 days in the refrigerator.

CHINOIS / ALSATIAN CINNAMON ROLLS

YIELD | 12 CINNAMON ROLLS

2-DAY RECIPE

INGREDIENTS	WEIGHT	MEASURE (APPROXIMATE) OR OUNCE WEIGHT
Brioche dough (PAGE 21)	½ recipe	½ recipe
Almond Cream (PAGE 43)	1 recipe	1 recipe
Ground cinnamon	1 gram	½ teaspoon
Walnut or pecan pieces	75 grams	¾ cup
Dark or golden raisins	70 grams	½ cup
Sugar Icing (PAGE 5)	75 grams (½ recipe)	½ recipe

These are perfect to enjoy for breakfast. Where I grew up bakeries are closed on Sundays, so families make or buy large breakfast cakes on Saturday to enjoy the next day. This is the Alsatian version of a cinnamon roll, made with brioche dough, a buttery almond cream, walnuts, and raisins. In Alsace we squeeze all of the rolls together in a pan and bake them as a cake, resulting in nice moist rolls. The cake is glazed with sugar icing as it comes out of the oven, which transforms the top into a shiny, luscious sugar crust.

METHOD

DAY 1

Make a recipe for brioche dough following the instructions on PAGE 21. After the first rise, press out the gases, cover the bowl with plastic, and refrigerate overnight.

DAY 2

1 Make a recipe of almond cream following the instructions on PAGE 43. Add the cinnamon to it at the end of the mixing process.

2 Grease two 9-inch cake pans or cake rings with soft butter; if using rings, place them on sheet pans lined with parchment paper.

3 Remove the brioche dough from the refrigerator, weigh it, and divide into 2 equal pieces. Wrap one half in plastic and freeze for another purpose (or make a regular brioche following the recipe on PAGE 21). Roll the other half out to a 10 × 16–inch rectangle. It should be about ¼ inch thick. Place the dough in front of you horizontally (with the long edge closest to you) and spread the

BEFORE YOU BEGIN

→ Get out the following equipment and allow all of the ingredients to come to room temperature:

Digital scale, set to metric weights
Equipment for Brioche (PAGE 21)
Equipment for Almond Cream
  (PAGE 43)
Plastic wrap
Two 9-inch metal rings or cake pans
2 sheet pans lined with parchment
  paper if using rings
1 chef's knife
1 rolling pin
1 rubber spatula
1 pastry brush
1 wire rack with parchment paper
  underneath it

→ Read this recipe through twice from start to finish.

almond cream evenly over the dough, leaving a 1-inch border along the top edge. Brush the uncovered border along the top edge with water.

4 Sprinkle the walnut pieces and raisins evenly over the almond cream. Starting with the edge nearest you, make a ½-inch fold in the dough and then roll up tightly, folding the dough over itself until the entire dough looks like a giant snake. Place the snake on its seam and, using a chef's knife, cut twelve 1⅓-inch slices. Take a slice and fold the tail end under it, and then place it, flat side up, tail underneath, in the cake pan. Repeat until you have 6 slices evenly distributed around the edge of the pan and 1 in the middle, 7 in all. Fill the next pan with the remaining rolls.

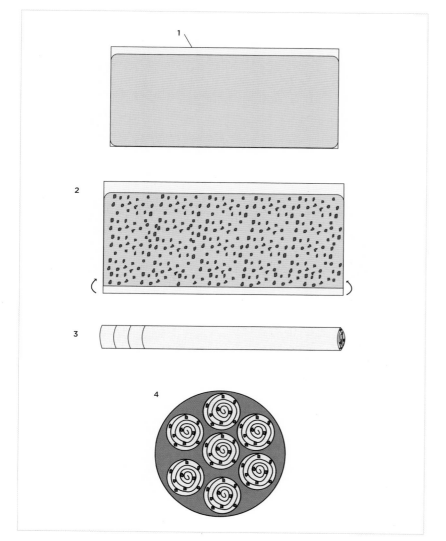

UNDERSTANDING INGREDIENTS

This dough should not be too fatty, as it will be filled with a rich almond cream; brioche is the right choice. Some cinnamon roll recipes call for croissant dough, but I think croissant dough is too rich.

Raisins and walnuts make a great flavor combination that complements the flavor of the almond cream. The raisins also bring an appealing fruitiness to the filling and the nuts contribute the crunch factor. Whatever you use as a filling, it should be dry and should not release any water during the baking process; fresh fruit, for example, would not work well.

1

Place the dough in front of you horizontally (with the long edge closest to you) and spread the almond cream evenly over the dough, leaving a 1-inch border along the top edge. Brush the uncovered border along the top edge with water. Sprinkle the walnut pieces and raisins evenly over the almond cream.

2

Starting with the edge nearest you, make a ½-inch fold in the dough and then roll up tightly.

3

Place the snake on its seam and using a chef's knife cut twelve 1⅓-inch slices.

4

Take a slice and fold the tail end under it, and then place it, flat side up, tail underneath, in the cake pan. Repeat until you have 6 slices evenly distributed in the pan and 1 in the middle.

5 Set the pans in a warm spot to rise for 1 hour or until doubled in volume. You can create a makeshift proofer if your oven does not have a pilot light by placing a small pan filled halfway with freshly boiled water on the oven floor and the pans inside the oven. Make sure that the temperature does not exceed 80.6°F/27°C or the butter in the dough will melt and ooze out.

6 While the cinnamon rolls are rising, prepare a recipe of sugar icing following the instructions on PAGE 5.

7 Once the rolls have doubled in volume, take the pan out of the oven if they were rising in it, and preheat the oven to 375°F/190°C. Bake the *chinois* for 35 minutes, until dark brown. Remove from the pans and place on a rack set over a sheet of parchment paper. Using a pastry brush, glaze the rolls, using up all of the icing. Allow the rolls to cool for 10 minutes and serve them warm.

NOTE: You can also serve these at room temperature or rewarm them in a 400°F/200°C oven for 2 to 3 minutes.

IT'S DONE WHEN IT'S DONE

The top of the rolls should have a dark and rich brown color. Once they are glazed they should look shiny.

STORAGE

Once baked the *chinois* can be kept at room temperature, wrapped in plastic, for 2 to 3 days or frozen for up to 1 month. The filled raw cinnamon roll slices can be frozen as well for up to 1 month. Let them defrost in the greased pans for 1 hour, proof them in a warm area for about 2 hours, until they double in volume, then bake as directed.

INGREDIENTS	WEIGHT	MEASURE (APPROXIMATE) OR OUNCE WEIGHT
ALMOND SYRUP		
Water	125 grams	½ cup plus 1 tablespoon
Granulated sugar	125 grams	½ cup plus 2 tablespoons
Almond flour, skinless	13 grams	2 tablespoons
Granulated sugar	13 grams	Scant tablespoon
Almond extract	2 drops	2 drops
Orange blossom water, optional	7 grams	1½ teaspoons
Melted butter, for brushing the rack	25 grams	A little less than 2 tablespoons
Day-old Brioche (PAGE 21)	½ recipe (1 brioche)	½ recipe (1 brioche)
Almond Cream (PAGE 43)	100 grams	3½ ounces
Sliced almonds	25 grams	Scant ¼ cup
Confectioners' sugar	13 grams	2 tablespoons

During bad times and wars, chefs and home cooks had to find ways to recycle day-old baked brioche. Solutions include *pain perdu* (French toast), *bettelman* (see Cherry Bread Pudding, PAGE 339), croutons, and bread crumbs. My dad would bring old stale bread to my grandmother, who raised rabbits on her farm. An exchange would take place and eventually end up on the family table as *lapin à la moutarde—Hasenpfeffer*, or rabbit in mustard sauce—with spaetzle.

A typical French recipe for reviving old croissants or brioches is brioche bostock. Slices of stale brioche are briefly dipped into an almond syrup, then topped with a thin layer of almond cream and sliced almonds and crisped up in a hot oven until golden brown. The finished product is to die for.

METHOD

1 Combine the water and the 125 grams of granulated sugar in a saucepan and bring to a boil. Meanwhile, mix the almond flour with the 12.5 grams of granulated sugar in a medium bowl. When the sugar has dissolved in the boiling water, pour the hot syrup over the almond flour mixture and add the

BEFORE YOU BEGIN

→ Get out the following equipment:

Digital scale, set to metric weights
Equipment for Almond Cream
    (PAGE 43)
1 medium saucepan
1 stainless steel hand whisk
1 medium mixing bowl that is larger
    than the saucepan
1 wire rack
1 sheet pan
1 pastry brush
1 serrated knife
1 sheet pan lined with parchment paper
1 small offset spatula

→ Read this recipe through twice from start to finish.

almond extract. Rinse the saucepan, add ½ inch of water to it, and place on the stove over medium heat. Create a bain-marie by placing the medium bowl containing the syrup on the saucepan, and let the syrup infuse for 15 minutes.

2 Take the bowl of syrup off the pan and set it aside until it has cooled to 95°F/35°C. Add the orange blossom water at this time, if desired, and stir together.

3 Place the wire rack on the unlined sheet pan and brush with a generous amount of melted butter.

4 Cut ½-inch-thick slices of brioche with the serrated knife and dip the slices into the syrup for no longer than 1 second. It is important to just dip the brioche briefly into and out of the syrup or the slices will get too soggy and fall apart. Place on the wire rack and allow to drip for 15 minutes to remove the excess syrup. Meanwhile, preheat the oven to 450°F/230°C.

5 Transfer the wire rack to the sheet pan lined with parchment paper. Using an offset spatula, spread a ⅛-inch-thick layer of almond cream on each slice. Sprinkle the top with sliced almonds and confectioners' sugar. Place the sheet pan in the hot oven and bake 10 to 12 minutes, until the slices are golden brown. Remove from the heat and dust the baked slices with additional confectioners' sugar. Serve right away.

STORAGE

The brioche bostock can be frozen at the raw stage. To defrost them, place on a greased wire rack and allow to sit for 30 minutes or until defrosted. Proceed with the baking instructions above. The slices can also be frozen after baking. In this case, defrost on a sheet pan lined with parchment paper and heat through at 475°F/250°C for 1 minute. Personally I prefer to eat them fresh from the oven.

BEIGNETS

YIELD | 15 BEIGNETS

2-DAY RECIPE

BASE TEMPERATURE | 54°C

INGREDIENTS	WEIGHT	MEASURE (APPROXIMATE) OR OUNCE WEIGHT
POOLISH		
Water	90 grams	⅓ cup plus 1 tablespoon
Dry yeast	5 grams	1¾ teaspoons
All-purpose flour	75 grams	½ cup plus 1 tablespoon
DOUGH		
Water	80 grams	⅓ cup plus 1 teaspoon
Granulated sugar	25 grams	2 tablespoons less 1 teaspoon
Bread flour	200 grams	1½ cups
Egg yolks	55 grams	About 3 yolks
Sea salt	5 grams	¾ teaspoon
Butter (French style, 82% fat)	50 grams	1⅘ ounces
Grapeseed or canola oil, for frying	1 to 2 liters, or as needed	1 to 2 quarts, or as needed
BEIGNET SUGAR AND FILLING		
Granulated sugar	100 grams	½ cup
Ground cinnamon	3 to 5 grams	1 to 2 teaspoons
Raspberry Jam (PAGE 80) or Pastry Cream (PAGE 39), optional	160 grams	½ cup

It's difficult to resist warm, freshly made beignets filled with raspberry jam. These, made with yeasted brioche dough that has much less butter in it than a regular brioche dough, are the type that I grew up eating around Mardi Gras, the only time of year that French *pâtissiers* produced them. They are usually shaped like round flying saucers and are filled with a delicious jam. Every semester my kids ask me when beignets are going to be taught at the French Pastry School, and when the time comes they never stop reminding me to bring some home. They like them so much that they request them for their birthday cakes.

Like doughnuts, beignets are deep-fried yeasted pastries, but the similarities stop there. My kids never eat or crave doughnuts, nor do I; the two are not comparable, even though the beignet, brought to New Orleans by the French more than 200 years ago, is the doughnut's ancestor. I've had a few good doughnuts in my life, but most are better off forgotten.

BEFORE YOU BEGIN

→ Get out the following equipment and allow all of the ingredients to come to room temperature (make sure that your butter is soft):

Digital scale, set to metric weights
1 digital thermometer
KitchenAid or stand mixer fitted with the hook attachment
1 rubber spatula
1 dough scraper
1 medium mixing bowl
Plastic wrap
1 large shallow pan or wok
1 sheet pan
2 hand towels
1 large mixing bowl
1 large pot or wok
1 wire rack set over a sheet pan
1 spider
1 timer
1 pastry bag fitted with a ¼-inch tip if filling the beignets

→ Read this recipe through twice from start to finish.

UNDERSTANDING INGREDIENTS

This dough is very similar to brioche dough, but the big difference is that water is used instead of milk, and there is much less butter in it than in brioche. Brioche relies on butter for good rich flavor, while beignet dough cannot have this luxury because it is fried. Fried doughs must always be low in fat because they will soak up a certain amount of fat during the frying process.

I like to use grapeseed oil for deep-frying because it has a neutral flavor. Canola oil will also work. The key to successful deep-frying is the temperature of the oil. It must be heated to 340°F/171°C before you add the items to be fried. This temperature is crucial, as the high heat will sear the skin of the beignets as soon as they hit the oil, preventing the oil from penetrating deeper into the beignets. If the oil isn't hot enough they will take too long to fry and become saturated with oil. Many deep-fried items are fried at a higher temperature (up to 375°F/190°C), but we cannot use such a high temperature for these because the bread needs time to "bake" inside the seared skin of the beignets. If the oil were too hot the outside would burn before the inside was sufficiently cooked and the beignets would be doughy—which is anathema to me. When you're ready to fry these, my advice is to fry one as a test to see how long it will take, especially if this is your first time making beignets.

That's because most doughnuts are made with shortening, and some are even fried in shortening. There are people who insist on the attributes of shortening when it comes to texture, but it can't do anything that butter or clarified butter can achieve.

I'm always encouraging my students to open their own pastry shops and make fresh beignets on a daily basis using this recipe. It has stood the test of time. If they want to they can always shape them like and even call them doughnuts, but these will be made with quality ingredients. The rest will be history; their bakeries will have lines around the block forever, as today Americans enjoy more than 10 billion doughnuts per year. Imagine if those 10 billion doughnuts were made with fresh, quality ingredients instead of shortening and chemicals?

METHOD

DAY 1

1 Make a *poolish* with a base temperature of 54°C. Take the temperature of the flour and the room (convert to Celsius) and add them together. Then adjust your water temperature (Celsius) so that the sum of the three ingredients is 54. Place the 90 grams of water in the bowl of your stand mixer and add the yeast. Stir together. Sprinkle the all-purpose flour over the top. Let sit undisturbed for 10 to 15 minutes, until cracks form on the surface of the flour. This signifies that the yeast is fermenting. The fermentation of the yeast creates a very slight acidic flavor that contributes a pleasant flavor to the dough.

2 Once the yeast has been activated you can mix and knead the dough. Before beginning the mixing process place an extra cup of water next to the mixer, just in case the dough is too dry. Bring the temperature of the water to the same temperature of the water you used for the *poolish*. Add the water, sugar, bread flour, egg yolks, and finally the sea salt to the *poolish*. Mix on medium speed for 30 seconds to a minute and observe the dough. If it looks very dry and lumpy add a very small amount of extra water to it. This can happen if you are in a dry environment where the flour is very dry; then it might need more hydration than usual. The dough should come together after 1 full minute of mixing on medium speed. Watch carefully and add liquid if necessary. Unattended yeast dough that is very dry in the early stages of the mixing will have lumps that will be impossible to get rid of later on. Mix the dough for about 5 minutes and stop the machine. Using a rubber spatula or a dough scraper, scrape the dough that is stuck to the bottom and sides of the bowl and add a tiny amount of all-purpose flour to that area. Mix again and repeat this 2 more times. Depending on the amount of dough, after about 15 minutes of mixing the dough you should hear a slapping sound and the dough should be very elastic and completely wrapped around the hook. It should now look shiny and you should be able to stretch out a small piece of it like a piece of cloth.

3 Add the soft butter to the dough and mix at low speed to incorporate it, about 2 minutes. At the beginning it will look like the butter will not incorporate, but that is normal. Stop the machine and scrape the butter together with the dough with a rubber spatula and mix for another 2 minutes. Eventually it will all be absorbed. The beignet dough should once again be elastic and shiny and the butter should now be completely incorporated.

4 Place the dough in a medium bowl, dust the surface with a small amount of all-purpose flour, and cover the bowl with plastic wrap or a towel. Let the dough rest at room temperature or in a warm place that is not hotter than 80.6°F/27°C until it doubles in volume. This can take 1 to 1½ hours depending on the temperature of the room. You can create an ideal environment for rising in your oven if it doesn't have a pilot light. Fill a medium saucepan halfway with boiling water and place in the cold oven. Set the dough in the oven along with the pan of steaming water. The hot water will provide heat and humidity. This system works very well, as it will keep the dough away from drafts. Just make sure that the temperature stays below 80.6°F/27°C or the butter will melt out.

5 Once the dough has doubled in volume it is time to press out the first gases created by the action of the yeast and place the dough in the refrigerator for at least 2 hours. Press down on the dough with your fist or the palm of your hand; you will hear the sound of the gases emerging from the dough. Cover and place in the refrigerator for 2 hours, after which time it should be cold and should have risen again.

6 Press out the gases again, cover, and let the dough rest in the refrigerator overnight.

DAY 2

1 After the overnight rest it is time to shape your beignets. Dust your work surface lightly with flour. Line a sheet pan with a towel and dust the surface lightly with flour. Using a bowl scraper, scrape out the dough and place it on your work surface. Cut 35-gram pieces of dough and place them on your work surface, leaving a lot of space in front of you for shaping the beignets.

2 Making sure that your work area is lightly dusted with flour, place 1 piece of dough in front of you. Lightly dust your hands with flour and place a hand over the piece of dough. Cup the dough and start pressing on it while making clockwise circles. At first you need to press hard so that the dough sticks to the table a little, and then you ease the pressing while tightening the cupping. This will take a few tries until you get the hang of it. Once you get comfortable shaping with one hand try shaping 2 pieces of dough at a time, 1 with each hand. When the shaping is done you should have perfectly round spheres of dough. If the dough sticks to the table too much, stop shaping and dust the work surface again with a very small amount of flour, remembering that over-flouring the dough will make the dough dry and impossible to shape. After you shape the beignet spheres, press them flat with the palm of your hand so that they have a flying saucer shape. Place them straight onto the towel-lined sheet pan, leaving 1 inch of space between each disk since they will expand when they rise. Dust a very small amount of flour on the beignets and place a second towel on top of them.

3 Set the beignets in a warm place (but not hotter than 80.6°F/27°C) to rise until they double in volume, 1 to 1½ hours. Meanwhile, mix the granulated sugar with the cinnamon in a large mixing bowl.

4 Pour 1 to 2 quarts of canola or grapeseed oil into a large but not too deep pot. The sides should be at least 3 inches tall and the pot should be wide enough to cover the entire burner and to accommodate several beignets at the same time. A flat-bottomed wok also works well. Wipe away any oil that might be on the side of the pot.

5 When you think that the beignets have risen enough poke one with a finger. If it bounces back rapidly it needs more time to rise; if it bounces back slowly and the finger leaves a slight mark, the beignets are ready. Place the pan over medium heat and warm up the oil to 340°F/171°C. Keep a thermometer in the oil during the entire frying process, as you will need to increase or decrease the burner heat to regulate the temperature so that it remains at 340°F/171°C. Place the sheet pan with the beignets on one side of the frying pan and a sheet pan topped with a wire rack on the other side. Always work from one side to the other.

6 When the oil is at 340°F/171°C, very gently slide in 1 beignet. Some people are afraid of hot oil and throw the beignet into the oil; this is a great way to hurt yourself. A safe way to do it is to place the beignet on a spider and slide it from the spider into the oil. If you use your hands, be very careful. As soon as the beignet is in the hot oil, gently flip it over with a spider or slotted spoon. Set a timer and fry the beignet for 2½ minutes; then gently flip the beignet over again and fry it on the other side for 2½ minutes. Using the spider, transfer the beignet to the sheet pan topped with a wire rack. Let sit for 3 minutes, then roll it gently in the cinnamon sugar. It is important to do

Flipping the beignets over as soon as you drop them into the oil ensures that both sides are seared and stops the beignet from expanding. If you forget to do that and place the beignet in the hot oil for 2½ minutes without flipping it right away you will see that the side that is not sitting in the oil is expanding and rising in a perfect round shape. When you try to flip it over it will roll and flip over due to the spherical shape. This problem is unfortunately difficult to correct; if it does happen, you will have to keep flipping the beignets over to ensure even frying.

this when the beignet is still hot because the residue of hot oil will make the cinnamon sugar stick nicely. Tear the first beignet in half to make sure that it is baked enough on the inside; this should set the standard for the timing for the rest of the beignets. If the surface gets too dark, reduce the time by 30 seconds on each side. If the beignet is doughy, increase the frying time to 3 minutes on each side.

7 Make sure to bring the oil back up to temperature between batches. After your test beignet you can fry the beignets 3 to 5 at a time depending on the width of your pan. Make sure that you do not put too many into the pot at once, as they will expand and crowd each other, which will slow down the frying process and make them sit longer in the oil than they should. Putting too many in at the same time will also make the oil temperature drop too much, which will also make them greasy. Remember to coat the beignets with the cinnamon sugar topping as soon as they have cooled for 3 minutes. Once all the beignets are fried, let the oil cool down overnight. Do not attempt to dispose of it while it is hot.

8 If you wish to fill the beignets, fill a pastry bag fitted with a ¼-inch round tip with raspberry jam or pastry cream, stick the tip into the beignet, and inject the filling until you see it begin to ooze around your pastry tip.

IT'S DONE WHEN IT'S DONE

The beignets should be golden brown on each side and they should be cooked and bready in the center.

STORAGE

Store the beignets at room temperature and try to enjoy them the day you make them. Technically you can freeze a beignet, but the flavor and texture will never be the same as when they are freshly fried.

JACQUY'S TAKEAWAYS

→ You can fill the beignets with different flavors of jam or pastry cream.

THE BEIGNET IS THE PASTRY that almost made me quit my apprenticeship. Looking back, it would have been a huge mistake, but at the time I considered it. I had begun my apprenticeship on September 1, 1976, when I was fifteen. Overnight I'd made a brutal switch from being a happy and worry-free teenager to a pastry professional responsible for a daily production.

In January, a relatively slow month, the bakery closed for one week, and I went on vacation in the French Alps with the other pastry workers. This was a far cry from a fancy Aspen trip; we were just a bunch of pastry cooks without any special gear who rented an old farmhouse and goofed around in the snow, trying to pretend to ski. The casualties were numerous but the *génépi*, a traditional liqueur from the Savoie region, eased the pain. I was in heaven after working so hard for the first time in my life.

Then it was time to go back to reality. The bakery was usually closed on Sunday afternoons and Mondays, our days off. But after a vacation a few of us would come in on Monday and prepare the recipes that required a two-day process. Making beignet dough was one of the preparations, and since I was in charge of making all the doughs, I was one of the lucky chosen ones who had to come in from vacation a day early.

I pre-scaled the ingredients as we were always asked to do. My boss, Jean Clauss, would then examine each amount and question them. "Are you sure this is 20 grams of yeast?" "*Oui, patron,*" I would say. If I had to put it back on the scale and it did not register exactly 20 grams, I would pay a very dear price.

I started to make the dough, but in my head I was still somewhere in the Alps, and my lack of concentration made me add too much liquid at the beginning, so that the gluten couldn't develop and the dough looked like soup. Jean Clauss was furious and screamed at me at the top of his lungs, "This dough is unfixable, you idiot!" I suggested adding more flour, which made him angrier. In his rage he explained to me that adding flour would completely change the recipe. Then he made me rescale the ingredients and stood behind me breathing down my neck. I was so nervous that this time I didn't add *enough* liquid, and the resulting dough looked like cottage cheese. Jean Clauss was livid and called me every name in the Alsatian insult repertoire. I fell down on my knees in the kitchen and broke down in tears, apologizing profusely. "*Je suis désolé, patron, je suis désolé!*" "You are good for nothing," he replied. "I will deduct the ingredients from your salary. Go back to your room!"

At the time my salary was $10 a month, which was not enough to pay for the ingredients that I had wasted—so that month I would have to pay him. I climbed up the six floors and stayed in the apprentice bedroom in tears for the rest of the day and night. That evening I was determined to pack my bags when everyone was asleep and escape. But eventually I calmed down and reminded myself that pastry was my passion and that leaving would be a terrible decision.

CARNIVAL FRITTERS /
PETITS BEIGNETS DE CARNAVAL

YIELD | TWENTY-FOUR 2 × 2-INCH DIAMONDS

1- OR 2-DAY RECIPE (DOUGH CAN REST OVERNIGHT; IT MUST REST FOR A MINIMUM OF 2 HOURS)

INGREDIENTS	WEIGHT	MEASURE (APPROXIMATE) OR OUNCE WEIGHT
Organic lemon zest	½ lemon	½ lemon
Organic orange zest	1 orange	1 orange
Butter (French style, 82% fat), melted	20 grams	⁷⁄₁₀ ounce
All-purpose flour	160 grams	Scant 1¼ cups
Baking powder	2 grams	½ teaspoon
Granulated sugar	35 grams	2½ tablespoons
Sea salt	1 gram	Rounded ⅛ teaspoon
Whole eggs	80 grams	1½ large eggs
Canola or grapeseed oil, for deep frying	1 to 2 liters	1 to 2 quarts
Confectioners' sugar, for dusting	As needed	As needed

Beignets fascinate me; they are so bad for you and yet everyone loves a warm piece of freshly fried dough sprinkled with sugar. Pastries made with fried dough date back at least as far as the time of the Egyptians, to whom dough expanding in hot oil symbolized rebirth and life in general. They are consumed around the world, especially on religious holidays. I have been lucky enough to work in and travel to many countries, and I always can find some form of fried dough. The dough is usually simple and not rich, because it will be sitting in some kind of oil while it's cooking.

Pastry chefs make different types of beignets in France. You have already seen the yeasted beignets, made with brioche dough, on PAGE 323. In Alsace we make fritters from January 6th, which celebrates Epiphany, to Mardi Gras Day, or Carnival. Carnival marks the last day of eating well before the Christian Lent, and it's a big day for beignets. These Alsatian fritters are not made with brioche dough, but with a simple dough leavened with baking powder and flavored with citrus zest.

METHOD

1 Scrub the lemon and orange with a brush under running water in order to remove the impurities, and wipe dry. Using a microplane, zest the half lemon and all of the orange. Place the zest in a small bowl.

BEFORE YOU BEGIN

→ Get out the following equipment and allow all of the ingredients to come to room temperature:

Digital scale, set to metric weights
1 vegetable brush
1 microplane
1 small bowl
1 small saucepan or microwave-safe bowl
1 sifter
KitchenAid or stand mixer fitted with the hook attachment
1 rubber spatula or bowl scraper
Plastic wrap
1 wide, shallow pan or wok
1 digital thermometer
1 spider
1 sheet pan lined with paper towel
1 rolling pin
1 fluted pastry wheel

→ Read this recipe through twice from start to finish.

UNDERSTANDING INGREDIENTS

This is a very simple dough that is made by placing the dry ingredients in a mixing bowl first and adding the liquid ingredients to them. Once the dough comes together it's rolled out, cut into diamond shapes, and fried. Since it's fried in hot oil the dough does not contain a lot of fat, as it would not make any sense to fry fat in fat.

The baking powder in this dough provides the rising agent that makes the fritters puff in the oil. Mixes or doughs that contain baking powder should be baked or fried no longer than 24 hours after the dough is mixed. Two things happen after that period: the baking powder becomes inactive, and it leaves an unpleasant salty and acidic taste in the dough.

I like to use canola oil or grapeseed oil for frying because they are both tasteless and have a high smoke point. These fritters are small and need to be fried quickly so that they stay soft in the center. For this you need a high heat in order to sear the skin of the fritters and keep them moist in the center. We bring the oil to a higher temperature (375°F/190°C) than we do for the beignets in the previous recipe because these are much thinner than the beignets and will cook through in no time. As with all fried dough, make sure the oil is hot enough—if it isn't, it will fail to sear the outside of the fritters and will seep through, making them very greasy.

The citrus zest brings a nice flavor to the dough. Make sure you zest the skin only and not the white part, because the skin is where the oils are and the white part is very bitter.

2 Melt the butter in a small saucepan or microwave-safe bowl and allow to cool to lukewarm.

3 Sift together the flour and baking powder into the bowl of your mixer. Add the granulated sugar and sea salt. Add the eggs, melted butter, and zest and mix with the dough hook for 60 seconds on medium speed. Stop the mixer and, using a rubber spatula or bowl scraper, scrape the mixing bowl to make sure that no dry ingredients are left on the bottom. Mix for another 30 to 45 seconds or until the dough comes together completely. Scrape out onto a sheet of plastic wrap and wrap airtight. Refrigerate for 2 hours or overnight.

4 Over medium heat in a wide, shallow pan or wok, slowly warm up 1 to 2 quarts of oil (depending on the size of your pan) to 375°F/190°C. The oil must be at least 1½ inches deep. Insert a digital thermometer into the oil and place a spider or deep-fry skimmer and a sheet pan lined with paper towels next to the pan.

5 Meanwhile, dust the surface of your counter with flour. Place the dough on it and dust its surface with flour as well. Roll out the dough for 5 seconds and check to see if it still slides on the counter. If it does not, dust the work surface with a little more flour. Roll the dough until it is ¼ inch thick. Using a fluted pastry wheel, cut 1-inch-wide strips. Repeat on an angle so that you obtain diamonds. Make a small horizontal cut in the middle of each diamond (SEE ILLUSTRATION). Take the tail of a diamond and slide it through the cut. Repeat with all the diamonds. They are now ready to be fried.

6 When the oil reaches 375°F/190°C carefully place 5 to 8 fritters (depending on the size of the pan) in the hot oil. Do not crowd them, as crowding will prevent them from frying nicely. The more fritters you put into the oil at once, the more you reduce the temperature of the oil, which can result in greasy fritters. Using the spider, flip them over right away so that they will rise evenly, and as they cook gently move the fritters around in the hot oil, flipping them over so that they fry evenly. After 3 minutes they should be golden brown. Remove from the oil with the spider, holding them above the pan for a few seconds to let the oil drip back into the pan, then place them on the paper towel–lined sheet pan. Repeat with the remaining pieces of dough. You can re-roll and fry the unused edges once, but not more than that because re-rolling activates the gluten in the flour and will make the fritters rubbery and tough. Dust the fritters with confectioners' sugar and serve.

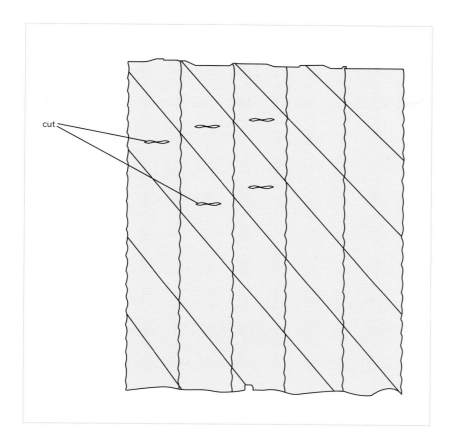

cut

IT'S DONE WHEN IT'S DONE

The fritters should be golden brown; the skin should be firm while the middle should be moist and soft.

STORAGE

Fritters are usually not kept longer than 1 day, as they get tough and rubbery in time. It's best to make them and serve them the same day, but you can make them a few hours in advance and reheat them in a 400°F/200°C oven for 2 to 3 minutes.

MY FIRST JOB ABROAD WAS as the pastry chef for Admiral Philippe Lejeune, the admiral in the French navy stationed in Djibouti in 1980 during the Iraq-Iran War. Our ship was a 200-yard-long oil tanker that was used to refuel the actual warships. I was there as part of my one-year compulsory military service; only the French navy sees the necessity of having a pastry chef on board a naval vessel in times of war.

Working on the ship, where there was no air-conditioning, was difficult. The tropical heat and humidity were incessant. We were required to wear only a T-shirt, a pair of shorts, and open-toe sandals—not the best uniform for a pastry chef working in a small kitchen with hot ingredients. My job was to make pastries for the admiral, who did a lot of wining and dining with admirals from the other navies. During my free time I baked for the crew, who knew that all the other ships were eating terrible canned, processed, or frozen bread and pastries. They regarded me as some kind of angel that had fallen from the sky.

That year on Mardi Gras Day I had the not-so-bright idea to make Beignets de Carnaval for my admiral. Our kitchen was outfitted to face the fury of the sea during the monsoon time, with metal bars installed on the edges of the large kitchen stove to prevent stock pots from flying off if a large wave hit our ship. But the sea was quiet that morning and nothing indicated that this would happen. I made the dough and heated up the oil. I fried the first batch without any problems, but as I worked on the second batch a huge wave suddenly came out of nowhere and rocked the ship, sending a splash of hot burning oil pouring out of the pot toward me. I managed to dodge most of it but was hit on my foot and toes; I can still feel the pain, and I can confirm that this really hurts!

I tried to find something to cool off my foot, but we had no air-conditioning and only cold water was available. The ship's doctor ordered me to follow a rigorous course of treatment to make sure that the wound healed well and quickly. Carnival fritters will always trigger this memory. My advice to you is: Enjoy them, but never wear open-toed shoes when you deep-fry, and certainly never deep-fry while you're sailing.

GINGERBREAD / PAIN D'ÉPICES

INGREDIENTS	WEIGHT	MEASURE (APPROXIMATE) OR OUNCE WEIGHT
SUGAR ICING		
Water	13 grams	2⅗ teaspoons
Lemon juice, freshly squeezed	2 grams	⅓ teaspoon
Confectioners' sugar	50 grams	½ cup
CAKE		
Flour and butter mixture, for coating pans (PAGE 8)	As needed	As needed
Clover honey	175 grams	½ cup
Brown sugar	20 grams	2 tablespoons
Whole wheat flour	62 grams	½ cup
Rye flour	62 grams	½ cup
Ground cinnamon	0.75 grams	Rounded ¼ teaspoon
Ground nutmeg	0.25 grams	½ teaspoon
Ground ginger	0.25 grams	¼ teaspoon
Ground anise	0.5 grams	¼ teaspoon whole seeds
Baking powder	5 grams	1⅓ teaspoons
Whole eggs	50 grams	1 egg
Whole milk (3.5% fat)	50 grams	3 tablespoons plus 2 teaspoons
Candied Orange or Lemon Peel (PAGE 87), cut in ¼-inch dice	37 grams	2 tablespoons
GARNISH		
Candied Orange or Lemon Peel (PAGE 87; optional), cut in ¼-inch dice	20 grams	1 tablespoon

Pain d'épices—spice bread—is the French version of gingerbread. It is usually made with flour, honey, and spices, and has a long shelf life because of its low water content and acidity. The bread was traditionally known as a *pain de voyage* because it could be taken on long journeys for sustenance. Armies as far back as the Middle Ages carried gingerbread on their campaigns.

Honey has been used in bread since Antiquity, but it was only during the Middle Ages that spices were introduced to Europe from the Middle East by the Crusaders. We find references to gingerbread made with

BEFORE YOU BEGIN

→ Get out the following equipment and allow all of the ingredients to come to room temperature:

Digital scale, set to metric weights
1 small mixing bowl
1 rubber spatula
One or two 1½-inch mini-muffin silicone molds or forty-five 1½-inch petit four molds or paper cups (or, for a cake, a 5 × 9-inch or 4 × 10-inch bread pan)
1 small saucepan
1 digital thermometer
1 sifter
KitchenAid or stand mixer fitted with the paddle attachment
1 stainless steel hand whisk
1 chef's knife
1 pastry bag fitted with a ⅜-inch round tip or spoon
1 pastry brush

→ Read this recipe through twice from start to finish.

UNDERSTANDING INGREDIENTS

Gingerbread is usually made with sugar and honey; some versions call for honey only. Both of these sugars are hydroscopic, which means that they absorb and retain moisture. This is especially true of honey—an important property, as it ensures that your gingerbread will remain moist for days. Honey is also acidic and contains very little water, so bacteria cannot easily grow in it. But it's important to store your honey in a sealed jar or it will absorb the humidity in the air and eventually will ferment. Honey is sweeter than most other sugars, and because of this it does not freeze well, but the spice bread, which contains other ingredients, freezes very well.

Whole wheat flour contributes an earthy flavor to the bread, and rye flour contributes an interesting, slightly acidic and sour taste. Whole wheat flour contains very little gluten, and rye flour contains even less; for this reason the cake will not become rubbery.

A fair amount of baking powder is added to the batter so that the cake will rise nicely.

The candied orange peels contribute a nice fruity flavor. Candied lemon peels can also be used.

honey and spices by German bakers from Nuremberg as early as 1108. The bread became such a delicacy that priests had to ask their parishioners to refrain from eating too much of it. Because the spices were also considered medicinal, doctors in the Middle Ages recommended gingerbread as a laxative and as a poultice for wounds.

For centuries gingerbread has been a celebration sweet bread in Alsace. It is eaten throughout the year, but especially around St. Nicolas Day and Christmas. There are two types: one that is made from a firm dough that is rolled out and cut into shapes, and a soft batter that is baked like a pound cake. I've decided on the second type for this collection, as the mix is versatile and gives you the choice of making either small cakelike cookies or a larger cake. I've added candied fruit to the mixture, as it's such a nice complement to the spices and honey. You can also add 50 grams of chopped nuts, such as almonds, hazelnuts, or walnuts.

METHOD

1 Prepare the sugar icing in a small bowl or container following the directions on PAGE 5 and set aside. Preheat the oven to 350°F/180°C. On a sheet pan, prepare forty-five 1½-inch paper cups or grease 45 small petit four molds with the butter and flour mixture. You can also use a mini-muffin silicone mold, which is very practical because it will not require paper cup liners or greasing.

2 Place the honey and brown sugar in a small saucepan and heat to 158°F/70°C while stirring with a rubber spatula.

3 Sift together the whole wheat flour, rye flour, spices, and baking powder and transfer them to the bowl of your mixer.

4 In a small bowl whisk together the whole eggs and milk. Turn the mixer on low and slowly add the milk and eggs to the flour mixture. Stop the mixer and, using a rubber spatula or a bowl scraper, scrape up any flour residue sticking to the bottom of the bowl. Add the warm honey mixture and finally the diced peel and mix on medium speed until incorporated.

5 Either spoon the mixture into the prepared molds or paper cups, about 1 teaspoon per cup, or scrape the mixture into a pastry bag fitted with a ⅜-inch round tip and pipe it into the molds or paper cups. The molds should be ¾ full. Make sure that the molds are at least ¾ inch apart so that the cakes can rise properly. See also my note about making the recipe in a loaf pan.

6 Place in the preheated oven and bake for 15 to 20 minutes.

7 Remove from the oven and immediately stir the sugar icing and brush the top of the cakes with the glaze. You must brush the cakes as soon as they come out of the oven so that the water in the icing evaporates and the icing

creates a nice white glossy sheen on the little cakes. Decorate with a square of candied peel if desired.

IT'S DONE WHEN IT'S DONE

The little cakes will rise and may crack open because of the action of the baking powder. They should have a deep and rich brown color.

STORAGE

Keep the cakes in an airtight container, or you can also freeze them for up to 1 month. Do not keep them in the refrigerator, as the honey will absorb the humidity in the cooler and the cakes will become soggy.

JACQUY'S TAKEAWAYS

→ You can play with different spices such as cinnamon, allspice, cloves, or black pepper, but use them very carefully, as some spices can be overpowering.

→ You can also make this recipe in a loaf pan that is greased and floured. Use a medium-sized pan so that it will be filled ¾ of the way and bake it for 40 to 50 minutes at 350°F/180°C, until deep brown.

CHERRY BREAD PUDDING / BETTELMAN AUX CERISES

YIELD | ONE 9-INCH BREAD PUDDING

2-DAY RECIPE (IF YOU HAVE THE TIME TO SOAK THE BREAD OVERNIGHT)

INGREDIENTS	WEIGHT	MEASURE (APPROXIMATE) OR WEIGHT IN OUNCES
Old brioche or kougelhof	100 grams	3½ ounces
Whole milk (3.5% fat)	180 grams	¾ cup
Vanilla extract	5 grams	1 teaspoon
Butter (French style, 82% fat), for the pan	As needed	As needed
Egg yolks	30 grams	2 yolks
Kirschwasser	2 grams	½ teaspoon
Ground cinnamon	0.5 grams	¼ teaspoon
Granulated sugar	15 grams	1 tablespoon
Almond flour, skinless	50 grams	½ cup
Egg whites	75 grams	2 whites
Sea salt	0.2 grams	Pinch
Granulated sugar	50 grams	¼ cup
Black cherries, pitted	250 grams unpitted or 200 grams pitted	8⅘ ounces unpitted or 7 ounces pitted
Sliced almonds	30 grams	¼ cup plus 2 teaspoons
Confectioners' sugar, for dusting	As needed	As needed

Bettelman means "beggar" in the Alsatian dialect, and this delightful dessert is a type of poor man's bread pudding made by reviving old brioche. It comes straight from the times when nothing was thrown away, and was a way to make a dessert with the ingredients at hand. Stale brioche or kougelhof is soaked overnight in a vanilla-flavored liquid custard, then the mixture is beaten, lightened with some meringue, and poured into a shallow dish, traditionally a cast-iron-skillet, but a ceramic dish works well, too. Dark cherries are added to it, almonds are sprinkled on top, and the dish is baked and served warm as is or with vanilla ice cream.

METHOD

1 Using a serrated knife, cut the old brioche or kougelhof into ¾-inch cubes on a cutting board. If you are using brioche that is glazed with egg wash, cut off the glazed part, as it does not soften easily (weigh out the 100 grams of bread after cutting off the glazed part).

BEFORE YOU BEGIN

→ Get out the following equipment and allow all of the ingredients to come to room temperature:

Digital scale, set to metric weights
1 serrated knife
1 microwave-safe bowl or measuring cup
1 rubber spatula
1 medium mixing bowl
Plastic wrap
One 9-inch cast-iron or ceramic dish or pan
1 stainless steel hand whisk
KitchenAid or stand mixer fitted with the whisk attachment

→ Read this recipe through twice from start to finish.

UNDERSTANDING INGREDIENTS

The better the bread, the better the bread pudding; if you make a bread pudding with bad supermarket processed bread, you will get bad supermarket bread pudding. I like to use old kougelhof or brioche to make this dessert, as they are breads that already have a great flavor. Regular white toasting bread can be used, but it will be not be as tasty. I like to cut my old bread in chunks and let it air dry so that it can soak in a lot of liquid and make a very moist bread pudding. The bread needs to be soaked for at least 2 hours, but if you have the time I would advise you to let it soak overnight so that the vanilla can flavor the custard and bread to its fullest. Almond flour is in this recipe because it is great at retaining liquids and will contribute to a moist, flavorful final dish. The original recipe that I grew up with did not contain whipped egg whites but I added them to obtain a much lighter dish. In season, dark cherries are great for this dessert as they will release their juice into the bread pudding.

You can substitute other fruits for cherries, but be mindful of how much water is released from each fruit. I recommend using peaches, apricots, raspberries, blackberries, or plums. Apples or pears could be used, but they would have to be precooked before incorporating them in the dish. I do not recommend using melon, watermelon, grapes, or strawberries since they release too much water and turn the dish to mush.

2 Combine the milk and vanilla in a microwave-safe bowl or measuring cup and warm up very slightly, for 20 seconds, in the microwave. Place the bread cubes in a medium mixing bowl and pour on the warmed milk and vanilla. Stir the mixture, cover the bowl with plastic wrap, and refrigerate for a minimum of 2 hours. In an ideal world you would let this mixture soak overnight to increase the exchange of flavor.

3 Preheat the oven to 375°F/190°C. Brush a 9-inch cast-iron skillet or baking dish or a 9-inch ceramic baking dish with soft butter. Beat the soaked bread mixture with a hand whisk until it becomes mushy. Even if the bread has soaked up all of the liquid you can break it down to a mush with a whisk. Add the yolks, kirsch, cinnamon, 15 grams of sugar, and almond flour.

4 Place the egg whites and sea salt in the bowl of your standing mixture fitted with the whisk attachment and whip for 10 seconds on low speed. Add the 50 grams of sugar and whip on high until they form a soft meringue, about 1 minute. (To understand soft meringue, see PAGE 69.)

5 Using a rubber spatula, gently fold the egg whites into the bread mixture. Transfer the mixture to the baking dish or pan. Arrange the cherries evenly in the pan, pushing them down into the mixture. Sprinkle the sliced almonds on top and dust with confectioners' sugar.

6 Bake at 375°F/190°C for 40 minutes, until it is puffed and the edges are golden brown; dust with confectioners' sugar again and serve hot, with vanilla ice cream if desired.

IT'S DONE WHEN IT'S DONE

The edges of the bread mixture and the sliced almonds should be golden brown and the cherries should have released their juice.

STORAGE

This dish is best eaten fresh from the oven, but you can keep it in a refrigerator for 2 days. In that case warm it up for 15 minutes at 400°F/200°C before serving.

JACQUY'S TAKEAWAYS

→ You can make the *bettelman* in individual dishes. Bake individual servings at 375°F/190°C for 25 to 30 minutes.

→ Other nuts such as hazelnuts or pecans can be substituted for the almonds.

BEER BREAD / PAIN À LA BIÈRE

YIELD | 2 LOAVES

2-DAY RECIPE | THE DOUGH REQUIRES A 2-DAY PROCESS.

BASE TEMPERATURE | LOW THE FIRST DAY (55°C) BECAUSE OF THE LONG FERMENTATION PROCESS, AND 65°C THE SECOND DAY.

INGREDIENTS	WEIGHT	MEASURE (APPROXIMATE)
FERMENTED DOUGH		
Water	63 grams	¼ cup
Dry yeast	0.4 grams	⅛ teaspoon
Bread flour	100 grams	¾ cup plus 1 tablespoon
Sea salt	2 grams	¼ teaspoon
DOUGH		
Potato flakes or unsalted mashed cooked potatoes	15 grams or 65 grams	2½ tablespoons or ⅓ cup
Water (only if using potato flakes)	50 grams	Scant ¼ cup
Water	120 grams	½ cup
Bread flour	125 grams	1 cup
Rye flour	60 grams	½ cup
Sea salt	5 grams	¾ teaspoon
Dry yeast	2 grams	¾ teaspoon
Butter (French style, 82% fat), softened, for the pan		
BEER MIXTURE		
Rye flour	25 grams	3 tablespoons
Beer	45 grams	3 tablespoons
Sea salt	1 gram	⅛ teaspoon
Dry yeast	0.5 grams	Rounded ⅛ teaspoon
Rye flour, for dusting	15 grams	2 tablespoons
Water, for steam	50 grams	Scant ¼ cup

BEFORE YOU BEGIN

→ Get out the following equipment and allow all of the ingredients to come to room temperature:

Digital scale, set to metric weights
1 digital thermometer
KitchenAid or stand mixer fitted with the paddle and hook attachments
1 rubber spatula
1 bowl scraper
Plastic wrap
2 or 3 small mixing bowls
1 chef's knife or a rectangular dough scraper
2 sheet pans, 1 of them lined with parchment paper
1 pastry brush
1 sifter
1 pizza stone
1 wire rack
1 small sheet pan
1 small cup or glass
1 oven peel

→ Read this recipe through twice from start to finish.

Beer bread—named because it is brushed before baking with a mixture of beer and rye flour that gives it its unique look and flavor—is a real symbol of Alsace, as the rye flour and potatoes in the dough are classic regional ingredients. And what could be more Alsatian than beer? The chef who put this specialty on the map is the late Joseph Dorffer, MOF *boulanger,* and I thank him for it every day. Of all the breads we make at the French Pastry School this is one of my favorites. It tastes wonderful with savory foods such as cheese or sausage but is, surprisingly, also delicious with butter and jam. The bread is very similar to the earthy, crusty bread that my dad used to make for our village.

METHOD

DAY 1

1 Make the fermented dough with a base temperature of 55°C. Take the temperature of the flour and the room (convert to Celsius) and add them together. Then adjust your water temperature (Celsius) so that the sum of the three ingredients is 55°C. Combine the water and yeast in the bowl of your mixer and stir together with a rubber spatula. Add the flour and the sea salt. Using the paddle, mix together at low speed until combined, then switch to the dough hook and mix for 5 minutes at medium speed.

2 Switch to a slightly faster speed and mix for 2 minutes. Scrape down the dough hook, cover the bowl with plastic wrap, and let rest at room temperature for 1 hour.

3 Press on the dough with the palm of your hand and shape it into a ball. Cover the dough with plastic wrap and place in a small bowl in the refrigerator overnight.

DAY 2

1 Remove the fermented dough from the refrigerator and bring to room temperature for 30 minutes. Meanwhile, mix the potato flakes with the 50 grams of water. Alternatively you can use 65 grams (about ⅓ cup) of unsalted mashed cooked potatoes. Set aside.

2 For the dough you will need a base temperature of 65°C. Take the temperature of the flour and the room (convert to Celsius) and add them together. Then adjust the temperature (Celsius) of your 120 grams of water so that the sum of the three ingredients is 65.

3 Combine the water, bread flour, rye flour, sea salt, dry yeast, and fermented dough in the bowl of your mixer and mix for 2 minutes on medium speed using the dough hook. Add the potato mixture to the dough and mix for 2 minutes on medium speed, until the dough is smooth. Using a spatula or a dough scraper, scrape the sides and bottom of the bowl, then mix on medium speed for 5 minutes, then on a slightly faster speed for 2 more minutes. The dough should now make a slapping sound and look smooth.

4 Cover the bowl with plastic wrap and let the dough rest for 1½ hours at room temperature. The dough will develop its unique flavor as the yeast ferments during this slow rise.

5 Dust your work surface with flour and turn out the dough. Weigh the dough and divide into 2 equal pieces. Take 1 piece of dough, cup your hands around it, and start pressing on it while turning the dough in clockwise circles. The sides of your hands should be touching the countertop as you cup and

UNDERSTANDING INGREDIENTS

Bread doughs all need yeast in order to rise, but there are many ways in which to introduce the yeast into dough. You can simply add yeast to the flour, salt, and water, which is the way it's done with most white breads; but these can be bland. A starter of some kind will add character to the flavor profile. You can use a liquid fermentation—a *poolish*, which we use in brioche and croissants (PAGES 21 AND 127) as well as the seeded bread on PAGE 346. Or you can make a *levain*, which is a starter made by using the natural yeast present in the flour. In this recipe you will make an initial dough, let it ferment overnight, and use it as your starter. All of these types of starters will contribute a slightly acidic and sour flavor that I like to the bread.

The crumb of this bread is very moist and flavorful because of the potatoes and the rye flour. When bread is baked the water in the dough turns to steam, which accumulates on the crust and decreases its temperature, allowing the bread to expand more during the first few minutes of baking. Steam also speeds up the melting of starch and sugar and allows a nice brown crust to develop. The trick is having the right balance, with enough moisture in the bread to create steam but not so much that a cloud of steam cools down the loaf. If the loaf is cooled too much, it will not

turn the dough. At first you need to press hard so that the dough sticks to the table a little, and then you ease the pressing while tightening the cupping. When the shaping is done you should have a perfectly round sphere of dough. Repeat with the other piece of dough. Cover with plastic and let rest for 20 minutes.

6 Shape the loaves. Line a sheet pan with parchment paper and grease the paper with butter. To obtain the triangle shape, fold in one side of the loaf and press it into the center (SEE PHOTO). Repeat with the other two sides so that you have a triangle, and pinch the seams. Flip the loaf over and place on one side of the parchment paper–lined sheet pan. Repeat with the other piece of dough and place on the other side of the sheet pan.

7 Prepare your beer mixture by mixing all the ingredients together in a small mixing bowl with a rubber spatula. Once mixed, spread over the top of the loaves using a pastry brush. Using a sifter, dust each loaf with a small amount of rye flour. At this point you cannot cover the loaves with plastic wrap as it will stick to the beer mixture.

8 Set your oven to 450°F/230°C and place your pizza stone on the rack set in the middle of the oven. Place a small sheet pan on the bottom rack of the oven or the oven floor. It is important to preheat the oven for at least 1 hour to ensure that the stone becomes hot enough to create a crust on the bottom of the bread.

9 Set the loaves in a warm place (not warmer than 80.6°F/27°C) to proof for 1 hour and 15 minutes. As the loaves rise the beer mixture will crack open and create the unique tiger skin look.

10 Have 50 grams of water ready in a small cup or a glass. When the dough is ready slide an oven peel under the parchment paper and place the loaves onto the stone. It is crucial that you do not have the oven door open for more than 30 seconds or you will lose too much heat and won't get a nice crust. Open the oven door quickly and pour the water onto the sheet pan on the bottom of the oven to create steam. After 10 minutes, open the door for 15 seconds, remove the sheet pan from the oven, and slide the parchment paper from underneath the loaves. After 25 minutes of baking, when the loaves are dark brown and respond to tapping on the bottom with a hollow sound, pull them out and let them cool on a wire rack.

IT'S DONE WHEN IT'S DONE

The loaves should have a dark brown color and the tops should be marked with a cracked dark and light tiger pattern.

STORAGE

It is important to know that after baking all bread loaves need to be allowed to cool for at least 1 hour, until all the water has evaporated. In very dry climates you will have to wrap them in plastic after they have cooled, but in more humid climates you can keep the loaves in a linen bread bag. Bread should never, ever be refrigerated, but it can be wrapped airtight and frozen for up to 1 month. To defrost it, unwrap and let it defrost overnight, then flash it in a 450°F/230°C oven for 1 minute. To defrost it quickly, microwave it for 1 minute and then flash it in a hot oven for 1 minute.

bake quickly and the crust will become very thick and tough.

Rye flour, which is grayish in color, comes from a grain that grows mainly in colder climates and poorer soils. It is a staple of Scandinavia, parts of France, and the countries of central and eastern Europe. Alsace, which is rich in Germanic culture, has also developed some nice recipes with rye flour. In addition to this bread we find rye flour in some Alsatian recipes for gingerbread, cookies, and waffles. Rye flour contains only a small amount of gluten and therefore is usually combined with regular flour so that the loaves will hold their shapes. It has a unique acidic, rustic flavor that distinguishes it from other flours.

In times of food shortages, such as during World War II, bakers used potatoes in their breads to make up for the shortage of flour. They called the replacement ingredient, be it potatoes or another type of flour, ersatz. The bakers soon realized the advantages of using potatoes in their dough, as the potato starch absorbs and retains water so that the resulting crumb is more moist than that of traditional white bread, as well as slightly sweeter and delicious overall.

The beautiful and unusual crust is created with flour, water, yeast, and beer. It contributes additional texture and character to the flavor profile.

JACQUY'S TAKEAWAYS

→ The best type of oven for making bread is a commercial oven where the loaves lie on a stone and there is no convection fan blowing. The stone slows down the baking and creates the crust. Convection fans can make bread get very dark in a short amount of time while leaving the middle undercooked. The best way to mimic a baker's oven is to use a stone (sold as pizza stones in the United States).

SEEDED BREAD

INGREDIENTS	WEIGHT	MEASURE (APPROXIMATE) OR OUNCE WEIGHT
SEEDS		
Sunflower seeds	25 grams	2 tablespoons plus 1 teaspoon
Sesame seeds	25 grams	2½ tablespoons
Flaxseeds	25 grams	2½ tablespoons
Rolled oats	25 grams	¼ cup
Pumpkin seeds	25 grams	2 tablespoons
Water	180 grams	¾ cup
POOLISH		
Bread flour	170 grams	1⅓ cups
Water	170 grams	¾ cup less 2 teaspoons
Dry yeast	3.5 grams	1 scant teaspoon
DOUGH		
Bread flour	250 grams	2 cups
Sea salt	13 grams	2 teaspoons

BEFORE YOU BEGIN

→ Get out the following equipment and allow all of the ingredients to come to room temperature:

Digital scale, set to metric weights
1 medium mixing bowl
1 rubber spatula
Plastic wrap
1 digital thermometer
KitchenAid or stand mixer fitted with the hook attachment
1 strainer
1 small cup
1 hand towel
1 large kitchen towel
1 sheet pan lined with parchment paper
1 pizza stone
1 pizza peel
1 razor blade or bread knife

→ Read this recipe through twice from start to finish.

Once I start eating a loaf of this delicious bread, it's difficult to stop! The different seeds make it so interesting, from the crunchy sunflower and pumpkin seeds to the nutty sesame seeds, the earthy flaxseeds and the chewy oats. The mildly acidic flavor created by a 2-hour *poolish* fermentation introduces a complex sourness and flavor profile to the bread. It's a very easy recipe to make, but does require 2 days due to the overnight soaking of the seeds. Soaking the seeds makes all the difference when it comes to seeded breads; they don't become too hard when you bake the bread, and they contribute much more flavor to the dough than dry seeds. The dough uses a base temperature of 60°C.

METHOD

DAY 1

Mix all the seeds and oats together with the 180 grams of water in a medium mixing bowl. Cover with plastic wrap and and let soak overnight in the refrigerator.

UNDERSTANDING INGREDIENTS

The array of seeds brings different flavors to this bread. There are a few reasons why they must be soaked in water over-night. One reason is that soaking breaks down phytic acid and protease inhibitors, naturally occurring substances in nuts, seeds, grains, and legumes that protect them until they germinate but can block enzyme function and reduce the absorp-tion of important minerals in your body. Soaking seeds also breaks down complex starches. Another reason we soak the seeds is that they can absorb 100 to 150 percent of their weight in water and they will retain the moisture in the bread, making the crumb very moist.

The amount of yeast is very low because I am using a long fermentation time, allowing the natural and wild yeasts in the flour to kick in. The amount of salt is quite high for the amount of dough, but it is needed to flavor the seeds. The bread will not taste salty.

DAY 2

1 Make a *poolish* with a base temperature of 60°C. Take the temperature of the flour and the room (convert to Celsius) and add them together. Then adjust your water temperature (Celsius) so that the sum of the three ingredi-ents is 60°C. For instance, if your room temperature is 70°F, convert to Celsius and you will get 21°C; if your flour is 72°F, convert to Celsius and you will get 22°C; 21°C + 22°C = 43°C. Subtract 43°C from 60°C. The difference is 17°C, the temperature you will need for your water. Once you have heated or cooled your water to the correct temperature, mix all the ingredients for the *poolish* together with a spatula in the bowl of your mixer. Cover with plastic and leave to ferment at room temperature for 2 hours or until it doubles in volume. Meanwhile, remove the bowl with the nuts and seeds from the refrigerator, drain through a strainer, and bring to room temperature.

2 Add the seeds, the 250 grams of bread flour, and finally the sea salt to the *poolish*. Have a cup of extra water next to the mixer. Start mixing on medium speed. The dough should come together in the first minute. If it does not, add a very small amount of water to help it along. Mix the dough for 5 minutes on medium speed, then turn the speed up to medium high and mix for another 7 minutes. The dough should be elastic and shiny. Stop the mixing and cover the bowl with plastic wrap. Set in a warm spot to rise for 1 hour. You can create a makeshift proofer if your oven does not have a pilot light by placing a small pan filled halfway with freshly boiled water on the oven floor and the bowl inside the oven. Make sure the temperature does not exceed 80.6°F/27°C.

3 Dust your work surface lightly with flour and scrape out the dough. Weigh the dough and divide into 3 equal pieces. To shape the loaves, take 1 piece at a time and press out the first gases created by the action of the yeast with the palm of your hand. Lightly dust your hands with flour, take the piece of dough in your hands, and fold it over itself to create a ball. Place the ball on the counter, cup it with your hands on each side, and start pressing on it while turning it in clockwise circles. At first you need to press hard so that the dough sticks to the table a little, and then you ease the pressing while tightening the cupping; the sides of your hands should always be touching the counter. When the shaping is done you should have a perfectly round sphere of dough. If the dough sticks to the table too much, stop shaping and dust the work surface again with a very small amount of flour, remembering that over-flouring the dough will make it dry and impossible to shape. Cover with a towel or lightly with plastic and let rest for 15 minutes while you shape the other 2 pieces of dough into balls.

4 Press the round piece of dough flat, then take the side closest to you and fold lengthwise upward, halfway to the center of the loaf. Lightly press down to seal. Take the top flap and bring it toward you over the first fold to the middle of the loaf and lightly press down to seal over the first fold. Flip over so that the seam is on the bottom and roll back and forth with both hands to form an oblong loaf with pointy ends. Place on a sheet pan lined with parchment paper and repeat with the other 2 loaves. Cover with a towel and place the loaves in a warm spot or in the makeshift proofer (reheat the water) for 1 hour. If you are using the oven as a proofer and only have one oven, take out the loaves and set in another warm spot to rise for 45 minutes while you preheat the oven.

5 Preheat the oven to 450°F/230°C with a pizza stone on the middle rack and a small sheet pan on the oven floor for 30 to 45 minutes. Have 50 grams of water ready in a small cup or a glass. If you have a large pizza stone, you can bake all of the loaves at once. If you have a standard home pizza stone, bake 1 loaf at a time and place the other loaves in the refrigerator to slow down the fermentation. Carefully slide 1 loaf of dough onto a pizza peel and, using a razor blade or a moistened bread knife, make a ½-inch-deep horizontal cut down the middle of the loaf from one end to the other. Using the pizza peel, slide the loaf onto the pizza stone and close the oven door. It is crucial that you do not have the oven door open for more than 30 seconds or you will lose too much heat and not get a nice crust. Open the oven door quickly and pour the water onto the sheet pan on the bottom of the oven to create steam. Set the timer for 5 minutes, and after 5 minutes take the sheet pan out of the oven. Bake the bread for a total of 25 to 30 minutes, until the loaf is dark brown and sounds hollow when you tap the bottom of it. Using the pizza peel, transfer the loaf to a wire rack to cool completely for 45 minutes. Repeat with the other 2 loaves. Once cool, the bread is ready to be enjoyed.

NOTE: If you have a large pizza stone and can bake all the loaves at once, place your first loaf on the left side of the stone, the next one in the middle and the third on the right side. Make sure that you leave 1 inch of space in between each loaf so that they don't touch when they bake.

IT'S DONE WHEN IT'S DONE

The loaf should "crack open" nicely in the center. The crust should be crispy; the baked loaf should feel light and sound hollow when you take it out of the oven and tap the bottom of it; this proves that enough water has evaporated.

STORAGE

You can keep this loaf for 2 to 3 days in a cloth bag; you can also freeze it for 1 month.

JACQUY'S TAKEAWAYS

→ You can play around with the seeds and substitute different types. Each type of seed or nut will bring a different texture and flavor to the bread.

PRETZELS / BRETZELS

YIELD | 9 PRETZELS

BASE TEMPERATURE | 60°C

INGREDIENTS	WEIGHT	MEASURE (APPROXIMATE) OR OUNCE WEIGHT
POOLISH		
Whole milk (3.5% fat)	90 grams	⅓ cup
Dry yeast	10 grams	2½ teaspoons
All-purpose flour	165 grams	1 cup plus 3 tablespoons
DOUGH		
Water	100 grams	7 tablespoons
Bread flour	165 grams	1 cup plus 3 tablespoons
Butter (French style, 82% fat), softened	35 grams	1⅕ ounces (1 tablespoon plus ¾ teaspoon)
Sea salt	7 grams	1 teaspoon
Butter (French style, 82% fat), softened, for the pans	As needed	As needed
Pretzel lye powder	15 grams	2¼ teaspoons
Cold water	500 grams	2¼ cups
Pretzel salt or coarse sea salt	25 grams or to taste	1½ tablespoons or to taste

I grew up eating pretzels in cafés. We call them *bretzels* in France. In Alsace they were always presented on wooden stands shaped like a tree, placed in the middle of the tables. They are so traditional in Alsace that they're part of the Alsatian bakers' emblem. The most prestigious award bestowed upon Alsatians who have promoted the region's culture through their work by the Institut des Arts et Traditions Populaires d'Alsace is called the Bretzel d'Or (an award that I was honored to receive in 2010).

There are many ways to enjoy pretzels. My parents would eat them while drinking a beer. When I came to the United States I noticed that people enjoyed them warm with mustard—which is a good reason to make them yourself. The best pretzel you could ever eat is one that has just come out of your own oven. Ask my family—they went crazy for them when I tested this recipe at home.

Soft pretzels are made with bread dough mixed with a small amount of butter. The butter makes the dough very moist and easy to manipulate. It's stretched into long ropes that are shaped in the traditional pretzel shape, which is said to symbolize a person's arms crossed in prayer, and then dipped into a special lye solution. The lye solution gives them their

BEFORE YOU BEGIN

→ Get out the following equipment and allow all of the ingredients to come to room temperature (make sure your butter is soft):

Digital scale, set to metric weights
1 digital thermometer
KitchenAid or stand mixer fitted with the hook attachment
Plastic wrap or hand towel
Pastry brush
2 sheet pans lined with buttered parchment paper
1 stainless steel hand whisk
1 medium glass mixing bowl or plastic container
1 large plastic trash bag or sheet of plastic wrap
1 flat plastic skimmer
Latex gloves
1 small saucepan

→ Read this recipe through twice from start to finish.

UNDERSTANDING INGREDIENTS

This is a very simple yeast dough. There is no long mixing and resting, as we are not looking for a sour character. Most of the flavor will come from the lye solution and the salt sprinkled on the pretzels. Some recipes call for oil rather than butter, but I will always lean toward butter since there is no comparison between the flavor of butter versus oil. I use a mix of all-purpose and bread flours, as using all bread flour would result in a very chewy pretzel because of all the gluten.

The one ingredient that you may be unfamiliar with in this recipe is the food-grade lye product that is used in the dipping solution. I have tried other recipes that call for a baking soda and water solution, but without the lye solution you will not get the unmistakable flavor of an authentic pretzel. The lye solution is made with caustic soda, and you must be sure that you buy a food-grade lye product made for pretzel dipping (see the buying guide on PAGE XXXI). This comes in a crystal form in a container and is added to water. Make sure to read the label and instructions before using this product. Once used, the liquid can be kept for months in a sealed plastic bucket. Label it properly and *make sure to keep it away from children and pets.*

Regarding the salt that will be sprinkled on the pretzels' surface, try to find a coarse pretzel salt (see the buying guide on PAGE XXXI), which is treated so that it does not melt when it comes into contact with moisture. Regular coarse sea salt is a decent second choice but it will have to be sprinkled on the pretzels just before baking or it will melt too quickly.

unmistakable rich nutty flavor with its addictive briny kick. They are then sprinkled with salt and baked in a very hot oven that will make them crispy on the outside and moist in the center.

METHOD

1 Begin by making a quick-acting starter (*poolish*) with a base temperature of 60°C. Take the temperature of the flour and the room (convert to Celsius) and add them together. Then adjust your milk temperature (Celsius) so that the sum of the three ingredients is 60. For instance, let's say that your room temperature is 70°F; converted to Celsius you will get 21°C and your flour is 72°F, converted to Celsius and you will obtain 22°C; 21°C + 22°C = 43°C. 60°C—43°C = 17°C, the temperature required for your milk.

2 When the 90 grams of milk is at the right temperature, put it in the bowl of your stand mixer and add the yeast. Stir together and sprinkle the all-purpose flour over the top. Let sit undisturbed for 10 to 15 minutes. After 15 minutes cracks should have formed on the surface of the flour; this signifies that the yeast is fermenting. The fermentation of the yeast creates a very slight acidic flavor that contributes a pleasant flavor to the dough.

3 Once the yeast has been activated it is time to mix and knead the dough. Adjust the temperature of the 100 grams of water to the same temperature as the milk. Before beginning the mixing process place an extra ¼ cup of water next to the mixer, just in case the dough is too dry. Add the bread flour, water, soft butter, and finally sea salt to the mixing bowl. Mix for 1 full minute on medium speed with the dough hook. The dough should begin to come together after 1 minute; if it does not, add a very small amount of water to it. Mix for 5 minutes on medium; stop the mixer and scrape down any dough sticking to the side or bottom of the bowl or that has risen up the hook. Mix for another 7 minutes on medium, until the dough is smooth and wraps around the hook.

4 Remove the dough from around the hook, shape it into a ball, and place it back in the bowl. Cover the bowl with a damp towel or with plastic wrap and let rest in a warm spot for 20 minutes. Meanwhile, using a pastry brush, generously grease the 2 sheets of parchment paper with soft butter.

5 Using a whisk, *carefully* mix the lye powder with the cold water in a glass bowl or a plastic container; do not use a metal bowl, as the solution might react with the metal. Set the mixture aside *away from children and pets.* Cut a large garbage bag open and cover an area of your counter that you will use as your dipping station. Place the lye bowl in the center of it and a sheet pan to its right.

6 After 20 minutes of rest, cut the dough into 60-gram (about 2-ounce) pieces; the next step is to shape them. You should not use flour during the shaping process. Take a piece of dough and fold it over itself to create a ball. Cup the dough and start pressing on it while making clockwise circles. At first you need to press hard so that the dough sticks to the table a little, and then you ease the pressing while tightening the cupping. When the shaping is done you should have perfectly round spheres of dough. Shape all of the pieces of dough into spheres and place them in the order in which you shaped them on the edge of the counter, leaving a lot of space in front of you. When you shape dough into balls, the gluten develops and makes the dough tight; before you continue shaping the pretzels you will need to let the balls rest for 5 minutes, so make sure to place them in order in a row so that you remember which one was shaped first. Cover them with a towel and let them rest for 5 minutes.

7 Take the first sphere that you worked on and roll over it with the palms of your hands to shape into a 3-inch-long log. Set it aside and repeat with the other spheres. Cover with a towel and let rest for 5 minutes. With both hands, roll each pretzel until it is 6 inches long; the shaping has to be done gradually or the dough will rip or shrink back. Repeat with the other pretzel logs. Cover with a towel each time and let rest for 5 minutes. Repeat rolling each log progressively longer, with a 5-minute rest between each rolling, until the logs are 21 inches long. The middle should be slightly thicker than the ends (SEE ILLUSTRATION).

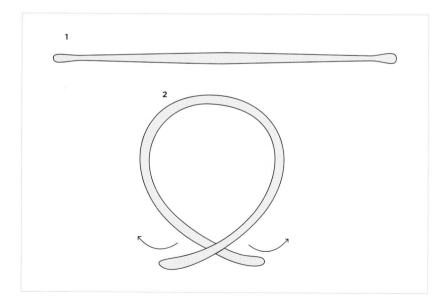

STEP 1

The middle of your log should be slightly thicker than the ends.

STEP 2

Cross the right end of the dough over the left.

8 To shape the pretzel, with the log lying on the countertop in front of you take an end in each hand, holding with your thumb and forefinger, and draw slowly toward the middle with both hands until your hands are centered in front of you; then cross the right end of the dough over the left. Let go of both dough ends, then take them up and twist the right end over the left end one more time. Fold the twist up toward the center of the circle and attach an end to each side of the round (SEE ILLUSTRATION).

STEP 3

Twist the right end over the left end one more time.

STEP 4

Fold the twist up towards the center of the circle and attach an end to each side of the round.

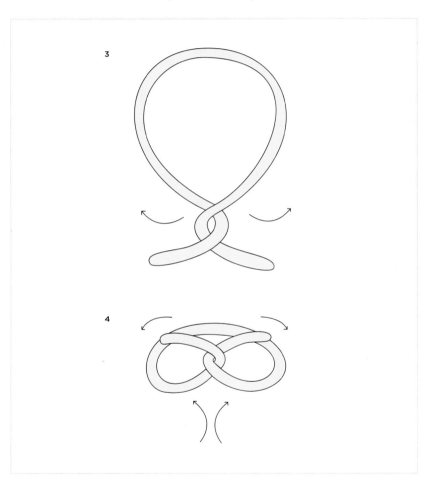

3

4

9 Line 2 sheet pans with parchment paper and butter the parchment. Once all the pretzels have been shaped, put on some latex gloves and set up your dipping station on the plastic garbage bag, with your shaped pretzels to the left of your lye solution and your prepared sheet pans to the right. Place a pretzel on the flat plastic skimmer and dip it into the solution for 1 second. Lift the skimmer out of the solution, hold the pretzel above the bowl so that it can drip for a couple seconds, and place on the sheet pan lined with buttered parchment paper. Sprinkle lightly with pretzel salt; repeat until you have 5 pretzels on the sheet pan, making sure that there is at least ¾ inch of space between them so that they can bake properly. Dip the rest of the pretzels and place them on the second sheet pan. Set in a warm spot to rise for 30 minutes. You can create a makeshift proofer if you have two ovens and your oven does not have a pilot light by placing a small pan filled halfway with freshly boiled water on the oven floor and the bowl inside the oven. Make sure the temperature does not exceed 80.6°F/27°C or the butter will melt out of the dough. Meanwhile, preheat the other oven to 450°F/230°C with the rack positioned in the center.

10   Bake the pretzels for 15 minutes, 1 sheet pan at a time. Serve hot or warm.

IT'S DONE WHEN IT'S DONE

The pretzels should be golden brown and the salt should not have melted.

STORAGE

The pretzels are best consumed the day they are baked, but they can be frozen for up to 1 month. You can then let them defrost at room temperature for 1 hour and reheat them for 1 minute at 450°F/230°C before you eat them.

JACQUY'S TAKEAWAYS

→ Pretzel salt is treated so that it does not melt after it is sprinkled onto the dipped pretzels. If you do not have pretzel salt, coarse sea salt is your second-best choice, but it will melt in contact with the lye solution. A trick is to let the pretzels rise without salt on them and, just before baking, brush them with a very small amount of water and sprinkle them with the salt, then bake them right away.

→ For a great sandwich roll, shape the dough into round or long buns, dip them in the same solution, and bake them at 375°F/190°C for 20 minutes.

Le Bretzel d'Or

Usually I am not much of a sentimental person, but when I was told that I was going to receive the coveted Bretzel d'Or my heart melted. The Bretzel d'Or is an award given every year to about 10 to 12 individuals who are in some way involved in promoting the Alsatian heritage. It could be a chef, a poet, an architect, or artist, an intellectual, a professor, or an artisan. Alsace is a region that is deeply anchored in its roots, be they artistic or culinary. It has had such a tormented history and has been on the verge of complete destruction so many times that it has always been crucial that our traditions be kept alive, and this has no doubt contributed to its survival. Our difficult history has made us fighters, but also people who know how to enjoy life and make the best of any situation.

Receiving this honor is akin to being named a general in the Alsatian army. As a Bretzel d'Or recipient you would not hesitate to go into battle as a representative of the region. These feelings have blossomed with time and experience; I thought traditions were boring when I was a kid, but I have come to realize that they are the essence of life. Alsace has put in place awards like the Bretzel d'Or in order to keep the flame of tradition alive. With this book I am hoping to pass on to you a little slice of the generous Alsatian way of life that has given me so much.

ONION TART /
TARTE À L'OIGNON

YIELD | ONE 9-INCH PIE

2-DAY RECIPE

INGREDIENTS	WEIGHT	MEASURE (APPROXIMATE) OR OUNCE WEIGHT
Pâte Brisée (PAGE 147)	One 9-inch crust (½ recipe, about 350 grams)	One 9-inch crust (½ recipe, about 12³⁄₁₀ ounces)
Bacon	100 grams	3½ ounces
Yellow onions	450 grams	1 pound (2 large or 3 medium)
Butter (French style, 82% fat)	50 grams	1⁷⁄₁₀ ounces or 3 generous tablespoons
Alsatian Riesling	50 grams	¼ cup less 1 teaspoon
Sea salt	To taste	To taste
Black pepper	To taste	To taste
Ground nutmeg	Pinch	Pinch
Whole eggs	60 grams	1 extra-large egg
Egg yolks	10 grams	About ½ yolk
Heavy cream (35% fat)	90 grams	⅓ cup plus 1½ tablespoons
Whole milk (3.5% fat)	90 grams	⅓ cup plus 1½ tablespoons
Sea salt	3.5 grams	½ teaspoon
Black pepper	0.5 gram	¼ teaspoon
Ground nutmeg	Pinch	Pinch
Egg Wash (PAGE 7)	1 recipe	1 recipe

This is a classic Alsatian savory tart that is usually served with a nice green salad on the side. It shows off the wonderful flavor of slow-cooked onions in butter, crispy smoked bacon, and pie dough. Serve it warm and all of these flavors will emerge in full force.

The pie dough crust is best rolled out the day before so that it will not shrink in the oven and collapse on one side. The onions should also be cooked a day ahead so that they can dry out slightly overnight. This way they won't release liquid into the custard when you bake the tart.

In our village having enough food for the weekend was everybody's mission because bakeries were not open on Sundays when I was growing up. Therefore all bakeries were very busy on Saturdays, selling huge amounts of bread, cakes, cookies, and savory tarts such as *tarte à l'oignon*. At our bakery there would already be a line in front as early as six a.m., and it would not slow down until noon.

BEFORE YOU BEGIN

→ Get out the following equipment and allow all of the ingredients to come to room temperature:

Digital scale, set to metric weights
Equipment for Pâte Brisée (PAGE 147)
Plastic wrap
1 chef's knife
1 wide, shallow sauté pan
1 rubber spatula or slotted spoon
1 sheet pan lined with paper towels
2 containers
1 rolling pin
One 9-inch tart ring or pan
1 dough docker or fork
Parchment paper or cheesecloth
Pie weights
2 medium mixing bowls
1 stainless steel hand whisk
1 strainer
1 pastry brush

→ Read this recipe through twice from start to finish.

UNDERSTANDING INGREDIENTS

This tart is similar to a quiche, and like a quiche it is usually made with *pâte brisée*, pie dough. Puff pastry does not bake well when it is in contact with a moist custard filling, which would be all the more moist because of the onions.

I like to cook the bacon lardons (little strips) in a frying pan and use the bacon fat remaining in the pan along with butter to cook the onions. It is important to cook the onions slowly and fully until they become slightly brown and translucent; this is how to bring out their best flavor. Also, when the Riesling is added, it is important to fully cook it out. Failing to do so will cause the onions to release liquid during the baking, resulting in a loose custard and a soggy crust. Alsatian Riesling, one of the great wines of France, is much drier than German or California Riesling. If you cannot get hold of it you can use another dry white wine.

Just as I prefer for a quiche, I like to use whole milk and heavy cream for the custard. Some recipes call for whole milk only while others use only cream; using only cream makes a very tasty but also

From the time I was about ten years old, on Thursday afternoons my mom and I would work in tandem (while my dad slept) to prepare the onion filling for our weekend tarts that my father would bake later that evening. I would arrive home from school at around four and we would begin our ritual, but my mom could only help if she didn't have customers to wait on at the bakery. I was the designated onion peeler, who had the honor of tackling two 10-pound sacks of onions that my mom would then slice up and cook slowly in butter for about 40 minutes, until they got their beautiful translucent shine. They looked gorgeous, and the slightly caramelized smell has always stuck with me. But I also remember how the onions would make us cry uncontrollably; it was hard work for a young boy, and I'm sure I probably wanted to go outside and play instead of peeling onions. My mom and I had so much fun working together, though, and now those days are a wonderful memory.

METHOD

DAY 1

1 Make a recipe of *pâte brisée*, divide the dough into 2 equal pieces, and wrap tightly in plastic wrap. Freeze half for another purpose. Let the dough you will use for the tart rest overnight in the refrigerator.

2 Using a chef's knife, cut the bacon crosswise into ¼-inch-wide sticks. Peel the onions and cut into ½-inch dice. Line a sheet pan with paper towels.

3 Heat a wide, shallow sauté pan over medium heat for 2 minutes, until hot. Add the bacon to the hot pan and sauté for 5 minutes, stirring occasionally, until the lardons start to brown and get slightly crispy. Using a slotted spoon or spatula, transfer the bacon to a sheet pan lined with paper towels. Keep the bacon fat in the pan and add the butter and the onions. Turn the heat down to low and cook for 20 minutes, stirring occasionally with a rubber spatula. It is important to cook the onions slowly so that they become translucent and do not caramelize too much or they will get too sweet. Add the Riesling and cook for another 10 minutes, until the wine evaporates. Season to taste with sea salt, pepper, and nutmeg. Take the pan off the heat and set it aside; allow it to air cool completely so that all the moisture evaporates. Transfer the mixture to a container and refrigerate uncovered overnight. Reserve the bacon lardons in a small container at room temperature.

DAY 2

1 Roll out the *pâte brisée* and line a 9-inch tart pan following the instructions on PAGE 147. Dock the dough by poking holes in it with a fork, 1 inch apart. If possible, refrigerate for 2 hours or longer to allow the crust to dry out further.

2   Preheat the oven to 325°F/160°C. Line the tart shell with a piece of parchment paper or a piece of cheesecloth. Fill it with pie weights, dry beans, or even rice. Bake for 55 minutes, then remove the pie weights and set aside to cool; the tart shell should be fully baked. If it is not, bake without the pie weights for another 10 minutes or until fully baked. Remove from the oven and allow to cool.

3   Meanwhile, remove the onions from the refrigerator and make the custard. Place the whole egg, egg yolk, cream, and milk in a mixing bowl and whisk together with a hand whisk. Season with sea salt, pepper, and nutmeg. Stir in the onions.

4   Brush the bottom of the pie shell with egg wash to make sure that the inside of the tart shell is sealed and that all of the holes are plugged. Bake for 5 minutes and let cool. Turn the oven up to 350°F/180°C.

5   Fill the tart shell with the custard and onion mixture and sprinkle the bacon on top. Place in the oven and bake 30 minutes, until set. Meanwhile, heat the broiler.

6   Remove the tart from the oven and set under the broiler for 1 to 3 minutes, watching closely so that the top doesn't burn, until the top is golden brown. Let cool for 30 minutes, remove the tart ring, and serve.

IT'S DONE WHEN IT'S DONE

The tart shell should be fully baked, the onions should be glossy and slightly brown, and the bacon should be golden brown and slightly crispy.

STORAGE

You can store the onion tart in the refrigerator for 2 days or in the freezer for up to 1 month. Reheat in a 450°F/230°C oven for 5 minutes. This will re-crisp the crust.

a very fatty quiche. I like to thicken and bind the custard with a combination of whole eggs and egg yolks. The yolk's lecithin is a great emulsifier that brings the water and fat together, while the white is a great binder. Using only egg yolks would work, but you would have to use a lot of them to make it set, and that would give the tart an eggy aftertaste. Using only whole eggs would introduce too much egg white, which could make the custard too firm.

The pie crust has to be fully baked because once it's in contact with the moist custard and onion filling it will not be able to bake easily. Since the onions, bacon, and tart shell are precooked, the baking time for the tart is not very long.

JACQUY'S TAKEAWAYS

→ The tart is best eaten with a green salad.

→ Never reheat a tart in the microwave, as this will make the crust mushy. The microwave draws moisture from the inside out.

→ If you want to make this a vegetarian tart, you can easily omit the bacon in the recipe.

→ You can also make a light variation of this tart by omitting the custard altogether. Make the onion filling and refrigerate overnight as directed. Fill the pre-baked crust, add the bacon (if desired), and bake as directed.

BEER QUICHE / QUICHE À LA BIÈRE

YIELD | ONE 9-INCH PIE

2-DAY RECIPE

INGREDIENTS	WEIGHT	MEASURE (APPROXIMATE) OR OUNCE WEIGHT
Pâte Brisée (PAGE 147)	One 9-inch crust (½ recipe, about 350 grams)	One 9-inch crust (½ recipe, about 12$\frac{3}{10}$ ounces)
Bacon	100 grams	3½ ounces
Yellow onions	200 grams	1 large or 2 medium
White mushrooms	125 grams	4½ ounces
Carrot	125 grams	1 medium
Butter (French style, 82% fat)	50 grams	1$\frac{7}{10}$ ounces or 3 generous tablespoons
Beer	250 grams	1⅛ cups
Sea salt	To taste	To taste
Freshly ground black pepper	To taste	To taste
Ground nutmeg powder	Pinch	Pinch
Whole eggs	60 grams	1 extra-large egg
Egg yolks	10 grams	About ½ yolk
Heavy cream (35% fat)	115 grams	½ cup
Whole milk (3.5% fat)	115 grams	½ cup
Sea salt	3.5 grams	½ teaspoon
Black pepper	0.5 gram	¼ teaspoon
Ground nutmeg	Pinch	Pinch
Egg Wash (PAGE 7)	1 recipe	1 recipe
Grated Swiss cheese	65 grams	2$\frac{3}{10}$ ounces (½ cup, tightly packed)

BEFORE YOU BEGIN

→ Get out the following equipment and allow all of the ingredients to come to room temperature:

Digital scale, set to metric weights
Plastic wrap
1 chef's knife
1 vegetable peeler
1 grater
1 wide, shallow sauté pan
1 rubber spatula or slotted spoon
1 sheet pan lined with paper towels
2 containers
1 rolling pin
One 9-inch tart ring or pan
1 dough docker or fork
Parchment paper or cheesecloth
Pie weights
1 medium mixing bowl
1 stainless steel hand whisk
1 pastry brush

→ Read this recipe through twice from start to finish.

Most pastry shops in France sell savory products as well as sweet ones, so they can serve as one-stop destinations for bread, dinner, and dessert. We have many traditional savory items in Alsace, and *quiche à la bière* is one of the best.

Everybody loves a nice warm quiche filled with mushrooms, carrots, onions, Swiss cheese, and a creamy custard. This one has a secret ingredient—Alsatian beer, which takes it to a completely different level. The slight bitterness of the beer brings a wonderful complexity to the quiche. Okay, I'll admit that other types of beer work as well, but I feel it's my duty to recommend a pale lager from Alsace. The tart evolved as

UNDERSTANDING INGREDIENTS

A regular quiche Lorraine is a pie filled with ham, Swiss cheese, and a custard made of milk, cream, and eggs as a binder. The dough is usually pie dough, *pâte brisée* (PAGE 147). Puff pastry does not bake well when it is in contact with a liquid custard. In this recipe, vegetables replace the ham. It's important to cook them well or they will release water during the baking and make the custard loose. Beer is added to the vegetables when you cook them and they absorb and retain its flavor. It is important to cook out all of the beer or it too will make the custard watery. For the same reasons as in the onion tart on PAGE 357, I like to make the custard with whole milk, heavy cream, egg yolk, and whole eggs.

The pie crust has to be fully baked because once it's in contact with the moist custard and vegetable filling it will not be able to bake easily. Since the vegetables, bacon, and tart shell are precooked the baking time for the tart is not very long.

a true *produit du terroir*, made with vegetables, dairy products, and beer from the region, all nurtured by the same soil. We Alsatians are very proud of what our land has to offer and have developed many specialties over the centuries that continue to boost the economy of our region.

This recipe requires a 2-day process because the pie dough needs to rest overnight and the cooked filling also needs to be refrigerated overnight so that it can dry out slightly. This way the vegetables won't release liquid during the final baking process.

METHOD

DAY 1

1 Make a recipe of *pâte brisée*, divide the dough into 2 equal pieces, and wrap tightly in plastic wrap. Freeze half for another purpose. Let the dough you will use for the quiche rest overnight in the refrigerator.

2 Using a chef's knife, cut the bacon crosswise into ¼-inch-wide sticks, called lardons. Peel the onions and cut into ½-inch dice. Clean the mushrooms and cut away the end of the stems. Cut the mushrooms in half and then cut each half into thick slices. Peel the carrot and grate it on the large holes of a grater.

3 Heat a wide, shallow sauté pan over medium heat for 2 minutes, until hot. Add the bacon to the hot pan and sauté for 5 minutes, stirring occasionally, until the lardons start to brown and get slightly crispy. Using a slotted spoon or spatula, transfer the bacon to a sheet pan lined with paper towel. Keep the bacon fat in the pan and add the butter and the onions. Turn the heat down to low and cook for 10 minutes, stirring occasionally with a rubber spatula. It is important to cook the onions slowly so that they become translucent and do not caramelize too much or they will get too sweet. Add the mushroom slices and continue cooking for 5 minutes, until they are tender and have released their moisture. Add the grated carrot and cook for another 5 minutes. Add the beer, turn up the heat to medium, and cook for another 10 minutes or until all of the liquid has evaporated. Season to taste with sea salt, pepper, and a pinch of nutmeg. Take the pan off the heat and set it aside; allow it to air cool completely so that all the moisture evaporates. Transfer the mixture to a container and refrigerate uncovered overnight. Reserve the bacon lardons in a small container at room temperature.

DAY 2

1 Roll out and line a 9-inch tart pan with the *pâte brisée* following the instructions on PAGE 147. Dock the dough by poking holes in it with a fork, 1 inch apart. If possible, refrigerate for 2 hours or longer to allow the crust to dry out further.

2 Preheat the oven to 325°F/160°C. Line the tart shell with a piece of parchment paper or a piece of cheesecloth. Fill it with pie weights, dry beans, or even rice. Bake for 55 minutes, then remove the pie weights and set aside to cool; the tart shell should be fully baked. If it is not, bake without the pie weights for another 10 minutes, or until fully baked.

3 Meanwhile, remove the vegetables from the refrigerator and make the custard. Place the whole egg, egg yolk, cream, and milk in a mixing bowl and whisk together with a hand whisk. Season with sea salt, pepper, and nutmeg.

4 Brush the bottom of the pie shell with egg wash to make sure that the inside of the tart shell is sealed and that all of the holes are plugged. Bake for 5 minutes and let cool. Turn the oven up to 350°F/180°C.

5 Fill the tart shell evenly with the cooked vegetable mixture. Sprinkle the bacon lardons over the vegetables and sprinkle the Swiss cheese evenly on top. Pour on the custard mixture, scraping all of it out of the bowl with a rubber spatula, and place in the oven. Bake 30 to 35 minutes at 350°F/180°C, until set. Meanwhile, heat the broiler.

6 Remove the quiche from the oven and set under the broiler for 1 to 3 minutes, watching closely so that the cheese doesn't burn, until the top is golden brown. Let cool for 30 minutes, remove the tart ring, and serve.

IT'S DONE WHEN IT'S DONE

The quiche should be golden brown and the custard set. The tart shell should be fully baked.

STORAGE

You can store the baked quiche in a refrigerator for 2 days or in a freezer for up to 1 month. Reheat in a 450°F/230°C oven for 5 minutes. This will re-crisp the crust.

JACQUY'S TAKEAWAYS

→ You can play with this recipe using different vegetables, as long as you remember to cook them fully before using them as a filling. You can also omit the bacon for a vegetarian quiche.

→ Never reheat a tart in the microwave, as this will make the crust mushy. The microwave draws moisture from the inside out.

→ You could use a dark lager beer instead of a pale lager, but then I would advise you to use half the amount or the quiche will be too bitter.

TARTE FLAMBÉE

(See page 294 for photo)

INGREDIENTS	WEIGHT	MEASURE (APPROXIMATE) OR OUNCE WEIGHT
CRUST		
Water	325 grams	1⅓ cups plus 1 tablespoon
Yeast	7.5 grams	2 teaspoons
All-purpose flour	500 grams	3⅞ cups
Sea salt	11 grams	1½ teaspoons
Canola oil	25 grams	2 tablespoons
TOPPING		
Crème fraîche	385 grams	1¾ cups
All-purpose flour	25 grams	2 tablespoons plus 2 teaspoons
Egg yolks	25 grams	2 tablespoons plus 2 teaspoons
Ground nutmeg	Pinch	Pinch
Sea salt	To taste	To taste
Black pepper	To taste	To taste
Yellow onions	300 to 360 grams	2 medium
Thick-cut bacon	8 strips	8 strips
All-purpose flour, for flouring the baker's peel if using	As needed	As needed
Canola oil, for oiling the pizza pan if using	As needed	As needed
Semolina or cornmeal, for dusting the pan	As needed	As needed

BEFORE YOU BEGIN

⇢ Get out the following equipment and allow all of the ingredients to come to room temperature:

Digital scale, set to metric weights
KitchenAid or stand mixer fitted with the paddle and hook attachments
1 rubber spatula
1 dough scraper
Plastic wrap
One 14-inch pizza pan lined with plastic wrap
1 rolling pin
Parchment paper or wax paper
1 pizza stone
1 medium mixing bowl
1 stainless steel hand whisk
1 chef's knife
1 pizza peel or lightly oiled pizza pan
1 small offset spatula

⇢ Read this recipe through twice from start to finish.

Tarte flambée is one of the signature dishes of Alsace. There are countless restaurants all over the region that specialize in the flat, crisp, thin-crusted pies topped with crème fraîche, bits of bacon, and thin slices of onions that is always served with Alsatian Riesling. The area that it comes from, the Kochersberg, which is where I too am from, is an agricultural region where farmers grow mostly sugar beets, hops, tobacco, and apples. Traditionally farmers had their own brick ovens and would bake bread once a week. The ovens would stay very hot for a long time after the bread was done, so the farmers would roll out bits of leftover dough into thin rounds, spread thick cream over them, and bake them quickly in the hot ovens. *Et voilà, tarte flambée* was born. *Flambée* refers to the wood fire in the oven.

These days one can buy steel *tarte flambée* ovens. Being the true Alsatian that I am, I shipped one to my house in Chicago so that I can enjoy a bit of Alsace with my friends and family. In this recipe the *tarte flambée* takes 5 minutes to bake in a home oven, but my oven gets much hotter than a regular home oven—650°F—and I bake my tart for just 60 seconds. Whether you bake in a home oven or a commercial one, the intense heat completely breaks down the gluten in the crust and makes it very crispy.

Because the dough is rolled so thin, it is easier to work with the rounds if they are frozen. When the oven is ready you pull them from the freezer one at a time, top them while still frozen, and put them directly onto the baking stone in the hot oven. You will need to make the crusts ahead so that they have time to freeze, which is a good idea anyway. Otherwise you'll spend the evening rolling dough instead of entertaining your guests. You can also pre-bake the crusts for 2 minutes before topping to stop the action of the yeast so that they are easier to handle.

METHOD

1 Take the temperature of the flour and the room (convert to Celsius) and add them together. Then adjust your water temperature (Celsius) so that the sum of the three ingredients is 65°C. For instance, if your room temperature is 70°F, convert to Celsius and you will get 21°C; if your flour is 72°F, convert to Celsius and you will get 22°C; 21°C + 22°C = 43°C. Subtract 43°C from 65°C. The difference is 22°C, the temperature you will need for your water. Once you have heated or cooled your water to the correct temperature, combine with the yeast in the bowl of a stand mixer and stir to dissolve. Add the flour, sea salt, and canola oil and mix together just to combine with the paddle. Turn off the machine, scrape all the dough from the paddle, and switch to the dough hook. Mix on medium-low speed for 5 minutes. Turn the speed to medium high and mix for another 2 minutes. Cover the bowl tightly with plastic and allow to rise in a warm spot for 1 hour.

2 Divide the dough into 8 equal pieces, approximately 100 grams each. Cover the pieces you are not rolling with a sheet of plastic or a towel. You will be freezing the crusts before baking them. To facilitate this, line a 14-inch pizza pan with a large sheet of plastic wrap. Roll 1 piece of the dough out into a very thin circle, approximately 12 inches in diameter. Place the rolled-out circle on top of the plastic wrap and bring the edges of the plastic wrap up over the edges of the dough. Place another sheet of plastic wrap on top to cover the round airtight. Place a piece of parchment paper or wax paper on top of the covered round, measure out another large sheet of plastic for the

UNDERSTANDING INGREDIENTS

Shop around for a good, thick crème fraîche. Some separate more than others during the baking process. We use the egg and flour as a binder to prevent that separation.

I like to use yellow onions, which I cut in small strips about ⅛ inch wide × ¾ inch long.

Use thick-cut, all-natural, smoked, center-cut bacon with no preservatives.

JACQUY'S TAKEAWAYS

→ If you don't have time to freeze your crusts, or if you are concerned that they might thaw and become sticky before you can get them into your oven, you can roll out the dough with the oven preheated and par-bake for 2 minutes. That will stabilize the dough, and you will not have to worry about it sticking to your baking peel or counter. Reduce the final baking time by 1 minute.

next round of dough, and place it on top of the parchment paper. Roll out the next round and place on the plastic. Wrap as directed and continue until all of the rounds of dough are rolled out and stacked on top of each other. Wrap the entire stack and place in the freezer for at least 2 hours or for up to 1 month.

3 One hour before you wish to bake, preheat the oven to 500°F/260°C, preferably with a baking stone in it, or prepare a hot wood fire.

4 In a medium bowl, whisk together the crème fraîche, flour, egg yolk, nutmeg, sea salt, and pepper. Cut the onions in half lengthwise (root end to stem end), then across the grain into thin slices. Separate the layers. Cut the bacon crosswise into ¼-inch-wide strips.

5 Lightly flour a baker's peel or very lightly oil a pizza pan and very lightly sprinkle with semolina or cornmeal. Place a frozen disk on the peel or pan and, using a small offset spatula, spread a thin layer of the crème fraîche mixture—about 3 rounded tablespoons—over the surface, leaving a border around the edge. Sprinkle about 60 grams of onions (2 ounces, about ¼ small onion) and slivered bacon from 1 slice of bacon over the top. Slide from the peel onto the baking stone, or place the pizza pan directly into the oven. Bake 5 minutes, until the edges of the crust are crisped and brown and the topping is sizzling. Keep your eye on the oven as the thin crust will burn quickly on the stone once it is crisp. Remove from the heat and serve at once.

IT'S DONE WHEN IT'S DONE

When the *tarte flambée* is done the crust is golden brown underneath and the edges are slightly burned and crisp. The onions and bacon should be cooked and the topping will be sizzling.

STORAGE

The frozen raw or par-baked disks can be kept in a freezer for 1 month. *Tarte flambées* are best eaten straight out of the oven. They can be frozen at the baked stage but they risk becoming soggy. They will need to be thawed out and re-crisped right away in a 400°F/200°C oven for 1 minute before serving.

VARIATIONS

In Alsace they also make a dessert *tarte flambée* with apples. Sliced apples are layered on the dough, brushed with melted butter, and sprinkled with sugar and cinnamon. It's baked in the hot oven and served with Calvados. At home I play around with different toppings like pesto, roasted tomato slices, portabello mushrooms, and mozzarella; not Alsatian at all, but very tasty!

ROLLING OUT YEASTED DOUGH

Because the gluten has been developed in a yeasted dough like a pizza dough, you must let it rest while rolling it out. Otherwise you will stretch the gluten too much and tear the dough apart. A good way to approach rolling out all of these tarte flambée disks is to roll 1 piece for about a minute, then put it aside to rest for 5 or 10 minutes while you go on to the next one, roll that piece for a minute, go on to the next, and so on. Stack the partially rolled-out rounds between pieces of parchment paper so they don't stick to each other. Then go back to the first disk and continue to roll out to a thin circle, and continue with the remaining rounds.

WARM ALSATIAN MEAT PIE / PÂTÉ CHAUD ALSACIEN

YIELD | 1 MEAT PIE, SERVING 8 PEOPLE

2-DAY RECIPE

INGREDIENTS	WEIGHT	MEASURE (APPROXIMATE) OR OUNCE WEIGHT
Puff Pastry (PAGE 28)	1 recipe	1 recipe
Pork butt (shoulder)	520 grams	1 pound plus 2 ounces
Veal shoulder	280 grams	10 ounces
Alsatian Riesling	80 grams	½ cup
Curly parsley, finely chopped	6 grams	2 tablespoons
Shallots	40 grams	2 medium
Sea salt	1 gram or to taste	¼ teaspoon or to taste
Cardamom seed	1 seed	1 seed
Ground black pepper	0.3 gram	Scant ¼ teaspoon
Ground nutmeg	0.2 gram	Scant ¼ teaspoon
Dried bay leaf	1 leaf	1 leaf
Fresh thyme	1 sprig	1 sprig
Fresh tarragon	2 sprigs	2 sprigs
Clove	1 clove	1 clove
Egg Wash (PAGE 7)	1 recipe	1 recipe

A good meat pie is absolute heaven to me, especially because it brings back fond memories of Sundays and summers spent at my grandparents' farm near the Vosges, a region of hills and small mountains in eastern France where I spent many a summer afternoon picking blueberries, wild raspberries, strawberries, and chestnuts with my brothers and sisters, my mother and my uncle. My grandparents, Lucie and Lucien Heinrich, had a huge garden with *mirabelle* and *quetsch* trees. They raised rabbits and chickens (my job as a boy was collecting eggs from the chicken coops) and had two milk cows and an enormous Ardennais draft horse that my grandfather used for his second occupation, lumberjacking. In those days, not too long after World War II, he cut trees by hand, without the help of a chain saw to section off the lumber. This he would do with an ax and a saw. He would then attach the tree trunk to a chain and use draft horses to haul the wood down the mountains, load it onto a carriage, and bring it to the local village.

BEFORE YOU BEGIN

→ Get out the following equipment and allow all of the ingredients to come to room temperature:

Digital scale, set to metric weights
Equipment for Puff Pastry (PAGE 28)
1 large chef's knife
1 large mixing bowl
Plastic wrap
1 large silpat
1 rolling pin
1 sheet pan lined with parchment paper
1 rubber spatula
1 colander
1 pastry brush
1 cookie cutter or paring knife
Parchment paper

→ Read this recipe through twice from start to finish.

The farm, like all the surrounding farms at that time, was self-sufficient, with an abundant supply of eggs, milk, cream, fruit, vegetables, and meat. In summer I would go there to help cut the hay and make haystacks, hard work for a kid in the August heat. I didn't appreciate it then, but now it is a wonderful memory. I will never forget the food I ate there. Nothing was raised or grown with chemicals, and the vivid flavor of these products will always be engraved on my palate. I've never tasted milk that compares to the super-fresh milk I drank at my grandparents' farm.

Alsatian *pâté chaud*, unlike other French meat *pâtés* that are served cold, is a warm meat pie made with pork or a mix of pork and veal wrapped in puff pastry. The meat is traditionally cut into strips, though it can also be cut into cubes, marinated for a day in Riesling with shallots, parsley, herbs, and spices, and arranged on a large rectangular strip of puff pastry. The pastry is gathered up around the sides of the filling like a package, and another rectangular sheet of puff pastry is set on top. Then the dough is decorated with the tip of a knife in a herringbone pattern and brushed with egg wash so that when it bakes it comes out shiny and ornate. A marvelous exchange of flavors takes place as the meat roasts inside the pastry, filling it with its juices while on the outside the pastry becomes crisp and flaky.

Until I began working on this book it had been a while since I'd made *pâté chaud*; there was little demand for it in the bakeries I worked in around the world. As a child, though, it was a special dish that we always had when we went to see my grandparents for family occasions. My grandma would marinate the meat and bring it to the village baker to wrap in puff pastry and bake in his big oven. I loved that delicious puff pastry filled with the warm, juicy meat filling. Little did I know then that years later I would be making *pâté chaud* by the hundreds when I worked for a caterer in Strasbourg.

When you make this pie, take care to roll out the puff pastry dough sufficiently so that you will have a wide edge on the sides and at both ends to wrap the meat. If the meat isn't carefully wrapped, the juices will escape during baking and your puff pastry will become soggy. Serve the *pâté chaud* hot or warm with a simple green salad and a good bottle of Alsatian Riesling.

UNDERSTANDING INGREDIENTS

During my testing for this recipe I was reminded that the quality of the meat is crucial for meat pies. I recommend that you go to a reputable butcher shop and that you make sure that you talk to your butcher about the recipe. Tell him how you are planning to use the meat, and how you need to cut it. For this meat pie you will need pork shoulder, also called pork butt. You will remove any bones and some of the fat (the fat on the outside), but not all of it. You will combine the pork with veal shoulder, again removing some but not all of the fat.

In Alsace we use local Riesling to marinate the meat, but you could use any other dry white wine, such as sauvignon blanc or pinot grigio. White wine is acidic, and any acidic liquid (such as vinegar or acidic fruit juice) will help tenderize meat. But to do so it has to get to the center of the strips or cubes, which is why it's important to cut them no wider than ½ inch. It's also important not to use too much wine. The meat should marinate in it but it shouldn't swim. Too much wine would mean too much acid, which would "cook" the meat and make it tough.

I prefer to use shallots instead of onions for this, as they have more character, but you can always use half shallots and half onions. In France we usually use curly parsley instead of flat-leaf parsley because it has a milder taste with hints of nutmeg. Regarding the spices, ask any Alsatian and he or she will have his or her own spice formula for *pâté chaud*, each person claiming that his or hers is the best one. You can always play with the spice and herb mix, but you should be careful with cloves, nutmeg, and cardamom, as these spices have a very powerful and persistent flavor. Also, if you use dried herbs instead of fresh, use them sparingly—half as much as fresh.

METHOD

DAY 1

1 Make the puff pastry and give it 4 folds.

2 Place the pork and veal on your cutting board and trim away the fat that is on the outside, leaving some of the interior fat. Cut the meat across the grain in slices, then cut the slices into ½-inch-wide strips. If the cuts of meat don't lend themselves to slices, cut it into ½-inch cubes. Place in a large mixing bowl and add the wine. Finely mince the parsley and dice the shallots. Add to the meat, along with the sea salt, spices, and herbs. Mix well and cover with plastic wrap. Refrigerate overnight.

DAY 2

1 Give the puff pastry 2 more turns, refrigerating for 30 minutes between turns. After the last turn refrigerate for 1 hour or longer.

2 On a lightly dusted counter or silpat, roll out the puff pastry until it is ¼ inch thick or a little thinner. Cut a 15 × 9–inch rectangle (this will shrink to about 14 × 8 inches) and place on a parchment paper–lined sheet pan. Wrap the remaining dough and refrigerate.

3 Stir the meat, then place it in a colander in the sink to drain. Remove the thyme and tarragon sprigs, the whole clove, the bay leaf, and, if you can find it, the cardamom seed. Taste a piece of shallot to verify the seasoning; add a little more salt if desired. Let the meat drain for about 10 minutes.

4 Meanwhile, make the egg wash.

5 Spoon the meat onto the middle of the puff pastry rectangle, then shape the block of meat into a rectangle, leaving a 1½- to 2-inch border all the way around. The meat block should be approximately 1¼ inches thick, 10 inches long, and 4 inches wide, but it may vary depending on how much your dough rectangle has shrunk. The important thing is to leave a wide enough margin to properly enclose the meat so that the juices don't run out when you bake the pie (SEE FIGURE 1).

6 Fold a long edge of the dough up over the meat rectangle and repeat with the other side. Brush the exposed edges at each end of the dough with egg wash and fold them in over the meat and the ends of the long edges. The meat should now be enclosed on all sides but still exposed on the top (SEE FIGURES 2 AND 3). Brush all the sides with egg wash and place in the refrigerator while you roll out the top piece of puff pastry.

7 Roll out another piece of puff pastry until it is ¼ inch thick. Cut a 13 × 7–inch rectangle (this will shrink by about 1 inch all around). Remove the meat pie from the refrigerator. Brush all of the sides again with egg wash and place

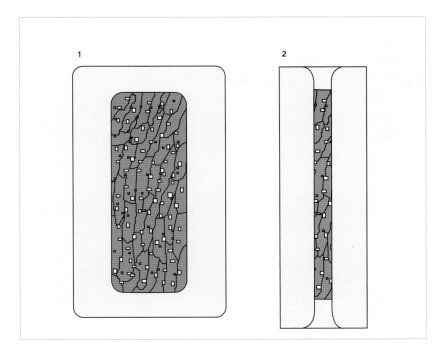

1

Place the meat in the center of the dough.

2

Fold each side in over the meat.

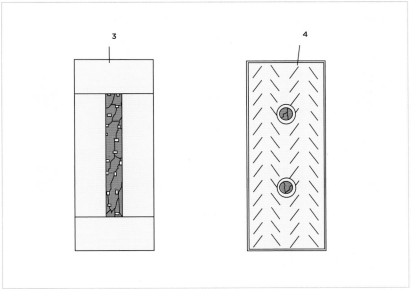

3

Fold in each end.

4

Cover the pie with a sheet of dough, egg wash and score with a paring knife.

Cut out two ¾-inch circles of dough from the top of the pie and place the 2 puff pastry rings around the holes.

the second rectangle on top. It should cover the pie completely. Gently press on all of the sides to make sure they are stuck together. Trim away the over-lapping dough at the corners. Brush all over with egg wash and refrigerate for 10 minutes.

8 Meanwhile, roll out a strip of puff pastry until it is ⅛ inch thick and at least 2 inches wide. Using a cookie cutter or a paring knife (a cookie cutter is easiest) cut out two 2-inch circles. Cut a ¾-inch hole in the center of each round using a knife, a very small cookie cutter, or a pastry tip. Set aside.

9 Preheat the oven to 375°F/190°C. Remove the meat pie from the refrigerator and brush again with egg wash. Using the tip of a paring knife, mark the sides and top of the dough with a herringbone pattern, cutting 1-inch lines at a slant at ½-inch intervals. Cut out two ¾-inch circles of dough from the top of the pie and, using egg wash, glue the 2 puff pastry rings around the holes (SEE FIGURE 4). Cut two 4-inch-long × 2-inch-wide strips of parchment paper, roll them around your pinky to make a tube, and insert 1 in each hole to make chimneys. This will allow steam to escape from the *pâté* as it bakes.

10 Place the meat pie in the oven and bake 50 minutes, until dark golden brown, turning the sheet pan front to back halfway through. Allow to cool for at least 10 minutes. Using a large chef's knife, cut in 1- to 1½-inch slices and serve.

JACQUY'S TAKEAWAYS

- If you don't like pork you can substitute all veal or even chicken for it.
- You can add some vegetables like mushrooms or carrots to the meat mixture. They must be cooked first, then added.
- The meat pie is best served warm as a main dish with a green salad.

IT'S DONE WHEN IT'S DONE

The dough should be golden brown on the outside; the meat should be cooked and tender.

STORAGE

The *pâté* can be baked several hours ahead, or refrigerated for up to 2 days. It is best served hot or warm. Warm in a 400°F/200°C oven for 15 to 20 minutes.

WHEN I WAS GROWING UP our family always spent Whitsunday, a religious holiday that occurs fifty days after Easter, at my grandparents' farm in Lutzel-house, a small, rustic village near the forests of the Vosges Mountains, about 20 miles away from our home. My father would install four garden chairs in the back of his delivery truck, our only vehicle at the time, put us kids in these improvised backseats, and off we'd go, setting out early so that we would arrive before noon. Alsatians have set rules about meal times, and lunch was at noon, period. You could not be late. It was an adventure for us to try to hold on to our sliding chairs every time we went around a curve; we were having so much fun it never occurred to us how dangerous that drive was.

When we arrived at the farm, we would be greeted by my godfather Armand, his wife, and their two daughters. My grandparents would give us a warm welcome, and while the adults drank a *picon bière*, the traditional Alsatian aperitif, we children would run off to play on the farm. First we would go and visit all of the rabbits in their cages, never bothered by the fact that these very rabbits would at some point end up on our plates as *lapin à la moutarde*—rabbit in mustard sauce. Then we would run around in the fields and gardens behind the house. It was an adventure for us, but we had to make sure not to get our good Sunday clothes dirty or there would be hell to pay for the remainder of the day.

At twelve thirty p.m. it was time for the men to go to the village bakery to pick up *d'flaischpàschtet*, the Alsatian word for the warm meat pie. Half the village of Lutzelhouse speaks the Alsatian dialect, a rough Germanic language that evolved over centuries of invasions and occupations in this disputed area at the German frontier. Lutzelhouse is typical of villages in the eastern part of Alsace; the people on one side of the village speak the Alsatian language, whereas those on the other speak only French (my grandmother spoke Alsatian and French, and my grandfather spoke only French).

I would get to go along with the men to the bakery. The day before, my grandmother would have marinated about six pounds of meat strips, enough to feed all thirteen of us, and brought it to the baker, who would wrap the meat in puff pastry, shaping the pie like a large flat log that was about ten inches wide and two feet long. He baked it in his huge brick oven, and when we came to pick it up it would be fully baked and golden brown. The aroma of the warm puff pastry and the pork that had been marinated with parsley, shallots, and white wine was absolutely delicious, and my grandmother's *pâté chaud Alsacien* would be the *pièce de résistance* of the entire meal.

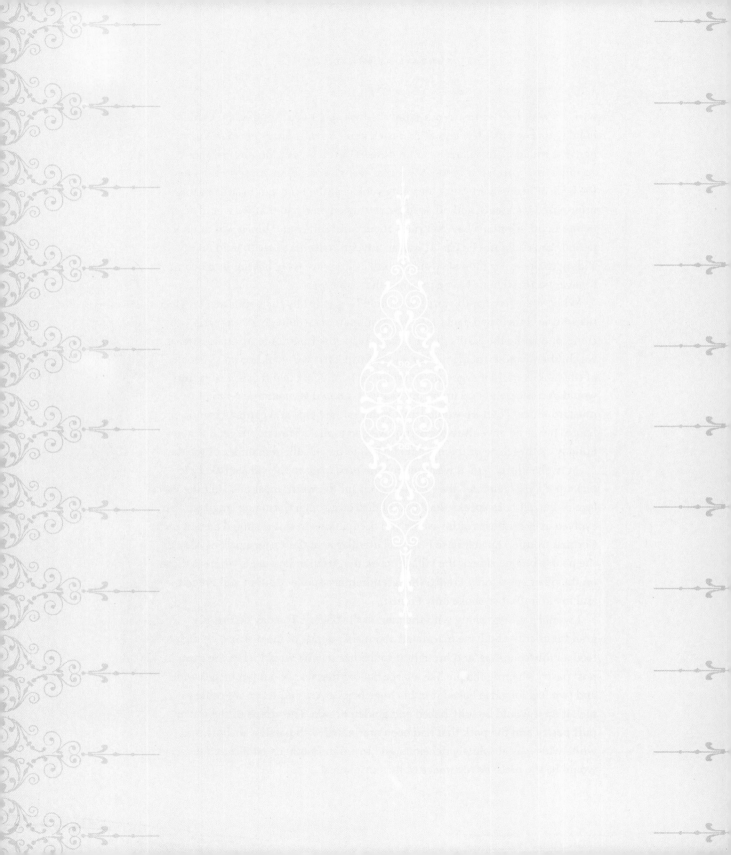

• A P P E N D I X •

FLOURISHES: LA CERISE SUR LE GÂTEAU

*I*n pastry we call decorations *"la cerise sur la gâteau"*—the cherry on the cake. They are never mandatory in my recipes, but they do embellish the final products. They make them even more special.

Some flourishes are as simple as a hazelnut dipped in caramel in such a way that the hot sugar dripping off the nut solidifies in the form of an elegant curl (SEE PAGE 376). Your decoration of choice can be simple: threads of candied peel (PAGE 87), a thin, crisp *tuile* (PAGES 217 AND 289), a shard or a square of chocolate nougatine crisp (PAGE 59), or something piped—butter cream, *mousseline*, whipped cream, or, once you get comfortable with tempering chocolate (PAGE 208), piped chocolate swirls. Chocolate offers a world of possibilities, from curls to swirls to simple chocolate shavings.

Most of the garnishes suggested in these recipes don't take a lot of time, but they do sometimes require practice and patience, like so many things in pastry. Using them will set your dessert presentations at a higher level and will impress your guests so much that before long they'll be placing orders with you.

HAZELNUT CARAMEL CURLS

INGREDIENTS	WEIGHT	MEASURE (APPROXIMATE)
Whole hazelnuts, skinned (PAGE 53)	8 to 15	8 to 15
Caramel (PAGE 47)	100 grams	About ½ cup

This is a clever and simple way to make a stunning decoration. All professional chefs look for ways to create beautiful things in efficient ways. We never have much time to complete our production of pastries, so when an idea like the hazelnut curl comes along, our eyes light up. What makes this such a smart system is the fact that the curls are made with simple ingredients that we usually have in the kitchen: two blocks of butter, sugar, nuts, toothpicks, and gravity. The blocks of butter are stacked on top of each other like a tower, and the nuts are stabbed with the toothpicks and dipped in hot caramel. We then stick the toothpicks into the top of the tower and allow the caramel to drip from the nuts in a thin caramel string. When the caramel is hard, we remove the toothpick and end up with a hazelnut with a long curvy tail. It's ingenious!

BEFORE YOU BEGIN

→ Get out the following equipment:

Digital scale, set to metric weights
Equipment for Caramel (PAGE 47)
1 small sheet pan lined with parchment paper
1 silpat
8 to 15 toothpicks
Two 1-pound blocks of butter (note that this is equipment, not an ingredient in the recipe)

→ Read this recipe through twice from start to finish.

UNDERSTANDING INGREDIENTS

Hazelnuts are my favorite nuts to use because they are round and are the easiest to stab. Macadamia nuts and almonds would be also good candidates. Other large nuts such as cashew nuts or Brazil nuts could also work, but I've never tried them. Pistachios, peanuts, or pine nuts would be too small and would not make much of a decoration.

METHOD

1 Preheat the oven to 300°F/150°C and roast the whole hazelnuts on a sheet pan lined with parchment paper for 15 to 20 minutes, until lightly toasted all the way through. Remove from the heat and let them cool completely.

2 Make a recipe of caramel following the instructions on PAGE 47. Cool for 5 seconds only by dipping the pan into a bowl of water as instructed in the recipe. Set aside for 5 minutes.

3 Stick a toothpick firmly into the side of each hazelnut.

4 Place a silpat on your work surface and create a tower in the middle by standing the butter blocks vertically one on top of the other. When the caramel gets slightly pasty, hold a hazelnut toothpick by the end and dip in the nut. Immediately stick the toothpick horizontally into the top of the butter tower so that the caramel-covered nut is suspended out to the side (SEE ILLUSTRATION). Let the caramel drip; it will make an elegant curl. Repeat with the rest of the hazelnuts. Once the caramel is cold remove the toothpicks from the hazelnuts and keep the hazelnut caramel curls in a dry place (see below), or lay them horizontally between sheets of parchment paper in an airtight container. Return the butter to the refrigerator to use in another recipe.

IT'S DONE WHEN IT'S DONE

It should look like a molecule with a head and a long tail.

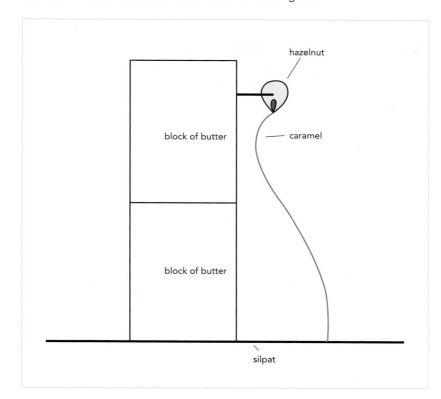

"Inventing" Pastry

I'm not sure if any single pastry chef invented caramel curls, but in any case it would be practically impossible to verify, as so many creative things take place at the same time and have taken place throughout history in the wide world of our profession. If you look at very old recipe books you'll see that sophisticated pastries were being created as far back as the sixteenth century. That's why I will never claim to invent a pastry item. I believe that every chef, whether professional or not, is here to share his point of view. It's the sharing of these new ideas, points of view, and techniques that makes our art so exciting.

STORAGE

It's best to keep these in an airtight box with a desiccant such as silica gel, which will help them stay dry for days. The main precaution to take is to be careful when you handle them, as the tails like to break off. See PAGE XXXI for a source for silica gel.

JACQUY'S TAKEAWAYS

→ These can be used to decorate a dessert in a glass (such as the *verrine* on PAGE 267), or a dessert on a plate. I have also used them to decorate mini pastries, 9-inch cakes, and even ice cream cakes.

CHOCOLATE CURLS

Chocolate curls are very appealing both because of what they are made of and because of their whimsical shape. A simple chocolate curl on a cake or a dessert completely changes its look and adds considerably to its attractiveness.

METHOD I: SHAVING A CHOCOLATE BLOCK

The simplest way to make chocolate curls is to use a large block of chocolate couverture that is at least 1 inch thick. It can be white, milk, or dark chocolate. If possible, leave the chocolate in a slightly warm area (between 75°F/23.8°C and 80.6°F/27°C) for 1 hour, until the chocolate softens a little but does not melt. Stand the block on its side and run a hair dryer over the opposite side once on low heat. Peel off curls by running a vegetable peeler along the warmed side. The idea is to soften the chocolate but not to melt it; then you should be able to make spiral curls. If it comes off in shavings it is not warm enough; run the hair dryer over the chocolate as needed. Never touch the curls with your hands, as they are warmer than the chocolate and will cause it to melt; the best way to pick them up is with a large spoon or an offset spatula. Place the curls on a sheet pan and put them in a cool place. A wine cooler is ideal, the best place there is to store chocolate. After making a few curls, if the chocolate is hard, rotate the block a quarter turn and make a curl on another side. The outside will still be warm enough for curls. The curls can be kept for weeks in a cool place after they are made.

METHOD 2

This is just a variation of the above method. Let the chocolate block warm up in a slightly warm room as instructed above. Place the block flat on the table and run the hair dryer over it once on low heat; use the sharp edge of a round cookie cutter to scrape the top. You should be able to make beautiful and very curvy curls using this method.

METHOD 3: USING TEMPERED CHOCOLATE

You need a minimum of 100 grams of chocolate for this method. See the section on tempering chocolate on PAGE 208. Temper your chocolate and, using an offset spatula, spread it 1/16 inch thick on a granite or marble counter. Spread it back and forth using a rocking motion of your wrist, as if you were painting a wall (I call it the wax-on, wax-off motion), until the chocolate starts to set up. At this point the chocolate should lose some of its dark color as the fat crystallizes on the table. Wait 2 full minutes. Using a large round cookie cutter, scrape the surface of the chocolate, scraping toward you. If the chocolate curls up, it is ready. If it does not, it is probably too soft and you should wait another minute or two. This method can be used with milk, dark, or white chocolate couverture but it requires more practice than the first version. I like to use it to make giant curls that are so curvy you could place sauce in them on a plated dessert.

ACKNOWLEDGMENTS

I have wanted to write this book for more than twenty years, but I could never get to it because I was so busy opening and running the French Pastry School. Finally I got to it, and now that it is done I want to make sure to acknowledge all of the people who have helped me directly and indirectly in my career. The recipes, advice, tricks, and comments in this book come from my deepest roots, and there have been many people along the way who have helped me to get to where I am now. I will try my best.

I can begin by thanking all of my family back in France. They have always been supportive, even when, at the age of fifteen, I chose to begin an apprenticeship in pastry rather than going on with my studies in school like most of the my other friends and fellow students. Throughout my apprenticeship and my subsequent travels they have always been there when I needed them. When I began working on this book, thirty-five years after beginning my apprenticeship, my mom, brothers, and sisters helped revive some of the old memories and stories that I have included with the recipes.

I owe a lot to Jean Clauss, the master pastry chef with whom I apprenticed. He taught me pastry in his own special way. His methods were ruthless and non-negotiable to say the least, but he instilled some common sense in me at a very young age and set my career on track by instilling in me the important core values of discipline, respect, and perseverance. My apprenticeship, though difficult on a personal level, changed my life and was the best thing that could have happened to me professionally.

I need to mention and thank all of the chefs I have worked with throughout my career, a journey that has taken me to four continents. They have all contributed something to this book, be it a technique, a trick, or a recipe. Chefs have a strong sense of brotherhood, and now it is my turn to share with you what they have shared with me. In the course of my quest for the title of Meilleur Ouvrier de France (Best Craftsman in France) I am grateful to have been associated with Chef Kurt Fogle, who was my outstanding assistant during this adventure. He was a model of perseverance and dedication, working with me day and night on perfecting the recipes and techniques needed for the task. You will find some of these in the pages of this book. That quest was depicted in a documentary called *Kings of Pastry,* and I would like to thank Flora Lazar, the outstanding producer and alumna of the French Pastry School, who was the originator of this project. Flora saw the need to document my journey and introduced me to the legendary documentary film makers D. A. Pennebaker and Chris Hegedus, who captured the essence of the experience and its true meaning.

I thank the entire team at the French Pastry School. They have been with us for the last eighteen years. Our employees do an outstanding job of taking care of our students on a daily basis, and during the book project they always stood behind me. Led by Franco Pacini, Anne Kauffmann and Maggie Fahey helped with some of the writing, and Joe Yakes helped me format the drawings that are included in the book. Chef Pierre Zimmermann and Chef Jonathan Dendauw, our two master bakers, helped me with details in the bread recipes, and Chef Dimitri Fayard tested the recipes and assisted me in the photo shoot.

Thank you to pastry chef Sherry Yard, who pushed me to finally write this book and introduced me to my coauthor, Martha Rose Shulman. Martha and I clicked right away when we met, and I must say that without her this book would not be what it is. She is based on the West Coast and I am in Chicago, and for an entire year, from a distance, she worked tirelessly at retesting and rewriting each recipe that I sent to her in my broken English. She has gone where not many have gone before, inside a male French chef's brain, and extracted the essence of my thoughts. It was an absolute delight working with her. I appreciate her fine touch, honesty, perseverance, and humor at the same time.

Thank you also to Christina Malach and the entire team at Knopf, who believed in the book from the start and did a great job editing it, and to Janis

Donnaud, my agent, who guided me through this entire process. I am grateful to Paul Strabbing, the French Pastry School's photographer for the last fifteen years. Only he can capture the essence of my pastries. Thanks to Johanna Lowe, who brought her European touch to the photo shoot and helped us with props and styling with such great attention to detail.

Saving the best for last, I am eternally grateful to my spiritual brother Sébastien Canonne, M.O.F., who created the French Pastry School with me in 1995. We were two young French chefs with no money but with a vision to create the best pastry school in North America, and after eighteen years I can say that we have never deviated from this goal. This perseverance and commitment to quality is what makes the school what it is today. Without Sébastien this book would not exist.

I want to thank my family in the United States, starting with Jo Kolanda and Bruce Iglauer, the best parents-in-law one could hope for. They gave me great feedback throughout the entire process and helped me tremendously during the editing process. I thank my two stepdaughters, Hailey and Gabrielle. Hailey's talent in pastry making still needs major improvement, but maybe this book will trigger culinary adventures for her. Hailey loves the English language and helped me edit the book. She also loves quality products and provided me with her honest feedback and comments whenever I presented her with a finished product, or when it came to the writing. Gabrielle is our vegetarian; she likes to cook and has a sweet tooth. She is always on my side when I try to convince people that sugar or chocolate should be served as a vegetable course. Alexandra, my daughter, who has a great nose and palate, was very helpful in recognizing flavors in the recipes I was testing. Her comments are always bluntly honest and to the point, which is what one needs when one writes a book; she too helped me with the editing part of the book. A big thanks to Oliver, our dog, who brought me joy when I was working long hours on this book every weekend for more than a year.

Finally, I want to thank my wife, Rachel, who clearly is the reason I don't live under a bridge. Some professions—that of airline pilots, surgeons, chefs—are not at all family-friendly. We chefs work long hours on weekends and holidays. Rachel, in her own special way, is always unconditionally supportive no matter what crazy idea I throw in front of her. Without her I would not have enjoyed many of my successes and I would not be the person that I am now. For this and so much more I will always be grateful.

Jacquy Pfeiffer
Chicago, 2013

INDEX

silpats, xvii, xx–xxi
Simple Syrup, 6
sorbets, 286–7
    fruits turning brown in freezer and, 287
    Pineapple, 281, 284
    sweetening amounts in, 287
    water-solid ratios in fruits and, 286
Sour Cream and Berry Tart, Alsatian / *Tarte au Fromage Blanc et aux Fruits Rouges*, 166–8, *167*
spatulas:
    flat and offset metal, xxii
    high-heat rubber, xxii
spice(d)(s), xxx
    flavoring chocolate custard filling with, 161
    flavoring ganache with, 74
    flavoring nougatine with, 60
    Gingerbread / *Pain d'Épices*, 335–7, *337*
    Whipped Cream, 289, 292
spiders, xxiii
Sponge, Chocolate, 259, 260, 262
    Flourless, 246–7
sponge cake / biscuit:
    Almond Biscuit Roulade, 243–5
    baked too long, making soft and usable again, 245
    use of term "biscuit," 241
sponge cake / génoise:
    baking on sheet pan, 241
    Cake Pan Version, 237–9
    flavorings for, 237
    freezing at baked stage, 242
    Jelly Roll / Roulade, 241–2
    use of term "génoise," 241
springerle, 191, 193, *193*
Spritz Cookies / *Spritz Bredele*, 194–6, *195*
stand mixers:
    KitchenAid, xx
    using, 30
starters for bread doughs, 344
    poolish, 23, 26, 128, 299, 344
steel bakeware, xvii
Stollen, *302*, 303–6
strainers, xxii

strawberry(ies):
    Alsatian Sour Cream and Berry Tart / *Tarte au Fromage Blanc et aux Fruits Rouges*, 166–8, *167*
    ice cream, 272
    making jam with, 83
    pairing with rhubarb, 182
    water released by, 144, 157, 172, 272, 340
    water/solid ratio in, 286
Streusel / Crumble, 9–10, *10*
    to absorb juices in fruit tarts, 157
    Brioche Streusel / *Streusel Brioche*, 307–9, *309*
    pre-baking, before using in fruit tart, 155
    Rhubarb Tart with Hazelnut Crumble, 179–82, *181*
    Wild Blueberry Tart, *152*, 153–5
succès, 122
sugar, xxvii
    brown, 48
    confectioners' (aka powdered sugar or 10x sugar), xxvii, 5, 139, 145, 244
    creaming butter and, 146
    Icing, 335, 336–7
    Icing, Lemon, 201, 202
    Icing Glaze, 5
    turbinado, 150
    vanilla-scented, 38, 155
sunflower seeds:
    roasting, 55
    Seeded Bread, 346–9
Sweet Dough / *Pâte Sucrée*, 138–42, 144
    creaming vs. sanding method and, 146
    see also pastry doughs
Swiss cheese, in Beer Quiche / *Quiche à la Bière*, *360*, 361–3
Swiss meringue, 66–7
Syrup, Simple, 6

tart crusts:
    creaming vs. sanding methods for, 146
    lining ring or tart pan with dough, 141–2
    Pâte Brisée / Savory Pie Dough, 147–8

Pâte Sablée, 138, 144–5, 146
pre-baking (blind-baking), 140
"resting" dough for, 142
rolling out dough for, 140, *141*–2
soggy, egg wash to prevent, 154
Sweet Dough / *Pâte Sucrée*, 138–42, 144, 146
Tarte au Chocolat with Nougatine Topping / Chocolate Tart, *158*, 159–61
Tarte au Fromage Blanc et aux Fruits Rouges / Alsatian Sour Cream and Berry Tart, 166–8, *167*
Tarte aux Framboises et Noisettes / Raspberry and Hazelnut Tart, 169–72, *171*
Tarte aux Quetsches / Plum Tart, *134*, 156–7
Tarte de Linz Ma Façon / Linzer Tart My Way, 173–7, *174*
Tarte Flambée, 294, 364–6
    dessert, with apples, 366
tarte Tropezienne, 311–12
tart rings or pans:
    buttering, 140–1
    lining with dough, 141–2
    metal, xxi–xxii
tarts, 135–82
    Almond Cream as filling for, 43–4
    Apple Nougat, 149–50, *151*
    Beer Quiche / *Quiche à la Bière*, *360*, 361–3
    brioche streusel / *streusel brioche*, 309
    Chocolate / *Tarte au Chocolat* with Nougatine Topping, *158*, 159–61
    Lemon Cream, with Meringue Teardrops, *162*, 163–5
    Linzer, My Way / *Tarte de Linz Ma Façon*, 173–7, *174*
    Onion / *Tarte à l'Oignon*, *356*, 357–9
    Plum / *Tarte aux Quetsches*, *134*, 156–7
    Raspberry and Hazelnut / *Tarte aux Framboises et Noisettes*, 169–72, *171*
    Rhubarb, with Hazelnut Crumble, 179–82, *181*
    serving warm, 135

The French Pastry School of Kennedy-King College at City Colleges of Chicago strives to offer an innovative, effective, intensive education in which students are equipped to achieve excellence in the pastry, baking, and confectionary arts.

The school was founded by chefs Jacquy Pfeiffer and Sébastien Canonne, M.O.F, in 1995 as a resource for intensive pastry education. The first session of the twenty-four-week professional baking and pastry program, L'Art de la Pâtisserie, started in 1999 when the chefs moved into their fully equipped, state-of-the-art kitchens at City Colleges of Chicago district headquarters in downtown Chicago. The school added its specialized sixteen-week cake decorating and baking program, L'Art du Gâteau, in August 2010, and its eight-week artisanal bread-baking course, L'Art de la Boulangerie, in June 2011.

Students travel from all over the world to take these programs at the French Pastry School and short-term continuing education courses offered year-round on a variety of subjects. The traditional master-apprentice method that the French Pastry School uses as its model—an intensive hands-on instruction from master pastry chefs, through the use of the finest ingredients and equipment currently available—optimally prepares students to pursue a career (or a hobby) in pastry.

Whether in the full-time certificate programs or continuing education courses, students are personally mentored by experts in their crafts. The French Pastry School's goal is to transmit the knowledge, commitment, and passion necessary for their students to continually elevate the art of pastry.

For more information visit www.frenchpastryschool.com.

A NOTE ON THE TYPE

This book was set in Celeste, a typeface created in 1994 by the designer Chris Burke. He describes it as a modern, humanistic face having less contrast between thick and thin strokes than other modern types such as Bodoni, Didot, and Walbaum. Tempered by some Old Style traits and with a contemporary, slightly modular letterspacing, Celeste is highly readable and especially adapted for current digital printing processes which render an increasingly exacting letterform.

COMPOSED BY NORTH MARKET STREET GRAPHICS,
LANCASTER, PENNSYLVANIA

PRINTED AND BOUND BY TOPPAN LEEFUNG PRINTING LTD.,
DONGGUAN, CHINA

BOOK DESIGN BY PEI LOI KOAY